Patient-Centered Care for Pharmacists

KIMBERLY A. GALT, PharmD, PhD, RPh, FASHP

Professor and Associate Dean
Creighton University
Omaha, Nebraska

MICHAEL A. GALT, MS, RPh, FASHP

Clinical Pharmacist
Coram Infusion Specialty Services
Lenexa, Kansas

American Society of Health-System Pharmacists®
Bethesda, MD

Any correspondence regarding this publication should be sent to the publisher, American Society of Health-System Pharmacists, 7272 Wisconsin Avenue, Bethesda, MD 20814, attention: Special Publishing.

The information presented herein reflects the opinions of the contributors and advisors. It should not be interpreted as an official policy of ASHP or as an endorsement of any product.

Because of ongoing research and improvements in technology, the information and its applications contained in this text are constantly evolving and are subject to the professional judgment and interpretation of the practitioner due to the uniqueness of a clinical situation. The editors, contributors, and ASHP have made reasonable efforts to ensure the accuracy and appropriateness of the information presented in this document. However, any user of this information is advised that the editors, contributors, advisors, and ASHP are not responsible for the continued currency of the information, for any errors or omissions, and/or for any consequences arising from the use of the information in the document in any and all practice settings. Any reader of this document is cautioned that ASHP makes no representation, guarantee, or warranty, express or implied, as to the accuracy and appropriateness of the information contained in this document and specifically disclaims any liability to any party for the accuracy and/or completeness of the material or for any damages arising out of the use or non-use of any of the information contained in this document.

Director, Special Publishing: Jack Bruggeman
Acquisitions Editor: Rebecca Olson
Senior Editorial Project Manager: Dana Battaglia
Production Editor: Johnna Hershey
Composition: Carol Barrer
Cover and Page Design: DeVall Advertising

©2012, American Society of Health-System Pharmacists, Inc. All rights reserved.

No part of this publication may be reproduced or transmitted in any form or by any means, electronic or mechanical, including photocopying, microfilming, and recording, or by any information storage and retrieval system, without written permission from the American Society of Health-System Pharmacists.

ASHP is a service mark of the American Society of Health-System Pharmacists, Inc.; registered in the U.S. Patent and Trademark Office.

ISBN: 978-1-58528-252-4

Dedication

We dedicate this book to our families. We hope that they benefit from the pharmacist's expertise in their times of need.

About the Authors

MICHAEL A. GALT, M.S., R.Ph., FASHP

Michael is Clinical Pharmacist at Coram Infusion Specialty Services. He received his pharmacy degree from North Dakota State University, completed a general pharmacy practice residency at Rush Presbyterian Hospital in Chicago, and received his M.S. in Hospital Pharmacy from the University of Houston College of Pharmacy with a combined pharmacy practice residency in the Veterans Affairs Medical Center in Houston, Texas. He has also completed the ASHP Executive Management Seminar Accrue Level III program at the University of North Carolina at Chapel Hill and the Metabolic Support Services Training Program through St. Mary's of Nazareth, Chicago, Illinois. His prior professional experiences include Director of Pharmacy at the Alegent Health System in Omaha, Nebraska, and Assistant Director of Pharmacy Services at St. Luke's Episcopal Hospital in Houston, Texas. He is experienced in managing patient care operations, pharmacy information systems, department budgeting, and coordination of clinical services in acute tertiary care hospitals; and coordinating specialized clinical home care infusion services to patients. He has a unique skill set, which combines management and clinical expertise, and he is recognized for his ability to implement progressive services and continuous change actions to reduce costs, enhance quality, increase margins, and improve customer satisfaction. During his tenure as Director, Michael established an ASHP-accredited residency program; implemented Intensive Care Pharmacy Satellite services as well as staff pharmacist coordinated Drug Use Evaluation and target drug programs; coordinated the development of clinical ladder programs for pharmacists; justified and implemented pharmacist-based decentralized programs; and developed and implemented specialized clinical services, including aminoglycoside and anticoagulation services. Michael is a Past President of the Texas Society of Health-System Pharmacists and has served at the national level of ASHP as both a delegate and ASHP Council member.

KIMBERLY A. GALT, PHARM.D., Ph.D., R.Ph., FASHP

Kimberly is Professor of Pharmacy Practice, Associate Dean for Research, and Director of the Creighton Center for Health Services Research and Patient Safety at the School of Pharmacy and Health Professions of Creighton University. She received her pharmacy degree from the University of Michigan and completed her Ph.D. in Qualitative, Quantitative, Psychometric, and Mixed Methods from the University of Nebraska–Lincoln. She has developed and managed pharmacist's primary care consultative ambulatory practice sites in the private and Veterans Affairs systems, supervised specialized drug information and clinical pharmacy services, and practiced general hospital, community, and long-term care pharmacy. She has extensive research and publishing experience in her career, with more than 60 publications and technical reports for use in translation of research to practice and policy and a funded research record exceeding six million dollars. As a methodologist she focuses on the use of qualitative, quantitative, and mixed methods as research methodologies and program evaluation tools applied in health services delivery and research. She is actively conducting research in patient safety with an emphasis on the impact of health information technology. She has held appointments as a member of the Health Information Technology National Resource Center Steering Committee for the Agency for Healthcare Research and Quality and a member of the Health Care Technology and Decision Sciences Study Section, Agency for Healthcare Research and Quality; served as an expert panel member on AHRQ Panels for Health Center IT, Medication Gap Research, Practice Based Research Network Resource Center, Health IT Demonstration Grant and Planning Grant portfolio; and as a reviewer for the National Institutes of Health. Dr. Galt chaired the Inter-professional Taskforce to Develop a Patient Safety Curriculum for Creighton University involving 18 individuals from a variety of health and professional disciplines resulting in a campus-wide offering to Creighton's students since 2005.

Table of Contents

Dedication iii
About the Authors iv
Publisher's Note..vi
Preface..vii
Chapter 1: The Patient 1
Chapter 2: The Pharmacist... 19
Chapter 3: The Practice Setting 43
Chapter 4: The Patient-Centered Care Plan 59
Chapter 5: The Patient–Pharmacist Encounter 79
Chapter 6: The Patient's Health Record.. 113
Chapter 7: Drug Information and Evidence-Based Practice..................... 155
Chapter 8: Application of Clinical Reasoning.. 209
Chapter 9: Designing the Patient-Centered Care Plan 241
Chapter 10: Implementing the Patient-Centered Care Plan 267
Glossary 311
Index 319

Publisher's Note

ACCESS BONUS CONTENT FOR THIS BOOK

What is this? It's a QR Code, or two-dimensional bar code. Below and following some of the chapters in this book you will find a QR Code. Using a free application for your smartphone, these codes can be used to connect to bonus content to accompany *Patient-Centered Care for Pharmacists*.

By downloading a QR Code reader on your smartphone, you can quickly go to the online location of this bonus material. To get a free code reader for iPhone, Android, or Blackberry, search in your smartphone app store for a QR code reader and download the app. "Scanlife" is one such app.

Once you have downloaded the app, start it and you will see it access the camera on your phone. Point the camera over the QR Code and you will be taken to bonus content.

Preface

HOW TO USE THIS BOOK

This book is designed to teach the content and application of basic patient-centered skills for pharmacists. The chapters of the book are presented in the order of the clinical process steps pharmacists follow to provide patient-centered care. The first three chapters introduce the reader to the context of providing care. This requires an understanding of the patient, pharmacists as providers, and the unique practice environment in which care is being delivered. Chapters 4 through 10 outline the process steps for assessing the patient, gathering information and documentation, using clinical reasoning, designing a care plan, and implementing it. Each chapter presents core practice knowledge that is complemented with brief case examples to illustrate practical application. Within some chapters, you will see a URL that can be accessed for additional web resources corresponding to the chapter's material.

The reader is introduced to four pharmacists and four patient case studies, each in a different practice setting and with varied scopes of practice. These four cases are developed longitudinally across the book. Each chapter is immediately followed by the four cases—each case progressing with application scenarios illustrating the knowledge in that chapter from differing practice settings, diverse patients, and diverse pharmacists' practices. The reader will follow these four cases through the entire book.

Patient-centered care is presented as a series of process steps that must be completed following a systematic model. Therefore, the book is designed to proceed through it sequentially and in its entirety.

IMPROVEMENTS IN SECOND EDITION

The *Introduction to Patient-Centered Care for Pharmacists* has been redeveloped to complement the changing emphasis of the pharmacists' practice to patient-centered care and the contemporary context of health care delivery. A major feature is the inclusion of brief case examples or vignettes throughout the chapters to illustrate practical application within varied practice settings.

Depth of information is offered about how health behavior and beliefs can be better understood in our patients, bringing contemporary theories to practice. New tools about cultural awareness and competency are expanded and enhanced to address greater detail and breadth about cultural variations in patients and how this relates to pharmacists' care delivery.

The growth of virtual practice models along with traditional practice settings has occurred in health care. An introduction to virtual practice is integrated into our care delivery discussions. Explanations differentiate patient-centered care from our previous models of care in pharmacy; additional information is provided about Medication Therapy Management Services as a specific method of delivering patient-centered care.

The pharmacist–patient encounter discussions have been expanded to include unique patient situations. Some examples include dealing with the difficult or angry patient, the mental health patient, or those who have cognitive, sensory, or motor impairments.

Access, management, and use of the patients' health information has become an area of explicit importance in the movement to deliver patient-centered care. New areas of the book that address pharmacists' needs and knowledge areas include handing security, privacy, and confidentiality while delivering care; the various types of health records encountered (electronic health record, electronic medical record, personal health records); patient empowerment to access health information through patient portals; and population records such as registries.

Evidence-based practice skills and how these relate to systematically using clinical reasoning has been incorporated using the most up-to-date guidelines in this evolving area. These skills are discussed with a focus on medication use assessment in patient care plan development.

While the fundamental process of assessment and care delivery has not changed, the tools and technologies have. It is our intention that these changes in contemporary practice are incorporated into the basic patient care skills presented in this book.

—Michael Galt and Kimberly Galt

The Patient

"Kindness is a language which the deaf can hear and the blind can see."
—*Anon*

CHAPTER OUTLINE
Purpose
The Patient
- The Patient as a Person

The Patient's Values and Beliefs
- The Patient's Concept of Health
- The Health Beliefs Model
- Health Behavior
- The Patient's Culture

The Patient's View of the Pharmacist
- Types of Patients
- The Pharmacist as Health Care Provider
- Optimal Patient Health Information

Summary
Assessment Questions
Introduction to Four Patients' Cases
- Patient 1—Lauren Smith
- Patient 2—Eduardo Montanez
- Patient 3—Huong Tran
- Patient 4—Samuel Robinson

OBJECTIVES
To gain knowledge of the:
1. patient as a person;
2. patient's perspective about health and illness;
3. importance of the person's values, preferences, and beliefs about health and the care he or she desires or needs;
4. imperative to provide care, either directly or as an advocate, that is consistent with the patient's values, preferences, and beliefs;
5. relationship between a person's beliefs and health behavior;
6. importance of gaining cultural competence; and
7. importance of understanding how the patient views the pharmacist as a health care provider.

PURPOSE
The purpose of this chapter is to assist you as a health care provider in developing a concept of the patient that is personal, rich, and human. Your understanding must be in the context of the patient's life and how he or she experiences it. From this perspective, patient-centered care skills will be taught. You will be introduced to four patients in this chapter. Their lives will be followed as we explain the concepts and skills applications important for your development as an expert pharmacist.

THE PATIENT
I once cared for a man who was 79 years old. He was frail, quiet, and solemn; he rarely smiled. His family made him come to the clinic. He had difficulty with his medication management. The last time he skipped his digoxin, his atrial fibrillation became worse and he wound up in the hospital. After three visits, the physicians who evaluated him decided he was not mentally competent. As the

clinical pharmacist, I was asked to "get his medications in order." We talked. At first we talked about his medications. I talked, and I learned little. Then I asked him what he liked to do. He assessed me with a keen look—the first engaging look I'd seen. He decided that I really wanted to know. He spoke of his painting, sculpture, and ceramics. Of his love for Native American art. Eventually he told me that he felt he was a burden to his son.

He stopped taking his medications because he thought it was time to let nature take its course. We talked about his medications again. This time he told me all about them, and I listened. He knew what each one was, what it was for, and how he was supposed to take it. He told me that he knew they were giving him a test (MMSE—mini-mental status exam) to see if his brain worked fine. "I know how to make it look the way they want," he said. I administered the MMSE to him again, and he scored a 29 out of 30. He agreed to let his son and physician come in and talk.

Kim Galt, 1994

This story illustrates how an understanding of the patient's perspective of his life drove his own behavior toward his health professionals. By relating to him at the most personal level, the pharmacist was able to effectively gain his participation in his own care. It was the pharmacist's effort to gain insight into this man's values, beliefs, and resultant behavior that led to the opportunity to improve his care. This is what patient-centered care looks like… one patient at a time.

The Patient as a Person

Who is this person who comes to you as a patient? What does this person want? What does this person need? We must understand the patient as someone who possesses certain strengths, vulnerabilities, preferences, worries and fears, hopes and joys. By virtue of our humanity, we possess the same fundamental dignity and value as any other human being. It is this viewpoint that is needed to serve all patients.[1] The patient is the central reason for your work and the only reason for a health profession.

Our values, beliefs, attitudes, and concepts define us as a person. These things create our frame of reference about how we approach life and the world around us. This critical frame determines our beliefs about our own health and health-related needs. If you think about your own health and health-related needs, you begin to understand how the patient who you serve thinks about them as well. You, as a pharmacist, provide services and care that the patient perceives as wanted or needed. This understanding also frames the context for the remainder of the work you will do as a pharmacist.

You will be expected to deliver patient-centered care as a pharmacist. Application of this approach requires understanding the meaning of patient-centered care. Multiple definitions have been offered over the last several years throughout the world literature (see Glossary). While these definitions continue to vary, all of them have in common the concept that the patient should be the judge of patient-centered care.[2] Recently the International Alliance of Patients' Organizations (IAPO) in collaboration with the United Nations NGO Health Committee issued the IAPO Declaration on Patient-Centered Healthcare.[3] In this declaration, the IAPO observes that:

"Patients', families' and health care providers' priorities are different in every country and in every disease area, but from this diversity we have some common priorities. To achieve patient-centered healthcare we believe that healthcare must be based on the following Five Principles:

1. **Respect**—Patients and health care providers have a fundamental right to patient-centered healthcare that respects their unique needs, preferences and values, as well as their autonomy and independence.

2. **Choice and empowerment**—Patients have a right and responsibility to participate, to their level of ability and preference, as a partner in making healthcare decisions that affect their lives. This requires a responsive health service which provides suitable choices in treatment and management options that fit in with patients' needs, and encouragement and support for patients and health care providers that direct and manage care to achieve the best possible quality of life. Patients' organizations must be empowered to play meaningful leadership roles in supporting the patients and their families to exercise

their right to make informed healthcare choices.

3. **Patient involvement in health policy**—Patients and patients' organizations deserve to share the responsibility of healthcare policy making through meaningful and supported engagement in all levels and at all points of decision making, to ensure that they are designed with the patient at the center. This should not be restricted to healthcare policy but include, for example, social policy that will ultimately impact on patients lives.

4. **Access and support**—Patients must have access to the healthcare services warranted by their condition. This includes access to safe, quality and appropriate services, treatments, preventive care and health promotion activities. Provision should be made to ensure that all patients can access necessary services, regardless of their condition or socio-economic status. For patients to achieve the best possible quality of life, healthcare must support patients' emotional requirements and consider non-health factors such as education, employment and family issues which impact on their approach to healthcare choices and management.

5. **Information**—Accurate, relevant and comprehensive information is essential to enable patients and health care providers to make informed decisions about healthcare treatment and living with their condition. Information must be presented in an appropriate format according to health literacy principles considering the individual's condition, language, age, understanding, abilities and culture."

How do you know as a pharmacist how to meet the patients' needs across these five principles? Incorporation of these principles into daily practice with each patient who seeks care requires you to see the patient "through the patient's eyes."[4,5] Putting yourself in the patient's place, genuinely wanting to know about him or her, and listening to the patient to understand what the patient says he or she needs is a great start. As you read on, you will see additional specific suggestions and examples of how to provide patient-centered care.

THE PATIENT'S VALUES AND BELIEFS

The ability to provide patient-centered care requires the pharmacist to fully understand the patient's values, preferences, and beliefs about health and wellness. The following sections will discuss the importance of the patient's concept of health, health beliefs, health behavior, and cultural influences.

The Patient's Concept of Health

How do you know what concept the patient has of health? Each of us has our own concept, but it is formed by many factors. Let's briefly examine factors that may influence one's concept of health. In future chapters, we will practice the skills needed to solicit and understand the patient's health concept.

Let's begin by understanding the ways that health professionals and patients conceptualize health. Health thinking, from the health professions' perspective, has historically been based on a disease concept founded in the traditional biomedical model. Disease is described in terms of negative symptoms combined with the directly related physical pathology that causes those symptoms. In this model, the concept of health is represented by "the absence of disease."[6]

Patients, on the other hand, come to us with a diverse set of concepts, ideas, beliefs, and values about what health is and what it means. Many patients understand their health in a way that is considered consistent with Western medicine where body, mind, cognition, emotion, and spirituality are seen as discrete entities. In contrast, they may also participate in Eastern philosophies of Buddhism, Taoism, or traditional Chinese medicine. These philosophies adopt a holistic conceptualization of an individual and his or her environment. In this view, health is a body–mind–spirit concept perceived as a harmonious equilibrium that exists between the interplay of "yin" and "yang."[7] Several traditions are practiced within our communities, such as Chinese herbal medicine, indigenous North American medicine, and chiropractic, acupuncture, homeopathy, and naturopathic medicine. The same patients who use these alternative approaches also participate in the mainstream Western philosophies. Although we as health professionals may attempt to provide professional care within a singular primary model of health, patients may perceive no need to actually choose among models. They often participate in multiple, seemingly inconsistent, health care models.

Differences in these understandings of health have led to a broader examination of the concept and its possible meanings. For example, one shift in recent years included the concepts of functionality and well-being in the overall concept of health. Historically, Western measures of health did not include a patient's perception of well-being. Measures of health are changing today to reflect this shift. Increasingly, we see writings about recognition of 1) diversity, 2) the value of the whole person and the richness of life, 3) broad concern about the person, and 4) the need for inclusion of spirituality.

Given the breadth of patients' beliefs and behaviors, why try to have a health model defined at all? Models help us frame our ability to serve the needs of patients by proscribing a context to the care they seek and we provide. Models help us behaviorally define our actions to be consistent with the beliefs and expectations consistent with the models that represent our patients' expectations. Four prominent models for defining health are shown in **Table 1-1**.[8] Not all concepts of health are represented to our satisfaction. However, these models recognize the various ways in which patients define health. If we know the model that best fits a patient, we can offer professional care that meets those needs and acknowledge the influences that modify one's expectations of care.

The Health Beliefs Model

To fully serve the person as a patient, you must understand his or her values and beliefs in relationship to the person's concept of health. It is a common theme in health profession literature to highlight the difference between the professional's understanding of the patient's disease and the patient's interpretation of feeling unwell. In this distinction, we see the patient's need for more than a scientific formulation and treatment of problems. Patients generally want to feel understood and valued and to be involved

TABLE 1-1.

Health Model Definitions[9]

Model	Definition
Medical:	The absence of disease or disability.
World Health Organization:	State of complete physical, mental, and social well-being and not merely the absence of disease or infirmity.
Wellness:	Health promotion and progress toward higher functioning, energy, comfort, and integration of mind, body, and spirit.
Environmental:	Adaptation to physical and social surroundings: a balance free from undue pain, discomfort, or disability.

in making sense of their health problems. Additionally, many patients want to be involved in decisions about care management.

A common model for understanding this phenomenon is the health beliefs model (**Table 1-2**).[9] It explains specific factors that may increase the likelihood of a person taking action to try to positively affect his or her health. Individual factors include perceived susceptibility to illness; perceived seriousness of illness; perceived barriers to action; and perceived benefits of action, motivation, and self-efficacy. Modifying factors include past personal and family experiences, information and advice from family and friends, age, knowledge, fitness levels, and the external influence of the media. The person intuitively decides if he or she is ready to take the health action perceived as necessary by weighing its costs and benefits. Moreover, the model recognizes that a person will finally act when a cue of some type occurs—usually a profound negative event (e.g., stroke after uncontrolled hypertension, hospitalization after uncontrolled hyperglycemia secondary to uncontrolled diabetes). This model has proven to be a practical representation of patient beliefs and holds up to both cultural variation and differing definitions of health.

Health Behavior

Health-relevant behavior and attitudes are products of culture and are viewed in the overall cultural context in which they occur. Fundamental to this new paradigm of practice is understanding behavior, its relationship to health, and methods by which it can be altered. Current concepts of health behavior have been heavily influenced by social learning theory, self-efficacy theory, and a biopsychosocial view of health and disease. The way that patients behave in relationship to treatment depends on a complex interplay of many psychological, social, and environmental variables. To assist them in reaching their goals, you must understand how behavioral techniques may be used.[10] Patients with less positive

TABLE 1-2.

Health Belief Model

Concept	Definition	Potential Change Strategies
Perceived susceptibility	Beliefs about the chances of getting a condition	■ Define what population(s) are at risk and their levels of risk ■ Tailor risk information based on an individual's characteristics or behaviors ■ Help the individual develop an accurate perception of his or her own risk
Perceived severity	Beliefs about the seriousness of a condition and its consequences	■ Specify the consequences of a condition and recommended action
Perceived benefits	Beliefs about the effectiveness of taking action to reduce risk or seriousness	■ Explain how, where, and when to take action and what the potential positive results will be
Perceived barriers	Beliefs about the material and psychological costs of taking action	■ Offer reassurance, incentives, and assistance; correct misinformation
Cues to action	Factors that activate "readiness to change"	■ Provide "how to" information, promote awareness, and employ reminder systems
Self-efficacy	Confidence in one's ability to take action	■ Provide training and guidance in performing action ■ Use progressive goal setting ■ Give verbal reinforcement ■ Demonstrate desired behaviors

health practices are more likely to be health illiterate.[11] Furthermore, the stronger a person's perceived capability to carry out behavior, the more successful he or she is in doing so.[12]

Readiness for Change. A common model applied in daily practice assesses a person's readiness to carry out a desired behavior to improve his or her health. This is called the stages of change model.[13] This model describes how patients progress through the decision process to make a change in behavior through to taking action and maintaining a behavior change. It is a model commonly used when designing educational programs for patients that are intended to assist them in making changes to health-related behaviors (e.g., smoking cessation). In this model, patients progress from having no intention to take action to eventually changing behavior. This model can help us understand how to behave ourselves to support the patient as he or she works to attain a new behavior. The model is shown in **Table 1-3**.

Medication Use. What does this person believe about the use of medication as a form of treatment? Many studies indicate that perceptions of the role of medication use are highly varied—as varied as the characteristics that affect concepts of health. Multiple studies have shown that patients from different ethnic and cultural backgrounds use alternative medicines or home remedies, while also participating in a formal health care system approach.[14-16] Your knowledge of the patient's beliefs and his or her evaluations of treatment options should be considered when developing therapeutic plans and monitoring patient outcomes. While you are trained to use traditional and evidence-based treatment approaches, the patient may participate in your approach while simultaneously participate in a culturally based approach unfamiliar to you. Gaining personal knowledge of your patient is essential to becoming aware of these situations in order to work effectively with both.

Patient Relationships. You also need to know who other decision makers are in relationship to your patient. A spouse may actually be the decision maker in care or may have great influence. A patient may make decisions through the family members as a unit. Both of these relationships are observed as routine in some cultures. The patient may have a caregiver, either voluntarily from relatives, friends, and neighbors, or formally through the health system. Finally, other people important to the patient may play a role in influencing him or her.

Self-Care. In recent years, self-care has become a prominent aspect of patient behavior. Self-care may sometimes be observed as an individual taking responsibility for both identifying one's problem and determining the preferred treatment. The over-

TABLE 1-3.

Stages of Change Model

Stage	Definition	Potential Change Strategies
Precontemplation	Has no intention of taking action within the next 6 months	Increase awareness of need for change; personalize information about risks and benefits
Contemplation	Intends to take action in the next 6 months	Motivate; encourage making specific plans
Preparation	Intends to take action within the next 30 days and has taken some behavioral steps in this direction	Assist with developing and implementing concrete action plans; help set gradual goals
Action	Has changed behavior for less than 6 months	Assist with feedback, problem solving, social support, and reinforcement
Maintenance	Has changed behavior for more than 6 months	Assist with coping, reminders, finding alternatives, avoiding slips/relapses (as applicable)

the-counter product market is one example where a person can, without ever consulting a health professional, self-diagnose and treat. The range of self-care products is broad and varied, including such things as herbal remedies, nutraceuticals, vitamins, minerals, and other dietary supplements.

The concept of self-care also extends to patients in hospitals. A recent study showed that 90% of hospital pharmacy departments allowed "own use" medications to be brought in by patients.[17] Prior literature has shown that between 35 and 64% of patients bring their own medications to the hospital, averaging three medications per patient.[18,19] Patients often do so to reduce anxiety and loss of self-control while being hospitalized.[20]

Individuals also "self-help" by identifying with self-help groups (e.g., Alcoholics Anonymous). These groups offer people both emotional support and practical advice about a common problem they share. The groups are almost always member run, voluntary, and fairly inexpensive. An estimated 15 million Americans are members of self-help groups, which often lead patients to seek health information.

With 70,000+ web sites disseminating health information, more than 50 million people are seeking health information online. Online information is frequently inaccurate, and people in general have poor information-evaluation skills. However, the fact that 50 million people use the Internet for this purpose illustrates the potential of the source as part of a larger health communication system. An investigation and understanding of the Internet's influence on health beliefs and behaviors is needed.[21] Awareness and access to information through the Internet has changed patient interaction with the pharmacist. Patients frequently use the Internet to learn more before coming for health provider interactions. They come with this information and verify what they are learning and determine how it is relevant to themselves and their loved ones through discussions with their pharmacist and their physician or primary providers. As a pharmacist, you are in a unique position to be accessible to the public yet have a high degree of expertise.

KEY POINT

With 70,000+ web sites disseminating health information, more than 50 million people are seeking health information online. Online information is frequently inaccurate, and people in general have poor information-evaluation skills.

The Patient's Culture

Cultural Influences. Culture is described as a property of society.[22] There is no such thing as a pure culture, because there is diversity often recognizable as subcultures. Within a large ethnic group, substantial variation may exist in education, socioeconomic status, and practiced religions. America continues to become a more ethnically diverse population. In addition to ethnic populations, other cultural subgroups must be considered such as the very young, aging, disabled, and lesbian/gay patients (**Table 1-4**).

The 2008 U.S. Census data identified 65.6% of the population as White; Asians represent 4.5%, African Americans 12.8%, and Hispanics 15.4%. Children below the age of 18 years old represented 24.3% of the population, and elderly persons over the age of 65 represented 12.8%. The population's average age is rising, with female life expectancy in

TABLE 1-4.

Examples of Cultural Sub-Groups in the United States

- African American
- Asian American
- Indian American
- Irish American
- Jewish American
- Hispanic/Latino American
- Native American (American Indian, Eskimo)
- Refugees/New Americans
- Biracial/Bicultural Americans
- Aging Americans
- Disabled Americans
- Gay/Lesbian/Bisexual/Transgender Americans

2025 averaging 81.2 years and male life expectancy averaging 77 years. It is currently estimated that 10% of the U.S. population is gay.[23] Almost one in five individuals living in the United States has a disability such as blindness, hearing loss, or a learning disability.[24] People with disabilities often develop a cultural of disability that is founded on similar experiences, values, and beliefs.[25]

How can we understand a person's culture in a way that helps to meet his or her health care goals and needs? One approach is to understand a patient's cultural view of illness. Values, attitudes, and ways of knowing the concept of illness vary in cultures, influencing the approach that a patient may take toward health care. Cultural understanding is passed down from one generation to the next. You must acquire a reasonable understanding of the culture as a whole before you can build and confidently apply this knowledge.

Cultural bias and ethnocentricity are two common problems that patients face amongst health professionals. Let's examine an example. In your initial assessment of an African American woman, you may automatically assume she is from the United States. As you begin to listen to her, you may realize that her dialect resembles a British accent. One of her cultural frames is actually from an area in Britain. You realize that you were applying your own cultural bias over hers. This example illustrates the problem of ethnocentricity or the interpretation of one culture using the norms of another, usually your own. Cultural bias may cause you to make errors in interpreting what a patient means. It may also cause you to communicate information that is misleading to the patient because he or she interprets the meaning one way and you deliver it with a different intention. Understanding another person through critical cultural norms unique to that person's community is important. Competence in cultural interpretation matters and is certainly true of health beliefs that dominate cultures. To illustrate this point, examples of health beliefs in two common cultures are provided.

Latinos will represent the second largest segment of the U.S. population by 2025. Research on 189 Latino cultures around the world has demonstrated all but four have a cultural belief that illness is caused by supernatural or spiritual agents.[26-28] Illness among Latinos appears to be influenced by moral and religious implications. It is also common to find that Latinos use folk healing. As Latinos integrate into U.S. cultures, their emphasis on these beliefs weakens but is never entirely gone.

People of Vietnamese descent are our fastest growing population within the Asian/Pacific Islander population. One strong cultural belief is the profound respect for authority, leading individuals to not question health care providers. Another belief is avoidance of promoting one's self, making it difficult for some Vietnamese to acknowledge their pain or suffering. This belief results in delays in seeking care. A common practice of this culture is to use traditional and Chinese medicines (**Figure 1-1**).[29]

Figure 1-1. Chinese Herbs Used for Medicinal Purposes

There is a great deal to know about the cultural context of the patients you serve. Health professionals should become culturally competent through the ongoing process of integrating cultural awareness, knowledge, skill, encounters, and desire. How does one become culturally competent? One way is to live within the group. For most people, this is not a realistic approach. Alternatively, learning can be accomplished through reading, convening focus groups, and participating in community activities. It is most important to remain open to learning from the patient what is culturally important and relevant.[30] Cultural competence is the discovery of the way in which a health care provider can move a relationship with the patient from parallel to mutual through increasing the provider's knowledge, skills, and understanding.[31] Refer to www.ashp.org/patientcare for a listing of resources you can use to assess and self-educate about cultural competency.

Campinha-Bacote described a model of cultural competence in health care delivery as a framework for developing and implementing culturally responsive care.[32] This model assumes that cultural competence is a process, not an event. It recognizes that there is more variation within ethnic groups than across groups. It assumes that the provision of culturally responsive care is directly related to the health professionals' level of cultural competence in the context of each patient. The model defines the concept as follows:

1. Cultural awareness is the self-understanding of one's own cultural and professional background.
2. Cultural knowledge is the process of seeking and obtaining an educational foundation about different cultural and ethnic groups.
3. Cultural skill is described as the ability to collect relevant cultural data about the patient's problem as well as perform a culturally based physical assessment.
4. Cultural encounter involves the health professional engaging in cross-cultural interactions with individuals from diverse backgrounds. This interaction is almost impossible when the patient and health provider speak different languages, the patient has a limited English proficiency, the patient is speaking from a different perspective, or the provider has a limited proficiency in the patient's language. Occasionally, cultural tradition may preclude a patient speaking directly to a provider. For these reasons, an interpreter is sometimes needed.[33]
5. Cultural desire is the motivation of the health care provider to engage in the process of culturally responsive care.

A culturally competent pharmacist will consciously adapt care for the patient in a way that is consistent with the patient's need from the context of a cultural framework.[34] A recent publication suggests concepts and practices that can improve a pharmacist's cultural competence in pharmacy practice.[35] Gaining knowledge about the cultures that your patients are from and also examining your own cultural background provide you with practical knowledge. It is important to recognize cultural differences, yet not to generalize or stereotype. Each patient is an individual with his or her own perceptions, beliefs, preferences, and needs. Part of understanding your patient and establishing a genuine relationship involves displaying a sincere interest in the patient's culture. This will help you to educate yourself to develop therapeutic plans that are compatible with cultural beliefs of your patient. Ideally, you should have culturally sensitive educational approaches and materials. You might even learn some phrases of the predominant non-English speaking persons who you serve. Sometimes language barriers exist as well. You might consider using pictograms to help you communicate. You might also engage a trained interpreter if your work environment provides this resource. It is also common to ask for a family member who speaks your language to accompany the patient when they visit with you.

An organized method to assist health care providers with diverse populations has been developed. The ETHNIC mnemonics model may be a useful tool to guide health care providers with interviewing patients in a culturally responsive manner.[36] The ETHNIC mnemonic stands for Explanation, Treatment, Healers, Negotiate, Intervention, and Collaboration. These are important steps in establishing knowledge about the patient's culture. **Table 1-5** provides examples of questions using the ETHNIC framework that may be adapted for a culturally competent clinical practice.

TABLE 1-5.

ETHNIC: A Framework for Culturally Competent Clinical Practice

EXPLANATION: Listen with sympathy and understanding to the patient's perception of the problem.	■ What do you think may be the reasons you have this problem? ■ What do you call this problem (sickness)? What name does it have? ■ What do you fear most about your sickness? ■ What do friends, family, others say about these symptoms? ■ How does a person from your culture view a person who has this sickness? ■ Do you know anyone else who has had this problem? ■ Have you heard about it on TV, radio, or the Internet?
TREATMENT: Know what treatment options the patient has tried or is expecting.	■ What kinds of medicines, home remedies, or other treatments have you tried for this illness? ■ What kind of treatment do you think you should receive? ■ Are there any practices in your culture or religion that keep you healthy such as prayer, wearing charms, or massage medicine? ■ Is there anything you eat or drink (or avoid) to stay healthy?
HEALERS: Understand traditional and alternative providers of health care.	■ Who are the healers or health care providers in your culture/religion? ■ Have you sought advice or treatment for your illness from alternative/folk healers, spiritual leaders, friends, or other non-doctors? ■ Who makes most of the health care decisions in your family? ■ Do you have preferences about your health care providers: do you prefer male or female, younger or older, or someone of a specific ethnicity? ■ How do you feel about health care providers who are not part of your cultural background?
NEGOTIATE: Negotiate options that are mutually acceptable that do not contradict, but rather incorporate your patient's beliefs.	■ What kind of treatment do you think you should receive? ■ What are the most important results you hope to receive from the treatment?
INTERVENTION: Develop an intervention with your patient.	■ What alternative treatments could be included in the treatment plan? ■ Are there any spiritual or cultural practices that may be included? ■ What foods or drinks should be considered in the treatment plan?
COLLABORATION: Collaborate with the patient, family members, other health care team members, healers, and community resources.	■ Is there someone I can call that you would like to help you with the treatment plan at home? ■ May I contact your family doctor (home care nurse, pharmacist, respiratory therapist) to let him or her know how you are doing? ■ Is there anyone else you would like me to discuss your care with (e.g., such as a neighbor, relative, or pastor)? ■ What pharmacist do you normally get your medicines from so I can contact him or her about your plan?

THE PATIENT'S VIEW OF THE PHARMACIST

Types of Patients

To optimally care for a patient, you need to determine what type of "patient" the patient is. Your goal should be to recognize and respect the patient's autonomy and support him or her in the determination of needs.[37] You might view the patient as coming from three different possible points of view:

- **The patient as a consumer.** The patient views you (the professional) as a competitor who has something he or she wants or needs, but views you as willing to give as little as possible for the most amount of money. In this case, the consumer shops around for the commodity (i.e., health care services, pharmaceuticals).

- **The patient who is dominated by the professional.** The patient views him- or herself as powerless in decision making and hands over in a highly dependent way the decisions to be made to you (the health professional).

- **The patient as autonomous and interdependent with the professional.** The patient views him- or herself as vulnerable and seeks care in an interdependent fashion. The patient wants to trust your (the professional's) expertise. However, he or she wants to participate in, rather than hand over, decisions to you.

As a pharmacist, you will encounter all three types of patients. Understanding them can help you to determine how to best meet their needs. Your professional responsibility remains the same in all three cases. The ways you meet your responsibility will vary.

CASE EXAMPLE

Pharmacist Care of the Self-Empowered Consumer

You are the pharmacist on duty at a professional retail pharmacy that offers expanded patient services, including medication therapy management services (MTMS). A well dressed middle-aged man unknown to you requests assistance in locating an over-the-counter (OTC) medication for his recent consistent heart burn and indigestion. He specifically requests the product omeprazole and has a $5.00 coupon from the manufacturer. You walk him to the OTC section in the pharmacy. While walking, you ask if this is a new problem and what has brought it on. The consumer goes on to explain that he has had a stent placed in his heart within the last 2 months, and perhaps the stress of the heart attack and the procedure has brought on his stomach distress. You ask the patient if his physician has put him on any medications after the procedure. The patient tells you he is on aspirin and clopidogrel. You advise the patient that omeprazole is a good product; however, it may not be the right medication to be given with his other medications. Although omeprazole will be less expensive for the patient, you inform him that omeprazole may counteract his antiplatelet medication and has been reported to increase the risk of another heart attack. You suggest generic famotidine 20mg twice a day as a safe alternative. You also advise the patient if his stomach symptoms persist that he should be evaluated by a medical professional and make sure to inform the professional of all his current medication use. The patient–consumer evaluates the information and selects famotidine as recommended based on his concern about the potential of a recurring heart attack.

The Pharmacist as Health Care Provider

Does the patient have a concept of the pharmacist as a care provider?

Expertise and Trust. Some research suggests that, from a patient perspective, pharmacist expertise is the main factor necessary for establishing quality relationships between pharmacists and patients. Also, mutual disclosure is critical for building trust in pharmacist–patient relationships. In a study of 200 patients who came to the pharmacist for prescriptions, 80% expressed the importance of confidence (professional trust), while only 58% thought that knowing and liking (personal trust) the pharmacist was important in their selection of a pharmacy. For a nonprescription remedy, 72% stated they would accept the pharmacist's advice. For prescription medication, 57% were willing to accept advice. A strong interrelationship exists between personal and professional trust in both selecting a pharmacy and accepting advice from a pharmacist.[38,39]

Understanding the Pharmacist as Healer. Some patients view you as a healer. Pharmacists occupy a specialized community role, holding the social status as a healer by the use of medications as treatments. Pharmacists are recognized as experts who hold the capacity to cure as well as harm. In general, as with other healers, the pharmacist is a trusted and respected member of the community. This status is granted by patients who give the pharmacist this power. When a patient seeks a pharmacist for advice, he or she is placing trust in the intention and skill of the pharmacist. Many patients understand the pharmacist has knowledge that is specialized for this purpose. For the patient who invests in relationships, a hand hold or touch to the forearm has meaning from you as a healer, every bit as much as the medications you dispense, monitor, and educate about.[40]

Understanding the Pharmacist as Merchandiser. Some patients may view you as a merchandiser, recommending a drug product from the point of view of sales. The 2001 National Pharmacy Consumer Survey found that 30% of patients view pharmacists as their first choice for information regarding medications, and only 4% view pharmacists as their first choice for information regarding diseases.[41]

These results suggest that individuals may have preformed ideas about the role and value of a pharmacist without ever having a direct experience with a pharmacist. A patient's perception of the pharmacist is formed by interacting with you. To change perceptions, you must change the patients' experiences by helping them realize all of the health care value you can provide.

Patients usually come to pharmacists to receive services, products, and/or care. It is usually their choice. However, as illness progresses or acute events require intervention, the patient's choices become limited. When patients come to the hospital to get care, they don't choose you. You are assigned or provided. Similarly, when patients are referred to home care services or long-term facilities, pharmacist services are assigned. As choice is eliminated, the patient becomes more dependent on the pharmacist's attributes as a care provider who advocates for patient needs.

Optimal Patient Health Information

The patient is a unique individual who brings the influences of culture, ethnicity, education, socioeconomics, spirituality, family and friends, values, beliefs, and attitudes. As we consider how to give care, we must establish knowledge of our patient as a person with a full life whose care includes management of illness. We will label this knowledge as the optimal patient health information, listing in detail all of the components in **Table 1-6**.[42] We will refer to this patient health information throughout the remainder of the book.

The data consists of both what the patient tells us or shows us through our interactions and basic information needed to provide care on his or her behalf. There are several common ways patients share information with pharmacists. Many patients just remember the information and verbally share it at the time of interaction with a pharmacist. Some write down information on paper and provide it for viewing when they visit. Yet others are more thorough and systematic. Today consumers are being asked to be directly involved in managing their own care. They should be sure that the accountability and accuracy of health providers match their own needs. Consumers are beginning to track their

TABLE 1-6.
Optimal Patient Health Information[43]

Demographic	Medical
Name	Family history
Address	Genetic history
Date of birth	Acute/chronic medical problems
Gender	Current symptoms
Religion and religious affiliation	Vital signs/other bedside monitoring information
Occupation	Allergies/intolerances
	Past medical history
	Laboratory information
	Diagnostic/surgical procedures
Social/Economic	**Administrative**
Social history	Physicians/prescribers
Family members	Other health providers sought by patient
Significant relationships with others	Pharmacist(s)/pharmacy(ies)
Living arrangement	Room/bed numbers (hospital/long-term care)
Ethnic background	Consent forms
Cultural influences	Patient identification number
Primary language/secondary language	
Financial/insurance	
Behavioral/Lifestyle	**Drug Therapy**
Health beliefs	Prescribed medications
Concepts of illness	Nonprescription medications
Diet	Medications prior to admission (if hospitalized/long-term care)
Exercise/recreation	Home remedies/folk remedies/herbal products/other types of health products
Tobacco/alcohol/caffeine/ substance use	
Sexual history/orientation	Medication regimen
Personality type	Adherence with therapy regimen
Daily activities	Medication allergies/intolerances
	Concerns or questions on therapy
	Assessment of understanding of therapy
	Pertinent health beliefs

health information electronically in a record similar to the electronic health record used by professionals. The consumer version of this is called the Personal Health Record (or PHR). We will discuss the PHR is greater detail in Chapter 6 of this book.

Today consumers are being asked to be directly involved in managing their own care. They should be sure that the accountability and accuracy of health providers match their own needs.

SUMMARY

Patient-centered care is care that is consistent with the person's values, preferences, and beliefs provided in a culturally competency manner. It is through relating to a person's beliefs, values, and preferences that you will have the optimal opportunity to help the person improve health behaviors. You also need to have access to the optimal patient health information in order to develop a therapeutic care plan that is responsive to the person's needs. Knowing your patients as people first and foremost will provide you insight into their perspectives about health and illness in order to develop this plan.

ASSESSMENT QUESTIONS

1. Review the definitions of the models for health shown in Table 1-1. Select the one that best represents your own health beliefs. Next, select the one that you think represents most patients' health beliefs likely to be in your care. Finally, if you work in a pharmacy setting, select the one that best represents the concept of health that prevails in that organization, as represented by organizational programs, services, and decisions about care provision. What do you think should be done to successfully provide care to the patient when there are differences among these models?

2. Ethnocentricity is the problem of interpreting one culture using the norms of another. How might ethnocentricity cause problems for you in delivering care to your patients?

3. Establishing a genuine relationship with the patient is emphasized in this chapter. Suggest three ways that establishing a genuine relationship with the patient aids you in your own abilities to provide patient-specific–centered care.

4. Patients have differing views of you as a pharmacist: expert, healer, or possibly merchandiser. What is the main factor needed by a pharmacist from the patient's perspective to establish a quality relationship?

5. A framework called "ETHNIC" provides a tool for guiding you to establish a culturally competent clinical practice. Table 1-5 provides an example of how this tool might guide you to form questions you may use with the patient to function in a culturally competent manner. Select a culture that you would like to become more knowledgeable about. Take the ETHNIC framework in **Table 1-5** and generate questions you might ask a patient of this culture that you believe would facilitate learning in a culturally competent way. Ask others to examine your questions and contribute feedback about the appropriateness of your questions.

INTRODUCTION TO FOUR PATIENTS' CASES

We will follow the lives of four patients and four pharmacists throughout this book as they work together in a pharmacy practice setting related to the patients' care needs. Let's meet the patients and hear their stories:

PATIENT 1

LAUREN SMITH

Ms. Lauren Smith is a 23-year-old Caucasian woman who seems too angry for her young age. She is from a privileged socioeconomic neighborhood just outside of Detroit, Michigan. She completed college to be an interior designer, with a minor degree in fine arts. Ms. Smith grew up with an unlimited amount of spending money, as her generous parents were two people who became successful business owners feeling that they should "give the children everything they never had."

Lauren was raised with a Lutheran upbringing, but she dropped any involvement in a church when she started college, telling her friends that "she wasn't sure she believed in a superior being." She is living in her own apartment, first year paid by her parents. Most of her social life is centered on some college friends. She has a varied cultural background, mostly a mixture of Irish, Polish, and German descent—a third generation American. Employment is a challenge for Lauren, as she tells her parents "she just hasn't found quite the right job yet … she is getting around to it." Her parents continue to pay for her medical insurance and any additional expenses incurred. She avoids doctors, and mostly treats her own illnesses by shopping for over-the-counter products if she thinks she needs them. We will get to know Lauren's other health issues a little later.

CASE-SPECIFIC QUESTIONS

Instructions: Complete the answer to each of the following questions.

1. Identify the health behavior that best describes Lauren's approach to health.
2. In the Health Belief Model, the term "self-efficacy" refers to the person's confidence in one's ability to take action. How would you describe Lauren's state of self-efficacy?
3. What do you think Lauren's concept is of the pharmacist as a health care provider?

PATIENT 2

EDUARDO MONTANEZ

Mr. Eduardo Montanez is a 68-year-old Latin American man originally from Matamoros, Mexico. He moved to San Antonio, Texas, 5 years ago because his son, daughter-in-law, and their five children wanted to take care of him. He has limited English skills but is able to navigate his way reasonably well. His son is a schoolteacher and has excellent health benefits. Mr. Montanez is a dependent; therefore, he is eligible to receive the full benefit of his son's health insurance plan.

All of his life, Mr. Montanez has been a deeply religious person. He was raised in the Catholic Church and went to a Catholic school in Mexico. His mother raised him to believe in the church as a spiritual basis for everything in his life. He also has traditional Mexican beliefs about the spiritual nature of illness. Mr. Montanez believes that any illness he develops is related to a failing or wrongdoing on his part. He was raised with folk medicines administered by his mother and spiritual healers. We will hear more about his condition later.

CASE-SPECIFIC QUESTIONS

Instructions: Complete the answer to each of the following questions.

1. What challenges does Mr. Montanez's traditional Mexican culture pose to his participation in the U.S. health care system?
2. What ethnic biases do you hold that could affect your assumptions about how Mr. Montanez's care should proceed?
3. What tool could you use to help you overcome these biases in order to learn of Mr. Montanez's health care beliefs and needs?

PATIENT 3

HUONG TRAN

Huong is an 8-year-old Vietnamese boy who arrived in the United States 4 years ago with his mother and father. He speaks English well; however, his mother and father are quite limited in their command of the language. Huong attends public school in Omaha, Nebraska. He is doing very well with all of his subjects. His schoolteacher and a friend in his neighborhood help him to learn his lessons because his parents are not able to correctly interpret the assignments in English. Huong interprets for his parents when they do life chores, such as purchasing items at the hardware or grocery store. He is their "window" to the English-speaking world. His parents frequent a shop that sells Chinese medicines.

CASE-SPECIFIC QUESTIONS

Instructions: Complete the answer to each of the following questions.

1. Describe two cultural beliefs that Huong Tran's parents are likely to hold that will influence how he receives care in the future.

2. How might you gain cultural competence that is relevant to your ability to provide care to Huong Tran? (This question assumes you have a different cultural background than Huong Tran.)

3. What resources might you use to learn more about Huong Tran's culture?

PATIENT 4

SAMUEL ROBINSON

Mr. Samuel Robinson is a 76-year-old African American male who has resided in Biloxi, Mississippi, since he was 12 years old. He and his wife, Georgia, were married for 40 years. Georgia died 1 year ago. He is having a difficult time keeping his life in order now that he lives alone. He has always been a self-sufficient man. However, Mr. Robinson had a deep love and interdependency with Georgia, as did she with him. She would prepare remedies when he did not feel well, exchanging and discussing several of the traditional comfort remedies with her friends. These remedies were not written down anywhere, and Mr. Robinson cannot help himself with it. He finds this discomforting. Georgia frequented a pharmacist in town regularly. She took care of her husband's needs with the pharmacist as far as he was concerned. Now he is forgetful and often distracted. Mr. Robinson attended a Baptist church with his wife. He has only gone to church twice since she died—at her funeral and at the 6-month anniversary of her death.

Mr. Robinson is on Medicare, his only form of health insurance coverage. He retired from being a farm worker 9 years ago with a very small pension and no supplementary health coverage. He has several health problems that will be presented a little later.

CASE-SPECIFIC QUESTIONS

Instructions: Complete the answer to each of the following questions.

1. What roles might the pharmacist who is familiar with Mr. Robinson's history play in his care, based on the history that is provided?

2. What are some questions you would ask Mr. Robinson based upon the ETHNIC tool to guide you in understanding his medication needs and health beliefs?

3. In the Health Belief Model, the term "self-efficacy" refers to the person's confidence in one's ability to take action. How would you describe Mr. Robinson's state of self-efficacy?

REFERENCES

1. Gormally L. Definitions of personhood: implications of the care of PVS patients. *Ethics and Medicine.* 1993; 9(3):44–8.

2. Stewart M. Towards a global definition of patient centered care. *BMJ.* 2001; 322:444–5.

3. Anon. International Patient Organizations Present First-Ever Patient-Centered Care Definition, Principles. http://www.prnewswire.com/news-releases/international-patient-organizations-present-first-every-patient-centered-care-definition-principles-51678717.html. Accessed March 2010.

4. The Institute for Alternative Futures. *Patient-Centered Care 2015: Scenarios, Vision, Goals & Next Steps.* Alexandria, VA: Picker Institute; 2004.

5. Gerteis M, Edgman-Levitan S, Daley J, et al., eds. *Through the Patient's Eyes.* San Francisco, CA: Jossey-Bass Publishers; 1993.

6. Woodhouse MB. The concept of disease in alternative medicine. In: Humber JM, Almeder RF, eds. *What Is Disease?* Totowa, NJ: Human Press; 1997.

7. Chan C, Ho PS, Chow E. A model in health: an Eastern approach. *Social Work and Health Care.* 2001; 34(3-4):261–82.

8. Preamble to the Constitution of the World Health Organization as adopted by the International Health Conference, New York, June 19-22, 1946; signed on July 22, 1946 by the representatives of 61 States (Official Records of the World Health Organization, no. 2, p. 100) and entered into force on April 7, 1948.

9. Rosenstock IM. The health belief model and preventive health behavior. In: Becker MH, ed. *The Health Belief Model and Personal Health Behavior.* Thorofare, NJ: Charles B Slack Co.; 1974:27–59.

10. Kehoe WA, Katz RC. Health behaviors and pharmacotherapy. *Annals of Pharmacotherapy.* 1998; 32(10):1076–86.

11. Christensen AJ, Moran PJ, Wiebe JS. Assessment of irrational health beliefs: relation to health practices and medical regimen adherence. *Health Psychology.* 1999; (18)2:1969–76.

12. Aljasem LI, Peyrot M, Wissow L, et al. The impact of barriers and self-efficacy on self-care behaviors in type 2 diabetes. *The Diabetes Educator.* 2001; 27(3):393–404.

13. Prochaska JO, DiClemente CC. Trans-theoretical therapy—toward a more integrative model of change. *Psychotherapy: Theory, Research and Practice.* 1982; 19(3):276–88.

14. Johnson RE, Pope CR. Health status and social factors in nonprescribed drug use. *Medical Care.* 1983; 21(Feb):225–33.

15. Brown CM, Segal R. Effects of health and treatment perceptions on the use of prescribed medication and home remedies among African American and white American hypertensives. *Social Science and Medicine.* 1996; 43(6):903–17.

16. Boyd EL, Taylor SD, Shimp LA, et al. An assessment of home remedy use by African Americans. *Journal of the National Medical Association.* 2000; 92:341–53.

17. Norstrom PE, Brown CM. Use of patients' own medications in small hospitals. *Am J Health-Syst Pharm.* 2002; 59:349–54.

18. Kostick J, Chidlow J, Plihal T. A program for controlling mediations through to the hospital by patients. *Am J Hosp Pharm.* 1973; 30:814–6.

19. Breau DJ, Nickerson AL. Utilizing home medication supplies for hospital patients. *Can J Hosp Pharm.* 1997; 50:224–8.

20. Hones L, Arthurs GJ, Sturman E. Self-medication in acute surgical wards. *J Clin Nurs.* 1996; 5:229–32.

21. Cline RJ, Haynes KM. Consumer health information seeking on the Internet: the state of the art. *Health-Educ-Res.* 2001 Dec; 16(6):671–92.

22. Sensky T. Eliciting lay beliefs across cultures: principles and methodology. *British Journal of Cancer.* 1996; 74:S63–5.

23. About.com: Gay Life. Ramon Johnson's Gay Life Blog. Available at http://gaylife.about.com/od/commingout/a/population.htm. Accessed March 25, 2010.

24. Kraus L, Stoddard S, Gilmartin D. *Chartbook on Disability in the United States, 1996. An InfoUse Report.* Washington, DC: U.S. National Institute on Disability and Rehabilitation Research; 1996.

25. Eddey GE, Robert KL. Considering the culture of disability in cultural competence education. *Acad Med.* 2005; 80:706–12.

26. Murguia A, Zea MC, Reisen CA, et al. The development of the cultural health attributions questionnaire (CHAQ). *Cultural Diversity and Ethnic Minority Psychology.* 2000; 6(3):268–83.

27. Garcia V. Hispanic health beliefs. *Texas Pharmacy.* 1999; Jul:14–5.

28. Williams DP, McPherson HA. Providing culturally sensitive care to Hispanic patients in Arkansas. *The Journal.* 2000; Jan (96):312–4.

29. Garcia V. Vietnamese health beliefs. *Texas-Pharmacy.* 1999; 118 (Jul):18–9.

30. Leonard B, Plotnikoff GA. Awareness: the heart of cultural competence. *AACN Clinical Issues.* 2000; 11(1):51–9.

31. Ehret D. Devising and nurturing effective crosscultural relationships between patients and caregivers. *Patient Care Management.* 2001; 16(12):8–9.

32. Campinha-Bacote J. The process of cultural competence in the delivery of health services: a model of care. *Journal of Transcultural Nursing.* 2002; 13(3):181–4.

33. Enslein J, Tripp-Reimer T, Kelly LS, et al. Interpreter facilitation for individuals with limited English proficiency. *Journal of Gerontological Nursing.* 2002; Jul:5–13.

34. Purnell L. The Purnell model for cultural competence. *Journal of Transcultural Nursing.* 2002; 13(3):193–6.

35. Zweber A. Cultural competence in pharmacy practice. *Am J Pharm Educ.* 2002; 66:172–6.

36. Levin SJ, Like RC, Gottlieb JE. Appendix: useful clinical interviewing mnemonics. Patient Care. *Special Issue—Caring for Diverse Populations: Breaking Down Barriers*; May 15, 2000: p. 189.

37. Ozar DT. Patients' autonomy: three models of the professional-lay relationship in medicine. *Theor Med.* 1984 Feb; 5(1):61–8.

38. Worley MM, Schommer JC. Relationship quality between pharmacists and patients. APhA-Annual-Meeting 1996; 143(Mar):6.

39. Riley DA, Baldwin HJ. Confidence in the pharmacist and acceptance of the pharmacist's advice. *Contemp-Pharm-Pract.* 1980; 3(1):18–23.

40. Thorne S. Health belief systems in perspective. *Journal of Advanced Nursing.* 1998; 18:1931–41.

41. Stergachis A, Maine LL, Brown L. The 2001 National Pharmacy Consumer Survey. *J Am Pharm Assoc.* 2002; 42:568–76.

42. Modified from Mason NA and Shimp LA. The pharmacist's patient information needs. In: Mason NA and Shimp LA. *Building a Pharmacist's Patient Database, Module 2.* Bethesda, MD: American Society of Hospital Pharmacists, Inc.; 1993:7.

The Pharmacist

"Only an open heart will allow you to float equally between everyone."[1]

CHAPTER OUTLINE

Purpose

The Pharmacist

Evolution of Pharmacy Practice
- Pharmaceuticals-centered care
- Disease- and condition-centered care
- Pharmaceutical care

Patient-Centered Care
- Method of Providing Patient-Centered Care

The Pharmacist as Practitioner
- Philosophy of Practice
- Personal Beliefs and Professional Judgments
- Relationship with Patient
- Identifying the Patient's Health Care Needs
- Clinical Practice Skills
- Clinical Reasoning

Types of Pharmacy Practice
- Pharmacy Practice Related to Direct Patient Care
- General Pharmacy Practice
- Specialized Pharmacy Practice
- Collaborative Drug Therapy Management
- Medication Therapy Management Services

Prioritizing Patient Care in a Busy Practice

Summary

Assessment Questions

Introduction to Four Pharmacists' Cases
- Pharmacist 1—Nasir Jabr, PharmD, RPh
- Pharmacist 2—Christine Johnston, PharmD, RPh
- Pharmacist 3—Luisa Rodriguez, PharmD, RPh
- Pharmacist 4—Michael Jones, MS, RPh

OBJECTIVES

To gain knowledge of:

1. how pharmacy practice has evolved through the last 50 years to types of pharmacy practices today;
2. influence of the pharmacy profession's culture on our ways of caring for patients;
3. patient-centered care as an approach to pharmacy practice;
4. contrast in our own values, the patient's values, and the structure-based values governing systems of health care for patients;
5. foundation knowledge, skills, and behaviors needed by a pharmacist for a patient-centered practice;
6. skills of clinical reasoning: empathy, moral reasoning, and metacognition in the context of patient-centered care; and
7. how expertise is gained by practicing pharmacists.

PURPOSE

The purpose of this chapter is to understand how pharmacists have come to provide safe, expert, patient-centered care within the context of the varied types of practice that pharmacists may participate in today. This chapter helps us understand how pharmacists are influenced by their own values and practice skills development in relationship to patient needs and the type of pharmacy practice they have. An overview of the clinical practice and reasoning skills is provided to set the stage for more in-depth presentation and application in later chapters.

THE PHARMACIST

Pharmacists are defining what business they are in and want to be in during the years ahead. Pharmacists occupy many possible roles, including a caring health professional, pharmaceutical product formulator and compounder, dispenser, counselor, consultant, prescriber, merchant, and entrepreneur. The choices of "role" have continued to increase as we have moved into the 21st century.[2] How will you choose to conduct yourself towards patients in these roles?

To be a pharmacist who can fill these roles and continually adapt to changes, you need to start with a basic framework for your own development. This framework is a solid foundation that includes a philosophy of practice, professional knowledge, skills, behaviors, and clinical reasoning. Governed by values and beliefs, this framework requires you to know your own values and beliefs that support this practice foundation. **Figure 2-1** shows a visual representation depicting the various components that construct "the pharmacist." This chapter emphasizes the importance of defining yourself as a pharmacy practitioner who is shaped and influenced by the components identified in this figure. *If you embrace your professional identity in this way, you will be able to make the right decisions in your professional development and future actions as a pharmacist.*

EVOLUTION OF PHARMACY PRACTICE

Pharmacy is a profession that has been historically responsible to society to assure that pharmaceuticals are of high quality, safe for consumption and use, and effective for their declared purposes. Substantial change in how the profession has fulfilled this societal responsibility is observed through the evolution of practice in the latter half of the preceding century until today. One way to describe the evolution is the movement of practice being centered on pharmaceuticals, then diseases and conditions and their management, to pharmaceutical care, and now patient-centered care. These changes are compared in **Table 2-1**. A brief description of these concepts and changes is described here to set the stage for understanding the contemporary practice approach that is continuing to grow for pharmacists today.

The pharmacist has been the recognized expert about drug products across health care for centuries. The discovery and practical development of a compound into a consumable product with predictable dose-related effects has been the bastion of the profession. This history is what has created the

TABLE 2-1.
Evolution of Pharmacy Practice

Pharmaceutical-centered practice—Emphasizes product identification, preparation, availability, and selection.

Disease- and condition-centered practice—Emphasizes the signs, symptoms, and outcomes of a particular disease and assesses how well the patient is progressing toward reduction of the disease impact or cure.

Pharmaceutical care practice—Emphasizes the responsible provision of drug therapy for the purpose of achieving definite outcomes that improve a patient's quality of life. These outcomes are 1) cure of a disease, 2) elimination or reduction of a patient's symptomatology, 3) arresting or slowing a disease process, or 4) prevention of a disease or symptomatology.

Patient-centered care practice—Emphasizes understanding the whole person and finding common ground regarding management of the provider's concepts of disease and the patient's concepts of illness. A realistic approach to time and resources is incorporated into care, and the relationship between the provider and patient is emphasized. Health promotion and prevention continues to be included in this concept of care.

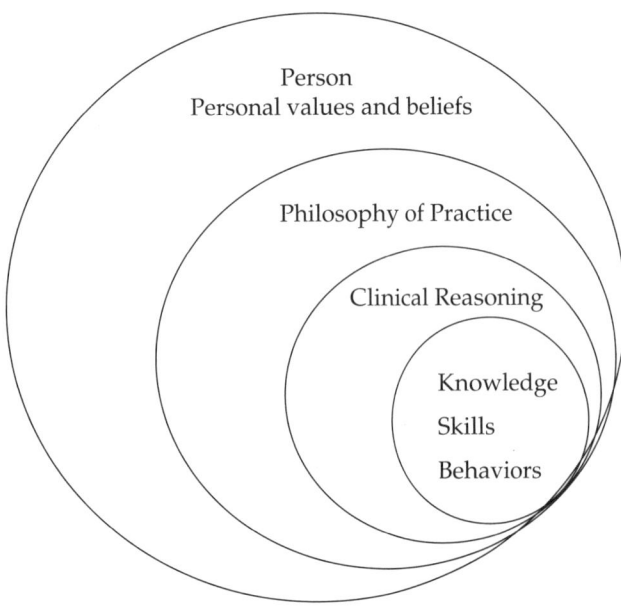

Figure 2-1. The Pharmacist: A Health Context

identity that society associates with the profession. The expert knowledge and recommendations of pharmacists to individuals seeking treatment, relief of suffering, cures and preventives has been sought and expected from the public. Pharmacists today are regarded as the premier expert on all forms of drugs. Discussion has occurred both in and outside the profession about the separation of functions among prescribing, counseling, and monitoring of drugs *for* patients and the compounding and dispensing of pharmaceuticals *to* patients. As systems of drug delivery continue to change, we see examples of such separation. However, the role and responsibilities of a pharmacist remain integrally linked with the patient and the pharmaceuticals both selected and used.

Prescription drugs have a status that requires the interaction between patient and pharmacist to ultimately deliver the pharmaceutical. The care associated with these products is interdependent between a patient and pharmacist. Over-the-counter products qualify as self care. As such, the pharmacist's involvement with the patient occurs because the patient desires an interaction with the pharmacist at some level (i.e., information expert, primary care provider, or advisor assisting the patient with carrying out another primary care provider's plan).

Pharmaceuticals-Centered Care

While expert knowledge accompanies this approach, that knowledge is expected by the public and freely provided to the public. Payment is based upon product sold.

Pharmaceuticals-centered care focuses on selecting, compounding, preparing, and dispensing the pharmaceutical for treatment. An emphasis is placed on product availability and selection. The attention paid to the patient emphasizes accurately identifying the correct patient and assuring that the dose, route of administration, and effects of therapy with other concurrent therapies taken by the patient will be safe and efficacious as it relates to the pharmaceutical being prepared and dispensed. Other aspects of the patient's needs in overall health care are secondary and often not considered within the scope of this form of practice by pharmacists. A limited use of clinical reasoning skills or direct communication with the patient takes place. Most communication is centered on verifying accuracy of basic information about the patient (name, height, weight, and so on) that is relevant to proper preparation and dispensing about the product for that patient. The pharmacist is the expert on the product. Without a doubt, no one else has the same knowledge as the pharmacist about products. It is both critical and uniquely valuable to patients that the pharmacist builds a practice philosophy around this approach.

Disease- and Condition-Centered Care

Disease-centered care focuses around the signs, symptoms, and outcomes of a particular disease and assesses how well the patient is progressing toward reduction of the disease impact or cure. Patients are not diseases, and their concerns are within a frame of illness and discomfort. No matter how hard you try, you can't assign a diagnostic label (e.g., ICD-10-CM code—see *Glossary*) to everything!

Common patient interview questions such as, "Hello Mr. Robeson, how is your asthma responding to the inhaler? And your blood sugar?" rather than, "Hello Mr. Robeson, how are you feeling today?" illustrate the point. If you are only concerned with the disease label, your patient will know it. In turn, the patient may not invest in you and the relationship you have to offer. The patient understands that you are not necessarily interested in his or her concerns, but, rather, progress with regard to a particular condition. To provide care that addresses Mr. Robeson's concerns, you have to ask questions that indicate to him that you care about his needs as he perceives them. This approach does not suggest that specialized care programs are inappropriate. Nor does it suggest that specific questions about a patient's response to drug therapy are wrong. These questions are critical to understanding the drug response aspect to the patient's disease, and it is your job to ask them. The distinction is in the emphasis.

> **KEY POINT**
>
> **If you only emphasize the disease, you missed the opportunity to respond to the patient's perceived needs. You must first find out about the patient's needs and then advocate for those needs to be addressed.**

Pharmaceutical Care

Pharmaceutical care is the responsible provision of drug therapy for the purpose of achieving definite outcomes that improve a patient's quality of life. These outcomes are 1) cure of a disease, 2) elimination or reduction of a patient's symptomatology, 3) arresting or slowing a disease process, or 4) prevention of a disease or symptomatology (see *Glossary*).[3] Pharmaceutical care is a necessary element of health care that should be integrated with other elements. However, pharmaceutical care is provided for the direct benefit of the patient, and the pharmacist is responsible directly to the patient for the quality of that care. The fundamental relationship is a mutually beneficial exchange in which the patient grants authority to the provider, and the provider gives competence and commitment (accepts responsibility) to the patient. The goals, processes, and relationships of pharmaceutical care exist regardless of practice setting.

As part of pharmaceutical care, a pharmacist cooperates with a patient and other professionals in designing, implementing, and monitoring a therapeutic plan that will produce specific therapeutic outcomes for the patient. This, in turn, involves three major functions: 1) identifying potential and actual drug-related problems, 2) resolving actual drug-related problems, and 3) preventing potential drug-related problems. The movement toward pharmaceutical care was a major step in the professional approach to advancing the pharmacist's role in patient care. What remained to be developed more fully is the appreciation of the patients' wants and needs. The outcomes identified in pharmaceutical care are most consistent with the biomedical model of health and leave secondary the patient's desires and needs.

PATIENT-CENTERED CARE

Patient-centered care places the care plan development around the patient's concerns and needs. Patient-centered approaches include applying clinical reasoning skills at the time of evaluating the prescribed medications, compounding and dispensing the medications accurately, reviewing the patient's medication history and use for drug interactions that should be addressed, and communicating with the patient about purpose, expectations, proper use, and follow-up plans. The pharmacist's dispensing role can be oriented in a patient-centered way. The pharmacist who will help patients make the best use of their medicines is one who provides patient-centered care with this expertise.

Patient-centered care places the care plan development around the patient's concerns and needs.

What does patient-centered care look like in pharmacy practice? You will make patients' expectations and needs an integral part of your work while facilitating patients to be central to determining their own care decisions. You will use your technical expertise to advise and inform patients and other care takers about the optimal choices in medication therapy management. These choices will be influenced by how patients perceive health—influenced by the personal beliefs and values they have and the behaviors they are willing to adopt. You will likely provide emotional comfort, insights, counsel, and advice as you provide your technical expertise.

Understanding the patients' concept of health and what is needed to achieve it becomes essential in patient-centered care. Knowing your own concepts about health is an important foundation for relating to patients and their health concept. The health beliefs and practices of patients are generally broader in concept and more inclusive of non-traditional options in care than what the biomedical model includes (see Chapter 1).[4] Most medical education does not extend past the biomedical model concepts, making it a challenge for many patients to receive care from a provider who accepts alternative approaches outside of this thinking.

Pharmacists are educated with an emphasis on the biomedical model as a basis for understanding disease and conditions, but a broader range of teachings about treatment approaches. Pharmacists are sought by patients for this expertise in treatment options, along with proper use and advice about those treatments prescribed by physicians and other providers. Pharmacy education extends past the biomedical model and is inclusive of many treatments that are oriented to physical, mental, and social well-being, health promotion, and adaptation. This is observed in the emphasis in education on over-the-counter medications for comfort and well-being, nutritional replacements and nutraceuticals, and physical aids, including durable medical equipment. Pharmacists in various settings emphasize the use of self-monitoring devices that empower patients and family members with self-care. A recent survey of pharmacy students revealed which health model most closely matched their personal belief system.[5] The results are shown in **Figure 2-2**. These results illustrate that few of the profession's future pharmacists have a personal concept of health which is as narrow as that ascribed to by the traditional biomedical model. Experienced pharmacists were more likely to select the wellness model, which includes interpretation of the mind, body, and spirit in defining health. As you make patients central to directing their own care decisions, you will discover that the biomedical model is increasingly inadequate in describing the comprehensive care believed to be pharmacy practice.

Method of Providing Patient-Centered Care

In the 1970s, the term "patient-centered medicine" was introduced. This concept was developed further into the patient-centered model and method by Levenstein in his own medical practice and refined at the University of Western Ontario.[6-8] The patient-centered model defines what health practitioners should do when they are helping their patients. Because the model is explicit about the behavior of an effective care provider, it provides a vocabulary and focus for teaching and learning. The model also provides a framework of caring as a description of specific behaviors that need to be learned as well as guidelines about when and how to use them. The model transfers to pharmacy practice easily. It applies to the majority of "ordinary" interactions between pharmacists and their patients when patients are seeking the pharmacist's help for consultation or care. It is supportive of a patient-centered philosophy of practice, regardless of the patient type being served. **Figure 2-3** illustrates the interaction model among the patient, pharmacist, and other factors of influence in

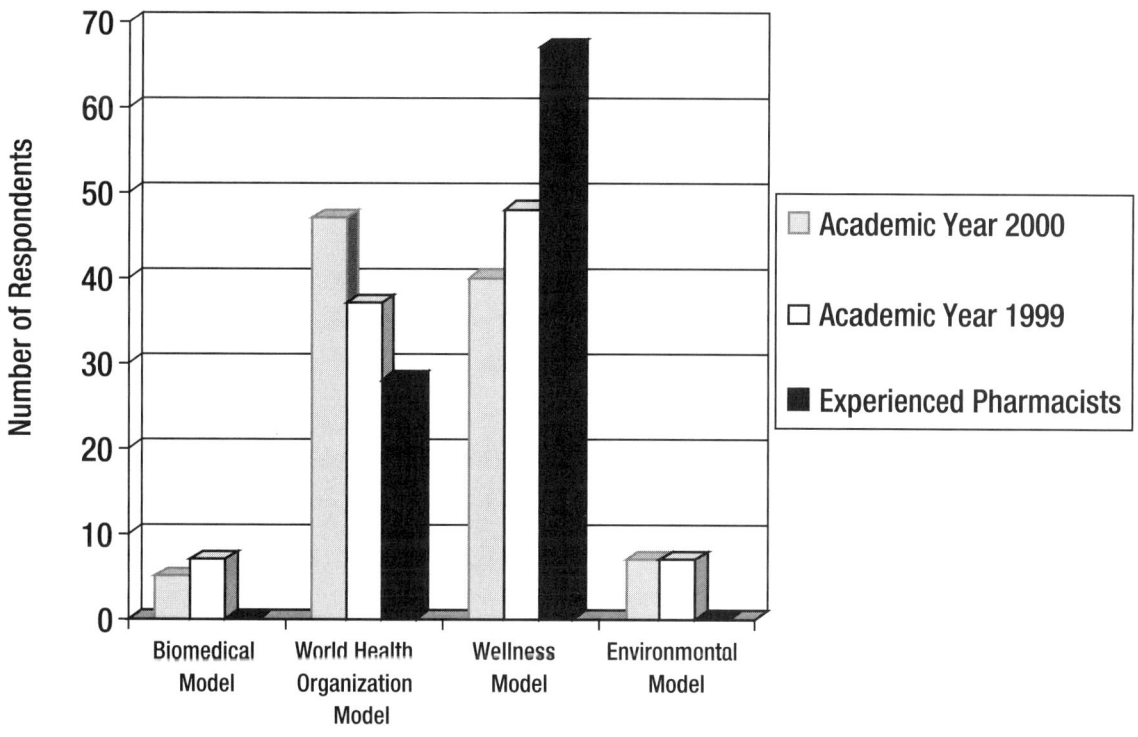

Figure 2-2. Health Models of First Professional Year Doctor of Pharmacy Students and Experienced Pharmacists (Adapted from Galt KA. The need to define care in pharmaceutical care: an examination across research, practice and education. Am J Pharm Educ. *2000; 64:223–33.)*

the patient-centered clinical method. This approach is consistent with the ways in which pharmacists' practices have evolved in more recent years.

The following six steps to patient-centered practice support the relationships in this model:

Component 1. Exploring both the disease and the illness experience. This first component involves the pharmacist's understanding of two conceptualizations of ill health: disease and illness.[2-4] *Disease* is a construct by which the health care provider labels a patient's problems in terms of abnormalities with a diagnosis. *Illness* refers to patients' personal experiences of ill health. The diagnostic label explains what each individual has in common with others with the same diagnosis, even though the illness of each per-

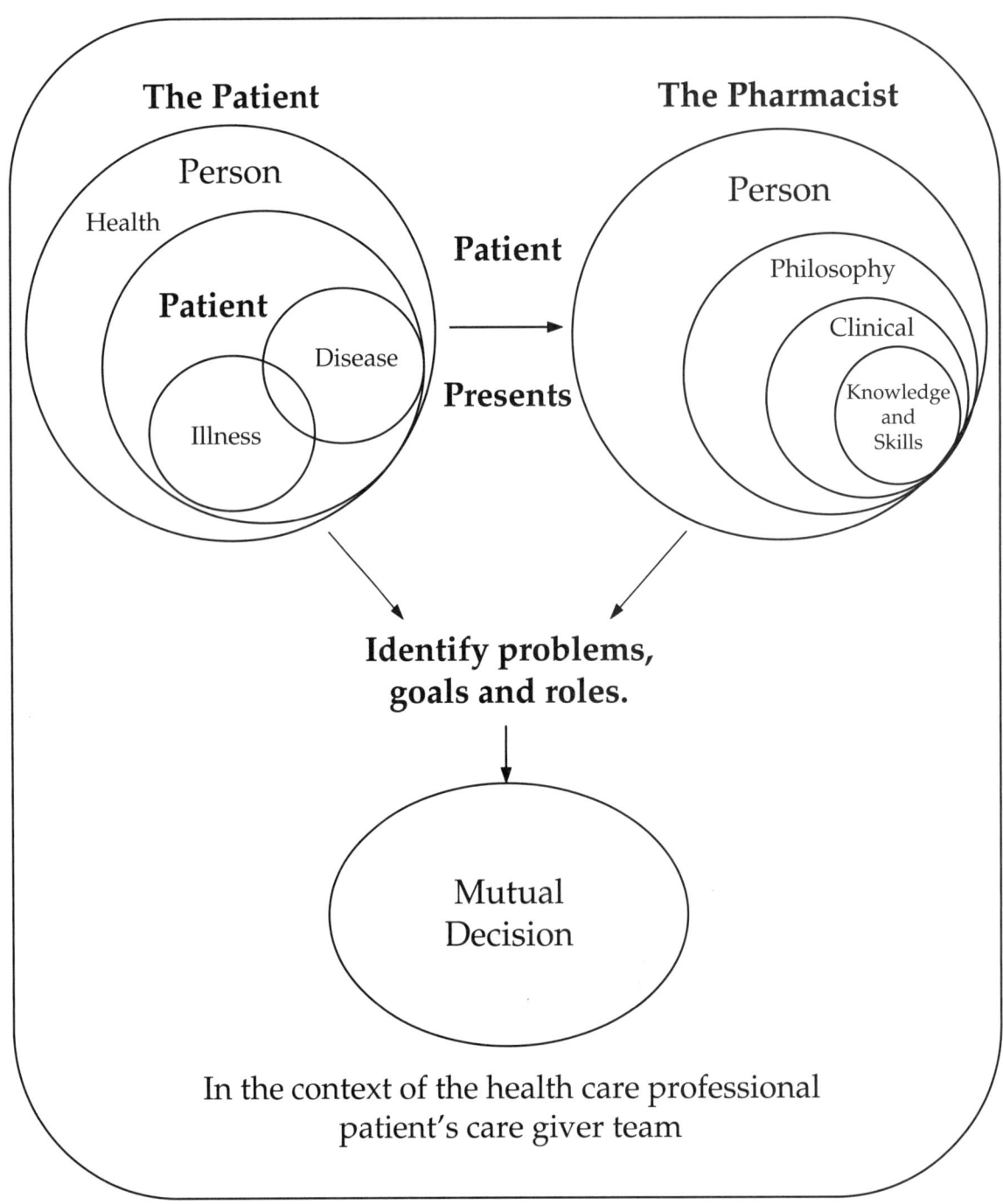

Figure 2-3. The Patient-Centered Clinical Method Adapted to Pharmacy Practice

son is unique. Effective patient care requires attending as much to patients' personal experiences of illnesses as to their diseases. A patient-centered method recognizes the identified disease as well as four principal dimensions of patients' illness experiences:

- Their ideas about what is wrong with them;
- Their feelings, especially fears about being ill;
- The impact of their problems on functioning; and
- Their expectations about what should be done.

A therapeutic understanding of patients' illness experiences requires skill in interviewing to enable the pharmacist to comprehend the illness from the patient's point of view. The pharmacist must be alert for any cues to the patient's ideas, expectations, feelings, or effects on function. Patients may prompt a pharmacist if they miss cues. Sometimes, a crucial comment is made only at the end of a personal interaction. These exiting remarks may indicate that the patient has finally summoned up enough courage to raise a fearful or embarrassing issue before it is too late.

Component 2. Understanding the whole person. The second component is an integrated understanding of the whole person. As you interact with the patient, you begin to know the whole person and, in doing so, come to understand the patient's disease and experience of illness in the context of his or her life and health beliefs. This knowledge of the person may include aspects of his or her life seemingly unrelated to pharmaceutical needs.

An understanding of the whole person can enhance the pharmacist's interactions with the patient at specific times—for example, when medication refills are picked up much later than expected for a chronic condition or the patient seems angry while you are counseling about optimal medication adherence. You will need to determine the reasons why the patient behaves or reacts in these ways. By understanding the patient's circumstances, you enhance your opportunity to assist him or her in achieving the desired behaviors needed to improve health.

Finally, understanding the whole person can deepen your empathic response, especially to those who are suffering or dependent upon your care. Your ethical obligation is to overlook nothing when determining a patient's drug-related problems. A thorough and systematic process will help to ensure that your assessment fulfills this obligation.

Component 3. Finding common ground. When a patient has been prescribed treatment, we as pharmacists initially assume that it is consistent with an effective management plan. However, oftentimes patients have not adequately participated in the initial plan determination with their providers and arrive to you with unmet needs. Developing an effective management plan requires that the pharmacist and patient reach agreement in three key areas:

- The nature of the problems and priorities,
- The goals of treatment, and
- The roles of the pharmacist and the patient.

Frequently, health care providers and patients have widely divergent views in these areas. Finding a satisfactory resolution requires pharmacists to incorporate patients' ideas, feelings, expectations, and function into treatment planning and care.

Component 4. Incorporating prevention and health promotion. The process of finding common ground with patients about opportunities for disease prevention and health promotion is an important component of pharmacist–patient interactions. With such a supportive process, pharmacists and patients together monitor areas related to medication use, disease, and illness in patients' lives that need strengthening in the interests of long-term emotional and physical health. Pharmacists also monitor recognized problems and screen for unrecognized problems. Finally, pharmacists implement health promotion and screening in practice with an emphasis on expert use and advice of patients' medications. This is done both independently with the patient and collaboratively with other health professionals.

Component 5. Enhancing the patient–pharmacist relationship. The fifth component of the patient-centered method is conscious attention to enhancing the patient–pharmacist relationship. At every visit, pharmacists strive to build an effective long-term relationship with each patient as a foundation for their work together and to use the relationship for its potential to heal and comfort. Pharmacists use self-awareness, unconditional positive regard, empathy, and genuineness to communicate with patients without always having to interpret or intervene. But the approach should be from an empathetic frame. Optimally, you should use your professional caring relationship for a healing purpose with patients. This relationship can provide healing by creating positive emotional support independent of drug treatment. However, this approach combined with treatment will improve the patient's ability to successfully adhere to drug therapy.

Component 6. Being realistic. Pharmacists frequently have competing demands for their time and energy. They must learn to manage their time efficiently for the maximum benefit of their patients. Pharmacists must develop skills of priority setting, resource allocation, and teamwork. Because pharmacists are often the providers with first entry into the health care system, they have an opportunity to steward the patient to needed resources. Pharmacists must also be able to determine reasonable outcomes for their patients. It is important to have the knowledge and expertise to achieve ideal outcomes; however, the patient's specific characteristics, circumstances, and overall health status contribute to what is actually achievable. Pharmacists have a key role in the care of a patient. The pharmacist must answer, "What role do I occupy with this patient at this time?" Roles include:

- The pharmacist as information expert and advisor. In this role, the patient is seeking information to further supplement his or her decision making needs.

- The pharmacist as a primary care provider. In this role, the pharmacist determines the patient's problems and possible treatment options with that patient. This role is illustrated in over-the-counter selections and counseling and in instances where the pharmacist receives delegated authority to manage a patient's drug therapy.

- The pharmacist as one who is carrying out the treatment plan on behalf of the primary provider. This role can include therapeutic drug monitoring as well as compounding and dispensing.

Understanding these roles provides us with a clear guide to our tasks while fulfilling our responsibilities to patients. Each role has specific features of practice that guide our actions by defining what is important. In each patient case, role definition helps us chart a course to effective action.

Although the six interactive components of the patient-centered clinical method have been presented as separate and discrete, they are in fact intricately interwoven. The skilled clinician moves effortlessly back and forth, following the patients' cues, among the six components.

THE PHARMACIST AS PRACTITIONER

A practitioner is someone who is actively engaged in an art, discipline, or profession. Pharmacists are practitioners in the field of pharmacy. The term also has legal and financial implications. A practitioner in a health care service field is licensed or otherwise identified as someone eligible to practice that discipline in each state in which he or she applies. This process of identification is associated with minimum standards in law and regulations governing a state and its citizens and/or the federal government in some practice settings and for patients who are recipients of health care services funded through federal programs. The term practitioner also is associated with both credentialing and privileging processes in organized health care systems and the military.[9,10,11] Licensed practitioners are subject to the laws that govern reporting requirements set by states and the National Practitioner Data Bank.[12]

The greater meaning of practitioner, however, resides with you and your patients. Being a practitioner means that you have an on-going process of developing expertise, skill, and engaging in the use of these tools for the betterment of your patients. The remainder of this section emphasizes core areas of development that are needed to be an effective practitioner. Each is discussed briefly. The effective practitioner is artful in how these areas are integrated to provide care for the patient.

Philosophy of Practice

Your philosophy of practice is your set of values and beliefs that determine the behaviors you demonstrate throughout your career. You will adopt a philosophy that transcends the many varied roles you will fill as a professional. What should your philosophy be?

"As the old man walked along the beach at dawn, he noticed a young man ahead of him picking up starfish and flinging them into the sea. Finally catching up with the youth, he asked him why he was doing this. The answer was that the stranded starfish would die if left in the morning sun. 'But the beach goes on for miles and there are millions of starfish,' countered the other. 'How can your effort make any difference?' The young man looked at the starfish in his hand and then threw it to safety and said, 'It makes a difference to this starfish.'"

—**Anonymous**

William Zellmer, one of our contemporary leaders in the profession of pharmacy, suggests that the life management advice of Steven Covey be followed. Covey recommends that we begin with the end in mind.[13] In other words, when you look back on your life as a pharmacist, what do you want to see and feel?[14] Will you adopt the three habits suggested to lead you down the road of being a fulfilled person in your chosen profession? The habits of being empathetic with your patients, making complex things simple enough to be effective for patients you serve, and caring enough to act on obvious things can make a difference for a patient.[14] Will you adopt a philosophy of caring, always having personal concern for the well-being of your patient?[5]

Personal Beliefs and Professional Judgments

All of your professional judgments are based on the beliefs and values held by you from a personal frame of reference. It is important to be aware of your own concept of health, your own values about what is appropriate and not appropriate with treatments, your own cultural beliefs, and your own beliefs about what your behaviors should be in response to a patient's needs. We all have boundaries that govern our beliefs and actions. Sometimes these boundaries conflict with the patient's own beliefs and needs. You may have ethical beliefs that conflict with the patient. In some circumstances, you may believe what the patient wants is wrong and you cannot participate in this aspect of care. If you have beliefs that prevent you from being able to serve a patient's preferences, you have a responsibility to inform the patient of this conflict.

Relationship with Patient

Patients sometimes seek pharmacists for help, and sometimes are in highly dependent situations where a pharmacist is part of the health system the patient has entered. Independent of how the pharmacist comes to care for the patient, the patient-centered pharmacist will remain committed to following through with medication management.

The Therapeutic Relationship—Use of Care as Prevention and Treatment. The use of care is another way of describing treatment of the whole patient—mind, body, and spirit as well as disease and illness. Caring is believed to bring comfort and healing, independent of the drug therapies you bring as a pharmacist. The healing relationship is founded in authenticity—a relationship in which the life experiences of both the pharmacist and patient are acknowledged and respected. The healing that occurs in a therapeutic relationship has been described as secondary to the use of therapeutic strategies by health professionals. Some strategies include displays of empathy, suggestion, touch, attending to adherence, and use of family, social supports, or community agencies. These strategies will be discussed further during a more in-depth review of the skills.[15]

There is healing power in the relationship between a health care provider and the patient. The greater emphasis on advanced diagnostic techniques and technologies has deemphasized the value of the therapeutic relationship, long known to the profession of medicine. Pharmacists can and do use their relationship to enhance the patients' therapeutic response to treatments and care. As we develop our relationships with patients, we should be cognizant of our power. An organized approach to the therapeutic aspects of the pharmacist–patient relationship should be integrated with the drug therapy evaluation to achieve optimal potential for patient healing. As we progress, we will incorporate learning about the therapeutic strategies that are commonly incorporated when a health care provider uses the therapeutic relationship to enhance patient healing.[16] Pharmacists must develop habits of thinking and acting that fully and accurately recognize the concerns of patients and that demonstrate the empathic commitment of pharmacists to patients.[15,17]

Responsibility as Patient Advocate. Your role as a patient advocate is substantive in today's pharmacist practice. You will increasingly be expected to provide advice, expertise, and direct care related to promoting wellness, improving medication access, and performing social service functions. This role is complementary to your role in the therapeutic relationship. These functions are the extrinsic actions that you take to advance the care necessary for the patient, while the therapeutic relationship is of intrinsic value to the patient.

Identifying the Patient's Health Care Needs

Are you and the patient a good fit? Do you offer what the patient needs? For the patient's preferences to be incorporated into the delivery of care, he or she must be able to express preferences. Your role is to support the patient's concepts of health and his or her values and beliefs. As a pharmacist, you must be prepared to care and advocate for, to the best of your ability, people from diverse backgrounds. Within this context, you should determine the following:

- Is the patient able to understand the information you provide about treatment?
- Does the patient demonstrate the ability to appreciate how that information applies to his or her situation?
- Does the patient have the ability to reason?
- Does the patient have the ability to make a choice and express it?

You must ensure that the patient is able to act on his or her own behalf, to an optimal capacity, given circumstances that will allow. If the patient is not capable of any of these four items, then it is the pharmacist's responsibility to work with a representative (e.g., interpreter or proxy) to best serve that patient's needs.[18]

Clinical Practice Skills

In addition to both your practice philosophy and health beliefs, you will integrate a unique set of clinical practice skills with clinical reasoning to practice patient-centered care. The knowledge, skills, and behaviors may be described as follows: physical assessment, clinical assessment, drug information and evidence-based practice, communication and patient counseling, caring behavior, professional behavior, and documentation skills. Clinical reasoning is built on three skills: empathy, moral reasoning, and metacognition. As you integrate the clinical practice and clinical reasoning skills with time, you are developing expertise in practice that is reflective of your continual development. Let's briefly review each area.

Physical Assessment Skills. Pharmacists perform limited physical examinations to diagnose patient complaints and monitor patient care progress. Training in physical assessment is provided in schools of pharmacy following the approach taught in schools of medicine. Physical examination is performed to determine the normal state of a patient and then any deviations from that state. Four basic assessment techniques used during physical examination include inspection, palpation, percussion, and auscultation. As you use each technique, you also pay attention to the appearance, sensation of touch, sounds, and smell. You observe findings and record these as part of the patient's record.

Clinical Assessment Skills. Pharmacy is built firmly on the concept of technical rationality.[19] This idea states that practitioners are primarily problem solvers who select technical ways to serve particular purposes. If you are a rigorous practitioner, you solve well-formed problems by applying theory and technique from systematic and scientifically derived knowledge. However, as you become oriented to the "fuzzy" problems of daily practice, you find that the problems you encounter are not well-formed but rather "messy indeterminate situations." It does not take long for novice practitioners to learn that they really don't know how to solve many problems they face in practice. They also learn quickly that defining the actual problem that needs to be solved is difficult and sometimes results in no clear resolution.[20] This book is designed to provide a systematic method to collect and assess the clinical information used to determine the patient's problems and health needs. With repetition and practice, you become proficient at "framing" the patient's problems, achieving concordance with your own professional viewpoint and the patient. (That's why it is called pharmacy practice!)

Drug Information and Evidence-Based Practice Skills. Comprehensive delivery of patient-centered care requires that you, as a pharmacist, provide and use accurate and pertinent information to recommend, design, and monitor therapeutic plans. A pharmacist who provides such information readily to patients and the health care team is a valuable contributor to the patient's care. Knowledge applicable to practice through evidence is more readily attained and used in health care today. Pharmacists are rigorously trained in the use of evidence related to treatments. Health care has identified evidence-based practice as the predominant approach to delivering high quality and safe care. Evidence based practice has been defined as, "The conscientious, explicit, and judicious use of current best evidence in making decisions about the care of individual patients. The practice … means integrating individual clinical expertise with the best available external clinical evidence from systematic research."[21]

Requests for drug information are frequent and require rapid follow-up. Time constraints may prohibit referrals to drug information specialists. Furthermore, many organizations do not have such specialists. Therefore, the pharmacist who is directly responsible for the care of a patient must be skilled in drug information retrieval and evaluation to contribute to or to make evidence-based decisions in practice.[22-24]

Communication Skills and Patient Counseling Skills. The pharmacist applies communication skills to interview patients, solicit information from other resources, counsel patients, and advise or consult with other health professionals. Interaction between the pharmacist and patient is essential to ensure that a relationship is established and maintained based on caring, trust, open communication, cooperation, and mutual decision-making. Similarly, the pharmacist must communicate with other health professionals to achieve optimal care for the patient. In this relationship, the pharmacist holds the patient's welfare paramount, maintains an appropriate attitude of caring for the patient's welfare, and uses all of his or her professional knowledge and skills on the patient's behalf. In exchange, the patient agrees to supply personal information and preferences and participate in the therapeutic plan. The pharmacist develops mechanisms to ensure that the patient has access at all times. Reviewing prescriptions, clarifying their appropriateness, and discussing the patient's care needs in relationship to the medication is central to providing care.

Caring Behavior Skills. One of your greatest challenges may be to balance a caring approach to the patient while simultaneously balancing the demanding responsibilities of taking a patient's history, performing drug information searching and retrieval, managing the dispensing process, overseeing the use of technologies, reconciling medication use, evaluating dosing, and preparing medications for administration. Yes, it is caring to use your knowledge, expertise, and quality delivery of pharmacotherapy and pharmaceuticals. But caring is also interpersonal. Professional caring behaviors have the value of healing, comfort, giving, and social support for those patients who are open to it. The pharmacist must attain the skills listed below to be a professional capable of routinely incorporating these behaviors into practice. For many of your patients, achieving the patient's desired outcomes requires both. Skills and attributes needed by a pharmacist include

- Learning to know and care for self.
- Learning to care for others personally and professionally.
- Seeing others as persons.
- Becoming more accepting of others.
- Seeking help from others.
- Gaining confidence.
- Coping effectively with stress.
- Learning to empathize.
- Supporting and helping others.
- Committing to the future.
- Displaying collegiality instead of competition.
- Treating people as unique individuals.

- Considering the whole picture.
- Being less judgmental.
- Valuing diversity.

In the *ASHP Statement on Pharmaceutical Care,* the following excerpt assists us in understanding that care means the context of pharmaceutical care.[25]

"**Care.** Central to the concept of care is caring, *a personal concern for the well being of another person.* At the heart of any type of patient care, there exists a one-to-one relationship between a caregiver and a patient. *In pharmaceutical care, the irreducible 'unit' of care is one pharmacist in a direct professional relationship with one patient.* In this relationship, the pharmacist provides care directly to the patient and for the benefit of the patient. The health and well being of the patient are paramount. *The pharmacist makes a direct, personal, caring commitment to the individual patient and acts in the patient's best interest.* The pharmacist cooperates directly with other professionals and the patient in designing, implementing, and monitoring a therapeutic plan intended to produce definite therapeutic outcomes that improve a patient's quality of life."

Other text in the statement helps us to better understand the depth and meaning of the term "care." Principal elements within the statement include medication-related, care, outcomes, quality of life, and responsibility. A specific, purposeful definition for care has been examined extensively by the nursing profession. Jean Watson has developed a framework that has been the primary influence on nurses. This framework is entitled the Carative Factors of Watson and translates fluidly to the practice of pharmacy.[26,27] When caring for a patient, these factors provide a values basis to the behaviors we choose to adopt. The factors are as follows:

1. Formation of a humanistic-altruistic system of values;
2. Instillation of faith-hope;
3. Cultivation of sensitivity to one's self and to others;
4. Development of a helping-trust relationship;
5. Promotion and acceptance of the expression of positive and negative feelings;
6. Systematic use of the scientific problem solving method for decision making;
7. Promotion of interpersonal teaching–learning;
8. Provision for a supportive, protective, and (or) corrective mental, physical, sociocultural, and spiritual environment;
9. Assistance with the gratification of human needs; and
10. Allowance of existential–phenomenological forces.

The major assumption underlying these factors is that caring can only be effectively demonstrated and practiced interpersonally. Caring itself consists of carative factors that result in the satisfaction of certain human needs. Effective caring promotes health and individual or family growth. Caring responses accept people not only as they are now but for what they may become. Furthermore, a caring environment offers the development of potential while allowing the person to choose the best action for him- or herself at a given time. Caring is more "healthogenic" than curing. The practice of caring integrates biophysical knowledge with knowledge of human behavior to generate or promote health and to provide ministrations to those who are ill. Therefore, a science of caring is complementary to the science of curing. The practice of caring must be central to pharmacy.

To be good, caring must be directed at the right things. Pharmacists should concentrate on how we care about patients and the way we express care through professional actions. Models of health illustrate the importance of incorporating caring behaviors into the training of pharmacists.

Professional Behavior Skills. Pharmacists are professionally socialized—a process of inculcating a profession's attitudes, values, and behaviors in an individual. The goal is to develop professionalism in all that a pharmacist does. Professionalism is a distinctive competence or an ability to provide a service that is valued by an individual as well as recognized by law and custom collectively.[28] Professional competence requires that the individual possesses skills based on technical and scientific information. This is the basis for expertise. Professional competence also requires that the individuals commit themselves to using their ability for the benefit of those they serve. This is the basis for trust. Finally, professional competence requires a commitment to colleagues to ensure that each individual in the profession meets its standards through self-monitoring and self-discipline. Knowledge, skill, and beliefs displayed by a professional include

1. maintaining the knowledge and skills of a profession.
2. remaining committed to self-improvement of skills and knowledge.
3. holding a service orientation.
4. displaying pride in the profession.
5. treating the relationship with the patient as covenantal.
6. demonstrating creativity and innovation.
7. demonstrating a conscience and trustworthiness.
8. displaying accountability for the work performed.
9. demonstrating ethically sound decision making.
10. leading.

Documentation Skills. Pharmacists communicate their own actions and their recommendations to other professionals through proficient documentation skills. Documentation serves as the primary method of both communicating what is needed or being done with a patient, or sharing about what has happened in a patient's life so that resources may be appropriately directed toward continued good care. Greater detail about documentation is provided in Chapter 4.

Clinical Reasoning

Clinical reasoning refers to the problem solving process that you employ with patient problems. Synonyms for the term clinical reasoning include "clinical problem solving" or "the clinical scientific method." Barrows defines the clinical reasoning process as a dynamic, cyclic, reiterative process in which observation, analysis, synthesis, deduction, induction, hypothesis generation, hypothesis testing, inquiry–strategy design, and skills of examination are interrelated.[29] Important skills that support clinical reasoning include empathy, moral reasoning, and metacognition. A representation of the Clinical Reasoning Process is shown in **Figure 2-4**.

Empathy. At the core of caring behavior in the pharmacist–patient relationship is empathy. Empathy is a reflexive understanding of patient and self.[30] In essence, the ability to empathize is to be able to put yourself in someone else's place, sometimes referred to as being able to "walk in someone else's shoes."

Moral Reasoning. Pharmacists who demonstrate the best clinical performance have high moral reasoning skills. A recent work provides an excellent discussion on the application of moral reasoning by pharmacists.[31] Moral reasoning skills are the processes an individual goes through to arrive at decisions. Kohlberg's stages of moral development (**Table 2-2**) describes moral reasoning in the context of development. Moral reasoning is a significant determinant of how pharmacists behave; pharmacists with higher moral reasoning skills demonstrate better clinical performance. Research has demonstrated that a person in the health professions who has more advanced moral reasoning skills will likely not be a poor clinical performer for patients. The idea of being inadequate as a caring professional is morally unacceptable. These individuals work at being competent and effective as a standard of practice behavior.[32,33]

Metacognition. Knowing intuitively is to have a direct understanding without reasoning. Metacognition refers to deliberation and reflection during problem solving. It is the hallmark of an expert clinical reasoner.

Scope of Practice. Standards of practice represent a consensus of professional judgment, expert opinion, and documented evidence that become society's specific expectations of what a professional should perform. They represent the behaviors for which a professional is accountable. These standards help us by providing guidance and direction to pharmacy practitioners and to other audiences that affect pharmacy practice. Professional organizations often write standards of practice to help practitioners comply with federal and state laws and regulations, to meet accreditation requirements, and to improve pharmacy practice and patient care. They are usually written to establish reasonable goals that can be attained while still being progressive and challenging. They generally do not represent minimum levels of practice but rather what the profession has tacitly or formally agreed represents expectations to achieve.

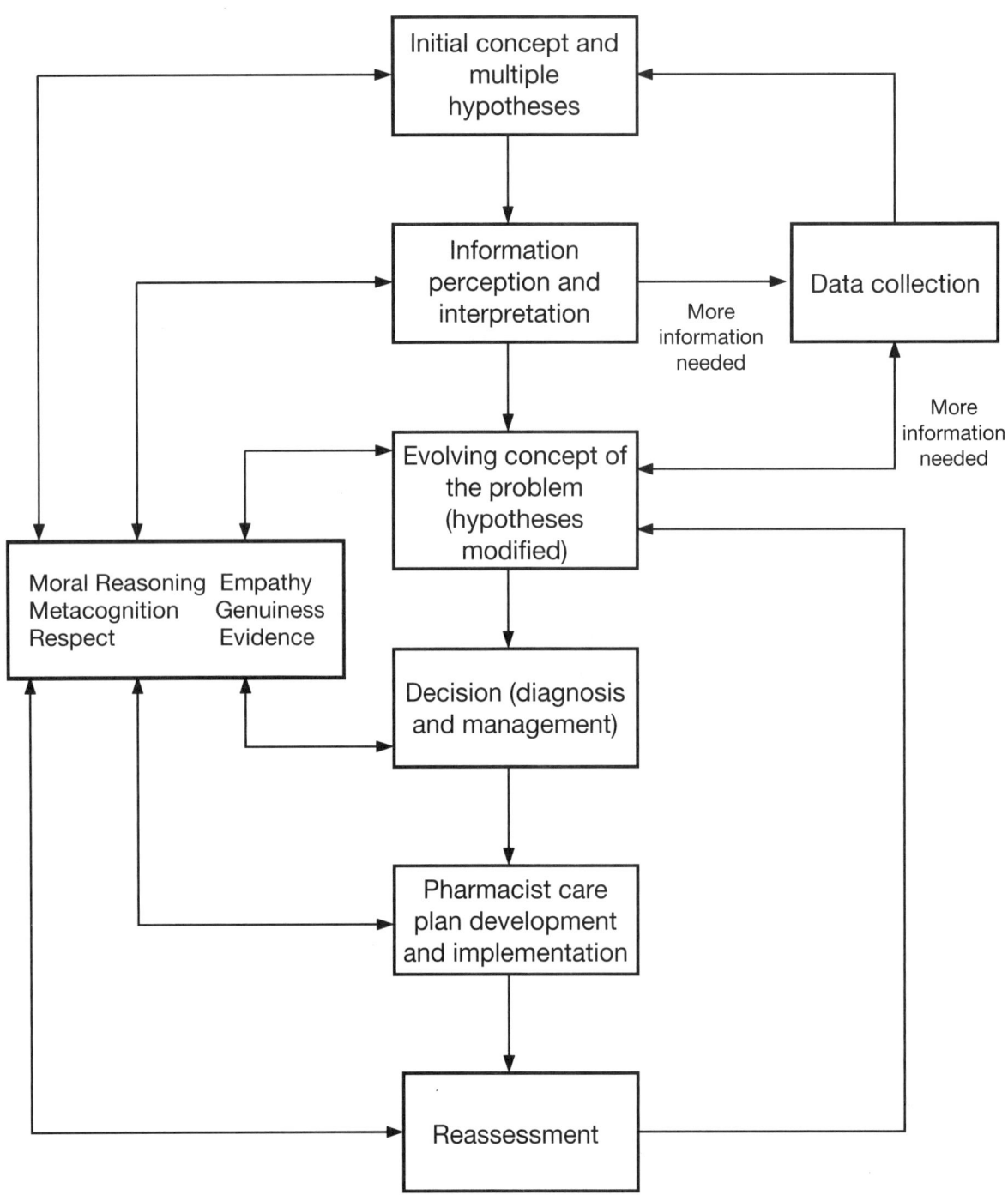

Figure 2-4. Clinical Reasoning Process for Pharmacists (Adapted from Jones MA. Clinical reasoning in manual therapy. **Phys Ther.** *1992; 72:875–84.)*

TABLE 2-2.
Kohlberg's Stages of Moral Development Complemented by Case Example

The following six stages of moral development are illustrated with a case example that might be observed in a routine pharmacy practice situation.

Stage 1: The morality of obedience—Do what you are told.
Pharmacy example: John the pharmacist is instructed by his regional pharmacy manager to not counsel patients unless they ask today because it will slow down the prescription turnaround time. The pharmacist obeys.

Stage 2: The morality of instrumental egoism and simple exchange—Let's make a deal.
Pharmacy example: John likes to counsel and works out a shift in responsibilities for dispensing to the other pharmacist, Marsha, in order to do it.

Stage 3: The morality of interpersonal concordance—Be considerate, nice, and kind, and you'll make friends.
Pharmacy example: Marsha, the pharmacist who accepted the dispensing role, did it to have a good working relationship with John. She finds counseling to be rewarding.

Stage 4: The morality of law and duty to the social order—Everyone in society is obliged to and protected by the law.
Pharmacy example: John and Marsha begin to discuss the fact that they feel they are not meeting their responsibilities to their patients by the way they handled this.

Stage 5: The morality of consensus-building procedures. You are obligated by the arrangements that are agreed to by due process procedures.
Pharmacy example: They contact the regional manager to discuss their viewpoints and to seek support for patient counseling. They discuss the obligations in the profession and the oath they took. He does not change his position.

Stage 6: The morality of non-arbitrary social cooperation—Morality is defined by how rational and impartial people would ideally organize cooperation.
Pharmacy example: Marsha and John restructure the work of the technicians. Even though the tasks they have delegated to the technicians are not all legally supported in the state, they are safe based on their 2 years' employment experience. Both counsel patients.

Modified from Rest JR, Narvaez D. *Moral Development in the Professions: Psychology and Applied Ethics.* Hillsdale, NJ: Lawrence Erlbaum Associates; 1994.

Standards evolve to meet several needs. A primary reason is to meet a collective need among practitioners for authoritative advice. Another reason is to document the stability often based on sufficient experience that a standard is reasonable. Standards of practice develop because they are relevant to the practice of a significant portion of a profession's members.[34]

The scope of practice is the breadth of responsibilities to the boundaries of what a professional is allowed to do under the legally recognized authority granted. Scope of practice is defined by the practice act of the health professional, and it is interpreted in the context of the standards of practice for that profession. Each pharmacist has the same scope of practice based on the licensure status of the pharmacist. However, some have broadened scopes of practice through collaborative practice agreements with other providers.

Development of Expertise. Pharmacists want to be able to solve problems encountered in clinical practice, and patients want to be treated by health professionals who are highly competent and have a high level of expertise. What elements contribute to development of expertise? Agreement exists that certain factors, identified across professions, distinguish experts from novices. Experts perform complex tasks in their areas of expertise more accurately than novices and solve problems with greater ease. They have superior memory for information related to their area of expertise. Experts are better at perceiving patterns among the cues in their data gathering than are novices and they hold knowledge in a highly specific area, making it readily retrievable when needed.

Experts are believed to have knowledge that is not the same as the knowledge taught in professional schools. The wise actions that professionals use involve practical knowledge. Practitioners add to a practical knowledge base not merely through experience but through a process of reflection. Professionals learn from experience by using reflective inquiry to think about what they are doing, what worked, and what did not work as they are doing it.

A representation model of expertise presented here incorporates elements of knowledge, skills, clinical reasoning, skill acquisition, and reflection similar to Sternberg's model of developing expertise (see **Figure 2-5**). Practical aspects to expertise development are discussed at greater length in a later chapter. The ultimate goal of a pharmacist should be to become expert as a patient-centered practitioner in all roles throughout one's professional career.[35]

Care Plan Development and Implementation. Care plan development and implementation are the "start with the end in mind" part of your work. The care plan is the application of your philosophy of practice, knowledge and skills, and clinical reasoning, integrated in a way that best serves the patient's need from the patient's point-of-view. The plan identifies 1) the patient's problems and illnesses, 2) the goals and outcomes expected, 3) care approaches to be implemented, 4) ways they are to be implemented, and 5) ways the patient will be monitored to determine if the needs are being met.

To achieve this, personal integrity in the relationship with the patient is essential. What you believe in must be matched by what you do. We know that empathy is important to being able to put oneself in another's situation. We must also understand that it is right to act on his or her behalf to do whatever we can to improve the person's situation. To achieve this, you may find that you need to involve as many caretakers as possible, when possible. Counsel to build the support structure around the patient while you provide pharmaceutical care.

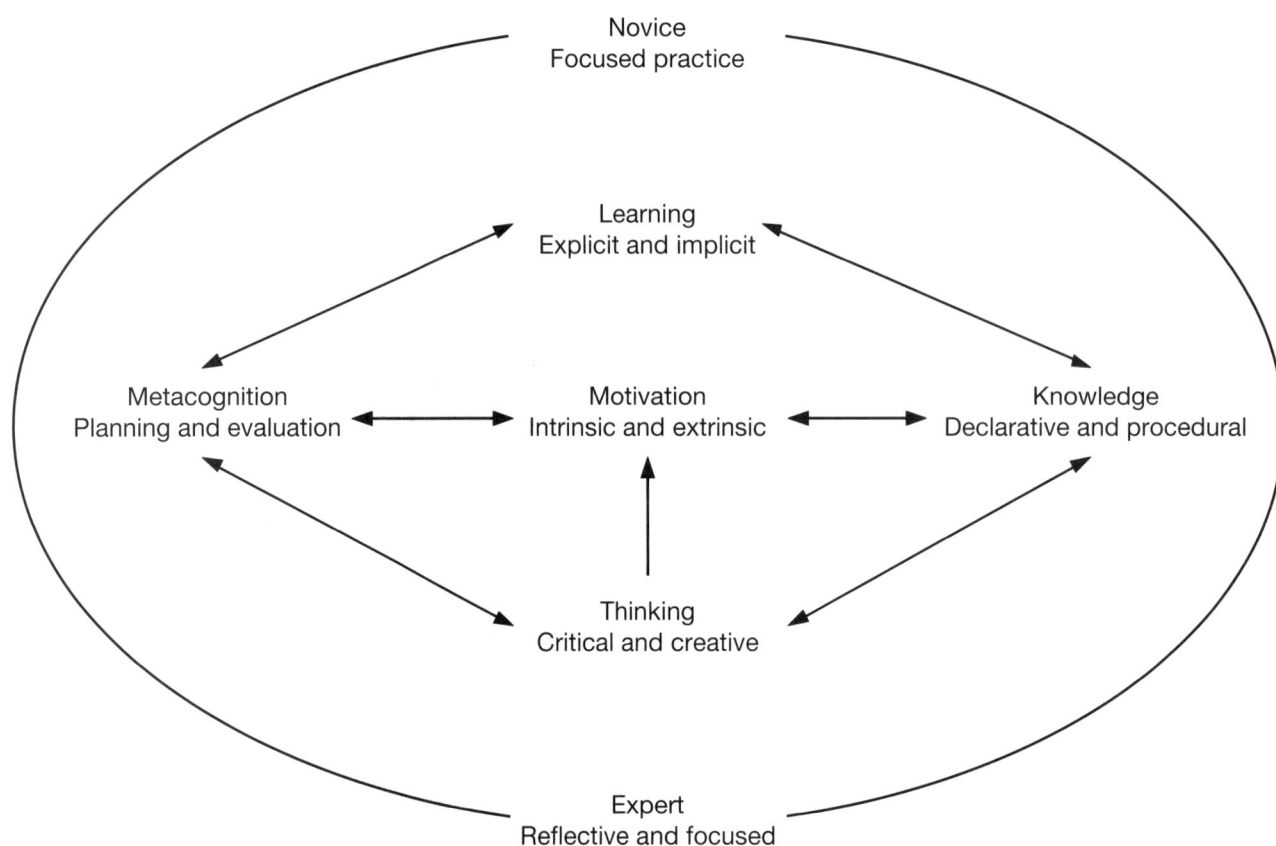

Figure 2-5. Model of Developing Expertise (Adapted from Sternberg R. Abilities are forms of developing expertise. **Educ Researcher.** *1998; 28:11–20.)*

CASE EXAMPLE
Pharmacist's Coordination of Care

Pharmacists practicing in the home care setting are responsible for monitoring and often coordinating many aspects of care plan delivery. Martha Jones is a home bound patient who is receiving 6 weeks of vancomycin administered by infusion pump into a peripheral central venous catheter (PICC line) for an infected knee following total arthroplasty. You receive a call from Martha complaining of an audible pump alarm when initiating the vancomycin infusion. You review the pump procedure with Martha and determine there is no operator error or pump failure issues. You ask Martha what is her procedure for flushing the double lumen PICC line. She reports the home nurse instructed her to flush the PICC line ports with saline before and after each infusion. She also reports that it is very difficult to push the saline flush into the catheter. You contact the home care nurse to discuss the patient's situation. The nurse reports on her last visit she was unable to get any blood return on either lumen and had to get weekly labs via vena-puncture rather than the PICC line. You ask the nurse if the patient was taught to use heparin for catheter maintenance. The nurse confirms teaching the patient to use saline before infusion, saline after infusion and then heparin to load the catheter.

As the home care pharmacist, you contact the orthopedic physician and report possible catheter occlusion related to the omission of heparin flushes. You recommend Cathflo® (alteplase) per package insert for each catheter to avoid pulling and replacement of catheter, which may require emergency room visit for this patient who is currently home bound. The physician gives you orders for Cathflo and for the home care nurse to administer the medication per pharmacist instructions. You contact the home care nurse to update the care plan, including patient/caregiver education on catheter maintenance. You call Martha Jones and explain the problem and to tell her to expect a nursing visit. You also offer to send Martha written information on how to flush her PICC line. You instruct Martha how and when to restart the vancomycin regimen once the catheter is functional.

TYPES OF PHARMACY PRACTICE

Pharmacy Practice Related to Direct Patient Care

The numerous roles you occupy as a pharmacist that we describe as "practice" sometimes do not involve the direct interaction and involvement of a patient. For purposes of this book, the term *pharmacy practice* will specifically apply to the roles you have as a pharmacist that directly involve patients. You will use the philosophy, knowledge, skills, behavior, and clinical reasoning to be effective in all roles. However, the concept of practice in the clinical context means the direct care of patients.

To know the ways you can use your clinical skills, you must understand your role for its potential breadth and depth of responsibilities as well as the expertise required to meet them. Your practice will take on characteristics that likely classify you as a *general pharmacy practitioner* or as a *specialized pharmacy practitioner*.

Responsibility for Dispensing. Both categories of practice may or may not involve the dispensing of pharmaceuticals directly; however, the majority of pharmacists' duties include dispensing as a basic responsibility. When dispensing takes place, it may be performed by the pharmacist or by a pharmacy technician or pharmacist intern directly under the supervision of a pharmacist. Functional models vary. In general, if your position is responsible for dispensing or its oversight, you have the broadest opportunities for care input, problem identification and resolution, problem prevention, and care delivery. If your position does not involve dispensing, then your ability to effect and implement changes to the care plan becomes one of recommending and following up (much like a quality assurance check).

General Pharmacy Practice

As a generalist, you are expected to have extensive knowledge about pharmaceuticals and treatments. Your role is to serve the varied and many—and respond to the multiple needs of patients quickly and simultaneously. In general, the practice responds "on demand." And, in this sense, it *is* demanding. Your scope of knowledge about pharmaceuticals and treatments is vast, and your ability to use drug information resources to continuously provide competent care must be well developed. The generalist represents most of us in practice. Examples of generalists include an inpatient hospital pharmacist, a community pharmacist, a nursing home consulting pharmacist, a home care pharmacist, or a clinical pharmacist.

Specialized Pharmacy Practice

As a specialist, you are expected to have depth about a narrower area of pharmaceuticals and treatments. Specialists are needed to serve those who have highly complex treatment needs. This complexity may be related to the clinical reasoning applied to product use, ongoing care processes related to product use, and/or complexity of product preparation, delivery, and administration. Examples of specialists include a hospital pharmacist whose primary focus is critical care, nutrition, or oncology. A pharmacist may run a specialty care clinic in anticoagulation, asthma, diabetes, or dyslipidemia in a health system or community pharmacy.

Collaborative Drug Therapy Management

The delegation of prescriptive authority to pharmacists has been successfully applied in acute care, long-term care, and ambulatory care settings. In public health and military settings, pharmacists have frequently been delegated prescriptive authority under protocol. This authority has been and continues to be a natural extension of the pharmacist's professional duties.

The professional pharmacy can be recognized as part of the solution to the three most significant problems in health care: escalating costs, insufficient access to medical care, and inconsistent quality of care. Pharmaceutical care provides several benefits, including the following: 1) patients receive care in drug therapy management from the most appropriate health professional, 2) efficiency of physician-directed care is enhanced by shifting appropriate drug therapy management functions to the pharmacist, and 3) more patients receive required medical services by increasing the amount of physician time available. Use of the pharmacist in this manner extends the availability of primary patient care service, enhances the overall quality of care, and is cost effective. In general, receiving delegated authority involves the following:

1. Authority granted to a pharmacist is delegated by a physician based upon the demonstrated knowledge and competence of the pharmacist;
2. Pharmacists and physicians voluntarily enter into professional arrangements resulting in prescriptive authority under protocol; and
3. The purpose of these arrangements is to improve the general public health by extending a higher quality of health care services to more patients than is currently available.

Health care services in which pharmacists' prescriptive authority under protocol is practiced demonstrate equivalent or higher levels of health care services and outcomes than when pharmacists were not involved in providing these services.[36,37] Prescriptive authority ranges from therapeutic interchange to complex functions such as initiating drug therapy, ordering laboratory tests, and performing physical assessments to determine a patient's response to therapy. Other examples include performing pharmacokinetic dosing consultation, modifying doses based on patient specific characteristics, writing discharge prescriptions, and authorizing medication refills. **Table 2-3** describes the usual arrangements for prescriptive authority privileges for a pharmacist.

Medication Therapy Management Services

Medication Therapy Management is a practice conducted by a health care professional with a patient to optimize the results obtained from medication therapies. This practice is a reimbursable form of health care service for Medicare beneficiaries. The legislation that authorizes this program is the Medicare Prescription Drug Improvement and

TABLE 2-3.
Implementation of Prescriptive Authority

Implementation of prescriptive authority usually involves the following:

1. A protocol between the physician and the pharmacist is written, which clearly defines the arrangement with respect to the delegated prescribing authority.

2. These protocols are generally readily retrievable from either of the parties involved in the arrangement. Individuals are generally not required to submit these protocols to any governing body for prior approval, although this varies by state or practice setting.

3. Core elements of the protocol should include the following:

    d. a written statement specifying that prescriptive authority of the stated physician or physician group practice is delegated to the pharmacist(s);

    e. the prescribing activities that are delegated must be clear to both the physician(s) and pharmacist(s);

    f. the scope of practice for the pharmacist should be defined for each protocol;

    g. limits are identified beyond which the physician must be contacted in order for the pharmacist to proceed;

    h. procedures are clearly defined for documenting the pharmacist's practice decisions and care provided;

    i. a time limit for each protocol arrangement should exist, beyond which the protocol should be reviewed and revised, if necessary;

    j. a system should exist in which the physician and pharmacist periodically evaluate the quality of care provided to patients who are treated using the protocol treatment guidelines; and

    k. pharmacists must demonstrate and maintain knowledge and competence needed to meet appropriate standards of practice.

In general, the minimum qualification of a pharmacist to practice prescriptive authority under protocol is a pharmacy license.

Modernization Act of 2003.[38] These services can and are offered to other patient groups; however, mechanisms for payment for services vary. While pharmacists are the most prepared professionals to offer these services, other health care providers may also offer these services if they are considered qualified to do so. This program is discussed at greater length in Chapter 3.

PRIORITIZING PATIENT CARE IN A BUSY PRACTICE

Depending on your practice, you may or may not be able to gather a comprehensive database on every patient. A clinical pharmacist in an inpatient dialysis service may see 10 to 20 patients each day. For the experienced clinician, the resources to efficiently develop a comprehensive database are likely available, so all patients will probably be evaluated. However, a lone pharmacist providing clinical services to 80 patients in a small community hospital would have to evaluate and prioritize patients to determine which have the greatest need or who would benefit most from direct care. In this setting, the pharmacist may create a modified database for every patient. Similarly, a community pharmacy that provides comprehensive drug therapy monitoring and education within delegated authority protocols will establish these databases on patients. However, a pharmacy providing extensive dispensing and compounding services combined with basic counseling services may need to create only a modified record to provide this service and care. Patients require a wide range of care surrounding their pharmaceutical issues. Whenever a pharmacist evaluates a patient's drug-related needs to determine the level of care, pharmaceutical care as a concept is maintained.

The pharmacist's professional expertise is put to its best use when this practice is applied in a patient-centered fashion with an adequate database to best serve the patient.

What types of patients may benefit most from your in-depth evaluation? Depending on your practice site, the following factors have been used to organize patient care delivery and determine priorities:

Patients Who Seek Your Care. These patients are a first priority. The therapeutic process begins when a patient decides to seek care.

Age. Geriatric patients tend to take more medication and have more medication-related problems. Pediatric patients need a substantially greater emphasis on individualized dosing of their medications.

Critical Care. These patients have complex medication regimens that require extensive monitoring as well as complex biotechnology considerations in both preparation and administration.

Consultations. Patients requiring the services of pharmacy consult teams (e.g., nutrition or kinetics) or patients referred by a physician should be monitored by a pharmacist to follow up the consultation.

Drug Use Review or Adverse Drug Reactions. You also may prioritize patients by targeting the medication they are receiving. For example, aminoglycosides or warfarins are often associated with dosing problems, adverse drug reactions, and patient education needs (e.g., warfarin).

Particular Disease States. Patients with renal failure, for example, deserve special attention because of the reduced dosages required for many medications and because some medications and other substances can exacerbate renal failure.

Multiple Prescription Medications or Complex Regimens. Some pharmacists working in ambulatory care settings target patients who take five or more prescribed medications because they often have difficulty managing their regimens.

Nonadherence. Patients who do not adhere to care plan regimens are often the ones who are referred to pharmacists for care. Pharmacists are optimally linked in professional communication networks, communities, and with the health care industry to help patients with medication assistance programs and referral to other professionals, services, and community initiatives. The in-depth interviewing abilities, communication skills, expertise in drug regimen design, and ready access to pharmacists greatly enhance a patient's opportunity to benefit from therapeutic regimens and professional care.

SUMMARY

As a pharmacist, you must adapt to the changing needs of patients and society. You must develop your own professional identity that includes a sound philosophy of practice as well as a solid set of skills, knowledge, behaviors, and adeptness at clinical reasoning. A patient-centered approach requires you to recognize and accept the patient's desires and expectations. To achieve patient-centered care, you must master the clinical practice skills of clinical assessment, drug information, communication, professional behavior, caring behavior, and clinical reasoning including empathy, moral reasoning, and metacognition. As you gain expertise, you will recognize the value of your relationship with the patient, and you will develop advocacy skills to improve the patient's outcomes.

ASSESSMENT QUESTIONS

1. Distinguish among disease-centered, pharmaceutical-centered, and patient-centered pharmacy practice.
2. Describe the care aspect of pharmaceutical care, as perceived by a patient.
3. What distinguishes a generalist practice from a specialist practice?
4. Describe the characteristics of a pharmacist that separate the novice from the expert.

INTRODUCTION TO FOUR PHARMACISTS' CASES

We will follow the lives of four patients and four pharmacists throughout this book as they work together in a pharmacy practice setting related to the patients' care needs. Let's meet the pharmacists and read their stories.

PHARMACIST 1

NASIR JABR
PharmD, RPh

Mr. Nasir Jabr is a 37-year-old man who has traveled far in his life journey. He immigrated from Jordan through Canada and is first generation in the United States. Mr. Jabr has worked extremely hard to obtain his education and find a meaningful career in the health professions. Raised in a family of six children, Jabr is the oldest and hopes to have his brothers and sisters join him in the United States. His family is highly educated. They are Muslims, and he is a devout follower of the Islamic faith. Mr. Jabr is generous to his neighbors and remains active in his community as a soccer coach and teacher of religious classes. He resides in Detroit, Michigan, where he has lived for 3 years. Mr. Jabr works for a community pharmacy chain. His own health beliefs are broad, and he emphasizes nutritional approaches to health. When Mr. Jabr injured his back during a soccer match several years ago, he consulted a chiropractor.

CASE-SPECIFIC QUESTIONS

Instructions: Complete the answer to each of the following questions.

1. Pharmacist 1—Nasir Jabr, PharmD, RPh. What model of health most likely describes the one to which Mr. Jabr relates?

2. What characteristics are likely to influence how he views the health needs of the patients he serves?

3. Which of the 10 carative factors of Watson are less likely to be understood and employed by Jabr?

PHARMACIST 2

CHRISTINE JOHNSTON
PharmD, RPh

Mrs. Christine Johnston is a 35-year-old Caucasian woman of German descent who moved to the San Antonio, Texas, area to complete a pharmacy residency when she was 22 years old. She stayed in Texas because she really enjoyed her ambulatory care clinic experience and was offered a position as an ambulatory care pharmacist after her residency.

Mrs. Johnston is married to a man who works full time at a law firm. They have two children—a 10-year-old daughter and a 7-year-old son. She is an active professional in the local health-system pharmacists' organization. She mentors pharmacy students and offers a clerkship experience. Conservative in her views about health, Johnston's own beliefs separate the spiritual nature of healing from those of the biomedical approach. She does not integrate these ideas for herself and does not connect spirituality to a healing process.

CASE-SPECIFIC QUESTIONS

Instructions: Complete the answer to each of the following questions.

1. Pharmacist 2—Christine Johnston, PharmD, RPh. What model of health most likely describes the one to which Mrs. Johnston relates?

2. What characteristics are likely to influence how she views the health needs of the patients she serves?

3. Which of the 10 carative factors of Watson are less likely to be understood and employed by Johnston?

PHARMACIST 3

LUISA RODRIGUEZ
PharmD, RPh

Ms. Luisa Rodriguez is a second-generation Mexican American woman who resides in Bellevue, Nebraska, just 8 miles south of Omaha. She is a single woman who is 42 years old. She enjoys her work as a hospital pharmacist with a split centralized/decentralized service model in a major hospital with a pediatrics and intensive care unit service.

Ms. Rodriguez lives near her parents and grandparents in the community. Her grandparents are traditional in their beliefs about health and spiritual healing. She is well aware of the cultural differences among her family members, herself, and the patients she generally serves. Ms. Rodriguez has never been sick enough to be dependent upon the health care system. Her mother and grandmother have always integrated their health needs into the traditional family approach and used remedies for comfort. Ms. Rodriguez understands the ways of her family as well as her own scientific discipline and evidence-based approach to her pharmacy practice.

CASE-SPECIFIC QUESTIONS

Instructions: Complete the answer to each of the following questions.

1. Pharmacist 3—Luisa Rodriguez, PharmD, RPh. What model of health most likely describes the one to which Rodriguez relates?
2. What characteristics are likely to influence how she views the health needs of the patients she serves?
3. Which of the 10 carative factors of Watson are less likely to be understood and employed by Rodriguez?

PHARMACIST 4

MICHAEL JONES
MS, RPh

Mr. Michael Jones has been a practicing pharmacist for 20 years. He has been a community pharmacist with long-term care experience but is presently a hospital pharmacist at a health system in Atlanta, Georgia. He is a 45-year-old white male who was born and raised in Boston, Massachusetts. His family goes back more than 10 generations in Boston. Extensive clinical care programs were not widespread where he trained 25 years ago. His relocation to Atlanta and his accumulated experiences motivated him professionally to complete a specialized training program in anticoagulation management. He has trained several other pharmacists over the years and is responsible for the pharmacy staff development program in this particular area at the hospital.

Raised as a Jehovah's Witness, Jones is an active follower of this faith and upholds many of the beliefs and practices. He occasionally finds conflicts between the medical treatment choices he is involved in and his own faith. He is married and has one 3-year-old child.

CASE-SPECIFIC QUESTIONS

Instructions: Complete the answer to each of the following questions.

1. Pharmacist 4—Michael Jones, MS, RPh. What model of health most likely describes the one to which Mr. Jones relates?
2. What characteristics are likely to influence how he views the health needs of the patients he serves?
3. Which of the 10 carative factors of Watson are less likely to be understood and employed by Jones?

REFERENCES

1. Albom M. *Tuesdays with Morrie: An Old Man, A Young Man, and Life's Greatest Lesson.* New York, NY: Double Day; 1997.

2. Bezold C, Halperin JA, Ashbaugh RR, et al. Pharmacy for the 21st century—planning for an uncertain future. *1984—A Guide to More Effective Diagnosis and Treatment.* New York, NY: Norton Medical Books; 1991.

3. Hepler CD, Strand LM. Opportunities and responsibilities in pharmaceutical care. *Am J Hosp Pharm.* 1990; 47:533–43.

4. Allen M. The health dimension in nursing practice, notes on primary care. *J Adv Nurs.* 1981; 6:153–5.

5. Galt KA. The need to define care in pharmaceutical care: an examination across research, practice and education. *Am J Pharm Educ.* 2000; 64:223–33.

6. Levenstein JH. The patient-centered general practice consultation. *South Africa Family Practice.* 1984; 5:276–82.

7. Levenstein JH, McCracken EC, McWhikkey IR, et al. The patient-centered clinical method: I. A model for the doctor-patient interaction in family medicine. *Family Practice.* 1986; 3(1):24–30.

8. Levenstein JH, Brown JB, Weston WW, et al. Patient-centered clinical interviewing. In: Stewart M, Roter D, eds. *Communicating with Medical Patients.* Newbury Park, CA: Sage; 1989.

9. The Health Center Program Policy Information Notice 01-16: Credentialing and Privileging of Health Center Practitioners. Accessed at: http://bphc.hrsa.gov/policy/pin0116.htm. April 30, 2010.

10. Joint Commission Approves Revised Medical Staff Bylaws Standard MS.01.01.01. Accessed at: http://www.jointcommission.org/NewsRoom/NewsReleases/nr_031810.htm. April 30, 2010.

11. Galt KA. Credentialing and privileging for pharmacists. *Am J Health-Syst Pharm.* 2004; 61:661-70.

12. National Practitioner Data Bank Healthcare Integrity and Protection Databank. Accessed at: http://www.npdb-hipdb.hrsa.gov/. April 30, 2010.

13. Covey S. *The Seven Habits of Highly Effective People.* New York, NY: Simon and Schuster; 1995.

14. Zellmer WA. The habits of successful pharmacists. *Am J Health-Syst Pharm.* 2000; 57:1794–6.

15. Novack DH. Therapeutic aspects of the clinical encounter. *Journal of General Internal Medicine.* 1987; 2:346–55.

16. Jensen GM, Gwyer J, Hack LM, et al. *Expertise in Physical Therapy Practice.* Woburn, MA: Butterworth-Heinemann; 1999.

17. Miller SZ, Schmidt HJ. The habit of humanism: a framework for making humanistic care a reflexive clinical skill. *Academic Medicine.* 1999; 74(7):800–3.

18. Tunzi M. Can the patient decide? Evaluating patient capacity in practice. *Am Fam Physician.* 2001; 64:299–306.

19. Shils E. The order of learning in the United States from 1865 to 1920: the ascendancy of the universities. *Minerva.* 1978; 16(2):159–95.

20. Schon DA. *Educating the Reflective Practitioner.* San Francisco, CA: Jossey-Bass Inc.; 1990.

21. David Sackett, Rosenberg WM, Muir Gray JA, et al. Evidence based medicine: what it is and what it isn't. *BMJ.* 1996; 312:71.

22. Galt KA. *The ASHP Clinical Skills Program Drug Information Series, Module 1: Analyzing and Recording a Drug Information Request.* Bethesda, MD: American Society of Health-System Pharmacists, Inc.; 1997.

23. Smith GH, Horton LL, Ferrill MJ. *The ASHP Clinical Skills Program Drug Information Series, Module 2: Evaluating Drug Literature.* Bethesda, MD: American Society of Health-System Pharmacists; 1995.

24. Sackett DL, Richardson WS, Rosenberg W, et al. *Evidence-Based Medicine—How to Practice and Teach EBM.* New York, NY: Churchill Livingstone, Inc.; 1997.

25. American Society of Hospital Pharmacists. ASHP statement on pharmaceutical care. *Am J Hosp Pharm.* 1993; 50:1720–3.

26. Watson J. *Nursing: the Philosophy and Science of Caring.* Boston, MA: Little and Brown; 1979.

27. Gramling L, Nugent K. Teaching caring within the context of health. *Nurse Educator.* 1998; 23:47–51.

28. Starr P. *The Social Transformation of American Medicine.* New York, NY: Basic Books; 1984.

29. Barrows HS, Pickell GC. *Developing Clinical Problem Solving Skills—A Guide to More Effective Diagnosis and Treatment.* New York, NY: Norton Medical Books; 1991.

30. More ES. Empathy as a hermeneutic practice. *Theoretical Medicine.* 1996; 17(3):243–54.

31. Latif DA. The link between moral reasoning scores, social desirability, and patient care performance scores: empirical evidence from the retail pharmacy setting. *Journal of Business Ethics.* 2000; 25:255–69.

32. Sheehan TJ, Husted SD, Candee D, et al. Moral judgment as a predictor of clinical performance. *Evaluation and the Health Professions.* 1980; 8:379–400.

33. Baldwin DC, Adamson E, Self DJ, et al. Moral reasoning and malpractice: a study of orthopedic surgeons. *American Journal of Orthopedics.* 1996; 25(7):481–4.

34. American Society of Health-System Pharmacists. Introduction. In: Deffenbaugh JH, ed. *Best Practices for Health-System Pharmacy 2000–2001 edition.* Bethesda, MD: 2001; xiii–iv.

35. Adapted from Holyoak KJ. Symbolic connectionism: toward third-generation theories of expertise. In: Ericsson

KA, Smith J, eds. *Toward a General Theory of Expertise.* New York, NY: Cambridge University Press; 1991.

36. Kroner BA. Anticoagulation clinic in the VA Pittsburgh healthcare system. *Pharm Pract Manag Q.* 1998 Oct; 18(3):17–33.

37. Fuller TS, Christensen DB, Williams DH. Satisfaction with prescriptive authority protocols. *J Am Pharm Assoc (Wash).* 1996 (Dec); NS 36(12):739–45.

38. Medicare Prescription Drug, Improvement and Modernization Act of 2003, Pub L. No. 108-173. 117 Stat. 2066 (January 7, 2003). Available at: http://www.cms.hhs.gov/MMAUpdate/downloads/hrl.pdf. Accessed April 30, 2010.

The Practice Setting

Be compassionate, and take responsibility for each other. If we only learned those lessons, this world would be so much better a place."[1]

CHAPTER OUTLINE

Purpose

The Structure of Health Care Delivery
- Physical Settings
- Virtual Settings
- Integration of Physical and Virtual Settings

Systems of Health Care Delivery
- The Medication Use Process, Patient Safety, and Quality of Care
- Methods of Pharmaceutical Product Availability

The Professional Work Environment
- Practice Settings and Patient-Centered Care
- Models of Pharmacists' Services Delivery
- Practice Infrastructure Needs
- Workforce Realities

Payment for Pharmacists' Services
- Salary for Employment Positions
- Reimbursement and Fees for Dispensing Services
- Reimbursement and Fees for Medication Therapy Management Services

Summary

Assessment Questions

Introduction to Four Pharmacists' Practice Settings
- Setting 1: Outpatient—general patient-oriented pharmacy practice
- Setting 2: Outpatient—collaborative drug therapy practice with delegated authority
- Setting 3: Inpatient—general patient-oriented pharmacy practice
- Setting 4: Inpatient—collaborative drug therapy practice with delegated authority

OBJECTIVES

To gain knowledge of:

1. structure of health care delivery in which pharmacy is practiced;
2. systems of health care delivery in which pharmacy is practiced;
3. professional work environment and workforce realities of practice;
4. practice settings where pharmacists provide patient-centered care;
5. range of responsibilities pharmacists may perform in the medication-use process; and
6. methods of pharmacists' payment for medications, services, and care delivery.

PURPOSE

The purpose of this chapter is to describe established processes and structure of contemporary health care delivery as we consider how patient-centered care is provided. Health information technology, pharmacy workforce issues, the medication use process, work environment, and payment considerations are presented to understand how these impact the pharmacist's practice. The medication use process is presented from both a patient safety and quality perspective.

THE STRUCTURE OF HEALTH CARE DELIVERY

Health care delivery is accomplished through a variety of systems and approaches. We often make reference to the "health care delivery system." However, there are many interconnected, and often not connected, systems and networks that provide the patient with the delivery of specific health care services. Patient-centered pharmacist care is one of these services. You and your patients have experiences directly influenced by your practice setting. The pharmacy practice setting provides the necessary resources to support patient safety and quality care that patients expect. A discussion of the physical, virtual, and integrated physical and virtual settings of health care delivery illustrates the varied ways in which health care is organized and structured.

Most physical facilities for health services delivery have health information technologies (HIT) integrated in ways that make health care delivery interdependent upon technology use. Health information technology is the use of technology for enhancing the treatment and care of patients. Use of HIT should facilitate ready access to information support, comprehensive management of medical information, and secure exchange of this information between patients and providers. Providers should be able to interact more closely with each other and improve the quality of care for their patients. Patients should be able to become more involved in their own care through use of HIT.[2]

The United States has been following a plan initiated in 2004 to develop and implement a nationwide electronic health information infrastructure that will allow authorized health care professionals to securely access relevant patient data from any location in the country at any time. This plan was initiated with Executive Order 13335 by the President of the United States. The order intent is to promote health information technology to improve efficiency, reduce medical errors, improve quality of care, and provide better information exchange for patients, physicians, and eventually all health care providers. The national goal of this plan is to have electronic health records for most Americans by 2014. Health information could be routinely exchanged among providers, provider organizations, and patients by establishing a standard for health information exchange and by using a planned health IT architecture.[3] This rapidly evolving technological framework is important to the way we conceptualize places where care is provided or received.

All physical facilities we discuss will incorporate some element of health information technology. The virtual place of receiving and delivering care is evolving rapidly. Pharmacists occupy roles and have responsibilities in all of these patient care settings. However, the majority of health care is provided at specific locations that patients must travel to in order to receive it. The next sections describe the settings where pharmacists commonly provide care.

Physical Settings

The most common physical settings include hospital, outpatient or community, ambulatory clinic, long-term care, home care, or provider office-based practices.

Pharmacists may provide services to these settings as consultants or provide services within these settings as employees. The practice setting itself determines the strategies needed to develop, implement, and sustain the patient-centered pharmacy services.

KEY POINT

The practice setting determines the necessary strategies for sustaining patient-centered services.

Hospitals. Most acute care hospital settings employ pharmacists. The common responsibilities of pharmacists include overseeing and managing medication ordering and product distribution, medication history taking and reconciliation, specialized consultation and rounding practices, policy development for therapeutics (e.g., formulary management, medication administration policies), management of medication use systems, and medication management through care transitions upon hospital discharge. Overall, 26.8% of pharmacists are employed in the hospital setting.[4] Health information technologies utilized in the hospital setting generally include computerized pharmacy records and manual or electronic medication administration records and automated dispensing devices. Additional technologies may include electronic health records, computerized order entry, bar code administration systems, robotic medication systems, and clinical decisions support tools found in a variety of software packages (e.g., drug information resources, drug interaction automated detection, and dosing guideline support). A workforce shortage of pharmacists exists in rural communities. It is common for pharmacists to be primarily employed in a community pharmacy and provide pharmacy services for smaller, critical access community hospitals and/or long-term care consultation.

Community Pharmacies. The most common setting that pharmacists practice in is the community pharmacy. This setting may be an independent pharmacy (14.4% of workforce), chain (24.9%), mass merchandiser (4.9%), or supermarket (9.6%). Pharmacists perform and oversee medication dispensing and patient counseling about proper medication use. Depending on the extent to which a pharmacist's practice is developed, the pharmacist may conduct medication histories, teach ambulatory drug therapy monitoring techniques, set appointments with patients to monitor drug therapy treatments, and operate under collaborative drug therapy practice agreements with physicians.[4] Common technologies encountered in community include automated dispensing systems, prescription vending machines, and electronic prescribing (e-prescribing). Additional technologies may include telepharmacy services in underserved regions of the country.

Skilled Nursing Facilities, Assisted Living Facilities, and Home Health Care. Pharmacists practice in these settings fulfilling a variety of responsibilities. Medication regimen review to assure optimal drug therapy management is the primary function in all. Pharmacists may be involved in medication dispensing and education, along with reviewing medication regimens. Several pharmacist practice models exist to service patients directly at home. There are home infusion companies where pharmacists manage the preparation and dispensing of products and assist in monitoring a patient's response to treatment. Home care pharmacies generally provide intravenous antibiotics, total parenteral nutrition, chemotherapy, and specialty blood products in the home. Home care companies may have pharmacists as a part of an interdisciplinary care provision model to patients. Pharmacists are also included in some home care visit programs to directly assist the complex care of patients on multiple medications to manage chronic conditions. Health information technologies utilized in these settings are typically limited to computerized pharmacy records and manual medication administration records. Some pharmacy settings may also incorporate automated dispensing or robotic technologies.

Virtual Settings

The use of health information technologies and health information exchange systems has led to the evolution of what has become known as *e-Health*. The term "eHealth" refers to the use of information and communication technologies (ICT) for health. It is recognized as one of the most rapidly growing areas in the health industry today. However, limited systematic research has been carried out to inform eHealth policy and practice. This is a rapidly emerging area of care in which pharmacists can have a critical role.

Telehealth Services. Telehealth services are provided through remote access connections to the local communities where people live. It is fairly typical to see a telehealth service supported through a local community hospital by making available a private consultation room. Telehealth services are delivered from practitioners in larger urban and tertiary care environments to smaller communities that do not have the fiscal or workforce capacity of specialists to serve the community. While this is an evolving area in the United States, these services are rapidly becoming one of the solutions in communities with the greatest health disparities.[5]

Telepharmacy Services. Telepharmacy services are provided through remote access connections to local communities where a pharmacy facility is available but no pharmacist is present. This is an emerging practice area where the pharmacist performs a quality assurance check to review medications and then view the product that is prepared by a local person who is a trained pharmacy technician. The technician provides the medication to the patient, and the pharmacist provides counseling and communication with the patient through an interactive web-based camera and display screen system. Medication regimen review and medication therapy management services are conducted using HIT and communication systems to interact with other providers in the community. Telepharmacy services are growing to meet the needs of rural communities in workforce shortage areas that do not have adequate pharmacists.

Integration of Physical and Virtual Settings

The global integration of advancing health information technologies and the Internet into our daily lives has changed the processes of care delivery in all settings. Health information technology has become a critical support infrastructure to pharmacists and integral to pharmacy practice and management. Computer use has evolved with wide access to patients as well as pharmacists. Recent public efforts have produced funding to increase computer availability and use in all sectors of our society. Pharmacists' models of care delivery will continue to change by incorporating technology support and increasing communication through this means to have relationships with patients. Geography will become less important and relationships more important to patients, particularly to those who participate in health information exchange systems built on electronic health record access availability.[6]

Internet-based Information Services. Patients and pharmacists have equal access to finding publicly accessible information on the Internet. Comprehensive expert information is available through consumer-centric approaches, replacing printable patient education materials. This large volume of sophisticated information empowers patients in ways not previously imagined. At the same time, the complexity and volume of information challenge patients to discerning what is useful and appropriate for their own needs. Pharmacists continue to be the most commonly sought after health care professional to assist patients with determining relevant information to their specific health care treatment needs. Pharmacists are responding to increasingly informed patients who call or visit to discuss health issues.

Secure E-mail Communications. Secure messaging technology provides a means for patients to send to and receive messages from health care providers in a manner that protects both the security and privacy of the information exchanged. E-mail provides patients with a 24 hour, 7 day per week method to communicate about their care needs to pharmacists asynchronously. Patients can proceed with the normal demands of life and receive back responses from their pharmacist at a later time. Pharmacists can take the needed time to organize their work and provide high quality, evidence-based responses using this mechanism while meeting the patient's needs in a timely manner.

Internet-based Clinical Support Services. Patients can receive updates about their progress in care and reminders to follow up on care services from their providers without ever leaving home. The use of automated reminders for medication refills through automated telephone or e-mail systems is being incorporated into many health care service systems. Patients can participate in monitoring of drug therapies using web-based services; online healthy lifestyle and wellness programs; self-care assessments and education; and focused programs such as weight loss, smoking cessation, and healthy eating, to name just a few.

The far reaching and gradual but extensive integration of HIT will continue to place ongoing demands on pharmacists. Successful use of HIT will improve the quality and safety of care for patients while enabling pharmacists to efficiently provide that care.

SYSTEMS OF HEALTH CARE DELIVERY

The Medication Use Process, Patient Safety, and Quality of Care

Pharmacists, Patients, and Medication Use Process. The medication use process starts from the time that a medication is determined as needed through the time that a patient has taken it and is being monitored for its effect on outcomes. The process is commonly described in five major steps: prescribing, preparation, dispensing, administering, and monitoring. Pharmacists accept direct responsibility for some or all aspects of the medication use process and indirect responsibility for all steps. Pharmacists may have direct responsibility for prescribing designated classes of drugs for which they have the authority to do so, or by the formation of a collaborative drug therapy management agreement between the pharmacist and an accepted, delegated authority from a licensed prescriber. This opportunity exists in almost all states through laws or regulation. Pharmacists also administer medication in many states. Nationally, pharmacists administer oral, topical, and parenteral products, and in various practice settings. This scope of responsibility places pharmacists in key roles to advance and assure patient safety and improved quality of care. Pharmacists have traditionally accepted the responsibility for monitoring medications. Many state practice acts require the pharmacist to perform medication regimen review. Advanced pharmacy practice models incorporate medication therapy management as a progressive medication monitoring service. Contemporary pharmacy practice requires the pharmacist to have expert knowledge in all aspects of the medication use process. Patients and other health providers expect the pharmacist to assume a shared responsibility for assuring quality and safety in the medication use process in all practice settings.

The Pharmacists' Role in Patient Safety. More than 1.5 million Americans are injured every year by drug errors in hospitals, nursing homes, and physician's offices that do not include estimates of patients' own medication mix-ups.[7] Your primary role as a pharmacist is to embrace patient safety as your first responsibility. Patient safety related to medication use is a primary concern of our nation. Medication errors are one of the most prominent health issues of concern today.[7] In 2006 the Institute of Medicine announced that prevention of medication errors is a primary area of emphasis that we must address. In their published report entitled, *Preventing Medication Errors,* the pharmacist was identified as central to achieving patient safety. Pharmacists were cited in 16 chapters 258 times as central to care strategies of the future to improve safety and quality.[8]

Your first responsibility as a pharmacist should be to patient safety.

The primary or root causes of medication errors are usually in systems of care delivery. The first process step that takes place in the medication use system is prescribing.[9] A 1992 study of 89 community pharmacists in five states documented the frequency and type of prescriber errors in the community setting.[10] The results revealed that for 1.9% of 33,011 new prescription orders, the pharmacists intervened to resolve a prescriber-related problem. Errors of omission, commission, and interactions accounted for 60.5% of these prescriber-related problems. Illegibility accounted for 6.4% of the errors identified. Expert evaluators concluded that 28.3% of the prescribing problems identified during the study could have caused patient harm if the pharmacist had not intervened to correct the problem.

A study by Gleason et al. demonstrated that pharmacists reviewing inpatient (hospital) medication histories determined that 36% of the patients over a 14-month period had avoidable errors in their medication regimens. Several (1.3%) were determined to result in a potentially longer hospitalization if not corrected, 10.4% as potentially causing temporary harm, and 52.4% rated as potentially requiring increased monitoring or intervention to preclude harm. The authors concluded that "hospital pharmacists can also be invaluable in obtaining complex medication histories and collaborating with physicians, nurses and other health care providers on medication reconciliation."[11]

Legibility of prescriptions is a widely recognized cause of medication errors.[12] Inability to correctly read a medication name, dose, or regimen has resulted in injuries and death. The issue is of such importance that the American Medical Association (AMA) studied the legal implications resulting from poor legibility of medication orders. The AMA publicly reported that misinterpretation of physician prescriptions was the second most prevalent and expensive malpractice claim listed on 90,000 malpractice claims filed over a 7-year period.[13] Through computerized physician order entry, printing, and e-prescribing, nearly all of these errors can be eliminated. These strategies resolve the difficulty of translating illegible orders and greatly reduce the need for duplication through transcription to enter information into the ambulatory care patient record.[14] However, this is only one aspect of how patient safety is affected. Clinical decisions resulting in duplications in therapy, inappropriately discontinued therapies, untreated conditions, and avoidable adverse drug reactions are all potential safety problems for patients that can be prevented through professional assessment and patient-centered care provided by the pharmacist.

The Pharmacists' Role in Continuous Quality Improvement in Patient Care. Continuous quality improvement suggests that quality problems emerge primarily from faulty procedures and processes, not from a lack of skill or learning of the part of individuals. Delivery of safe, quality care is dependent upon complex systems. And the quality of health care is based upon safe care, a relationship long known. Studies have clearly demonstrated that quality and safety are intimately related.

The problem is clearly identifying what quality is. The definition from the Institute of Medicine offers a sound framework for all health care providers: Quality is the degree to which health services for individuals and populations increase the likelihood of desired health outcomes and are consistent with current professional knowledge.[15] Quality is frequently described as having three dimensions: quality of input resources, quality of the process of services delivery (the use of appropriate procedures for a given condition), and quality of outcomes of service use (actual improvement in condition or reduction of harmful effects).

This operational definition makes the pharmacists' roles in achieving quality apparent. Pharmacists work to meet the three quality dimensions by being: 1) expert practitioners who are patient centered in care delivery, 2) responsible participants in assuring the quality and safety of the medication use processes, and 3) explicit in practice expectations to achieve improved outcomes for those patients served. Pharmacists occupy functional roles to achieve this and need to continue to learn tools that assist in accomplishing these roles. Examples of such tools include to become expert at interpreting evidence from the published literature to apply to practice, become a human factors knowledgeable professional to assist in analyzing root causes of errors, learning six sigma, and becoming expert at applying total quality management principles such as plan-do-study-act (PDSA).

CASE EXAMPLE

The Pharmacist's Role in Protecting Patient Safety and Improving the Quality of Care

You are the pharmacist in a very busy, independent pharmacy. The pharmacy utilizes pharmacy technicians but is without any bar-coding technology in the filling process. Mr. Carlson calls and asks to speak to the pharmacist. He reports experiencing significant drowsiness since the last time his prescriptions were refilled. The patient wants to know if any of his medications can cause drowsiness. An inspection of his medication profile indicates he is on hydrochlorthiazide, hydralazine, lansoprazole, and enalapril. He recently refilled 2 of his medications: hydralazine and lanzoprazole. You ask the patient to describe the color, shape, and any coding on the hydralazine tablet. You verify using drug information references that the medication is actually hydroxyzine. You inform the patient that a medication error (dispensing error) has occurred and to stop taking the medication. You offer to deliver, to his home, the correct medication. You also contact the prescriber to report the medication error and request any follow-up care.

A careful review of the medication use process revealed that a technician selected the wrong medication and filled the prescription with hydroxyzine rather than hydralazine. The pharmacist's manual double check did not catch the error, and the error reached the patient. Further investigation identified that the two medications are stored in very close proximity to each other. It was determined that a look-a-like/sound-a-like type medication misadventure had occurred. A root cause analysis of this error revealed a high probability of re-occurrence. A review of the error by the quality committee made up of pharmacists, technicians, and management recommended that all look-a-like/sound-a-like medications be identified with a large orange sticker to alert pharmacy personnel of a potential name mix up. The pharmacy management plan to implement the procedure took effect immediately.

Methods of Pharmaceutical Product Availability

Inpatient Setting. Patients receive drug therapy treatments in the inpatient setting by either direct provision from the pharmacy department or by the patient using his or her own medications, which were brought from home.

The vast majority of medications that are administered to patients in the inpatient setting are purchased, compounded, distributed, and dispensed under the supervision and direct services of licensed pharmacists. Pharmaceuticals that are purchased and overseen by pharmacists meet legal requirements for standards of safety and quality.

Occasionally, patients want to take medications that they have brought in from their home settings. This practice is discouraged because of the risks associated with incorrect medication identification and potential mix ups and also concerns about being responsible for the product integrity as a result of not being handled through the routes of pharmaceutical purchasing and delivery that services the inpatient facility. This approach may also bypass established medication safety technologies like bar coding and drug interaction screening. If a patient's request is honored, there is usually a policy and procedure for how to incorporate this practice into the care of the patient within the facility.

Outpatient Setting. The outpatient setting provides more diverse ways to receive pharmaceuticals. Patients can visit pharmacists directly, receive home delivery from a pharmacy or home administration from a home care provider, receive pharmaceuticals through the mail, attend an outpatient setting such as a pharmacy or clinic to have medications administered, and receive them through vending systems.

Visiting the local pharmacy continues to be the predominant way in which patients receive their medication. Many patients find this desirable because of the close relationship developed with the pharmacist, with ready access to the expertise and information provided at a personal level.

A long-standing custom of community pharmacies has been to deliver medications to patients' homes. Some pharmacies have organized home delivery services; others do so for patients with special needs, such as for elderly persons with restricted transportation.

The mail order method of receiving pharmaceuticals and health supplies has become a large sector of the proportion of prescriptions that are refilled. An estimated 30% of all prescription refills are provided in this way. The advantages of mail order include convenience for the patient for non-urgent refills. Some insurance providers encourage mail order use by allowing payment for up to 90 days of medication refilled at a time compared to 30-day limits they impose when a patient comes into the pharmacy directly. Home care pharmacies frequently ship chronic intravenous medications to the home for self administration by patients or family members.

Specialty clinics (e.g., oncology, dialysis) and specialty pharmacies (e.g., on site infusion) provide another method for patients to receive medications. These models have formed to support the complex medication administration needs of patients. Often these models also provide access to expensive medications with follow up billing after the medicine is administered to the patient.

Home care services for administering medications is most commonly a specialty service to provide infused medications and home parenteral nutrition therapies. Typically registered nurses deliver the home therapy, assess the patient, administer the medication, obtain required laboratory samples, and monitor the patient while in the home. Long-term therapies may require the nurse to teach the patient or designated caregiver how to administer home therapies.

Prescription vending machines are found more commonly within community pharmacies or in rural community emergency rooms. The purpose is to provide access to prescription medication after the pharmacist is off the practice site premises or community pharmacies are closed so patients do not have to wait to start therapy. Patients receive written medication teaching sheets from the device as a form of medication counseling. Strict laws and regulations are in place in order to assure safety and quality of the product. As electronic ordering and e-prescribing emerge, it is anticipated that these dispensing devices will receive these types of orders directly, making it possible to have patients go directly to these devices and get started with their medications. The profession of pharmacy has also taken a leadership role in designing guidelines for the safe use of automated dispensing devices.[16]

The emergence of Internet pharmacies over the past decade has been controversial. This form of pharmacy can be practiced legally by conforming to all state rules and regulations. The Internet pharmacy gained a bad reputation because of counterfeit products and widespread illegal distribution emerging visibly through this route. The National Association of Boards of Pharmacy formed the VIPPS accreditation program (Verified Internet Pharmacy Practice Sites) to provide pharmacists and consumers with an indicator of an Internet pharmacy's compliance with state and federal laws and regulations and NABP's criteria. The VIPPS Seal demonstrates public accountability—it is also intended to be a symbol of a pharmacy's commitment to its patients' health and safety. The VIPPS accreditation process provides for ongoing evaluation of an Internet pharmacy's practice. Internet pharmacies function in much the same way as traditional pharmacies and are subject to the same rules, regulations, and patient care requirements as brick-and-mortar pharmacies.[17]

THE PROFESSIONAL WORK ENVIRONMENT

Practice Settings and Patient-Centered Care

The professional service implied by the setting in which you encounter the patient provides an implicit contract. The setting creates certain expectations in the patient's mind. It can either promote or hinder your use of therapeutic strategies with patients. It also implies a specific set of goals for you. For example, a community pharmacy practice setting usually encountered by a patient may or may not provide a place for a lengthy evaluation of complex or chronic medical or psychosocial complaints. It may or may not provide a physical area that offers privacy and security of your communications with the patient. Such an environment can minimize the importance of this role to the patient and make it more difficult for you to practice patient-centered care in this physical setting.

You should assess the professional work environment you are functioning in and determine where the strengths and weaknesses of the environment are to support your service delivery model. Very few practice sites are ideal. However, you may be able to make realistic modifications in the environment to facilitate and support the models of care delivery that are a necessary part of your practice.

Few practice sites are ideal, but you may be able to make modifications in the environment to facilitate and support the models of care delivery in your practice.

Models of Pharmacists' Services Delivery

Medication Therapy Management (MTM) Services. Medication therapy management services are a core set of services designed to optimize a patient's use and response to medications. The core functions of MTM have been defined by the American Pharmacists Association and National Association of Chain Drug Stores Foundation. These functions include 1) comprehensive review of current prescribed and self-care medications for usage and patterns; 2) systematic assessment of each medication for appropriateness, efficacy, safety, and adherence to achieve optimal therapy goals; 3) development of a personal medication care plan with self-management goals and medication management recommendations; and 4) documentation and communication of the care plan to the patient and all health care providers.[18]

Specialty Therapies—Inpatient and Outpatient Anticoagulation Services. Pharmacists have been leaders in management of several specialty therapies associated with high risk of untoward reactions. One area we have selected for discussion here is anticoagulation. Patients managed in anticoagulation services by pharmacists have improved anticoagulation control, reduced bleeding, and reduced thromboembolic event rates when compared to usual medical care delivery.[19,20] The Joint Commission has set the expectation that every accredited health care facility must have a coordinated anticoagulation management program as part of the National Patient Safety Goals.[21] As the demands for safety continue, the pharmacist's responsibilities for development and care of these special therapeutic needs patients will also continue.

Employer-Based Medication Management Service.
Employer-based services have begun to expand as a practical method of improving medication use by patients through pharmacist-provided, patient-centered care. This practice model was developed and established through the Asheville Project. This project was started in 1996 by the city of Asheville, North Carolina. The city is a self-insured employer that carries the expenses of employees with chronic health problems. Employers are now adopting this model of care delivery for chronic conditions because it empowers persons to manage their conditions in ways that both reduce health care risks and costs.[22]

The Asheville Project model was used as a source of evidence and education for other communities to adopt. Polk County, Florida, did so through implementing the Polk County Pharmacist Intervention Model to engage patients with diabetes. Pharmacists provide on-site care to counsel patients with diabetes. Each patient's care plan is individualized by the pharmacist. The pharmacist visits with each patient with multiple episodes of counseling and assessment integrated into the patient's self-care program. Clinical and health care delivery outcomes are monitored over the time. In the first year of the program, significant decreases in clinical indicators for improvement in blood glucose control, blood pressure, and acute health care service use were observed.[23]

A MTM program was initiated 10 years ago at Fairview Pharmacy Services, a subsidiary of Fairview Health Services in Minnesota. This program is structured to serve targeted patient populations including Medicaid patients taking four or more prescription medications to treat or prevent two or more chronic conditions, Medicare patients who use Part D, self-funded employer beneficiaries, and private-pay patients. There were 85% of the patients identified as having one or more drug therapy problems detected on the first visit. Over the 10-year period, the program produced an estimated return-on-investment of $1.29 for every $1 in MTM costs. Patient's therapy goals were set by the pharmacist, patient, and physician. As patients received MTM services, improvement was observed for 55% of the medical conditions; no change in condition was observed for 23%, and 22% worsened.[24]

Inpatient Rounding and Consultation Services.
Pharmacists participate on inpatient rounding services in the hospital setting with multidisciplinary teams. Common functions include reconciling medications throughout a patient's hospital stay, providing target medication or disease management programs, and providing evaluation of all medication therapy. Examples of target medication/disease management programs may include pharmacokinetic monitoring services, intravenous nutrition monitoring, intravenous to oral conversions, antibiotic use monitoring/streamlining, deep vein thrombosis prophylaxis, and stress ulcer prophylaxis. Pharmacists contribute to improved quality of care through optimizing drug therapy related outcomes and reducing avoidable adverse events. While pharmacists' recommendations are often accepted if the pharmacist conducts independent reviews, increased acceptance of recommendations occurs when the pharmacist is present on the collaborative team during rounds.[25] These teams provide services to general medicine, cardiology, oncology, pediatrics, transplant, surgery, intensive care, geriatrics, and other teams as formed within the inpatient health care setting. There is a sustained body of literature documenting these recommendations; they are 1) associated with overall reduced health care costs and 2) their greatest impact can be found in the intensive care setting.[26]

Practice Infrastructure Needs

Pharmacists need a physical and technological environment to support efficient and expert practice. A setting that provides areas to communicate with patients in a private and confidential manner, perform limited physical assessment to evaluate patients' concerns (e.g., examine a rash, check a patient's blood pressure and pulse, examine the eye), and monitor responses to therapies is essential for future practice. Pharmacists need access to expert information sources at the point of care with patients. Pharmacists also need adequate computer software and technology to support a patient health record, interact with a patient's personal health record, and exchange health information among providers. Facilities and equipment to properly assess patients and to assure patients' comfort during the process is essential for providing patient-centered care. For example, the setting should include a clean, private space with sinks to hand wash and latex gloves for conducting finger sticks or palpation. Consideration for essential practice infrastructure needs is critical to support a patient-centered pharmacy practice.

Workforce Realities

The day-to-day challenges of implementing patient-centered care are both numerous and imposing. First and foremost, patient-centered care must be in the organization's mission and philosophy for pharmacists to expect to perform duties at that level. But several other barriers may also be present. Barriers that individual pharmacists can overcome include personal practice philosophy, competency, and commitment to patient-centered care. Other barriers the pharmacist can influence, but may not control, include the administrator's attitude, knowledge and/or commitment to patient-centered care, and the characteristics of the practice setting.

In all settings today, excessive workload is a major barrier as is the financial obstacle to employing adequate numbers of pharmacists and support staff. Certainly managing pharmaceutical prescription or medication order volume is a challenge for the limited human resources dedicated to pharmacy. Organizational downsizing is occurring concurrently with an increasing portion of the population that needs the pharmacists' care. This problem is further exacerbated by the projected pharmacist shortage over the next 10 years, particularly in the hospital setting.

The outpatient practice setting also has challenges. The financial methods of reimbursement in the business of pharmacy depend upon the prescription volume to profit. With the recent incorporation of Medicare Part D benefits from our federal government, a substantial decrease in remuneration to pharmacies occurred. This policy has caused increased pharmacy closures (reported) or shortened hours of service availability (through rural pharmacy providers). This model creates an economic disincentive if pharmacists decrease time spent dispensing prescriptions to provide more comprehensive patient care. Several models are being explored for pharmacists to achieve a successful patient-centered care practice that overcomes the economic challenges.

Home care practice encounters similar barriers to community practice. Payment for pharmacist services is indirectly linked to product dispensing and reimbursement because pharmaceuticals in the home care setting have been drastically reduced over recent years. Moreover, pharmacists in the home care setting generally do not make home visits and are sometimes a distance from their patients.

Hospital setting barriers often include proximity. The pharmacist has an opportunity to work directly with patients if he or she works in a decentralized practice model. This form of practice places the pharmacist on the patient care unit, participating in direct activities with the patient and other health care providers. In contrast, centralized services trade off direct patient care contact opportunities for product preparation and dispensing efficiencies. Pharmacists work together in one central location, often a substantial distance from the patient care area, making systematic care programs more difficult to implement. The pharmacist has far fewer opportunities to interact directly with the patient.

PAYMENT FOR PHARMACISTS' SERVICES

Payment mechanisms for pharmacists' services have been integrally linked to both practice setting and drug product. These mechanisms are evolving from these product-based fee structures to service-based fee structures and salaried positions. Many pharmacists who provide clinical services to patients are still being paid as salaried employees. Some occupy staff positions in corporations, others in academic positions who offer assistance to patients as a service to the facilities that are providing sites for professional internships and faculty role-modeling and teaching. The majority of pharmacists practice and conduct these services to provide students with an opportunity to observe and practice with an experienced instructor. A few have organized practice-based networks or formed practice plans that integrate a network of pharmacist providers to offer

MTM services. The next section briefly describes the current methods of pharmacists' service payment mechanisms.

Salary for Employment Positions

Pharmacists who provide patient-centered care as employees in health care organizations (e.g., hospitals and health systems) are shown to reduce excess and inappropriate medication use. This reduction in drug costs has been associated with reduced hospitalizations, adverse events, length of stay in inpatient settings, and general burden on patients. The vast majority of pay for pharmacists' professional services is done by paying pharmacists a salary and benefits as an employee in a health care organization of some kind. In the inpatient setting, the costs of pharmacists' salary and benefits are included in the overhead of the health care business. As payment mechanisms evolve, the pharmacist is becoming recognized as a provider and fee structures for some MTM services have been formed. This trend will increase in scope and adoption.

Reimbursement and Fees for Dispensing Services

Drug costs have been increasing at double-digit rates for several years, and they show no signs of decreasing.[27] As pharmacists shift the emphasis from dispensing to decreased pharmaceutical use, it is cheaper for health care payers to reimburse for the professional patient-centered care services of a pharmacist than pay for both the excessive and unnecessary use of therapies and the untoward sequelae that occur from inappropriate use.

Increasingly we see pricing methods and fees for pharmaceutical care services. This is particularly true in the outpatient pharmacy settings. A mixture of payment methods is likely for a successful health care organization. These methods include direct payment from patients, payment for services incident to a physician's care billed through Medicare, or reimbursement from third-party payers such as private insurance. Demonstration projects concerning pharmacists' reimbursements for patient-centered care services have been developed, and the early signs indicate that they are successful.[28] This method of reimbursement is expected to continue growing. Additional work to advance mechanisms for payment is planned in the future, but the direction has been taken and growth in adoption is increasing nationally.

Reimbursement and Fees for Medication Therapy Management Services

Current Procedural Terminology (CPT) codes are the mechanism for charging for health care services by providers to Medicare and private payer entities. In 2005 the American Medical Association established CPT codes for reimbursement of MTM services by a pharmacist.[29] There are organized MTM programs in both the inpatient and outpatient settings. These programs involve enrolling patients into the MTM program, assessing the patient and developing a follow up care plan, and monitoring the patient's progress and outcomes as the practice progresses. Payers in these programs are a mixture of private pay, Medicare Part D, and Medicaid in some states with legislation authorizing pharmacists to receive payment for services.

SUMMARY

A systemic approach to a patient-centered practice provides a clear guide to the skills and knowledge necessary to fulfilling the pharmacist's patient care responsibility. Role definition in each patient's case helps the pharmacist in documenting a course for effective patient care. The pharmacist needs to prioritize patient care needs in all employment settings. It is effective to determine these general priorities so the most critical medication issues are addressed first. Workforce realities pose daily challenges that the pharmacist must navigate to effectively serve patients. Maintaining a patient-centered approach will provide the context to overcoming these day-to-day problems and setting specific challenges.

ASSESSMENT QUESTIONS

1. Why do some organizations waver in their support of pharmacists in the provision of patient-centered care?
2. What can the physical layout of a pharmacy or health care facility suggest to a patient?
3. What barriers to the delivery of patient-centered care can you identify? List them. What strategies might be considered to overcome them?
4. What are the social advantages of having telepharmacy services available today?
5. How is technology affecting the delivery of patient-centered care?
6. Describe the infrastructure needs to support a pharmacist's practice.

INTRODUCTION TO FOUR PHARMACISTS' PRACTICE SETTINGS

Throughout this book, we follow the lives of four patients and four pharmacists as they work together in a pharmacy practice setting related to the patients' care needs. Let's learn about the settings:

SETTING 1

Outpatient—general patient-oriented pharmacy practice

Werbert's Pharmacies, a national chain of drug stores, advertises itself as a full-line pharmacy. In addition to traditional pharmaceuticals, the pharmacy also offers a comprehensive nutritional supplement selection, natural products, and durable medical equipment. Nasir Jabr, PharmD, RPh, works at Werbert's. It averages 270–290 prescriptions a day and is staffed with two technicians and another pharmacist overlapping for 6 hours of the day. Jabr started a counseling program for smoking cessation and a medication refill telephone reminder system for chronic medication users. On request, the pharmacists all agree that they will do semi-private counseling of patients. Appointments are made with the pharmacist for smoking cessation. Jabr is learning about reimbursement for professional charges and will implement some form of payment soon for these services. His store management is lukewarm on the idea of expanding much further on these programs.

CASE-SPECIFIC QUESTIONS

Instructions: Complete the answer to each of the following questions.

1. What structural and environmental infrastructure support would you expect to find available at Werbert's, based upon the services that the pharmacists provide?
2. What services should be added during patient visits to make this an MTM service?
3. How could the pharmacists be paid for these services?

SETTING 2

Outpatient—collaborative drug therapy practice with delegated authority

Christine Johnston, PharmD, RPh, works for a large organized health care system in San Antonio, Texas. Seven ambulatory care pharmacists hold various clinics to manage patients with chronic conditions who need extensive drug therapy monitoring and adjustment to their regimens. Management is dedicated to this form of patient care and believes the pharmacist is the right person to do it. All of the pharmacists complete an internal privileging process for doing this work. Johnston sees patients by appointment upon formal referral from the physicians who delegate authority to her to perform some practice functions. For specific conditions, Johnston orders laboratory tests, performs physical assessment, and develops a comprehensive pharmaceutical care plan, including the prescribing of medications for this purpose.

CASE-SPECIFIC QUESTIONS

Instructions: Complete the answer to each of the following questions.

1. Identify patient safety issues that are likely to be present in this practice.
2. Describe the practice environment needs that these pharmacists have in order to provide a patient-centered care practice.
3. What resources and tools might these pharmacists need to maintain this patient-centered practice?

SETTING 3

Inpatient—general patient-oriented pharmacy practice

Luisa Rodriguez, PharmD, RPh, is a pharmacist at the general tertiary care hospital in Omaha, Nebraska. The hospital pharmacy director has worked several years to build adequate staff to achieve decentralized pharmacy services Monday through Friday from 7 a.m. to 6 p.m. A small drug information support service is available for in-depth questions related to patient care. Rodriguez has access to mainframe drug information sources and carries a personal digital assistant with a few handbooks and key references. It is paid for by the department of pharmacy. She maintains an active practice of 60 to 90 patients a day, with a preference for the pediatric population. She is responsible for medication management, including order review and entry, dispensing, compounding, and distribution. She has a technician assigned to her for working together throughout the day.

CASE-SPECIFIC QUESTIONS

Instructions: Complete the answer to each of the following questions.

1. What criteria might Rodriguez use to prioritize her patient assessments?

2. What has the practice setting provided to support Rodriguez's patient-centered practice?

3. In what areas of the medication use process does Rodriguez have direct oversight for patient safety?

SETTING 4

Inpatient—collaborative drug therapy practice with delegated authority

Michael Jones, MS, RPh, works at a large hospital in Atlanta, Georgia. Forty-five pharmacists are on staff, all of whom are expected to carry out systematic clinical programs such as drug usage evaluations and target drug programs. Every clinical program undergoes a privileging process for determination of delegating authority under protocol. Jones is responsible for one such program, anticoagulation, that has gone through this process.

CASE-SPECIFIC QUESTIONS

Instructions: Complete the answer to each of the following questions.

1. What organization expects a hospital to have a formal anticoagulation therapy management program to assure both patient safety and quality of care?

2. What infrastructure support would you expect to see provided to this group of pharmacists in order to carry out this formal anticoagulation management program?

3. What aspects of the medication use process are these pharmacists responsible for in this program?

REFERENCES

1. Albom M. *Tuesdays with Morrie: An Old Man, a Young Man, and Life's Greatest Lesson*. New York, NY: Double Day; 1997.

2. U.S. Department of Health and Human Services. Health information technology initiative major accomplishments: 2004–2006. Accessed at: www.hhs.gov/healthit/news/Accomplishments2006.html#2004. September 2, 2007.

3. Bush Administration: Executive order: incentives for the use of health information technology and establishing the position of the National Health Information Technology Coordinator. Accessed at: www.whitehouse.gov/news/releases/2004/04/20040427-4.html. September 2, 2007.

4. Midwest Pharmacy Workforce Research Consortium (2009). Final report of the 2009 national sample survey of the pharmacist workforce to determine contemporary demographic and practice characteristics. March 1, 2010.

5. eHealth Capacity Building (2008). Chapter 3: From silos to systems. Accessed at: http://www.rockefellerfoundation.org/uploads/files/7e99cb0d-ea8f-4666-82d2-5ab193d3768d-silos-to.pdf. April 30, 2010.

6. Downard S, Galt KA, Reel AB. Pharmacists' use of electronic health records: silent leaders no more. *JAPhA*. 2007; 47(6):680–92.

7. Kohn KT, Corrigan JM, Donaldson MS. *To Err is Human: Building a Safer Health System*. Washington, DC: National Academy Press; 1999.

8. Committee on Identifying and Preventing Medication Errors Board on Health Care Services. Aspden P, Wolcott J, Lyle Bootman J, et al., eds. Institute of Medicine of the National Academies. Released July 15, 2006. Supported by a Contract No. HHSM-500-2004-00020C between the National Academy of Sciences and Department of Health and Human Services.

9. National Wholesale Druggist's Association. Industry profile and healthcare factbook. Reston, VA; 1998.

10. Rupp MT, DeYoung M, Schondelmeyer SW. Prescribing problems and pharmacist interventions in community practice. *Medical Care*. 1992 Oct 30; (10):926–40.

11. Gleason KM, McDaniel MR, Feinglass J, et al. Results of the medications at transitions and clinical handoffs (MATCH) study: An analysis of medication reconciliation errors and risk factors at hospital admission. *J Gen Intern Med*. 2010 May 25; (5):441–7. Epub 2010 Feb 24.

12. Galt KA, Siracuse MV, Rule AM, et al. "Physician Use of Hand-held Computers for Drug Information and Prescribing." *Advances in Patient Safety: From Research to Implementation*. 2005; (4):93–108.

13. Cabral JD. Poor physician penmanship. *JAMA*. 1997; 278:116–7.

14. Bates DW, Leape LL, Cullen DJ, et al. Effect of computerized physician order entry and a team intervention on prevention of serious medication errors. *JAMA*. 1998 Oct 21; 280(15):1311–6.

15. Institute of Medicine. *Crossing the Quality Chasm: A New Health System for the 21st Century*. Washington, DC: National Academy Press; 2001.

16. ASHP guidelines on the safe use of automated dispensing devices. *Am J Health-Syst Pharm*. 2010; 67:483–90.

17. VIPPS. Accessed at: http://www.nabp.net/programs/accreditation/vipps/. April 30, 2010.

18. American Pharmacists Association and National Association of Chain Drug Stores Foundation. Medication therapy management in pharmacy practice: core elements of an MTM service model (version 2.0). Washington, D.C. and Alexandria, VA; 2008.

19. Witt DM, Sadler MA, Shanahan RI, et al. Effect of centralized clinical pharmacy anticoagulation service on the outcomes of anticoagulation therapy. *Chest*. 2005; 127(5):1515–22.

20. Chiquette E, Amato MG, Bussey HI. Comparison of an anticoagulation clinic and usual medical care: anticoagulation control, patient outcomes, and health care costs. *Arch Intern Med*. 1998; 158:1641–7.

21. The Joint Commission. 2010 national patient safety goals. Accessed at: http://www.jointcommission.org/pateintsafety/nationalpatientsafetygoals/. April 30, 2010.

22. American Pharmacists Association Foundation. Asheville Project. Accessed at: www.aphafoundation.org/programs/Asheville_Project. April 30, 2010.

23. Iyer R, Coderre P, McKelvey T, et al. An employer based pharmacist intervention model for patients with type 2 diabetes. *Am J Health-Syst Pharm*. 2010; 67:312–5.

24. Ramalho de Oliveira D, Brummel AR, Miller DB. Medication therapy management: 10 years of experience in a large integrated health care system. *J Manag Care Pharm*. 2010; 16:185–95.

25. Patel R, Butler K, Garrett D, et al. The impact of a pharmacist's participation on hospitalist's rounds. *Hosp Pharm*. 2010; 45(2):129–34.

26. Schumock GT, Butler MG, Meek PD, et al. Evidence of the economic benefit of clinical pharmacy services: 1996-2000, *Pharmacotherapy*. 2003; 23(1):113–32.

27. Mehl B, Santell J. Projecting future drug expenditures—2001. *Am J Health-Syst Pharm*. 2001; 58:125–33.

28. Farris KB, Kumbera P, Halterman T, et al. Outcomes-based pharmacist reimbursement: reimbursing pharmacists for cognitive services part 1. *J Managed Care Pharm*. 2002 Sept-Oct; (8)5:383–93.

29. Gonzales J, Noga M. Medication therapy management. *J Manag Care Pharm*. 2008; 14(6 suppl S-c):8-11. Accessed at: http://www.amcp.org/data/jmcp/Aug%20C_S8-S11.pdf. April 30, 2010.

The Patient-Centered Care Plan

There are many ways of caring, and many ways in which patients need caring. We need to know just what it is a patient most needs and what is, in our relationship to that person, in us to give.[1]

CHAPTER OUTLINE

Purpose

Determining the Patient's Care Needs
- Gathering Background Information
- Gathering Drug Information and Published Evidence
- Gathering Expert Opinions
- Developing the Problem List
- Determining the Therapeutic Options
- Applying Clinical Reasoning

Designing the Patient Care Plan
- Specifying Care Goals
- Designing the Pharmacotherapeutic Regimen
- Designing the Monitoring Plan
- Determining the Support Needed by Patients

Implementing the Patient Care Plan
- Recommending the Patient Care Plan
- Initiating Care
- Documenting Care Provision

Assessing the Patient's Response to Care
- Evaluating the Results from Implementation of the Plan
- Redesigning the Patient Care Plan Based Upon Patient Progress and Outcomes

Summary

Assessment Questions

Introduction to Care Plan Development for our Patients
- Case 1: Lauren Smith visits Werbert's Pharmacy and meets Nasir Jabr, PharmD, RPh
- Case 2: Eduardo Montanez attends his outpatient primary care clinic appointment and is referred to Christine Johnston, PharmD, for followup
- Case 3: Huong Tran is admitted through the Emergency Room to Midcity Hospital and meets Luisa Rodriguez, PharmD
- Case 4: Mr. Robinson meets Michael Jones, MS, RPh, while hospitalized for an exacerbation of congestive heart failure

OBJECTIVES

To gain knowledge of:

1. interpersonal nature of determining the patient's care needs to develop a patient-centered care plan;
2. components of a patient-centered care plan;
3. role of gathering relevant evidence to support development of a patient-centered care plan;
4. role of applying clinical reasoning to prepare a patient-centered care plan;
5. design and implementation of a patient-centered care plan; and
6. assessment of a patient's response to care and redesign of a patient's care plan in response to progress and outcomes.

PURPOSE

The purpose of this chapter is to present the patient-centered care process that you should follow to provide care. This chapter provides an overview of this process as a step-wise approach. You should apply this process to the best of your ability under the circumstances you are working within each time you provide care to a patient. Think of it as a cycle that is repeated whenever you are involved in any step of care. The process is iterative. You learn to update the patient database and evaluate how it influences the patient's care plan as well as how to modify it as you and your patient participate in the care process together.

DETERMINING THE PATIENT'S CARE NEEDS

Your ability to determine the patient's needs is dependent upon the quality and comprehensiveness of the background information you obtain. Information is compiled from various sources. You gather and assess information to determine its relevance to the patient. You *integrate this information in your mind* to form a personalized understanding of the patient data specific to the person you are caring for. A comprehensive listing of patient information is presented in Chapter 1 in Table 1-6, Optimal Patient Health Information. You may find it helpful to refer back to this table throughout the remainder of your reading. Typically, various components of the patient's health information are recorded into numerous health care records that are created in different care settings. Increasingly, however, we see patient health data integrated into records from multiple providers and settings. Providers of care usually allow other providers to view or exchange health information from each other in order to improve the continuity and quality of care. The information you gather for a patient is important in this emerging change in health care delivery.

Gathering Background Information

Key sources of information that you can use to form this database include (a) your patient encounter, (b) the patient's medical chart or patient profile, (c) information provided by other health professionals caring for the patient, and (d) information provided by family members and caregivers who are not health professionals. You will also gather expert evidence. These sources include published information from the clinical literature and expert opinions.

The skills required to gather information vary depending on the type of source. Information may be gathered from the patient, caregivers, and other health care providers. Obtaining this form of information will involve patient or professional communication skills, listening, direct observation, empathy, and a comprehensive knowledge of disease states and therapeutics. Skills required for compiling material from drug information and clinical literature include knowledge of available resources, searching strategy, literature evaluation proficiency, and discerning relevance. Expert patient-centered practice involves mastering the skills needed to gather and use the information to advance your patient's care.

The Patient Encounter. The patient encounter is your first opportunity to form a relationship with the patient. Psychologist Carl Rogers identified what he termed the *therapeutic core qualities* of a clinician—*respect* (also described as unconditional positive regard), *genuineness* (congruence), and *empathy*.[2] During the first encounter, the patient must immediately detect these qualities in you. Through your demonstration of these qualities, the patient will give you the privilege of observing his or her problems or concerns and grant you access to all aspects of who he or she is, including physical access through visual inspection, touch, smells, and sounds. If this relationship is not established, you will not succeed in assessing the patient's needs and ultimately developing an effective care plan. The encounter may be broken into two main sections: the interview and the physical assessment.

The interview is your opportunity to gather key information directly from the patient. Data are available immediately that you begin to reason with clinically, such as 1) the patient's concerns, comments, and responses to your initial questions; 2) the patient's appearance, age, sex, dress, and posture; 3) the patient's movements and speech characteristics (e.g., animation, clarity, and the rise and fall of the voice); and 4) the appearance and manner of the people who accompany the patient (spouse, friend, parent, guardian).[3] It is taught in medicine that 90% of a diagnosis is based on history alone and that most of the care needs are found in the patient's story. This observation counters the commonly held belief by pharmacists that having no access to the other provider's medical charts precludes the delivery of sound care. It is very helpful to have access to the data gathered by other care providers, including their impressions and observations. However, your interaction with the patient is focused on unique aspects that may not be typically addressed in the scope of practice of other providers.

KEY POINT •

Reviewing the data and observations of other care providers is helpful, but keep in mind that your interaction with the patient is unique and issues may arise that may not be addressed in the scope of practice of other providers.

The purpose of physical assessment is to determine the health status of the patient through physical examination. It is the central source of data for a complete health assessment. Four assessment techniques are used during the examination process: inspection, palpation, percussion, and auscultation. These techniques are usually applied in this order. In the aggregate, they are referred to as observation. Physical assessment begins immediately upon seeing and hearing the patient. You observe such things as skin color and tone, behaviors, attitude, alertness, and physical comfort level. The physical examination is often used to confirm what you have already discerned during the patient interview.[3] Specific physical assessment functions are used to assess a patient's condition and monitor response to treatment and care. Drug therapy monitoring provides most improved outcomes for patients when you track the desired responses from drug therapy treatment and continually adjust the care approach to achieve them. Chapter 5 will discuss in detail the skills required in the patient encounter.

The Medical Chart. The medical chart documents the health information of your patient. The chart is the primary vehicle for communicating among health care professionals involved in a particular patient's care. This information is used as a resource by health care providers for treatment planning and care provision. Use the medical chart as a primary source of information when the chart is available to you.

The medical chart is a legal document of the patient's health information. The chart also has educational value to health professional students in training who are learning about patient care. The chart is also used as a research data source for projects or studies that use a chart review technique to provide data relevant to answering a research question. It may be audited as a primary source of data when assessment or evaluation of programs and services occurs by a health provider organization, or when answers to important questions of safety and effectiveness of patient care practices are sought. Obviously, the medical chart would be the primary source of information during a medical–legal investigation.

All patient care settings and services maintain some form of the patient medical chart. Charts are maintained in hospitals, clinics, home health care services, extended care facilities, and other practice settings. Historically, they have remained within the physical premises of these settings and services rather than with the patient. Charts are composed of paper materials, can be fully electronic in format, or, commonly, are a combination of both paper and electronic records. The chart may also be a virtually organized document—pulling together the various records from the different providers and locations where your patient has been cared for. The organization of charts varies; however, certain elements exist in each. Chapter 6 will concentrate on the organization and use of the patient's chart.

Charts are physically found in several locations within the practice setting. Typical locations of printed charts in the hospital are at the end of the patient's bed, in a holder on the room door, in a wall or cabinet by the patient, or by the centrally located patient care area (sometimes called nursing station). Electronic charts are usually accessible through computer screens in locations such as the patient room, hall area just outside the room, centrally in the patient care station, or through mobile computing devices. In clinic settings, printed charts are usually placed on the door or in the examination room just prior to the patient's visit. In home care practices, charts are maintained and carried by the health professional involved in care delivery. Charts not being used are archived or stored in central locations in hospitals, clinics, home care services, or extended care facilities in printed version and as digital repositories.

The chart is a private patient document that contains personal health information. The Health Information Privacy and Accountability Act (HIPAA), passed in 2002, provides additional assurance that individuals who do not have a reason to access the patient chart do *not*. In the context of HIPAA, the patient's chart includes the actual medical chart, pharmacy profile and records, and any official medical documents.

Pharmacists in the hospital setting usually maintain an electronic record of patient medication orders that provide the source of information for active medication orders while a patient is hospitalized. This electronic record is used to generate a manual document commonly called the medication administration record (MAR). This record is printed and placed in the patient's active medical chart and used by nurses, physicians, pharmacists, and other health professionals to document the time of drug administration to the patient and details of the drug regimen. In many facilities, the MAR is created and maintained electronically and is accessible as part of the electronic medical record. Similarly, MARs are usually prepared and maintained for extended care facility and home care patients.

The Patient's Profile. Pharmacists in the community setting maintain records about patient care, often referred to as the patient's profile or pharmacy profile. At a minimum, these patient records contain abbreviated demographic information similar to the medical chart, a prescription list, a listing of conditions or diseases, and general comments related to patient counseling or drug therapy management for the patient. These items are common to most outpatient computerized pharmacy systems that support dispensing activities. In general, the comment areas in computer systems are limited in length, making it difficult to track the care delivery process. Software programs that adequately track pharmacists' dispensing and basic counseling activity are evolving to include documentation features. Most pharmacists maintain two separate systems: one for managing the dispensing process and one for clinical care documentation and monitoring. As software systems and workflow processes improve, integrated software systems that track all aspects of the pharmacists' services to a patient are emerging in the community practice setting. Chapter 6 will cover the patient's profile in detail.

Other Health Professionals Caring for the Patient.
Both past and present health care providers are excellent sources of information. However, their evaluations and interpretations of patient data are a product of their experience, cultural background, attitudes, and opinions. The information obtained from health care providers can be written in medical charts and other archived records or communicated verbally. The primary provider who has cared for a patient over time is a key source of information about that person's past medical history. In addition, the primary provider's assessments of the patient's personality type and interests in various modes of therapy may help you. As you develop your practice, you become a primary care provider for some patients whose needs include ongoing medication management.

Health care professionals can be sources of information on numerous topics. For example, dietitians can provide information on nutritional measures instituted by a patient, and social workers may provide insight into the patient's psycho-social situation and financial status. A valuable resource for the institutional pharmacist is the patient's community pharmacist. Dispensing records kept by the community pharmacist often help determine what medications are being taken, and refill frequencies can provide a good approximation of compliance. Collaborative care is now recognized as an important approach to improving the patient's care.[4] The public has identified the training of health professionals for collaborative care as a priority. Communicating with the various health providers involved with your patient becomes increasingly important as you focus on the patient-centered care process.

Caregivers Who Are Not Health Professionals.
Caregivers assist with a patient's health care needs. A caregiver is often a family member such as the parent of a young child, the adult child of an elderly person, or the spouse of an ailing person. However, caregivers can also be neighbors, friends, or paid companions. Caregivers are sources of primarily subjective information. In some cases, they may clarify or elaborate on the information that patients report or they may become the spokespersons for patients who cannot speak for themselves.

Caregivers are often in a better position to assess therapeutic success or failure than are health care providers because of their regular contact with the patient. For example, a caregiver may be able to describe the improvement in a patient who recently began an antidepressant or confirm the limitations of a person with uncontrolled angina. The caregiver is often the first person to observe and identify medication side effects.

Caregivers are often in a better position to assess therapeutic success or failure than are health care providers because of their regular contact with the patient.

The caregiver is often a reliable source of information regarding social drug use and can confirm or deny patient reports on amounts and frequencies of substance use. Objective information that a caregiver may provide could include home blood glucose test results or blood pressure measurements, the patient's medical history, medication use and needs, adherence behaviors, and frequency of self-treatment with over-the-counter products, remedies, and alternative therapies. Friends, coworkers, good Samaritans, or law enforcement officers may provide information relevant to a specific situation, such as an accident or injury, particularly when patients cannot speak for themselves.

When questioning individuals about a patient, you must be aware of the potential to breach privacy. You must approach it in a manner that is consistent with HIPAA rules and regulations. Privacy can be breached if the wording of your question conveys confidential information (unless the patient decides to share it). For example, an appropriate way to inquire about possible illicit substance use of an adolescent would be to ask, "Tell me about your niece's use of illicit street drugs." In contrast, a breach of privacy would occur if you said, "In addition to marijuana, which your niece told us she smoked, do you know what other illicit street drugs she may have used?" Sometimes friends and coworkers may be needed as sources of information and/or participants in a patient's treatment. Information concerning work attendance and performance may be important in assessing a patient's possible overuse of alcohol. Friends and coworkers also may be asked to participate in intervention therapy for alcoholic or addicted patients.

Gathering Drug Information and Published Evidence

When you are directly responsible for patient care, you must be skilled in obtaining medical-based information and evidence efficiently and effectively. You must be able to formulate a search strategy by retrieving pertinent literature and selecting appropriate drug information. To develop this strategy, you must identify available drug information sources, critically evaluate the information, and select what is immediately and most useful to your patient care needs. Your skills must be so accomplished that you are able to define a framework for your need that reflects the urgency, scope, and depth of information to serve the patient.

Drug information is commonly found in tertiary textbooks (or electronic media versions), secondary resources (bibliographic search systems), or primary literature (published studies in journals). Information is also accessed through resources such as drug or poison information centers and through the assistance of medical librarians, pharmaceutical manufacturers' medical information departments, professional associations or organizations, and government agencies that disseminate evidence and information. You must take ownership of the skills required to comfortably select and draw upon these resources as the needs arise. Chapter 7 will focus on the application of drug information skills to patient care.

Gathering Expert Opinions

Oftentimes, you are unable to find the exact information required to proceed with the care planning process. There are two likely reasons for this problem: 1) you do not have access to the resources you need to find the information or evidence and 2) the information or evidence is not known in the published literature. Clinical knowledge is often tacit, gained through your cumulative experiences with patients. Some information resides with experts who have confidence from prior experience. Experts from other disciplines can be of great assistance too. Pharmacists who work in specialized care areas have expertise in comprehensive management of their patients. Areas such as burn units, transplant units, oncology, eye, neurology, pediatrics, intensive care, geriatric units, rehabilitation, and others often have pharmacists who concentrate in the special needs of these patients. If you have exhausted all resources and require expedient information, you should consult these resources for advice.

Developing the Problem List

The next step in developing a patient-centered care plan is to generate a problem list. You will generate a list of problems and concerns on behalf of your patient using clinical reasoning applied to the patient-specific information learned through the patient encounter, gather pertinent drug information and evidence, and consult other expert resources. The problem list must be accurate and consistent with the patients' needs. This list is the format used to determine the therapeutic options for consideration, set patient care goals, and design the care plan. It is documented in the medical chart, patients' profile, or existing documentation system to track the provision of care.

Determining the Therapeutic Options

As you gather information, you develop possible approaches to assist the patient with managing problems. Your options may include recommending a new therapy or modifying an existing therapy. The therapeutic choice may include the use or no use of over-the-counter treatments or prescription medications. You may also recommend supportive care approaches that optimize the patient's existing therapies (e.g., dietary modifications, exercise, or when to use medications to optimize effectiveness). Your accurate knowledge of the possible therapeutic choices to be considered is essential to delivering expert patient-centered care. In some situations, the most appropriate option is to refer the patient to another health professional for the problem. This inter-professional approach will optimize the patient's outcome by ensuring that competent and appropriate care takes place.

Once you have developed all the potential therapeutic options, you need to determine the patient care goals, reasonable outcomes to expect, and implementation of the therapeutic options. These steps are involved in designing the patient's care plan.

Applying Clinical Reasoning

Clinical reasoning is a major component of expert clinical problem solving. It is a dynamic, cyclic, reiterative process in which observation, analysis, synthesis, deduction, induction, hypothesis generation and testing, inquiry-strategy design, and the skills of examination are all interrelated.[3] Expert clinical performance is effective problem solving. It is accomplished by combining clinical reasoning with accurate knowledge of background information and evidence. The use of clinical reasoning skills continues throughout each step in the care process. Your ability to use clinical reasoning skills is critical to preparing a patient's care plan incorporating both the individual's health care needs and his or her values. These skills help you determine the best approach that is specific to the patient's needs. Your approach will vary with each patient based upon the values and specific concerns for that person.

DESIGNING THE PATIENT CARE PLAN

Specifying Care Goals

Optimal care goals will be established between you and your patient through a successful interpersonal care approach. This is a critical step in decision making. It requires your application of clinical reasoning skills to integrate your knowledge about the patient, the identified problems, potential therapeutic options, and relevant evidence-based information with the patients' values, preferences, and beliefs. You should prioritize the goals that require more immediate attention and assess the patients' interest in achieving them. Remember that the patient's care plan drives the patient's care process. As a result, it needs to be modified in response to how the patient reacts to the treatment approaches implemented. This process has the same core elements independent of care setting. However, the care plan process changes rapidly in the acute care setting compared to the ambulatory care setting where it is typically more prolonged.

Designing the Pharmacotherapeutic Regimen

Designing the therapeutic regimen takes place in all settings. However, the degree of authority you have to implement is dependent upon the formal arrangements with the patient's physician or the

CASE EXAMPLE

Patient-Centered Care

As a pharmacist with a decentralized hospital practice on the general internal medicine floor, your responsibilities include conducting admission histories and documenting a patient's medication use on admission, a part of the process called "medication reconciliation." Your first patient of the day is Mr. George Lucas. You first review Mr. Lucas's medical chart and document key information for yourself. The admitting physician has identified three medical conditions, three prescription medications, and two over-the-counter medicines. You look at the pharmacy record portion of Mr. Lucas's chart and also identify a prior history of admission that includes a note indicating Mr. Lucas is allergic to penicillin. No description of the allergic reaction is described. You plan to visit Mr. Lucas to conduct a brief interview, but first make a quick stop at the nurses' station and speak with Ruth, the floor nurse in charge of Mr. Lucas's care on this shift. Ruth tells you that Mr. Lucas did not bring any medicines into the hospital from home and that he is complaining of significant GI distress. You consider this information as you go to meet Mr. Lucas. You introduce yourself and explain the purpose of your visit—that you are there to understand his medication needs and would like to ask a few questions. After completing the interview, you determine that omeprazole was omitted from his admission medication list and that the penicillin allergy was described as nausea/GI upset by the patient. You evaluate the information you have learned and develop a list of the best therapeutic and care options to consider, and you form an opinion about which of them is best suited for Mr. Lucas at this point.

---

medical staff of your employment setting. Meeting *some* goals may require only a minor adjustment to a patient's existing medications. Other goals may require that you recommend all aspects of drug treatment. Sometimes these goals can be met with you and the patient developing a self-care approach with nonprescription medications and supportive care. Other times, you will be recommending the therapeutic approach desired by another provider with the authority to prescribe. You may establish a practice that involves receiving delegated authority from a physician to direct a complete pharmacotherapeutic plan for a patient.

In the outpatient setting, it may warrant a discussion of the optional approaches with the patient and an agreement with the primary prescriber. In the inpatient setting, you are more likely to discuss the approaches directly with the physician to seek agreement. You may also have been delegated the authority to modify the treatment regimen by the medical staff without prior approval required.

Designing the Monitoring Plan

The monitoring plan is the tool that allows you and your patient to track your patient's progress and the outcomes associated with that care. You should determine if you have achieved the goals that the patient desires through the plan. You should also determine what parameters can be measured (either quantitatively or qualitatively) as indicators that a given goal has or has not been achieved. It is essential that every element in the therapeutic plan has a defined monitoring parameter and goal. The monitoring plan should provide you and the patient with feedback, signaling if a redesign of the care plan is warranted. At a minimum, the monitoring plan should include specifying drug therapy monitoring parameters, identifying desired endpoints, determining the frequency or schedule for monitoring, and educating the patient about how to participate in the plan. The monitoring plan will also be influenced by the needs of other professionals caring for the patient and policies of the health care setting itself.

Determining the Support Needed by Patients

Patients should be included in the decisions about the care processes chosen and educated about how to achieve established care goals. Patient needs for supportive behavior and assistance vary. It may not be possible for the patient to independently participate in all aspects of care, requiring a support system to be designed into the care plan. Examples include periodic phone call reminders about the patient's drug therapy monitoring responsibility or education of the caregiver about specific responsibilities needed to successfully implement the care plan. The support system for achieving the health goals should be designed along with the pharmacotherapeutic regimen. The details of designing the care plan will be emphasized in Chapter 9.

IMPLEMENTING THE PATIENT CARE PLAN

Recommending the Patient Care Plan

To implement the patient-specific care plan, you may need to communicate various recommendations to the appropriate person. For example, suggesting that a prescriber change his or her pharmacotherapeutic approach to treatment requires you to select the appropriate drug–disease information to convey and the optimal communication style to convey it to the practitioner. Key elements of the recommendation include reviewing the patients' health care needs that you are addressing and identifying as the therapeutic goals; the treatment recommendations; and your suggestions for monitoring. These same guidelines govern recommendations to the patient or a caregiver. However, the content and perhaps the communication style would need to be modified to the patient's level of understanding. You may also have to negotiate the final treatment and monitoring plan when another health care professional or caregiver is involved. It is advantageous to know this from the outset so that a successful approach can be implemented.

Oral Communication. Oral communication can take place face to face or over the telephone. These responses are more personal than written communication. An oral medium also allows for immediate clarification if someone does not understand a particular issue. Moreover, oral communication provides an open forum to facilitate discussion about a recommendation. Face-to-face interactions allow both people to interpret and evaluate important nonverbal cues. These cues include a nod of one's head, a smile, a crossing of arms, and a raised eyebrow. A limitation of telephone communication is that you do not have the opportunity to process nonverbal cues from the requester.

Oral communication is not without its limitations. Misinterpretation of information is dangerous and more likely to occur with this method. Additionally, oral consultations are time consuming. The depth of your response also may be limited due to time constraints imposed by your other work responsibilities.

The level of information and the terminology in your response should be appropriate for the person to whom you are communicating. If the request is initiated by a physician, your communication should include professional terminology and scientific evidence. Your goal is to provide expert guidance necessary for the physician to modify the patient's care plan in the physician's area of respon-

---

CASE EXAMPLE

Implementing Care Plan

You assess what you know and decide you have adequate knowledge to recommend care goals for the medication-related problems of Mr. Lucas. You describe for Mr. Lucas a brief summary of the problems, potential plan, and goals. You explain that you will be discussing these with Mr. Lucas's physician and will return to share the findings with Mr. Lucas. You prepare a brief consultation note to have Mr. Lucas's physician review an action plan for approval. In this note you write the findings from your background assessment and interview; the care goals; the therapeutic care options you recommend; and a recommended monitoring plan and your plan to follow through with Mr. Lucas. One of your recommendations requires physician authorization to add esomeprazole 20mg at bedtime, which is the formulary alternative to omeprazole in your hospital. The other is information regarding the penicillin allergy to keep penicillin as a therapeutic option if needed. You continue on to assess the seven other patients admitted that morning.

sibility. This communication will ultimately influence the physician's decision to make the recommended change by reviewing your evidence and feedback to determine that the change is optimal for the patient's care and health care goals. Your recommendation should improve the patient's care plan from this present state. A summary of skills to optimize the physician–pharmacist encounter is described in **Table 4-1**.

A response to a patient should include lay language. When dealing with a patient, you should know the advice that the patient has received from the primary provider so you do not offer confusing information and recommendations. You also must consider the impact of your response on a patient. Be sure that you are providing useful and pertinent information. The decision about what and how much information to impart depends on your relationship with the patient, the amount of background information you have about that patient, and the role of other involved providers. You may need to be selective about what you communicate. The most effective communication will include a combination of both written and verbal forms of information.

Initiating Care

Through the process, you monitor all aspects of what has been agreed upon and take responsibility for the patient's safety and care. A key to ef-

TABLE 4-1.

Optimal Skills for the Physician–Pharmacist Encounter

Skill	Category Criteria
Environment	■ Pick a location that ensures privacy between you and the physician when you communicate.
	■ Do not communicate in front of the patient. This may cause the physician to feel you are being confrontational. It may cause discomfort—reducing your potential for success.
Preparation	■ Prepare your communication to: • state your recommendation first. • provide a brief summary of the background and evidence that supports the recommendation. • anticipate the questions the physician may have. • prepare your recommendation to emphasize patient centeredness.
Greeting	■ Introduce yourself; identify who the patient is; indicate you are contacting the physician to make a recommendation.
Body of Communication	■ State recommendation.
	■ Provide a summary of the background and evidence that supports it.
	■ Answer any questions the physician poses.
Closure	■ Confirm the physician's agreement with the recommendation.
	■ Thank the physician for supporting the change.
Documentation	■ Record the key elements of the encounter in the appropriate patient records.
Assessment of Barriers	■ If the physician rejects your recommendation: • solicit the physician's reasons. • acknowledge the legitimacy of these. • reconsider your recommendation.
General Guidelines	■ The physician may be aware of other information that is not familiar to you; accept and consider this additional information.

fective patient-centered care is communication. You should provide the direct care you are responsible for, communicate all relevant information to other providers proactively, and pay attention to and monitor the patient's progress as needed.

Documenting Care Provision

Care provision should be recorded in the medical chart, patient profile, or existing documentation system. Documentation is the primary method of communicating the approach to the patient's care, what care has been provided, and information useful to other health professionals. All basic care and services provided to patients should also be documented for legal reasons. For example, a well-documented allergy history can be useful in determining if an untoward event is drug related. If it is a standard of practice in your facility to conduct medication histories and identify agents that patients bring to the hospital, documentation of this information could be regarded as a minimum standard of practice. You should also document any therapeutic preferences expressed by patients. This documentation can provide a rationale for therapeutic decisions and decrease overall liability. You must always take care in what you document in a patient record. The note should express the care provided and observations made in an objective and patient-centered manner. The note is not a forum to record opinion or conjecture, debate a medical issue, or assign blame for an undesired outcome in the care of the patient. Written responses may also be a letter or a memorandum, a pharmacy newsletter, or a communication from your department's Pharmacy and Therapeutics Committee.

You should find out your institution's policy governing use of the patient chart. Because of sensitive and legal issues, some institutions restrict who can write in the chart. However, with an increased emphasis on documentation of patient care, pharmacists should expect to record their recommendations. *How* and *where* the pharmacist documents care varies widely by the individual patient care setting.

Documentation provides specific information and becomes a formal record for both you and the patient and for the health setting or facility where care is provided. Although it may seem that oral communication is less time consuming, writing sometimes can be more expedient. Written communication also allows you to explain as much information in as much depth as desired, including the use of tables, graphs, and charts to display data visually. One limitation of the written method is that it usually is not as immediate as oral communication. However, it is an essential method for documentation of care.

Although no rules are absolute for selecting the method of response, certain situations are better suited to a formal written format. Written notes in the patient chart allow you to evaluate the existing literature on a topic and to synthesize a patient-specific response. If the content of your documentation is complex or requires a lengthy answer, the best way to communicate it may be in writing. Written responses also are useful because they provide documentation about what types of services you provide in your practice setting.

Methods of Written Response. After you decide that a written note is warranted, the amount of information you provide depends on the purpose of your note. Two methods can be used: medical chart entry or a letter/memorandum format. Chart entries are appropriate when:

CASE EXAMPLE

Initiate Care

A couple of hours later you review the physician's orders on Mr. Lucas and see the physician's countersignature and approval of your recommendations. You return back to visit Mr. Lucas. You explain the care plan to Mr. Lucas, including the use of a therapeutic alternative to his home medication omeprazole and invite him to ask any questions or state any concerns he may have. You provide Mr. Lucas with your business card and the phone number you can be reached at.

- An official consultation requests your services.
- The patient's physician requests it.
- You need to communicate information to the health care team.
- You have delivered care directly to the patient and need to document the care provision and plan for follow-up.

You may record your medical chart entry on a consultation document, form, or progress note. In certain circumstances such as the home health care setting, a letter or memorandum may be appropriate.

A formal consultation is a written request for expert services. When you are asked to conduct an official consultation, you usually write on the report or findings section of a consultation form. A formal consultation requires an expert evaluation of a patient for a specific purpose. It must include a comprehensive discussion of findings and recommendations. Furthermore, the level and depth of expertise applied to these requests must be documented. Conversely, a brief communication in the Progress Notes section of a chart is not comprehensive. Its primary purpose is to provide key facts for determining any necessary changes in the patient's care plan. A brief written note may also be used in follow-up to a previous formal comprehensive consultation. You should prioritize your information to determine its importance. Your background information, including literature summary, should be clearly separate from your conclusions and recommendations. If attachments are needed, refer to them in the body of your consultation and label them accordingly.

Suppose that you are the pharmacist who provides decentralized services to the general medicine inpatient floor of a hospital. At 2:00 p.m., a clerk on the patient care unit pages you to provide a pharmacy consultation on behalf of a physician's written request. This physician needs to know the likelihood that a patient's thrombocytopenia is drug related. In this case, you should evaluate the urgency of this request, determine an information-gathering strategy, conduct an evaluation, and formulate a response. Ultimately, you should write your response and recommendations on the consultation form that was originally generated by the physician. This form should then be placed in the chart.

A physician may verbally request a consultation and ask that you "leave a note in the chart." At the beginning of the medical chart note, you should indicate that the note is provided at the physician's request. A chart entry is the only way of ensuring that your information is communicated to everyone who may need it. This entry becomes essential when the patient is transferred among different providers or levels of care. For example, when a patient is preparing for discharge, your information may be needed by outpatient or home care providers. Therefore, it should be part of the documentation supporting the discharge plan.

A chart note is useful when you want to provide a brief reply to a question. However, information placed in the medical chart becomes the patient's legal document. Because some issues are sensitive, chart information should include only what is essential to deliver appropriate patient care. Some situations may require determining if the response to the question should be provided in the patient record or in the form of a written memorandum. Although you may have expertise in a particular area, the note you write in the chart could result in litigation.

For example, a pregnant patient on the obstetrics/gynecology (OB/GYN) floor asks the pharmacist whether phenytoin can cause fetal malformation. The pharmacist researches the literature and discovers that phenytoin is indeed a possible culprit; however, the pharmacist is unable to reach the physician responsible for her care. Although this pharmacist could write about phenytoin-induced fetal malformation in the chart, the pharmacist lacks adequate patient specific knowledge to advise the patient about the actual risk associated with this medication and her medical condition. Before submitting a chart note, you must contact the provider to work out an appropriate collaborative response to the patient's concern. If your recommendations conflict with other providers, you must understand your role and obligations in the total care of the patient. Include a notation in your chart entry that the primary care provider was consulted and then summarize the comments pertinent to your recommendation. Limit the extent of your chart entry to reflect what you are asked.

If your recommendations conflict with an organizational policy, you should identify the issue and determine if you can modify it to conform. If you cannot conform, evaluate the purpose of the policy and determine if your recommendations are a reasonable exception. An example of this might be recommending a non-formulary medication in a closed formulary health care system. Include these explanations in your entry to substantiate your recommendations and to protect yourself as a practitioner. In these situations, a countersignature from a physician or supervisor may ensure all professionals that appropriate orders or activities can be performed. The endorsement by suitable authorities also strengthens the credibility of controversial or highly judgmental recommendations.

You should document your oral response to a request in the patient care plan of the pharmacy department. Consequently, all pharmacists who provide care to the patient will know about your recommendations. Moreover, the data are recorded in the workload statistics of the department. Not all oral responses require chart documentation. You should document oral responses if you believe that they are essential for proper patient care or the physician has requested them.

If you decide that documentation should appear in the patient's medical chart, your entry should be placed in the Progress Notes or Consult section of the record. The documentation must include

- Date and time the note is entered.
- Purpose of the note.
- Person who requested services or consultation.
- The content summarizing your findings, assessment, and recommendations. It is usually prepared in S.O.A.P. note format.
- Your contact information for additional follow-up.

Documentation Using the S.O.A.P. Note Format. The most common method for documenting information about the patient encounter is the "S.O.A.P." note. This acronym describes both the type and order of information that should be included in the note. The "S" represents subjective information or information told to you by the patient or others. Subjective information is reported to you. Objective information, represented by "O," is the information that you directly observe. This includes your physical and mental assessment of the patient and measurable data (e.g., blood pressure, temperature or heart rate, and laboratory data). Assessment information, represented by "A," is the clinical opinion of the patient's problems and an evaluation of how the patient is progressing based upon the subjective and objective information. Outcomes evaluation of a patient's response to a prior plan is expressed here. This section also incorporates relevant published evidence or guidelines to be applied in a patient's case. The Plan, represented by "P," summarizes the care approach you will use with the patient. The plan includes a prioritization of the patient's problems, care steps intended for each problem, monitoring indicators and timeframe for evaluation, and the future period for follow up. A forward thinking approach to the plan is helpful to you and others. A comprehensive care plan involves patient and provider education and documents communication to other health care providers when relevant. **Table 4-2** provides an overview of the information elements that are included in a S.O.A.P. note. The order of these elements suggests the organization of the S.O.A.P. note. If the information is not relevant or available for a specific note, it is omitted.

When a written response is provided in the medical chart, you also should document it in the pharmacist's care plan if available. Documentation in the pharmacist's care plan varies, depending on what is used by your organization. Remember to be concise. If your written response to an information request is a letter or memorandum, it may or may not be appropriate to refer to it in the patient's medical chart. You must decide whether it can add to the quality of a patient's care and/or provide the minimum documentation to ensure that other providers are properly informed. Again, you should document the fact that you provided a letter or memorandum response to a particular request in the pharmacist's care plan.

Example S.O.A.P. Note. Suppose that a clinic physician asks your advice about how to properly dose allopurinol in Mrs. Alicia Caines, a 67-year-old white female with a history of gout. Her only other

TABLE 4-2.

Information Elements Included in a S.O.A.P. Note

Section	Information Element
Subjective	■ Chief complaint (CC). Description of the complaints and symptoms that a patient describes in his or her own words.
	■ History of present illness (HPI). Recent history provided by the patient that relates to the chief complaint.
	■ Past medical history (PMH). Past information about the patient's medical conditions, prior complaints.
	■ Medication history (MH). Current medication use and past medication use. Includes behavioral history related to adherence and untoward reactions.
	■ Allergies. Current allergies and past reports to medications, foods, environment, and description of reaction when exposed.
	■ Social history (SH). Description of lifestyle.
	■ Family history (FH). Description of family relationships, including genetic predispositions.
	■ Review of systems (ROS). Description of symptoms of problems in patient's own words based upon interviewer prompted questions by clinician.
Objective	■ Vital signs (VS). Vital signs include body temperature, pulse, respiratory rate, blood pressure.
	■ Physical examination (PE). A head-to-toe sequence of observation.
	■ Laboratory results (Lab). A profile of laboratory values obtained from serum, urine, and fecal bodily substances to aid in diagnosis and monitoring.
	■ Drug concentration results. Drug level concentrations in serum or urine aid in drug therapy dosing and monitoring.
	■ Diagnostic test results. A summary of findings from tests for diagnosing and monitoring a patient's progress. These include such examples as x-rays, CT scans, MRIs, and others.
	■ Medication profile. A current printed version of the patient's active medication list. Examples include a hospital, long-term care facility, home care service, and ambulatory care pharmacy.
Assessment	■ A description of the health status, current problems, and health outcomes is prepared based upon your clinical reasoning.
Plan	■ A systematic description of the actions that need to be taken in response to each problem is identified. The actions should include treatment approach, monitoring parameters to evaluate, education and behavioral guidance for the patient, and followup plan with a recommended time interval for reassessment.

medication is indomethacin for acute gout flares. Her creatinine clearance, estimated at 30 ml/minute, has remained stable for at least 1 month. Her serum uric acid concentration is 9.8 mg/dl, and her serum creatinine is 2.4 mg/dl. Six months ago Mrs. Caines was hospitalized for an elective surgical procedure to remove nasal polyps. You should adequately research information on allopurinol used for the treatment of gout and then continue to develop recommendations. In this example, it is appropriate to provide your recommendation orally and follow up with written documentation as a S.O.A.P. note. You should prepare a brief progress note that identifies the patient, confirms the creatinine clearance estimate and stable but impaired renal function, and states the information you are using to recommend a dose adjustment. Then, you should sign and date the note. You also should document on the pharmacist's care plan that this recommendation was recorded in the patient's medical chart. The example of this S.O.A.P. note is provided in **Figure 4-1**.

A letter is the usual format for communicating information to someone outside of your employment setting. Letters can be sent to health care professionals, patients, administrators, government agencies, and media professionals. Conversely, a memorandum usually communicates a response to someone in your employment setting. It is a brief, formal communication and usually does not exceed two pages. A memorandum is used to

- Document a communication for several people who need a common understanding of content.
- Provide information for later reference.
- Disseminate important information rapidly.
- Communicate important changes in policy.
- Communicate expectations about a behavior.
- Communicate information about a patient or patient care that is not appropriate for the medical record.

The implementation of the care plan will be detailed in Chapter 10.

Physician Request for Consultation about Allopurinol Dose

Date: 8/20/20XX **Time:** 3:20 p.m.

Patient's Name: Alicia Caines

AC is a 67 year old white female who is being initiated on allopurinol therapy.

S: CC: AC describes herself as having "gout."

PMH: Recent elective surgery for nasal polyps.

MH: Use of indomethacin for swollen painful joints from gout.

O: PE: Weight = 72.5 Kgs.

Lab: Serum creatinine (SCr) is 2.4 mg/dl.

Serum uric acid concentration is 9.8 mg/dl.

A: Creatinine clearance (CrCl) estimated at 30 ml/min—stable for 1 month using Cockcroft-Gault formula of (140 – age)(lean body weight in kgs)/72(SCr).

Allopurinol dose in normal renal function (CrCl> 80 mls/min) is recommended at 250 to 300 mgs/day. Dose is recommended at 100-150 mgs/day when CrCl is between 20 and 40 mls/min.

P: Initiate allopurinol at 100 mgs/day. Reduction in serum urate levels may take between 1 and 3 weeks. Serum uric acid target is < 6 mg/dl. Assess serum urate level at 7 days after initiation of therapy. If no reduction in serum urate observed, increase daily dose to 150 mgs. Reassess serum urate levels in 2 weeks after dose increase.

After serum urate concentrations are controlled, consider dose reduction. Allopurinol therapy should be continued indefinitely.

Pharmacist Signature/Telephone or pager number

Figure 4-1. Sample SOAP Note

CASE EXAMPLE

Assessment of Care

The next day you reevaluate Mr. Lucas's response to the plan that was implemented. His primary nurse for the day informs you that Mr. Lucas has not complained of any GI distress since started on esomprazole. You visit Mr. Lucas and learn that he has no concerns and is comfortable with how his care is progressing. You note that the plan is progressing as expected, and Mr. Lucas is having a positive outcome from the treatment plan. You prepare a progress note to inform the other health professional team members involved in Mr. Lucas's care.

ASSESSING THE PATIENT'S RESPONSE TO CARE

Evaluating the Results from Implementation of the Plan

Your evaluation of progress should be documented in the appropriate patient care records. The evaluation should assess progress based on the treatment goals and monitoring plan previously developed in the patient care plan. Not all care situations require this follow up such as a patient who seeks information for self-treatment in a community setting. However, the offer to be available to a patient for further follow up may be just what was needed to have that patient return for assistance in the future.

Redesigning the Patient Care Plan Based Upon Patient Progress and Outcomes

You should change the patient care plan if the desired goals are not being met. The care process is iterative. New patient information about progress and outcomes should be used, and clinical reasoning skills should be applied to redesign the care plan with the intent for success. All changes to the plan as a result of outcomes assessment should be documented in the patient profile or medical chart. The redesign of the care plan will be detailed in Chapter 11.

SUMMARY

Your success in determining the patient's needs is directly dependent upon your ability to gather relevant patient-specific information. You formulate your own patient database from the patient encounter, the medical chart or patient profile, other health care professionals caring for the patient, and family members and caregivers who are not health professionals. Clinical reasoning skills are applied to develop a problem list, determine therapeutic options, design a care plan, and then implement and monitor the care plan. You document and communicate about the care provided. You will assess the patient's response and redesign the care plan based upon the patient's progress and outcomes. These steps are essential to developing and implementing a patient-centered care plan.

ASSESSMENT QUESTIONS

1. What are the therapeutic core qualities of a clinician? Why are they so important to patient care?
2. When do you obtain expert opinions in the delivery of patient care?
3. Describe the reasons why you document care provision in writing.
4. What is the purpose of a S.O.A.P. note?
5. What circumstances warrant redesigning a patient's care plan?

INTRODUCTION FOR CARE PLAN DEVELOPMENT FOR OUR PATIENTS

CASE 1

Lauren Smith visits Werbert's Pharmacy and meets Nasir Jabr, PharmD, RPh

Lauren decides to visit Werbert's Pharmacy because she is having some uncomfortable symptoms (i.e., itching and burning when she urinates). She decides that her discomfort is too great and wants to seek some relief. She hopes that there is an over-the-counter product that she can use. This pharmacy is the one she frequents most, once every few months.

Lauren first browses through the Analgesic/Pain Management section of the store. Advil® has worked for her in the past, so she picks up another bottle of 200mg strength tablets, 100 count. Then she reconsiders, because she thinks that she might have a vaginal infection. Lauren uses Internet access at home to look at consumer-oriented health sources. Consequently, she decides to purchase Vagisil Gel®, so she takes these products to the prescription checkout area to pay for them. Nasir Jabr is the pharmacist on duty and offers to assist her.

As he is completing the checkout process, Nasir Jabr asks: "Can I assist you with any information or help?"

Lauren: "No thank you. I think I have what I need for today."

(Dr. Jabr quickly evaluates her overall appearance, facial expressions, general appearance of health, and attitude. These observations, along with her strong individualist approach to communication, suggest that she will not be responsive to further offers.)

Nasir Jabr: "Our phone number is listed on my business card. Do not hesitate to contact me if you decide you would like assistance. I would be most pleased to answer any questions or conduct a preliminary clinical evaluation about your concerns. Call me if you decide you would like further assistance."

Lauren: "Thank you very much. I appreciate your concern. I'll consider this." (She was surprised and impressed by his professional approach and politeness toward her.)

CASE-SPECIFIC QUESTIONS

1. In Chapter 1, we discussed three types of patients you generally will encounter. What type of patient does Lauren Smith seem to be?
2. To what extent do you think Nasir Jabr's professional services will be used by Lauren?
3. What impact will the interaction between Nasir Jabr and Lauren Smith have on her likelihood of returning to the pharmacy? Seeking counsel from Nasir Jabr?
4. Determine the sources of information that were used by Jabr.

CASE 2

Eduardo Montanez attends his outpatient primary care clinic appointment and is referred to Christine Johnston, PharmD, for follow up

Mr. Montanez was taken to his primary care physician, Dr. Mattis, at Heart of Texas Health System Clinics, by his daughter-in-law Maria. Dr. Mattis spoke with him and his daughter-in-law in some detail about his health status and health practices. Dr. Mattis concluded that a more individualized drug therapy management approach would likely benefit Mr. Montanez. He obtained agreement from both Mr. Montanez and Maria to visit Christine Johnston, PharmD, ambulatory clinical pharmacist who assists patients with chronic condition drug therapy management. Dr. Mattis gets Christine Johnston from her work area to facilitate introductions.

Christine Johnston: "Buenos dias, Señor Montanez and Maria! Mr. Montanez smiles, and Maria responds: Buenos dias, Señora Johnston."

Christine Johnston: "It is my great pleasure to have the opportunity to work with you, Mr. Montanez. I speak very little Spanish. However, I am able to provide information in writing that has been translated from English to Spanish. I can also arrange for a translator when you come to visit. Would you prefer that I do this?"

Mr. Montanez (looks slightly confused): "Translator? Won't Maria come?" (Mr. Montanez speaks with limited confidence.)

Maria: "Yes, Señora Johnston. Please let me serve as a translator for my father-in-law. He has some beliefs about his health and problems that I could help to explain. He is very comfortable coming here. This would be best."

Christine Johnston: "Very well. I appreciate the support and care you are providing Maria and will look forward to both of you visiting. When you return to visit, Mr. Montanez, will you please bring all of your medications and treatments with you?"

Maria: "Oh, I take care of all of that for him. I will make sure to do this."

Christine Johnston: "Good. I enjoyed meeting you both and look forward to your visit."

She turns to leave the room thinking Mr. Montanez seems to understand most of what she is saying. She makes a mental note to speak directly to him and not allow Maria to distract her from this approach. (She also notes the very close caregiving relationship Maria has with her father-in-law.)

CASE-SPECIFIC QUESTIONS

1. What background sources of information are accessible to Christine Johnston to learn about Mr. Montanez before his next clinic visit?
2. What is likely to be the primary method of documenting care provided to Mr. Montanez?
3. Who should Christine Johnston be sure to communicate with each time she has a care visit with Mr. Montanez?
4. Determine the sources of information that were used by Johnston.

CASE 3

Huong Tran is admitted through the Emergency Room to Midcity Hospital and meets Luisa Rodriguez, PharmD

Dr. Mooris, the Emergency Room physician, evaluates Huong's respiratory status. He hears severe wheezing through the stethoscope. Huong is trying to take deep breaths, but he is unable to because of severe restriction of his airways.

Dr. Mooris: "Huong, do you have asthma?" (Huong nods his head yes, as it is too difficult for him to answer. Huong's parents came with him. They appear frightened. Unable to speak English, they depend on Huong to tell them what they need to know. They try to treat Huong's respiratory condition with herbal remedies and an acupuncturist.)

Dr. Mooris: "I want you to inhale this medication by spraying it directly in front of your mouth and breathing deeply."

(Huong appears to have difficulty manipulating his handheld inhaler. Luisa Rodriguez, PharmD, was delivering another medication to the Emergency Room and noticed Huong struggling with self-administration of the albuterol.)

She approached Dr. Mooris and asked: "Dr. Mooris, I noticed this child is having a difficult time using this device. Would it be alright if I showed him how to use it?"

Dr. Mooris: "That would be terrific. Huong, this is Luisa Rodriguez; she is a pharmacist. She will help you to use this medicine correctly. Please do what she says. It will make you feel much better in just a few minutes."

(Ms. Rodriguez works with Huong while Dr. Mooris completes Huong's hospital admission process. Once Huong is stabilized, the pharmacist informs him and his family that she will be working with him while he is in the hospital. Huong's parents look worried and frightened, and she feels badly that she cannot speak with them to alleviate their fears and concerns.)

CASE-SPECIFIC QUESTIONS

1. What are the cultural and language considerations that have affected Rodriguez's ability to establish a productive relationship with Huong and his parents?
2. What are some actions she can take to minimize the negative impact of these considerations on caring for Huong? What should she do in order to prepare for caring for Huong?
3. Determine the sources of information that were used by Rodriguez.

CASE 4

Mr. Robinson meets Michael Jones, MS, RPh, while hospitalized for an exacerbation of congestive heart failure

Mr. Robinson rings the bed alarm from his semiprivate room on the 3rd floor on the internal medicine ward.

Nurse Charlotte (over speaker): "What is it, Mr. Robinson?"

Mr. Robinson (over speaker): "Yes, nurse. I think I am supposed to take my blood thinner this morning. It is almost noon, and I am sure I didn't get it."

Nurse Charlotte (over speaker): "Thanks Mr. Robinson. I'll check and see what is happening with your medication and get right back to you."

(Michael Jones, decentralized pharmacist, was just getting to his patient care rounds when the nurse stops him in the hallway.)

Nurse Charlotte: "Michael, Mr. Robinson in Room 347 believes he should receive his warfarin and thinks that it is late. I did not give him any because I saw that you were consulted by Dr. Rangert to manage his anticoagulation."

Michael Jones: "Thank you Charlotte. I will go and speak with him right away. I have not met him yet."

(Michael goes to see Mr. Robinson. He knocks on the room door.)

Mr. Robinson: "Hello . . . come on in . . . it's okay, I'm dressed."

Michael Jones: "Hello Mr. Robinson. My name is Michael Jones, and I am a pharmacist. Dr. Rangert, your physician in the hospital, asked me to see you and take care of your warfarin and other blood thinner medication while you are in the hospital."

Mr. Robinson: "It's nice to meet you, Michael. I didn't know there were pharmacists in the hospital. I guess I shouldn't be surprised . . . I just never really thought about it."

Michael Jones: "Yes Mr. Robinson. There are several pharmacists on duty, and we staff the hospital 24 hours a day. Most of our work is behind the scenes, ensuring that your medication is being dosed correctly, preparing it for your use, and watching how you respond to the medicine you are taking. We make recommendations to adjust medications as we see areas for improvement."

Mr. Robinson: "Great. Well . . . I think you guys are late with my warfarin."

Michael Jones: "That is why I am here. I will be evaluating some information about your response to warfarin and deciding the correct dose for you while you are here. This will take me another 15 minutes or so. I will get back to you to let you know what I recommend."

Mr. Robinson: "Thank you. I just don't want anyone to make any mistakes. My wife used to watch everyone for me . . . she really took care of me . . . but now I have to do this on my own. She taught me well though!"

Michael Jones: "She certainly did. And you are doing a good job. I will communicate with you shortly. Thank you Mr. Robinson."

(Jones leaves the room.)

CASE-SPECIFIC QUESTIONS

1. What did Michael Jones do well in relationship to managing Mr. Robinson's case?
2. Do you think that Nurse Charlotte did the right thing in response to Mr. Robinson's request?
3. Determine the sources of information that were used by Jones.

REFERENCES

1. Callahan D. *The Lost Art of Caring*. Baltimore, MD: Johns Hopkins University Press; 2001.
2. Coulehan JL, Marian RB. *The Medical Interview: A Primer for Students of the Art*, edition 3. Philadelphia, PA: F. A. Davis Company; 1997.
3. Barrows HS, Pickell GC. *Developing Clinical Problem Solving Skills—A Guide to More Effective Diagnosis and Treatment*. New York, NY: Norton Medical Books; 1991.
4. Committee on the Health Professions Education Summit. Board on Health Care Service. Institute of Medicine. *Health Professions Education: A Bridge to Quality*. Greiner AC, Knebel E, eds. Washington, DC: The National Academies Press; 2004.

The Patient–Pharmacist Encounter

"I walked into the patient's room and instantly realized how fragile this patient was. She lay in the hospital bed looking thin and nearly as flat as the mattress itself. She couldn't be more than 5 feet tall and weighed no more than 100 pounds. But it was her slow, methodical, labored breathing…her pale, faded thin skin…her thin white hair, her sunken cheeks, and her colorless lips that told me her condition. She was poorly nourished and dehydrated. I didn't need her chart to identify this."
—Kim Galt

CHAPTER OUTLINE

Purpose

The Patient Encounter
- The Interview
- Physical Assessment

Documenting the Encounter

Special Situations
- The Pediatric Patient
- The Geriatric Patient
- Working with an Interpreter
- The Visually Impaired Patient
- The Hearing Impaired Patient
- The Angry or Difficult Patient
- The Mentally Incompetent Patient

Summary

Assessment Questions

Pharmacist–Patient Encounter with Our Four Cases
- Case 1: Lauren Smith calls Nasir Jabr, PharmD, RPh, 2 days after her visit to the pharmacy
- Case 2: Christine Johnston, PharmD, RPh, conducts the initial patient encounter with Mr. Montanez in the clinic
- Case 3: Luisa Rodriguez, PharmD, RPh, conducts an admission history on Huong Tran in the Emergency Room
- Case 4: Michael Jones, MS, RPh, conducts a patient interview and limited physical examination with Mr. Robinson

OBJECTIVES

To gain knowledge of:

1. the purpose, structure, and processes of the various types of patient encounters;
2. the unique aspects of the patient encounter to consider with special populations;
3. how to conduct and document your findings from a patient interview;
4. how to use different communication techniques with the patient;
5. how to use physical assessment for problem identification and drug therapy monitoring;
6. the value and use of clinical assessment in the patient encounter; and
7. how to conclude the patient encounter.

PURPOSE

The purpose of this chapter is to describe the structure and process of the pharmacist–patient encounter. You will learn about the two major components: the patient interview and physical assessment. You will learn how to properly prepare for the interview; construct an organized approach; open and close the interview properly; and listen, respond, and use questioning strategies appropriately. The role of physical assessment and ways to incorporate this important

*Many of the forms in this chapter are available online at www.ashp.org/patientcare.

skill into the encounter will be discussed. The importance of documenting the encounter is also discussed.

THE PATIENT ENCOUNTER

The patient encounter is the primary event that guides your understanding of the patient's health condition and concerns. No matter what the circumstances and setting, therapeutic care is the purpose of your encounter with the patient. During patient encounters you gather information, determine the care a patient needs, and provide care. With each patient, you have the opportunity to form a *therapeutic relationship*.[1] A patient encounter consists of the patient interview and physical assessment. These are your tools to directly learn from the patient. You will learn the types and severity of the patient's problems, determine treatment options that are acceptable to the patient, and monitor treatment response. The patient encounter may take on several forms. The encounter may be brief, focused on a specific concern, and limited in extent of communication and assessment. Alternatively, the encounter may be more developed. You may conduct a formal, systematic interview and/or a comprehensive physical assessment.

When you first see the patient, you will pose questions that encourage a conversation intended to have the patient describe his or her concerns. As you continue to listen and observe the patient, you will form an initial impression or concept of this patient's problems. Then you will formulate an inquiry strategy to focus on the emerging areas of need. Inquiry involves conversation, observation, and physical assessment to generate data. You will use your clinical reasoning skills to analyze this information and eventually synthesize your concept of the patient's needs with a degree of confidence that draws you to the next step—development of the care plan.

You will have patient encounters in almost all employment settings. In the hospital setting, the encounter may occur initially to gather an admission history, compile specific information in response to you being asked to consult, solve a problem you or another professional has identified, or prepare a patient for discharge. Other reasons may include gathering information to participate in an interprofessional care planning session, counseling a patient about medication for self-use, or responding to a request from a patient to discuss an issue with a pharmacist.

In the community setting, patient encounters routinely occur when a prescription is presented for filling and when a patient receives the dispensed medications. Encounters occur when you are resolving a conflict or problem on a prescription, or when a patient requests advice or guidance on self-treatment. In some community settings, pharmacists provide comprehensive care evaluations, drug therapy monitoring, and drug therapy management. In this role, you will have patient encounters that require complete privacy. You will conduct physical examinations and assessments important to drug therapy management.

Figure 5-1 provides guidance about the usual patient-specific information collected during a patient encounter. You should refer to it as you progress through the chapter. You may use this as an actual interviewing tool.

The Interview

Good patient–pharmacist communication is essential to pharmacy practice. The interview is the direct method to determine the patient's needs in all practice settings. Previous research has shown that many of the difficulties that patients experience with their medications are due to inadequate patient–provider communication.[2] Specifically, many patients are reluctant to ask questions about medications and do not want to be counseled or advised by providers.[2,3] While interactions with patients may be brief or lengthy, the interaction can be guided by the key elements of a structured interview. Adapting this approach, you should develop an expert approach to the communication aspect of your patient encounter. Coulehan and Block describe the fundamental skill of the interview as "understanding exactly."[4] Interviewing is a basic skill that can be broken down into its component parts and be learned. **Table 5-1** provides an overview of the communication skills that are relevant to any patient interview.

You will use both interpersonal skills and communication skills during your interviews. The key interpersonal skills should be to build and maintain

Demographic and Administrative Information:		Room No.	ID No.	
Date:		Gender:	Primary Language:	
Name:		DOB:	Height:	Weight:
Street Address:		BP:	Temp:	Pulse:
City, State, Zip		Race/Ethnicity:	Religion:	
Home Phone #:		MD/Phone No.		
Work Phone #:		Pharmacist/Phone No.		
Occupation:		Insurance:		
Family Members/Care Givers:				
Problem List:	**Pharmacist's Recommendations/Plan:**			
1.				
2.				
3.				
4.				
5.				
6.				
7.				
8.				
9.				
10.				

Pharmacist's Name: _____ Date: _____ Phone/Pager #: _____

Chief Complaint/History of Present Illness:	
Past Medical History/Surgery/Genetics:	
Family and Social History (significant relationship/co-habitants):	
Physical Examination/Review of Systems:	
ADL:	
Lifestyle/Diet/Exercise:	
Acute and Chronic Medical Problems/Associated Symptoms:	
1.	6.
2.	7.
3.	8.
4.	9.
5.	10.
Describe Patient's Health Beliefs and Values:	

Figure 5-1. Patient's History Form—Pharmacist's Recommended Care Plan

Does Patient Receive Assistance in Medication Administration? Describe:

Allergies/Intolerances: ( ) No Known Drug Allergies		
Allergen:	Reaction:	Treatment:
Allergen:	Reaction:	Treatment:
Allergen:	Reaction:	Treatment:

Social Drug Use:	Alcohol:	Caffeine:	Tobacco:	Other:

Current Drug Therapy (prescription and over the counter, vitamins, remedies, alternative treatment):						
Drug Name Strength/Route	Problem Number	Usual Schedule	Describe PRN Use	Does Med Work?	Side Effects or Concerns	Compliance Issues
1.						
2.						
3.						
4.						
5.						
6.						
7.						
8.						
9.						
10.						
11.						
12.						
13.						
14.						
15.						

Past Drug Therapy:

Time Line: Circle administration times and record appropriate medications and meals below:
Patient's Actual Use: 6 7 8 9 10 11 12 1 2 3 4 5 6 7 8 9 10 11 12 1 2 3 4 5   am   noon   pm   midnight   am
Prescribed Schedule: 6 7 8 9 10 11 12 1 2 3 4 5 6 7 8 9 10 11 12 1 2 3 4 5   am   noon   pm   midnight   am

Costs of Meds/Month:	$	Insurance:	( ) Yes	( ) No	
	Co-pay:	Medicaid:		Annual Income:	
Completed by: _____			Date: _____		

Figure 5-1 (continued). Patient's History Form—Pharmacist's Recommended Care Plan

TABLE 5-1.
General Communication Skills for the Patient Interview

General
- Communication conveys care for the other person.
- Communication conveys an open and non-judgmental attitude.

Non-verbal communication
- Maintains eye contact with the patient (exception: cultural considerations).
- Keeps arms open, not folded across body.

Listening skills
- Is attentive to the patient.
- Responds to the patient's comments and requests.

Speaking skills
- Present information at a level of understanding that matches the patient's abilities and needs.

Questioning strategies
- *Communication style:* Responses show respect for the interviewee's attitudes and feelings.
- *Close-ended questions:* Uses close-ended questions to obtain precise, narrow-focused information.
- *Open-ended questions:* Uses open-ended questions when obtaining as much information as the interviewee is willing to provide.
- *Probing questions:* Probing questions are assertive, not aggressive.
- *Indirect questions:* Chooses indirect questions when the goal is to encourage the interviewee to elaborate on a particular matter.

Quality of questions in interview
- Questions are appropriate for the care needs of the patient.
- Questions are productive, i.e., yield useful information needed to optimize patient care.

Verbal caring behaviors
- Verbally responds to an expressed concern.
- Explains procedure/touch of patient prior to initiation.
- Verbally validates patient's physical status.
- Verbally validates patient's emotional status.
- Shares personal observations or feelings (self-disclosing) in response to patient's expression of concern.
- Verbally reassures patient during care.
- Discusses topics of patient's concern other than current health problems.

Non-verbal caring behaviors
- Sits down at bedside.
- Touches patient exclusive of procedure.
- Sustains eye contact during patient interaction.
- Enters patient room without solicitation.
- Provides physical comfort measures.

a therapeutic relationship and demonstrate caring and respectful behaviors. These skills involve making a personal connection to the patient, eliciting the patient's perspective on the illness, and expressing empathy and a desire to work with the patient. The key communication skills you will use involve listening effectively, eliciting information with effective questioning skills, providing information using effective explanatory skills, counseling to educate, and making informed decisions based on patient information and preferences.

You will use both interpersonal skills and communication skills during your interviews.

Preparing for the Interview. Your opportunity to conduct a patient interview may occur in an unplanned way. Most often, interviews in community pharmacy are initiated by the patient, making it impossible to prepare ahead of time for the unplanned interaction. But if you have ready access to the patient pharmacy profile and are prepared with skillful questions, you can efficiently and effectively turn the interaction into a meaningful interview, consistent with the patient's expectations. Brief encounters usually do not provide an opportunity to prepare. Planned encounters do. For the planned encounter you should review your patient care records to determine where you and the patient are at in your care plan. If you are preparing for a new patient, then you should review the available records and form your initial impressions and area of inquiry. An alternative plan can be developed, if required. You may be able to gather information in advance of an actual interview. A brief review of the medical chart or the patient's pharmacy profile may improve your efficiency in your interview strategy through familiarizing yourself with the known history of this patient, alerting you to areas of inquiry, and providing you with insight into what you may need to know prior to the interview (e.g., unfamiliar medication in patient's current regimen). **Table 5-2** provides an overview of the skills needed to conduct the interview.

Environment. The environment surrounding an interview implies what is expected of you to the patient and what you can provide to the patient. This environment is referred to as the patient care setting. In general, patients expect certain services from you based upon the practice setting. Patients who are interviewed by you in the community pharmacy, at a minimum, expect their questions to be answered, to be given a recommendation for care or referral, and possibly to receive a prescription or over-the-counter treatment. Patients who are interviewed in the hospital, outpatient clinic, and home care or nursing home setting may be unclear about what to expect from you at your first interaction. You may have to assist the patient with this understanding.

Ideally, the environment should be private and relatively quiet to enhance communication between you and the patient. A sense of privacy can be created by drawing curtains between beds in a hospital or nursing home or sitting away from other people in a waiting area. This same sense of privacy can be created in a community pharmacy by having an area slightly separate for interviewing and counseling. If you are involved in using physical assessment skills that involve directly touching the patient, manipulating clothing to assess or view an area, or some other act that is perceived as personal or intimate, a private area that blocks the view of others is necessary. If such an area is not available, you will be limited to fewer methods of drug therapy monitoring and outcomes assessment.

Questioning Skills. Good communication during your interview involves use of questioning skills. You can enhance the quality and efficiency of your interview by understanding how to use different types of questions. Use different types of questioning to get the patient to tell you what you really need to know. **Table 5-3** provides an overview of different types of questioning strategies that will help you conduct an effective interview. The basic types of questions that we will review here are open-ended, close-ended, direct, indirect, and probes.

Let's discuss open- and close-ended questions first. In general, express your questions in a way that elicits more than a "yes" or "no" answer. For example, you will learn more information by asking

TABLE 5-2.
Skills for the Patient Interview

Environmental preparation

- Assure adequate patient privacy.
- Appropriate level of privacy for the clinical care occurring in the encounter. A completely private area is required for physical assessment.
- Is away from physical barriers (glass windows, high countertops).
- Area is relatively quiet.

Interview preparation

- Reviews background sources of information, i.e., medical chart or pharmacy profile.

Greeting

- Introduces self; explains purpose; assures confidentiality.
- Establishes rapport; demonstrates respect, genuineness, empathy, competence.
- Determine patient's willingness to participate.

Assessment of patient communication barriers

- Primary language and interpretation is known. If you are unable to communicate effectively, seek another person known to the patient for assistance or an interpreter.
- Assesses visual impairment. Alternatives to assist the patient's vision are available and used when needed (magnifying glass, large print patient education, supplementary written instructions to medication labels).
- Assess hearing impairment. Communicates by looking directly at the patient and not covering mouth during speaking.
- Assess physical limitations. Determine if patient has inadequate strength or dexterity to open medication containers or handle small medical devices. Does patient require a wheel chair, walker, or cane? Is patient limited in gait and distance he or she can walk?
- Assess if having others present during the encounter is desired by the patient.
- Determine the need for an interpreter.

Establishment of therapeutic relationship

- Responsiveness to patient's questions.
- Display intent to advocate for the patient's needs.

Assessment of patient expectations

- Communicates in a way that demonstrates you understand the patient's expectations.

Closing the encounter

- Reviews findings of importance.
- Generates problem list and priorities.
- Reaches agreed upon action plan with patient.

Documenting the encounter

- Writes summary of care in S.O.A.P. format for medical chart and pharmacy care plan or pharmacy profile.

TABLE 5-3.

Questioning Strategies

Type	Purpose	Usual Response	Example
Open Ended	Encourage patient to talk; elicit additional information	Conversational / large quantity of information	How do you manage a headache?
Close Ended	Gather specific, narrow-focused information	"yes"–"no" short phrases	Does your headache respond to aspirin?
Direct	Learn information	Specific information	What medication do you take for a headache?
Indirect	Elaborate or clarify information	Information about feelings or concerns	I hear you saying it bothers you that your headaches don't respond to aspirin.
Probe	Elicit specific information about a portion of something already said	Detailed information	What is the most aspirin you've taken at one time for a headache? And you've never felt relief from this?

"How do you remember to take your medicines?" than by asking "Do you use a reminder package to help you remember to take your medicines?" In this example, the first question—known as an open-ended question—encourages the patient to talk, but the second question is closed and can be answered with one word or a short phrase. Close-ended questions are most useful when gathering precise, narrowly focused information. They can help fill in details after open-ended questions have established a general framework within a topic area. Let's examine a short interview where the pharmacist combines both types of questions:

Pharmacist: "Now, I'd like to discuss the non-prescription medicines you use. Can you tell me what you would take if you got a headache?"

Patient: "I'd most likely use some Tylenol™, maybe Advil™."

Pharmacist: "Do you ever take any aspirin?"

Patient: "Yes sometimes. My wife swears by Bufferin™ and sometimes gives me that."

Pharmacist: "How do you manage constipation if it occurs?"

Patient: "I try to manage it by watching what I eat. I've been eating a couple of prunes every morning."

Pharmacist: "What if the prunes don't work? Do you take any laxatives?"

Patient: "If I need something, my wife gives me some of her Nature's Remedy to take. That's something else she swears by—says it keeps her regular as a clock, and it's natural."

Pharmacist: "Tell me about the vitamins and minerals you use."

Patient: "Well, I take a B-complex pill because the lady at the health shop at the mall said most people like me have stress and it would help. She also said the body needs more minerals than what were in regular vitamins, so I'm taking a pill that has calcium, magnesium, and zinc in it."

Pharmacist: "Any others?"

Patient: "No. No one seems to agree about how much vitamin C is a good idea, so I just drink some orange juice every day. I figure that it can't hurt me."

This combination of question types elicits the most complete information. The close-ended questions were most effectively used to follow up on the open-ended questions.

With direct questions, you attempt to learn information. With indirect questions or reflective statements, you encourage a patient to elaborate or clarify a previous comment. A reflective statement summarizes or simply restates the idea or feelings that were expressed. It demonstrates interest and understanding but does not imply approval. Indirect questions are most useful for eliciting a patient's feelings or concerns.

The following examples illustrate how both direct and indirect questions might be used to gather information on a patient's negative feelings about taking several medications. Direct questions on this topic include "Why are you unhappy about taking all of these medicines?" or "What bothers you about taking these medicines?" The direct question limits the patient's response to what you specifically want to know. Comparable, reflective statements might be "So, you're unhappy about taking all of these medicines" or "What you seem to be saying is that it bothers you to have to take all of these medications." In this situation, the strength of the indirect question is that it is not too instructive to the patient as to how to express concerns or feelings.

A probe is a direct question designed to elicit specific information about a portion of what was said. There are two main purposes for probes: one is to redirect the patient's attention on something in order to ask about it again, and the other is to clarify a statement or obtain more detailed information. Probing is really a way of eliciting sufficient detail for an assessment. A common example is asking a patient to provide more information about the frequency of medication use. You may ask "How often do you take aspirin?" Then a patient may reply "Oh, just occasionally." This answer is not detailed enough for you to decide if the patient's aspirin use has any therapeutic implications. A suitable probe in this case might be "Which would describe how often you take this medication—a couple of times a week, a couple of times a month, or almost every day?" More than one probing question may be necessary to obtain enough detail for assessment purposes.

Listening Skills. Listening to the patient's response to your questions is a critical skill for conducting a successful interview. Through listening you will gain the information you are seeking from the patient. Listening is a complex activity that requires openness and sensitivity. In many ways, an opportunity to listen can be lost. One common way is to talk. If you are talking, you are not listening. To maximize your opportunity to gather information, the person you are interviewing should be talking. Some keys to effective listening include

- Give the person 100% of your attention.
- Begin listening with an open, neutral mind.
- Respond either verbally or nonverbally (nod, express interest) to demonstrate that you heard and understand. If your response is verbal, speak at approximately the same energy level.
- Respond to the person in a way that shows you understand what he or she was saying.
- Pay attention to the logical content of what the patient says, but also pay attention to how he or she says it. It reveals one's true feelings on the subject.
- Demonstrate respect for the person's point of view.

Facilitation means to encourage patients to say more but do so without directing the conversation. Facilitation can be done either verbally or nonverbally. The message behind facilitative gestures is that you are interested in what the patient is saying. A common verbal facilitative gesture is to repeat the last words said by the patient (reflection) or to say a short phrase such as "go on," "I see," or "mm-hmm." These gestures encourage the patient to provide greater detail.

Attentive silence is an important facet of skillful interviewing. Silence essentially provides the opportunity for the patient to talk; as long as the patient is sharing relevant information, you are gathering important data. However, the word "attentive" is critical. Although you are not speaking, you must provide nonverbal cues that demonstrate your interest and encourage the patient to continue. In this way, silence is a nonverbal facilitative gesture or technique. Silence may also occur because the patient is confused, resistant, embarrassed, or has strong emotion. If the patient is confused, rephrase your question. If the patient is resistant to answering the question, acknowledge the patient's reluctance and explain the usefulness of the information to the pharmacy assessment. You might say, for example, "I know that you are reluctant to discuss the frequency of use of your inhaler. However, I think that you are using it more often than what is intended. Knowing how often you use it now will help us determine how to change your medications to control your shortness of breath." A silence from embarrassment should be acknowledged. You might consider saying "I can see this is hard for you to talk about." Finally, if a strong emotion is evoked in the interview, a patient may become silent. If given a moment, most patients will "collect" themselves and continue with the interview.

Responding to Patients' Questions. Patients and others often raise questions during an interview. In fact, you may be seen as more accessible than physicians or as able to offer a "second opinion." However, these questions can create an uncomfortable situation if you do not know how much information has been shared with a patient or if the response would reveal unpleasant information. In general, it is appropriate to refer many questions about care or procedures to either a nurse or physician; questions on prognosis or medical problems should be referred to the patient's physician. You can acknowledge the patient's concerns, encourage him or her to seek the appropriate professional, and also let that professional know about the patient's concerns. Taking responsibility for interdisciplinary communication is an important part of the patient-centered care process.

You will often have requests for information as a pharmacist. However, patients also sometimes pose questions as a way of expressing concerns or underlying feelings. Before answering a question, think about what it might imply and then try to elicit the person's true concern. For example, if a patient asks "What are the effects of this blood pressure medicine?," you might describe its pharmacologic actions. But if you respond with "The medication has several effects—why do you ask?," the patient has the opportunity to share a concern such as "Well, I read that it might cause memory problems."

Similarly, a question may convey an attitude that you should acknowledge. For example, a recent pharmacy school graduate is asked by an older patient, "How old are you?" This question may convey the attitude that the pharmacist is too young to be giving advice. The pharmacist may respond to the presumed attitude rather than to the factual question by saying "I realize that I may seem young, but I am a licensed pharmacist and am knowledgeable about your medicines." An alternative response may be, "I can help you get the most out of your medicines and stay safe while using them."

Patients and caregivers frequently ask a health professional for advice, and these questions can be taken at face value and answered accordingly. However, people also ask about personal situations where your advice would be inappropriate. For example, a man whose mother is having difficulty managing her medications at home may ask, "Do you think she should be placed in a nursing home?" While you may have an opinion, it is inappropriate to share it; the decision must be made by the family, not the pharmacist. If you have access to the resources, you can offer to connect the caregiver to a social worker or pastoral care worker that may be in a better position to discuss many of the factors that need to be assessed. As a reply, "Many factors have to be considered before you decide how best to care for your mother. In terms of her medication management, several options could be tried to improve her medication compliance at home. I could assist you with understanding these and how to implement them. If you would like to discuss the larger issue of placing your mother in a nursing home, I can make arrangements for you to visit with the social worker while in the hospital."

Interpreting Nonverbal Communication. Both you and the patient communicate with words and behavior. Communication via behavior is a nonverbal exchange. Just as you carefully select the wording for a question, you must also control your nonverbal messages. Nonverbal messages are expressed by posture, facial expressions, gestures, activities, voice quality, and eye contact. A patient also may form impressions based on your personal appearance (just as you are likely to do in return). The general demeanor that facilitates communication conveys an unhurried calm style and interest. If you are collecting more than a small amount of information, it is appropriate to sit while talking with the patient; standing often implies being "too busy to spend time talking." Likewise, if you do other things while talking (e.g., leafing through a chart or fidgeting), the patient can interpret your behavior as indicating a lack of interest. Attentiveness and interest can be communicated by leaning forward, by maintaining eye contact, and by voice inflection. Open-body posture (arms extended or hanging loosely at the side) suggests to the patient that you are relaxed. Closed-body posture (limbs crossed or held in a defensive position) suggests mistrust or anxiousness. One gesture that will inhibit almost any conversation is looking at a watch.

Facial expressions are an important nonverbal behavior. Your expressions might be misinterpreted and negatively affect a patient's willingness to communicate. If you frown, for example, a patient may interpret this as indicating anger or annoyance. Your expressions may also convey judgmental feelings, such as embarrassment, disapproval, or boredom, about what the patient is saying. Although you may experience these feelings, nonverbal expression of them is likely to inhibit further sharing by the patient.

Making eye contact is generally regarded as a positive way to engage the patient in communication. However, eye contact and its meaning vary by culture. In Asian, Native American, Indochinese, Arab, and Appalachian cultures, directly looking at someone may indicate a sign of disrespect or aggression. In some cultures, it is not acceptable for women or younger people to make direct eye contact.[5]

In summary, Platt and Gordon recommend the following behaviors.[6]

▶ KEY POINT

Avoid outside interruptions when you are speaking with a patient. Look like you're listening. Look like you are there for a while. Sit down when speaking with the patient. Use touch appropriately. Even when you are not talking, your body language is talking for you.

Assessment of Patient Communication Barriers.
Communication at eye level improves comfort for patients. Therefore, you should sit across from the patient to enhance interaction. Physical barriers, such as glass windows or relatively high counter tops separating you and the patient, should be eliminated. Communication barriers can also result from language (e.g., the patient is not able to speak or understand your language), sensory impairments (e.g., dementia), or affective disorders (e.g., depression). And always, you should determine the patient's willingness to participate in this process. Patients will participate when they are ready.

If a patient's family member is present, either include that person in the conversation, if appropriate, or ask that person to return after the interview. The patient may feel uncomfortable discussing certain topics in the presence of another person; in that case, politely ask the individual to leave. In other situations, the patient may prefer to have a family member present. For example, a patient's spouse may be able to confirm or expand on the information being provided by the patient. One important caveat is to avoid shifting your attention away from the patient when another person is speaking. While you may record information from both sources, it is usually best to direct your questions primarily to the patient. For example, when the patient is a child who is old enough to speak with you, you should keep focused on the child even when the parent speaks.

Developing an Organized Interview Approach. During an interview, you must gather a considerable amount of information by using a written history or interview document or by adhering to a structured or ordered sequence of questions. Figure 5-1 provides you with a history-taking form that is complementary to Table 1-6, the pharmacist's database model. Use of such tools will help to improve your efficiency of documentation and prompt you to not miss important aspects of questioning. However, the structure itself is only part of the interview process. When patients have concerns, you always start with insufficient information. The process of inquiry is inductive, and it requires you to solicit information that reveals insight into the patient's needs. In essence, you hypothesize the patient's problems as you conduct the inquiry and formulate a questioning strategy to further support or refute your hypotheses.[7] Your ability to define and revise the definition of the patient's problem is a skill that develops with increasing expertise. Some problems remain ill-defined, challenging you as a clinician to develop a plan for care. Equally challenging is knowing what the optimal plan choices are for managing a particular problem. Some treatment choices have greater uncertainty of the outcomes that are achievable than others. The process of inquiry is the feedback loop that makes the pharmaceutical care process cyclic, allowing you to redesign your care plan as is needed based upon these outcomes.

Opening the Interview. Start with a broad-based question or statement that elicits the patient's concerns right away. When the patient initiates the interview, you might consider examples such as "I understand you want to speak with me about medications" or "What might I assist you with today?" However, if you have initiated the interview, it is best to begin with questions that fit a patient's expectations of a pharmacist. For example, after introductions and statement of your purpose for interviewing the patient, you might consider "Do you have any concerns or questions about your medications?"

Interacting with the Patient. Greet the person initially, introduce yourself, and briefly explain the purpose of the interview. You also may want to assure the patient that the information shared is confidential. In many instances, you may offer the patient a document to sign that is a consent allowing you access to the medical information and health data you need to properly care for him or her. This is a requirement induced by the HIPAA legislation approval in 2002. Work to establish rapport at the outset by establishing the therapeutic core qualities with the patient through demonstration of respect, genuineness, and empathy as well as competence.[5] Rapport is also enhanced by a clean, neat, professional appearance and, where customary, a white coat and nametag. Use proper names and titles, such as Mr., Mrs., Miss, or Ms.; when referring to colleagues, use their titles (e.g., Dr.).

Some patients will respond to a genuine personal relationship more than a professionally distant one. You may find that if you show interest in the person's life outside of the medication related areas of mutual concern, the patient will receive this effort and realize the personal approach you are taking is one that is genuine. The patient may want to know more about you and your life as well. You will need to be prepared to share enough to convey a caring approach while not getting so emotionally involved that you can no longer properly work with the patient's treatment needs.

KEY POINT

Be prepared to share information about yourself with the patient to gain trust, but be careful to not become emotionally involved.

Learning the Patient Characteristics. As your conversation with the patient unfolds, you should stay alert to the patient characteristics that may influence the interview. How a person reacts and performs in the role of patient or caregiver will be influenced largely by social, familial, cultural, spiritual or religious and socioeconomic background, age, and gender. Refer to Chapter 1 about the patient for a review. The specific influences of each are discussed here in the context of the interview.

Social Background. Social distance is a term used to describe the social, cultural, and economic differences between a patient and health care provider.[4] The greater the social difference, the more difficult it is to establish an open and trusting relationship, and the more likely it is that misinterpretations will occur. Work and lifestyle considerations should be brought out in order to understand the influences they may have on problem identification and care planning. Refer to Chapter 1 for a more detailed discussion.

Cultural Background. Language barriers exist if the patient does not speak or understand your language. Translation by a family member may allow for communication, but it also may alter either the questions asked or the patient's responses. Studies of reporting styles have demonstrated differences among various cultural groups. Different ethnic groups are apt to respond to and describe pain differently; some are more vocal, while others more stoic. An important consequence of these differences is the interpretation by health professionals. You need to consider your own cultural competency when interacting with patients. Refer to Chapter 1 to review the ways in which you can work to achieve cultural competence in your practice.[8]

Spirituality. Spirituality is an important source of meaning for many patients. Your understanding of the patient's spiritual history is a critical element to understanding the ways in which you will be perceived by the patient. Spiritual tradition may dictate that perception. Again, it is the patient's values and beliefs that must determine how you approach your communication with the patient. If you are a devout Catholic, communicating about birth control may be a substantial challenge for you. But you must place the values of the patient first. You must find an acceptable way to serve the patient. It might include, for example, finding another pharmacist who feels capable of working with these patients and their needs. But the spiritual basis of a person's belief system might be more subtle. For example, an individual's concepts of death may determine their choices in life. It is possible that a patient chooses non-adherence to a regimen because he or she believes that medication use is prolonging life in a way that is inconsistent with personal beliefs. These understandings of the person further explain why we see conflict or discord between a patient and one's family members. Family members may want something different (i.e., they may want to not lose this loved one, no matter what the "price" of treatment). This difference is often observed in what are termed "code" situations in hospitals. A code situation means an urgent, lifesaving call to have a trained interprofessional team rapidly respond to manage it. A code is commonly called when a patient stops breathing or develops a life-threatening cardiac arrhythmia.

Alternative approaches to healing and health may involve shamanism, faith healers, and medicine healing. Shamanism is the practice of a native healer. This person acts as a spiritual advisor, medical care provider, and counselor. Shamans exist in cultures worldwide. Similarly, faith healers are a common health provider in many areas of the world, including South Africa, Australia, and in the Pennsylvania Dutch communities across the United States. Shamans and faith healers commonly use prayer in their modes of treatment.

Socioeconomic Background. Some evidence shows that the reporting of symptoms and the seeking of medical attention occur less frequently for certain symptoms among patients of lower socioeconomic classes.[8] This difference is referred to as health disparities. Health disparities are differences in the incidence, prevalence, mortality, and burden of diseases and other adverse health conditions that exist among specific groups in the United States.[9] It is the outcome of racial and ethnic differences in rates of access, utilization, and prescription health care services. Recent reports indicate differences in the kind and quality of health care both sought and received by different race or ethnic groups. You may elicit more information if you actively inquire about symptoms, such as potential adverse drug effects, rather than assume that the patient will mention significant ones. Patients with limited incomes may have difficulty adhering to their medication regimen because of insufficient funds to purchase medicine. Moreover, patients in lower socioeconomic classes experience higher illiteracy rates and complete fewer years of formal education. This is particularly true for the elderly on fixed incomes. To ascertain literacy and correct usage, ask patients to demonstrate medical use rather than just describe it. You should ask the patient to read the medical label back to you, draw insulin in a syringe, or use an inhaler to show true understanding.

Family Background. During the interview, you may be able to gather information that provides insight into family dynamics and social support. For example, the person's role in the family may influence his or her reaction to a chronic illness. Reluctant to accept this role, the patient's attitude may translate to non-adherence with medications. Family members may also be the care providers needed to support the patient. For example, a grandson may organize his grandmother's medications so that she can continue to live in her own home.

Family history is relevant to the probability that a patient presents with certain conditions due to genetic predisposition. The role of the family history, when interpreted in combination with genetic testing, is emerging as an important component to this future method of diagnostics, treatment, and prevention. An excellent source to assist care providers with comprehensive, reliable family history is the My Family Health History Tool Kit found on the federal government website: http://www.hhs.gov/familyhistory/. One disadvantage to the family history is the amount of time it takes to construct it. Experienced clinicians report 30–45 minute sessions to accurately complete them. If this information is already available for use in records, it is well worth saving time to not repeat it.

> **KEY POINT** ....
>
> Use proper judgment to determine if the value of what you will learn can substantially contribute to your ability to perform care responsibilities.

Gender and Age Considerations. Men tend to report fewer symptoms or problems than women. Elderly people are less likely to report symptoms and problems than younger people. Because of the overlap between common drug side effects and symptoms (e.g., upset stomach, fatigue, drowsiness, dizziness, headache, constipation, and diarrhea), you should actively inquire about symptoms rather than wait for older patients to volunteer information. Pediatric patients may not be able to accurately express the symptoms (e.g., scratching at ear for otitis), and younger pediatric patients will require an adult to describe the patient's history and presentation. The content of the interview changes from small children to teenagers to adult and elderly based upon the needs and concerns present.

Literacy. *Illiteracy* is the complete inability to read or write. Only 5% of the U.S. residents are illiterate. *Functional illiteracy* refers to adults who read, write, and understand material below the 5th grade level. This causes adults to have difficulty in coping with many aspects of daily existence that require interpretation of written material. Low *literacy* refers to adults who can read, write, and understand information up to the 8th grade level. For these adults, functioning in society can be difficult. More than 90 million U.S residents have functional or low literacy. These conditions have a substantial impact on your ability to effectively communicate with the patient to both gather information and to provide it back.[10]

Health literacy is defined as the degree to which individuals have the capacity to obtain process and understand basic health information needed to make appropriate health decisions and services needed to prevent or treat illness. A patient's health literacy may be affected by low educational skills, cultural barriers to health care, limited English proficiency, and by health care providers who do not care to speak using a vocabulary that patients can understand. The American Medical Association published results of a task force that reviewed and analyzed the literature regarding health literacy. They concluded that the consequences of poor health literacy are more serious than revealed through the research data and that it is critical for all clinicians to improve communication with patients at risk for having low health literacy.[11]

You can continue to enhance your communication skills as a health care provider by preparing yourself through studying the Unified Health Communication (UHC) approach.[12] The UHC approach acknowledges cultural diversity, accommodates low English proficiency, and addresses low health literacy through adapting communication abilities or enlisting appropriate resources to meet patients' needs in these areas.

Continuing the Interview. Once you have started the patient talking, use a focused approach to inquiry and design the questioning strategy based upon your hypotheses of the patient's problems or needs. You must look, listen, be aware of odors, and pay attention, while trying to be as objective as possible about what you are observing. Sometimes, knowing exactly what the patient means by the words they are using is difficult. You can easily misinterpret or *translate the patient's words incorrectly*. A way to avoid this mistake is to inquire until you know what it would be like yourself to experience what the patient is telling you. Do not assume anything about the patient.

CASE EXAMPLE

How to Open and Interview and Secure Information Quickly

You are the pharmacist assigned to a family practice ambulatory clinic. Your primary responsibilities are to facilitate a prescription refill clinic and to assist with medication problem resolution. Doris Black, a 75 y/o/female who lives alone, is referred to you by the family practice resident for non-compliance. You meet the patient in the designated counseling room. You begin with a greeting. "Good morning Mrs. Black. My name is Mike, and I am a pharmacist here at the clinic. My job is to help people with their medications. How are things going for you today? Did you have any problems finding the clinic? Your doctor has requested that I visit with you today. Is it ok for us to discuss your medications?" The patient affirms. "How have you been doing taking your medications?" The patient explains she is on 8 different medications that are taken 2-3 different times a day. You respond " that must be really hard. I know I would have a difficult time with all those medications. Many people I visit with have a difficult time with that many medications. Do you have anyone to help you at home?" The patient replies that she does her own daily activities and that a daughter stops by once a week to check on her. She further shares with you that she does not want to leave her home. You review her medication regimen and are able to simplify administration times by changing two of the medications. You determine that a weekly medication organizer set up with the patient's revised medication regimen would be beneficial for patient compliance. "Doris, would it be okay if we set up your medications in this container system with your daily medications? Do you think your daughter could help you with this each week?" Mrs. Black agrees with the plan. He says, "Is it okay with you if I call your daughter to discuss the medication organizer? Doris, I would like to call you in 2 weeks to see how things are going. Would that be okay? Do you have any questions or other things you want to discuss?" The patient is dismissed from clinic. You place a call to the daughter to update the treatment plan.

Physical Assessment

Physical assessment activities are used to assist patients with determining their self-treatment needs (e.g., selecting an OTC product or referring to another provider), monitoring drug therapy response, and determining the success of the care plan or recommendations you have made. In this context, physical assessment will provide you with valuable baseline data about your patient. If your patient is being managed for hypertension, taking the patient's blood pressure at the initiation of therapy will provide you with a frame of reference to monitor his or her response to treatment. If your patient is being treated for atrial fibrillation, assessing the patient's pulse for rate and rhythm will provide you with a simple monitoring parameter to determine treatment response.

The skills of physical assessment include observation or inspection, palpation or manipulation, percussion, and auscultation. The skill used most by pharmacists to collect physical data is observation. Physical data collected by pharmacists includes age (as birth date), weight, height, pulse rate and rhythm, respiratory rate, and blood pressure.[13]

Review of Systems Approach. You may use the review of systems (ROS) approach to elicit a more complete assessment of symptoms that a patient may be experiencing as you are interviewing the patient to gather data. The ROS approach asks questions by geographically beginning at the head and working down through the body systems, ending at the toes. This approach is sometimes used when you are not getting adequate and specific information to assist you in further determining the patient's problems or response to treatment.

Mental Status Assessment. Physical assessment includes those assessments related to the mental state. Conducting a mental status examination for a patient who appears to have inconsistencies with memory and substantial medication non-adherence problems may reveal findings that should be used in plan redesign and possible referral to a primary care physician. Coulehan and Block state that you can quickly and non-intrusively assess cognitive function of a patient at the start of the interview without a formal mental status examination.[3] When you first meet a patient, you should assess the level of alertness demonstrated. You should also pay attention to the person's general appearance and behavior. As the patient begins to speak, assess the verbal output or speech. As the person converses with you, determine if the patient demonstrates a pattern of thought process that is logical and of appropriate content. Notice the patient's mood and affect. Many patients who have cognitive difficulties will give the impression of being oriented to time, place, and person. However, as you continue to talk, the patient's ability to remember may become more apparent when specific questions are asked. This approach gives you insight into the patient's mental state without a formal test or measurement. Alternatively, the Mini-Mental Status Examination (MMSE) can be used to rapidly quantify the patient's overall cognitive function.[14] Pharmacists have found it useful as an indicator of cognitive impairment in relationship to medication use (see **Figure 5-2**).

Activities of Daily Living (ADLs) and Instrumental Activities of Daily Living (IADLs) are methods to assess a patient's inability to manage the basic tasks of everyday life. ADLs are in the form of questionnaires and assess such things as eating, bathing, dressing, toileting, and transferring. The IADLs assess the functional capabilities such as using the telephone, traveling, shopping for meals, doing housework, managing money, and taking medicines. The goal of using these instruments is to determine how well and in what areas your patient is able to maintain personal independence in daily life. This tool is commonly used by nurses or occupational and physical therapists—individuals who often manage the long-term adaptation abilities of patients. The IADL is a useful tool for pharmacists' general assessment of a patient's ability to take medications independently of assistance and to determine one's mobility in getting to the pharmacy and obtaining medication. There are many versions of the ADL and IADL, but a representative IADL is included in **Figure 5-3**.[15]

Closing the Encounter. Closing the encounter is an important communication that outlines your understanding of the patient's needs and the responsibilities you have to the patient. In most situations, the closure should include reviewing what your findings of importance are—the problems you have identified and the signs and symptoms that support it. If you are ready at this time, you should also generate the problem list with priorities. From this, you should agree on an action plan and determine your responsibilities and the patient's responsibilities. This should culminate in patient education and answering any last questions from the patient. The appropriate point to end the encounter and how long the encounter should take depend on the nature of the patient's problem, its urgency, and your own constraints.

DOCUMENTING THE ENCOUNTER

Once you have heard the patient's story, you should document it in writing. How do you do this given the breadth of information, symptoms, experiences, and feelings shared with you? What do you write—knowing it will be included in the permanent record? You must select the facts or observations that appear most important from all of the information you can access. As you gain experience, you will almost automatically decide what problems have surfaced. You should record your findings in a way that will facilitate your own work with the patient and enlighten others also caring for the patient who have access to your documentation records. Chapter 4 introduced you to documentation; more detail will be presented throughout the case studies.

SPECIAL SITUATIONS

The Pediatric Patient

Parents or guardians are a usual source of information when a child is evaluated. For the very young, adults may describe the child's health experience as what they observe rather than how the child feels. Coulehan and Block point out that participation in the pediatric interview changes when children

Items	Points
Orientation	
1. What is the Year?	1
Season?	1
Date?	1
Day?	1
Month?	1
2. Where are we? State?	1
County?	1
Town or city?	1
Hospital?	1
Floor?	1
Registration	
3. Name three objects, taking one second to say each. Then ask the patient all three after you have said them. Give one point for each correct answer. Repeat the answers until the patient learns all three.	3
Attention and calculation	
4. Serial sevens. Give one point for each correct answer. Stop after five answers. *Alternate:* Spell WORLD backwards.	5
Recall	
5. Ask for names of three objects learned in Question 3. Give one point for each correct answer.	3
Language	
6. Point to a pencil and a watch. Have the patient name them as you point.	2
7. Have the patient repeat "No ifs, ands, or buts."	1
8. Have the patient follow a three-stage command: "Take the paper in your right hand. Fold the paper in half. Put the paper on the floor."	3
9. Have the patient read and obey the following: "CLOSE YOUR EYES." (Write it in large letters.)	1
10. Have the patient write a sentence of his or her own choice. (The sentence should contain a subject and an object and should make sense. Ignore spelling errors when scoring.)	1
11. Enlarge the design printed below to 1–5 cm per side and have the patient copy it. (Give one point if all sides and angles are preserved and if the intersecting sides form a quadrangle.)	1

Reproduced from Folstein MF. The Mini-Mental State Examination. In: Crook T, Ferris S, Bartus R, eds. Assessment in geriatric psychopharmacology. New Canaan, CT: Mark Powley; 1983:50-51. With permission.

Figure 5-2. The Mini-Mental State Examination

Patient's Name: _____   **Date:** _____

I = Independent   A = Assistance Required   D = Dependent

Obtained from Patient	Obtained from Informant	Activity	Guidelines for Assessment
I	I	**Using Telephone**	I = Able to look up numbers, dial, receive and make calls without help
A	A		A = Unable to use telephone
D	D		D = Able to answer phone or dial operator in an emergency but needs special phone or help in getting number, dialing
I	I	**Traveling**	I = Able to drive own car or travel alone on buses, taxis
A	A		A = Able to travel but needs someone to travel with
D	D		D = Unable to travel
I	I	**Shopping**	I = Able to take care of all food/clothes
A	A		A = Able to shop but needs someone to shop with
D	D		D = Unable to shop
I	I	**Preparing Meals**	I = Able to plan and cook full meals
A	A		A = Able to prepare light foods but unable to cook full meals alone
D	D		D = Unable to prepare any meals
I	I	**Housework**	I = Able to do heavy housework, i.e., scrub floors
A	A		A = Able to do light housework, but needs help with heavy tasks
D	D		D = Unable to do any housework
I	I	**Taking Medicine**	I = Able to prepare/take medications in the right dose at the right time
A	A		A = Able to take medications, but needs reminding or someone to prepare them
D	D		D = Unable to take medications
I	I	**Managing Money**	I = Able to manage buying needs, i.e., write checks, pay bills
A	A		A = Able to manage daily buying needs but needs help managing checkbook, paying bills
D	D		D = Unable to handle money

Adapted from Lawton MP and Brody EM. Assessment of older people: self-maintaining and instrumental activities of daily living. Gerontologist 1969; 9:179-186.

Figure 5-3. Instrumental Activities of Daily Living (IADL)

reach the age of 5–6 years. These children are able to broadly speak about their concerns but may need an adult to provide accuracy and precision. Adolescents take an active role in their own health care and may need to speak with you in confidence. Local regulations govern confidentiality issues.

The Geriatric Patient

Older patients are more likely to have multiple conditions and complex medication regimens that challenge the patient and you in successfully managing medication use. A larger proportion of the elderly population have low income, decreased mental acuity, impaired memory and access to care, or reliance on caregivers. These patients need you to spend more time initially in assessing their health and medication management needs. You are more likely to encounter adverse drug events, under-treatment of conditions, and over-treatment of conditions in this population. These patients often go to multiple providers for their varying problems and may use multiple pharmacies. Constructing an effective history may require the input of people who know the older patient well enough to fill in the details. You are likely to interact with caretakers to obtain information and make decisions when dealing with elderly patients. You must discern who has the authority to make decisions on behalf of the patient and take care to manage these relationships appropriately.[16]

Working with an Interpreter

It has been argued that every clinical encounter with a patient is actually a cross-cultural event.[17] We might classify this in two ways. Patients may not speak your language nor you theirs, and many patients lack conversational English language skills. Alternatively, you may both speak the same language but use the words for different ideas about the problems that the patient is experiencing. In both situations, translation is needed, and it always involves both language and culture.[13]

The roles of interpreters vary. Interpreters may translate the meaning of words in a neutral way; alternatively, they may advocate or negotiate for the patient by controlling and filtering information between you and the patient. Therefore, it is important to communicate to the interpreter what you want and expect from the encounter, such as the following:

- Tell translators what you need to obtain good and useful information.
- Determine the translation technique that you would like (simultaneous, consequential, or summary).
- Encourage the translator to ask questions when clarification is needed for the translator or patient.
- Tell the translator that you expect the patient to be assured of confidentiality and privacy.
- Determine how the exchange is progressing. Ask the translator to provide feedback about the patient's comprehension of the exchange.

Translation will take time and may create distance between you and the patient. To make the most of the encounter, communicate to the patient that you are interested in doing your best to understand and also ask that of the patient. Keep eye contact with the patient, rather than the translator, as much as possible. This may best be accomplished by sitting next to the translator, with both of you across from the patient. This way the patient can make contact with both of you, and you keep your eye contact directed toward the patient. Use touch and nonverbal communication techniques to enhance your understanding as cultural considerations permit.

In general, family members, especially children, and friends make poor translators for communication about personal and private matters. However, a family member may be the only available translator. There may be a need for you to provide brief training about the role of a translator and the need to communicate in a neutral and non-filtered fashion.

The Visually Impaired Patient

Visually impaired patients are more dependent upon the auditory form of communication. Speak clearly, not necessarily louder, so that the patient can understand you and confirm it is important. Large print reading materials may also help those patients who have partial vision or uncorrected vision. A practical tool is the magnifying glass. Some patients may find it a helpful assist device. There are also effective teaching tools/aids for visually impaired individuals. However, the poorer the vision, the less useful the visual aids. Make sure to introduce yourself as the pharmacist so the patient knows who he or she is speaking with. If you intend to touch the patient, let him or her know your intentions and request permission to do so beforehand. Warm your hands briefly so that you do not startle the patient. Make sure to speak to the patient while you are performing any physical contact to keep him or her informed of your intentions.[18]

The Hearing Impaired Patient

Sensory loss ranks second as a cause of low morale among the elderly, with 1 out of 4 people over the age of 65 affected by some degree of hearing loss.[19] Take responsibility for enhancing communication with a person who is hard of hearing. Background noises such as conversation, radios, television, or traffic make it more difficult to hear. Hearing impaired patients are more dependent upon visual forms of communication. Having written and pictorial materials available can be good assists. Gestures are helpful. In general, you should be directly in front of the patient for the benefit of the person who uses lip reading as a technique. Get the patient's attention before you speak by a gentle touch on the arm. Medications may affect the patient's ability to pay attention. Speak clearly in short sentences and not too quickly. If the patient asks you to repeat yourself more than once, find a different way to say what you want. Be sure to continue looking at and speaking directly to the patient rather than to others who are present. Patients who are hard of hearing only know what they are capable of hearing. For patients who are deaf, the use of sign language interpreters may be effective if available.[19] Generalizations should be applied cautiously and tentatively since they have the potential to become stereotyping. Be observant of these possible influences during the interview and decide their impact and relevance.

The Angry or Difficult Patient

Patients who are angry or difficult to work with may be so because they are experiencing a loss or feel threatened about the health condition or circumstances they are coping with. Patients may experience anger in response to many aspects of their health or health care situation that you are not directly aware of. Common reasons known are: (a) delays in diagnosis, (b) depression, (c) family conflict over health issues, (d) untreated pain, (e) disappointment and hurt in key relationships about health issues, (f) feelings of being abandoned by God when coping with illness and bad news, (g) frustration at being out of control when sick, (h) difficulties in dealing with uncertainty of illness, (i) disappointed hopes, (j) multiple losses, and (k) feelings of being trapped. Anger is a common reaction because when patients become overwhelmed with bad news they are usually not equipped emotionally to put the information into proper perspective. And patients may not even consider that they need extraordinary help to cope. This may be true of persons who have never needed assistance before. The notion of asking for help is not a welcome option for them. These patients may experience stress, anger, and fear and not understand why they are feeling these things.

Anger can seem irrational or of inappropriate magnitude when the patient is in an interaction with you, making it difficult for you to assess and determine how to best interact with the patient. Even if you do understand the patient and the reaction, you may still find it disturbing to be around. A common reaction to this is to respond defensively and withdraw from interacting. You may be tempted to abandon your role of developing the therapeutic relationship and instead engage in a negative response with the patient about what he or she is expressing anger about. This will not be productive.

There are behaviors that are constructive. Nonjudgmental listening and validating the patient's feelings can help the patient to regain perspective. If your care and concern is felt by the patient, the patient is likely to move the conversation to the causes of the anger. Often when a patient feels heard and understood the anger will disappear. If this does not result in improvement, the patient may have other causes that require additional therapeutic intervention (e.g., depression, untreated pain, substance dependency, other psychiatric disorders, unresolved grief). You may identify other therapeutic strategies to suggest and triage the patient to medical intervention. Rather than waiting for the patient to request help, you could suggest counseling with a social worker or mental health care professional, participating in a support group, or seeking medication management through a medical provider.[20]

The Mentally Incompetent Patient

Patients may have pre-existing psychiatric illness, personality disorders, or conditions such as Alzheimer's disease. All of these conditions may impair your ability to assess the patient through asking questions and listening. Similarly, these conditions may impair the patients' ability to receive information and learn from you when you conduct your interview or provide counseling. When the traditional strategies for communication are not working, you should consider these causes. Patients with these conditions often exhibit disruptive, demanding, manipulative, impulsive, or angry behavior. These patients require complex treatment strategies and the care of an interdisciplinary team. You may confront limitations quickly if you work alone and independently from other providers. You should also be in a safe setting in order to handle your own emotions generated by interacting with this challenging patient group.

SUMMARY

This chapter has provided an introduction to the structure and process of the patient encounter. No matter what the circumstances or setting, therapeutic care is the purpose of your encounter with the patient. The well conducted interview is a primary source of information to determine the patient's needs. You should now be able to properly prepare for the interview, construct an organized approach, open and close the interview properly, and listen, respond, and use questioning strategies appropriately. Your interaction with the patient (and others) should be broad and open based upon the patient's cues. Physical assessment may be an important component to some patient interviews. Once completed, the interview should be documented in retrievable records for you and others involved in the care of the patient if appropriate.

ASSESSMENT QUESTIONS

1. Describe the optimal environment for conducting a patient interview.
2. What should you communicate to the patient when you first meet him or her?
3. What will you evaluate about the patient when you have your initial interaction?
4. Describe ways to enhance your communication with a visually impaired patient.
5. Describe ways to enhance your communication with a hearing impaired patient.
6. What key points should you communicate with the patient about when you close the patient encounter?

ASSIGNMENT

1. Interview a friend or family member, practicing the communication skills and clinical observation skills presented in this chapter. You may use the Patient's History Form—Pharmacist's Recommendations/Plan document (Figure 5-1) to keep track of your observations.
2. Conduct a Mini-Mental Status Examination on three different people. Reflect on the variation you observe in the responses from these individuals.

PHARMACIST–PATIENT ENCOUNTER WITH OUR FOUR CASES

CASE 1

Lauren Smith calls Nasir Jabr, PharmD, RPh, 2 days after her visit to the pharmacy

Lauren decides to contact Nasir at Werbert's Pharmacy because after self-treatment, her symptoms are not going away. She is trying to make a decision about what she should do next. Lauren makes contact with Nasir by telephoning into the pharmacy, rather than coming in and having a face-to-face encounter. Nasir is available when she calls.

Pharmacy Technician (answers telephone): "Hello, you have reached Werbert's Pharmacy. This is Nancy, Pharmacy Technician, how may I help you?"

Lauren: "This is Lauren Smith. Is Nasir Jabr available?"

Nancy, Pharmacy Technician: "Yes, just a moment; will you hold please?"

Lauren: "Yes."

Nasir Jabr, Pharmacist: "Hello Lauren; it is nice to hear from you. What may I help you with?"

Lauren: "Nasir, you mentioned to me if my symptoms did not go away to give you a call. Well, they haven't."

Nasir Jabr: "Tell me what symptoms you are having."

Lauren: "I am having a burning sensation when I go to the bathroom."

Nasir Jabr: "Do you mean when you urinate?"

Lauren: "Yes. And it has worsened. It hurts so much that I just can't stand it anymore."

Nasir Jabr: "Lauren, it sounds like you have an acute urinary tract infection. I would like to refer you to a physician so that he can confirm this and start antibiotic treatment."

Lauren: "I never have experienced anything like this before. Do you think I should go to the Emergency Room?"

Nasir Jabr: "No, this is a common problem that many women of your age experience. There are several things you can do to reduce your chances of having this problem again. In the meantime, you need to get in to see a physician and start treatment. Do you have a physician that you see?"

Lauren: "No, I really haven't had any problems that I haven't been able to treat on my own. Would you refer me to someone?"

Nasir Jabr: "Dr. Joyce Miller is nearby and has a general family practice. The office phone number is 501-2963. You need to tell the office when you call that you are having this pain and that the pharmacist referred you to the physician."

Lauren: "Good. Thank you Nasir."

Nasir Jabr: "You are welcome. I would also like to know a few additional things. Do you have any other medical problems that you are self-treating?"

Lauren: "No."

Nasir Jabr: "What about birth control? Do you use birth control pills?"

Lauren: "Why do you ask?"

Nasir Jabr: "Women often are more susceptible to urinary tract infections if they are currently on birth control pills."

Lauren: "I didn't know that. Yes, I do."

Nasir Jabr: "Please tell that to Dr. Miller. Do you smoke?"

Lauren: "Well, yes. Why do you ask that?"

Nasir Jabr: "I noticed you bought cigarettes when you were in here last. I also noticed that you bought Advil™. Do you use this for any other problems beside the pain that you describe now?"

Lauren: "Well, yes again. I often get headaches and find that this relieves most of my discomfort."

Nasir Jabr: "Lauren. Let Dr. Miller also know this history. Will you please let me know how it goes after you see her?"

Lauren: "Yes, Nasir; I will. Thank you so much for your help."

CASE 1: SPECIFIC QUESTIONS

Evaluate the initial encounter, the main encounter, and the closure to the encounter.

1. What were the correct communication skills demonstrated in this encounter?
2. What improvements in the communication skills would you recommend?
3. What types of information were not accessible to you because of the telephone communication?

CASE 2

Christine Johnston, PharmD, RPh, conducts the initial patient encounter with Mr. Montanez in the clinic

Mr. Montanez and his daughter Maria return to Christine Johnson's medication assessment clinic for a visit at the Heart of Texas Health Systems Clinics. Christine Johnston maintains an evaluation area in a clinic examination room with assessment tools and patient teaching materials, including the Patient History Form (Figure 5-1). Christine Johnston greets Mr. Montanez and Maria through a face-to-face patient encounter. In this visit, Christine conducts a thorough patient interview and also gathers information from Mr. Montanez's family member, Maria.

Christine Johnston: "Buenos dias Señor Montanez and Maria. It is very nice to see you. Please have a seat and make yourself comfortable."

Maria: "I have brought everything that you asked of us last time when we met. I wrote down this list of medications my father takes and have also brought his prescription bottles."

Christine Johnston: "This is wonderful Maria. Thank you for bringing all of this. Let me take a few moments to look them over."

[Christine reads the list of medications and finds the following:

Glucotrol 1 tablet every day

Glucophage 1 tablet twice a day

Zocor 1 tablet every day

Vicodin 1 tablet if leg pain

She examines the medication bottles and finds the following on the labels:

Glipizide 5 mg. Take one tablet by mouth every day.

Metformin 500 mg. Take one tablet by mouth every 12 hours.

Simvastatin 40 mg. Take one tablet by mouth every evening.

Vicodin ES (750 mg acetaminophen/7.5 mg hydrocodone). Take one every 4 hours if needed for leg pain.

She thinks about what she is seeing and asks a few questions of Mr. Montanez.]

Christine Johnston (hands Mr. Montanez each medication container as she asks the questions): "Mr. Montanez, can you please tell me what this medication name is and how you take it?"

Mr. Montanez (looks at Maria with an alarmed expression): "I take this one in the morning. This one is (he moves the medication container back and forth like he is trying to focus his vision) well, I think this one is for my diabetes."

(Maria looks a little embarrassed for her father-in-law.)

Christine Johnston: "What about this one Mr. Montanez? Tell me what it is and how you use it."

(Mr. Montanez repeats the same episode. Christine decides not to pursue this further and asks a different line of questions.)

Christine Johnston: "Okay then Mr. Montanez. Thank you very much. Have you ever been told that you have allergies to any medicine?"

Mr. Montanez: "Yes. I was told I am allergic to codeine."

Christine Johnston [pulls out her opioid allergy decision tree developed by the pharmacists at her facility **(Figure 5-4)**]: "Do you have asthma?"

Mr. Montanez: "No."

Christine Johnston: "Why do you think you are allergic to codeine?"

Mr. Montanez: "Because the last time I had some I had an upset stomach and was dizzy. I called the pharmacy, and the pharmacist said I might be allergic to codeine. He told me I might need to switch to some other medicine."

Christine Johnston: "Have you ever had codeine before that?"

Mr. Montanez: "I am not really sure."

Christine Johnston: "When you had that upset stomach and were dizzy, did you develop a rash or itching?"

Mr. Montanez: "No."

Christine Johnston: "How about difficulty breathing soon afterward?"

Mr. Montanez: "No."

Christine Johnston: "Did you have to go into the emergency room or hospital for any reason right after taking it?"

Mr. Montanez: "No, oh no, not at all. I just didn't really feel good in my stomach, and I would get a little dizzy when I stood up. That's all."

Christine Johnston: "Mr. Montanez, do you find that you must use the bathroom to urinate frequently?"

Mr. Montanez: "I usually go every hour or two…I guess that's a lot. But I am thirsty and drink a lot of water too."

Maria interjects: "And beer too!" (she laughs)

Christine Johnston: "How many beers a day do you drink sir?"

Mr. Montanez: "Well, usually 1 or 2." (Maria confirms by nodding her head "yes.")

Christine Johnston: "Do you lose the feeling in your hands or feet?"

Mr. Montanez: "Sometimes. Mostly I get pain in my feet and lower legs…it comes and goes."

Christine Johnston: "What do you do when you get this pain?"

Mr. Montanez: "Sometimes I take one of those medicines."

Maria: "I usually give him one of the Vicodin™ tablets."

Christine Johnston: "Do you test your blood sugar at home?"

Maria (interjects): "Yes, I do this for him once a week with a machine."

Christine Johnston: "Did you bring this with you today?"

Maria: "No."

Christine Johnston: "Is there anything else that you do to take care of your health that we haven't discussed?"

Mr. Montanez (joking): "Well, I come here a lot." (everyone laughs)

Christine Johnston: "Okay Mr. Montanez. Thank you so much. I am going to have the nurse check your urine for protein and check your blood sugar too. Let me escort you to the laboratory area."

(Christine walks Mr. Montanez to the outpatient stat lab and returns to discuss the case further with Maria.)

Christine Johnston: "Maria, is there anything else that your father-in-law takes or is given to him for his health?"

Maria: "Well, I probably should not talk to you about this, but I am not sure if this is good for him or not. You see, he is from the old country…and he has beliefs about his health that are different than what goes on here in this clinic. He believes that his diabetes was caused by 'susto.' This is the word for him having a 'fright' or 'scare' many years ago. This is commonly believed by my older relatives. So he has also been told to use some of the plants to get better."

Christine Johnston: "What do you mean 'plants'?"

Maria: "Well, his sister started him using cactus flowers, from the prickly pear cactus."

Christine Johnston: "How does he take this?"

Maria: "She says to broil the stems and eat them each day. She says if he feels worse, to eat them three times during the day; if he feels better, to eat one. I tell him not to do this, but he ignores me and tells me I am not helping him. So I buy these at the market and help him with it."

Christine Johnston: "Is there anything else that he uses?"

Maria: "His sister also buys him yucca root from the store and brings it over. She boils it into a tea and has him drink

PATIENT INTERVIEW PROTOCOL

Do you have asthma? _____Yes _____No (Patients with asthma are more likely to develop difficulty breathing because of opioid induced histamine release.)

If yes, consider pretreatment of asthma patients who have previously reacted to opioids with diphenhydramine or prednisone. Continue on with patient interview.

If no, continue on with patient interview.

Have you ever been told that you are allergic to or should not receive codeine, morphine or other opioid medication?

_____Yes _____No *(Common brand names to prompt patient with:* Vicodin®, Lorcet®, Percocet®, Tylox®, Roxicet®, Percodan®, Oxycontin®, Darvon 65®*, Darvon N®*, Darvocet N-100®*, Demerol®, Duragesic®, Dilaudid®, Numorphan®, Talwin NX®)
*No longer commercially available in the United States.

If yes, continue on with patient interview.

If no, correct allergy status documentation in the chart. No further interview necessary.

Did you (patient) report any of the following symptoms or did any of your health care providers observe one or more of the following symptoms after taking codeine/morphine or drug(s) identified by patient above? (Check all that apply from both list A and list B)

List A

_____ Upset stomach
_____ Dizziness
_____ Previous history of taking codeine/morphine
_____ Mild, localized itching
_____ Difficulty breathing (due to laryngeal edema or bronchospasm)

List B

_____ Drug-related fever
_____ Severe systemic rash or itching
_____ Localized hives (late onset urticaria > 72 hrs)
_____ Immediate hypotension or hypertension
_____ Major total body rash (early onset urticaria within 1–72 hrs)
_____ Documented anaphylaxis to codeine/morphine
_____ Hospitalization/emergency room visits from opioid allergy

If yes to any symptoms in list A, and no to any in List B, then the risk of anaphylaxis approximates that of the general population. Continue with current agent.

If yes to any symptoms in List B, then risk of anaphylaxis is greater than that of the general population. Opioid agents are listed in three distinct classes below. If allergy is confirmed, switch to an alternative from one of the other two available classes.

  I. **Most structurally similar to morphine/codeine:** hydromorphone, hydrocodone, oxymorphone, oxycodone, buprenorphine, butorphanol*, nalbuphine, pentazocine**

  II. **Less structurally similar to morphine/codeine:** meperidine, fentanyl, sufentanil, alfentanil

  III. **Least structurally similar to morphine/codeine:** methadone***, propoxyphene[a] (Propoxyphene is no longer commercially available in the United States.)

References: 1) Baumann, T. Therapy consultation: Analgesic selection when the patient is allergic to codeine. Clinical Pharmacy. 1991;10:658; 2) Drug Consult.Opioid Analgesics-Cross Allergenecity. Micromedex Database 2001; 3) Ginsberg GS. Managing a patient with morphine allergy. Drug Therapy. 1985;June:147-158; 4) DeSwarte RD. Drug allergy—problems and strategies. J Allergy Clin Immunol. 1984;74(No.3 part 1): 209-221; 5) Levy JH, Rockoff MA. Anaphylaxis to meperidine. Anesthesia and Analgesia. 1982;61(3):301-303; 6) Fahmy NR. Hemodynamics, plasma histamine, and catecholamine concentrations during an anaphylactoid reaction to morphine. Anesthesiology.1981;55(3):329-331; 7) Fukuda T, Cohi S. Anaphylactic reaction to fentanyl or preservative. Canadian Anesthetists' Society Journal. 1986;33:826-827; 8) Bennett J, Anderson LK, McMillan JC, et al. Anaphylactic reaction during anaesthesia associated with positive intradermal skin test to fentanyl. Canadian Anesthetists' Society Journal. 1986;33:75-78.

Figure 5-4. Opioid Allergy Decision Tree: Standard Method to Determine the Likelihood of True Allergy and Cross-Sensitivity to Opioid Derivatives

a few cups each day. She taught me how to do this. We do it some days."

Christine Johnston: "I really appreciate you telling me about this. I will need to check on whether there is any evidence that this is helpful to diabetes; or for that matter, whether this may cause harm."

Maria: "Thank you so much. No matter what you find, it will be difficult for my father-in-law to believe what you tell him about these things. These beliefs are strong and founded in his culture and family."

Christine Johnston: "I understand. Why don't I go get your father? In the meantime, if he has a worsening of symptoms, including dizziness, thirst, or the frequency of his urination, please call me. What I plan to do is evaluate the information you have provided to me today and have you return in 1 week for a follow-up plan."

Maria: "Very good. We will do this."

CASE 2: SPECIFIC QUESTIONS

Evaluate the initial encounter, the main encounter, and the closure to the encounter.

1. How was communication affected by the language and cultural differences among Mr. Montanez, Maria, and Christine Johnston in this encounter?
2. How might the information revealed through this visit be affected by the use of a professional interpreter?
3. What possible communication problems emerged about Mr. Montanez through this routine encounter?

CASE 3

Luisa Rodriguez, PharmD, RPh, conducts an admission history on Huong Tran in the Emergency Room

Luisa Rodriguez visits with Huong to assist him with learning to correctly manipulate his handheld inhaler. Huong Tran is having difficulty with self-administering this medication after Dr. Mooris has instructed him to do so in the Emergency Room. Rodriguez demonstrates in this face-to-face encounter how to interact with Huong, and in turn, how to communicate with his non-English speaking parents through Huong during the patient encounter. She further engages the services of an interpreter after it is determined that Huong will be hospitalized. During this encounter, Rodriguez learns of alternative medicines and the care practice of acupuncture that Huong is also receiving because of guidance by his mother.

Rodriguez visits with Huong in the Emergency Room to assess his medication needs. She grabs a spacer device to help Huong with his metered dose inhaler of albuterol.

Luisa Rodriguez: "Huong, I am attaching this to the inhaler...all you have to do is breathe as soon as you push it down. I would like you to do this now."

[Huong does this, trying to breathe deeply. Rodriguez has him repeat this each minute three more times. Huong's breathing improves substantially within 5 minutes. She has him wait 5 minutes and repeat the 4 inhalations one minute apart each. Huong's breathing improves further. While she is working with Huong, the Emergency Room nurse was administering solu-medrol 40 mg (1 mg/kg dose) intravenously. Huong's parents became frightened. Rodriguez tries to reassure them that Huong is receiving the right care, but they do not understand and watch in great fear.

The metered dose inhaler process is repeated again in 20 minutes. By the end of one hour, Huong is breathing normally.]

(Huong speaks to his parents in Vietnamese.)

Huong: "It is okay Mom and Dad. I am better now. These people have done the right things for me."

(His parents are relieved and ask him what will happen next. Huong translates this back to Rodriguez.)

Luisa Rodriguez: "Well Huong, because you have been here three times in these past 2 weeks, the doctor wants to admit you to the hospital. I need to interview you about any medicines you are on and how you take care of yourself. Then we will provide you with medication and send you home. But, I am concerned that your parents will not understand everything that we have to discuss. Is there anyone else in your family that speaks English and Vietnamese… an older brother, sister, or a relative of your parents?"

Huong: "No. It is just us. There are other people in the neighborhood. But I pretty much do all of the translating for our family."

Luisa Rodriguez: "We have a translator who speaks Chinese. I wonder if this is close enough to be helpful to your parents. In addition, there is a social worker who may be able to contact a volunteer translator in the community. Dr. Mooris will be back in a minute to explain to your parents what will happen. I will let him know that you are the family translator."

(Huong is transferred to the general pediatric floor in the hospital. Rodriguez visits him to conduct a medication admission history.)

Luisa Rodriguez: "Hello again Huong, Mr. and Mrs. Tran. I hope you are comfortable here. This is the area of the hospital I usually work in. Huong, tell me what medicines you are supposed to take."

Huong: "I have the inhaler just like the one you had me use in the Emergency Room. But I don't have one of those things that you put on it…that really worked better."

Luisa Rodriguez: "That is called a spacer device. We will get you started with that in the future. How do you get this medicine?"

Huong: "Well the school nurse has been working with a doctor in our neighborhood. She worked it out so that I could see her after school sometimes. She gives me the inhaler from her cabinet."

Luisa Rodriguez: "Do you run out of medicine?"

Huong: "Yes. I tell the nurse and she works it out for me to get some more. That is what happened about 2 weeks ago. I ran out and told her about it, but she couldn't find any yet. So I have been having trouble."

Luisa Rodriguez: "What other medicines do you take?"

Huong: "My mother gives me something that she gets from Vietnam. Mom, what is it called?"

(Huong asks his mother in Vietnamese.)

Mrs. Tran: "Bai guo ye."

Huong: "I do not know what it is exactly. She takes a powder and mixes a little bit of water with it. She grinds it up and lets it soak into the water. Then I drink the small amount of liquid."

(Rodriguez makes a note to herself to look up this substance and find out what it is.)

Luisa Rodriguez: "Does she do anything else for you?"

Huong: "There is a doctor; he uses the needles."

Luisa Rodriguez: "Does he call it acupuncture?"

Huong: "Yes. That is it. And sometimes she takes me there. It's okay; it really doesn't hurt or anything."

Luisa Rodriguez: "Thank you Huong, Mr. and Mrs. Tran. I will be back later to discuss your medicines with you."

CASE 3: SPECIFIC QUESTIONS

Evaluate the initial encounter, the main encounter, and the closure to the encounter.

1. What were the difficulties that Luisa Rodriguez was faced with during this emergency room encounter?
2. What issues in patient care management might Rodriguez face, even if she is able to arrange for an interpreter that speaks their language?

CASE 4

Michael Jones, MS, RPh, conducts a patient interview and limited physical examination with Mr. Robinson

Michael Jones conducts a face-to-face interview with Mr. Robinson to collect the needed patient health information for properly managing Mr. Robinson's anticoagulation therapy along with his other medications during his hospital stay. Michael goes to Mr. Robinson's room to conduct his initial patient interview. Before entering the room he checks to make sure that he has his pocket notepad and his stethoscope and that his pager is on vibrator mode so it doesn't disrupt Mr. Robinson during the interview. He also thinks about how he will physically interact in a respectful manner during the interview prior to entering Mr. Robinson's room. He knocks on Mr. Robinson's door to greet him and initiate the patient encounter.

Michael Jones, Pharmacist: "Hello Mr. Robinson. It's me, Michael the pharmacist. May I come in to speak with you?"

Mr. Robinson: "Yes. I've been anxious for your return. Please come in."

Michael Jones: "Mr. Robinson, I'd like to ask you several questions. I need some information from you directly to be able to recommend to Dr. Rangert the best approach for your anticoagulation while you are hospitalized. This means I need to know information about how you are feeling, how your body is responding to this medicine, and about other general aspects of your health. I would also like to respond to any questions you have. Please be assured that whatever you and I discuss will remain private."

(As he is speaking, Jones finds a chair and brings it up alongside Mr. Robinson's bed so that he can face him at eye level. He also partially closes the room door to assure privacy in the conversation. He sits down.)

Mr. Robinson: "Go ahead. I'm not going anywhere."

Michael Jones: "Thank you. I'm going to ask you some general questions, and then I will follow up with specific questions about your blood thinner medicine."

[Jones uses the Patient's History Form (**Figure 5-5**) first to guide his questions and take notes and record relevant information from the interview.]

Michael Jones: "Tell me about yourself. How old are you?"

Mr. Robinson: "I am 76 years old."

Michael Jones: "Where do you live?"

Mr. Robinson: "At my home. It's been mine and my wife's now for over 50 years."

Michael Jones: "Are you still working?"

Mr. Robinson: "Well, not really. I retired several years ago from farming. I have a pension, but I still take fresh vegetables to the market for a little extra when they are in season."

Michael Jones: "Does your wife help you with your medicines?"

Mr. Robinson: "Well she used to. But she died 1 year ago, and I am having a very hard time keeping track of things. I live alone now."

Michael Jones: "I am sorry to hear that. Do you have anyone who helps you with your work around the house?"

Mr. Robinson: "Not really. There are a couple of lady friends of my wife who look in on me now and then. They pick up my medicines or take me to see Joe Daly, the pharmacist at Daly Apothecary in town. He's been the most help to me."

Michael Jones: "What is the main problem that caused you to come to the hospital Mr. Robinson?"

Mr. Robinson: "I was having a real hard time breathing, I just felt like I was gonna suffocate. I called Joe, and he asked me a few questions. He said he'd call me right back. When he did, he said that he talked to Dr. Friedland in town who said that I should get to the hospital right away."

Michael Jones: "Who is Dr. Friedland?"

Mr. Robinson: "He's the doctor I usually see. He works with Dr. Rangert."

Michael Jones: "What medical problems have you been told you have?"

Demographic and Administrative Information:		Room No.	ID No. 02946372
Date:		Gender: M	Primary Language: ENGLISH
Name: SAMUEL ROBINSON		DOB:	Height:	Weight:
Street Address: 1362 MOCKINGDALE LANE		BP:	Temp:	Pulse:
City, State, Zip BILOXI, MISSISSIPPI 78023		Race/Ethnicity: AF-AMER	Religion:
Home Phone #: (901) 468-4832		MD/Phone No.	
Work Phone #: N/A		Pharmacist/Phone No.	
Occupation: RETIRED		Insurance: MEDICARE	
Family Members/Care Givers: WIFE DECEASED			
Problem List:	**Pharmacist's Recommendations/Plan:**		
1.			
2.			
3.			
4.			
5.			
6.			
7.			
8.			
9.			
10.			

Pharmacist's Name: _____ Date: _____ Phone/Pager #: _____

Chief Complaint/History of Present Illness:	
Past Medical History/Surgery/Genetics:	
Family and Social History (significant relationship/co-habitants):	
Physical Examination/Review of Systems:	
ADL:	
Lifestyle/Diet/Exercise:	
Acute and Chronic Medical Problems/Associated Symptoms:	
1.	6.
2.	7.
3.	8.
4.	9.
5.	10.
Describe Patient's Health Beliefs and Values:	

Figure 5-5. Patient's History Form—Pharmacist's Recommended Care Plan—Samuel Robinson

Does Patient Receive Assistance in Medication Administration? Describe:

Allergies/Intolerances: ( ) No Known Drug Allergies		
Allergen:	Reaction:	Treatment:
Allergen:	Reaction:	Treatment:
Allergen:	Reaction:	Treatment:

Social Drug Use:	Alcohol:	Caffeine:	Tobacco:	Other:

Current Drug Therapy (prescription and over the counter, vitamins, remedies, alternative treatment):

Drug Name Strength/Route	Problem Number	Usual Schedule	Describe PRN Use	Does Med Work?	Side Effects or Concerns	Compliance Issues
1.						
2.						
3.						
4.						
5.						
6.						
7.						
8.						
9.						
10.						
11.						
12.						
13.						
14.						
15.						

Past Drug Therapy:

Time Line: Circle administration times and record appropriate medications and meals below:

Patient's Actual Use:
  6 7 8 9 10 11 12 1 2 3 4 5 6 7 8 9 10 11 12 1 2 3 4 5
  am   noon   pm   midnight   am

Prescribed Schedule:
  6 7 8 9 10 11 12 1 2 3 4 5 6 7 8 9 10 11 12 1 2 3 4 5
  am   noon   pm   midnight   am

Costs of Meds/Month:	$	Insurance:	( ) Yes	( ) No
	Co-pay:	Medicaid:		Annual Income:

Completed by: _____   Date: _____

Figure 5-5 (continued). Patient's History Form—Pharmacist's Recommended Care Plan—Samuel Robinson

Mr. Robinson: "I was told I had a congested heart…and bad blood pressure…and that my heart beats in a funny way, so they give me a blood thinner for that problem."

Michael Jones: "Could you tell me what medicines you take?"

Mr. Robinson: "Well I can never remember names. But I know my blood thinner, my heart pills, there are three of them…and my thyroid medicine too. You know I put all of these medicines in a bag and brought them to the hospital. That nurse, you know, Charlotte, she has them."

Michael Jones: "Okay Mr. Robinson. I will get them and be back with a couple more questions. Thanks. That will help us to do better with your medicine. Do you remember the last time you took your blood thinner?"

Mr. Robinson: "I don't miss that one. I took that yesterday morning."

Michael Jones: "Now Mr. Robinson. I'd like to take a closer look at you. Do you mind if I take your pulse and blood pressure?"

Mr. Robinson: "No—that's fine. Go ahead."

(Michael Jones measures his blood pressure. It is 156/102 mm Hg at rest. He then takes his pulse rate of 110 beats/minute-rhythm irregular. While he is doing this, he examines Mr. Robinson's skin and eyes for evidence of bleeding or bruising. There is no evidence of a problem.)

Michael Jones: "Mr. Robinson, your blood pressure is higher than normal and your heart rate, which I am checking by monitoring your pulse, is higher than we like to see it. The rhythm of your heart is also irregular. Have you been told you have atrial fibrillation?"

Mr. Robinson: "Yes…that's it. That's what it's called."

Michael Jones: "Do you drink alcohol sir? Beer or whiskey or anything?"

Mr. Robinson: "No sir—don't touch it." (He frowns at Jones with displeasure.)

Michael Jones: "How about smoking?"

Mr. Robinson: "Well yes, I do smoke. I smoke cigarettes."

Michael Jones: "How many cigarettes do you smoke in a day sir?"

Mr. Robinson: "Well—for sure about 20 or so—1 pack a day or so."

(Michael switches to his Anticoagulation Assessment Record, **Figure 5-6**.)

Michael Jones: "Have you had any bleeding of any kind recently Mr. Robinson?"

Mr. Robinson: "What do you mean?"

Michael Jones: "Do you have bleeding of your gums when you brush your teeth?"

Mr. Robinson: "No."

Michael Jones: "Have you noticed any blood in your stool or urine when you use the bathroom?"

Mr. Robinson: "No."

Michael Jones: "Okay then. Do you take any over-the-counter medicine?"

Mr. Robinson: "What is that?"

Michael Jones: "The kind you can buy without a prescription. For example, do you use any acetaminophen? Some people know it as Tylenol®."

Mr. Robinson: "No."

Michael Jones: "How about ibuprofen? Some people know that as Advil®."

Mr. Robinson: "You know…some times when I get a headache, I think I take that Advil® medicine."

Michael Jones: "How about vitamins. Do you take any?"

Mr. Robinson: "Yes. I know that I take a once-a-day vitamin of some kind. And also vitamin E. My wife told me that vitamin E was good for my heart."

Michael Jones: "I have a few things to look at in your medical record, and then I will recommend what to do to both you and your doctor."

Mr. Robinson: "Thank you Michael."

ANTICOAGULATION ASSESSMENT RECORD

Patient's Name _____ Date of Birth _____ Race _____

Home Telephone ( ) _____ Alternate Telephone ( ) _____ Emergency Contact Person _____ Telephone ( ) _____

Habits (describe pattern of use): Smoking _____ Alcohol _____ Drugs _____

<u>Consider for dose determination:</u> Indication for anticoagulation/Target INR   Bleeding history/risk factors for bleeding   Drug Interactions
Conditions requiring dosage adjustment   Dietary/alternative sources of Vitamin K

Indication for Anticoagulation	Check One	INR Goal
Prophylaxis of DVT		2-3
Treatment of venous thrombosis		2-3
Treatment of PE		2-3
Prevention of systemic embolism		2-3
Tissue heart valves		2-3
Acute MI		2-3
Valvular heart disease		2-3
Bileaflet mechanical valve/aortic position		2-3
Mechanical prosthetic valve		2.5-3.5
Antiphospholipid syndrome		2.5-3.5
Acute MI (prevent recurrence)		2.5-3.5

Bleeding History/Risk Factors for Bleeding	Check if present
Hospital admission for bleed	
Falls	
Oral bleed	
Vaginal bleed	
Lower GI bleed	
Upper GI Bleed	
Rectal bleed	
Guaiac + - _/_/_ ND	
Hemorrhoids/Ulcer	
Seizure	
Urinary bleed	
Hct <30%	
Hematuria	

Conditions Requiring Dose Adjustment	Dose Change
ETOH Acute	No change
ETOH Chronic	Inc dose
Advanced renal disease	Dec dose
> 65 years old	Dec dose
Liver disease	Dec dose
Congestive heart failure	Dec dose
Thyroid disease	Dec dose
Baseline Hematology	**Value**
Hemoglobin	
Hematocrit	
Platelets	
WBCs	
Stool Guaiac	

Vitamin K Food Intake History (Foods High in Vitamin K)

Food Source	Amount	Consumption Qty	Food Source	Amount	Consumption Qty
Fats and Dressings			Green scallion—raw	2/3 cup	
Mayonnaise	7 tbsp		Kale—raw	3/4 cup	
Oils: cannola, salad, soybean	7 tbsp		Lettuce—raw bib, red leaf	1-3/4 cup	
Vegetables			Mustard greens—raw	1-1/2 cup	
Broccoli	1/2 cup		Parsley—chopped	1-1/2 cup	
Brussel sprouts	5 sprouts		Spinach—raw leaf	1-1/2 cup	
Cabbage	1-1/2 cup		Turnip greens—raw	1-1/2 cup	
Collard greens	1/2 cup		Watercress—raw chopped	3 cup	
Endive—raw	2 cup				

Figure 5-6. Anticoagulation Assessment Record

ANTICOAGULATION ASSESSMENT RECORD (page 2)

Concurrent Medications Known to Interact with Warfarin (Prescriptions and OTC—name, dose, frequency):

Drug	Using	Action to be Taken	Drug	Using	Action to be Taken
Acetaminophen—large dose>1week		None	Dicloxacillin		Inc W dose
Alcohol—acute ingestion		Redraw INR in 24 hrs	Diflunisal		DecW dose
Alcohol—chronic ingestion		Inc W dose-stop ETOH	Disulfiram		DecW dose
Allopurinol		?Inc W dose	Fluconazole		DecW dose
Aminoglutethimide		Inc W dose	Griseofulvin		Inc W dose
Aminoglycosides		?DecW dose	Isoniazid		DecW dose
Amiodarone		DecW dose—delayed effect	Ketoconazole		DecW dose
>500 mgs/day ascorbic acid		?Inc W dose	Lovastatin		DecW dose
Azathioprine		?Inc W dose	Metronidazole		DecW dose
Azithromycin		?DecW dose	Miconazole		DecW dose
Barbiturates		Inc W dose	NSAIDS-varies with each agent		Inc/DecW dose
Carbamazepine		Inc W dose	Omeprazole—slight increase in INR		DecW dose
Cephalosporins		?DecW dose	Phenytoin		Inc/Dec W dose
Cholestyramine		Inc W dose/displace time of administration	Quinidine		DecW dose
Chloramphenicol		DecW dose	Simvastatin		DecW dose
Cimetidine		?DecW dose	Sulfinpyrazone		DecW dose
Ciprofloxacin		?DecW dose	Tamoxifen		DecW dose
Clofibrate/Gemfibrozil		DecW dose	Thyroid hormones		DecW dose
Colestipol		Inc W dose/displace time of administration	Tricyclic antidepressants		?DecW dose
Corticosteroids		Unpredictable	TMP-SMX		DecW dose by 1/3
Cyclophosphamide		Inc W dose	Vitamin E		DecW dose
Cyclosporine		IncW dose	Valproic acid		DecW dose
Danazol		DecW dose	Zafirleukast		DecW dose

Date	Dose	INR	RP Initials	Comments

Initial dose recommendation taking into consideration all factors: _____

Date	Dose	INR	RP Initials	Comments

Figure 5-6 (continued). Anticoagulation Assessment Record

CASE 4: SPECIFIC QUESTIONS

1. Evaluate Jones' initial greeting in the encounter with Mr. Robinson. What did he do to "set the stage" correctly for the interview?
2. What additional questions could Michael Jones have asked to learn more about Mr. Robinson's Advil® use?
3. Is Mr. Robinson someone who should be assessed with the IADL? The MMSE?

REFERENCES

1. Cipolle RJ, Strand LM, Morley PC. *Pharmaceutical Care Practice*. New York, NY: McGraw Hill; 1998.
2. Sleath B, Roter D, Chewning B, et al. Asking questions about medication: analysis of physician-patient interactions and physician perceptions. *Medical Care*. 1999; 37(11):169–73.
3. Katajavuorn NM, Valtonen SP, Pietila KM, et al. Myths behind patient counseling: a patient counseling study of non-prescription medicines in Finland. *Journal of Social and Administrative Pharmacy*. 2002; 19(4):129–36.
4. Coulehan JL, Block MR. *The Medical Interview: Mastering Skills for Clinical Practice*, 3rd ed. Philadelphia, PA: F.A. Davis and Company; 1997.
5. Bernstein L, Bernstein RS. *Interviewing: A Guide for Health Professionals*, 4th ed. Norwalk, CT: Appleton-Century-Crofts; 1985.
6. Platt FW, Gordon GH. *Field Guide to the Difficult Patient Interview*. Baltimore, MD and Philadelphia, PA: Lippincott Williams and Wilkins; 1999.
7. Barrows HS, Pickell GC. *Developing Clinical Problem Solving Skills—A Guide to More Effective Diagnosis and Treatment*. New York, NY: Norton Medical Books; 1991.
8. Zweber A. Cultural competence in pharmacy practice. *Am J Pharm Educ*. 2002; 66:172–6.
9. Anon. Addressing racial and ethnic disparities in health care fact sheet. AHRQ Publication No. 00-P041. Rockville, MD: Agency for Healthcare Research and Quality; February 2000. www.ahrq.gov/research/ disparit.htm.
10. Dreger V, Tremback T. Optimizing patient health by treating literacy and language barriers. *AORN Journal*. 2002; 75(2):280–93.
11. Health literacy: report of the Council on Scientific Affairs. Ad Hoc Committee on Health Literacy for the Council on Scientific Affairs, American Medical Association. *JAMA*. 1999 Feb 10; 281(6):552–7.
12. Health Literacy. Access: http://www.hrsa.gov/publichealth/healthliteracy/ Accessed June 2010.
13. Barkauskas VH, Stoltenberg-Allen K, Baumann LC, et al. *Health and Physical Assessment*. St. Louis, MO: Mosby-Year Book, Inc.; 1998.
14. Folstein JF, Folstein SE, McHugh PR. Mini-mental state: a practical method for grading the cognitive state of patients for the clinician. *J Psychiatry Res*. 1975; 12:189–98.
15. Lawton MP, Brody EM. Assessment of older people: self-maintaining and instrumental activities of daily living. *Gerontologist*. 1969; 179–86.
16. Clark M. *Culture and Aging: An Anthropologic Study of Older Americans*. Springfield, IL: Thomas; 1967.
17. Myerscough PR. *Talking with Patients—A Basic Clinical Skill*. New York, NY: Oxford University Press; 1989.
18. Billings JA, Stoeckle JD. *The Clinical Encounter—A Guide to the Medical Interview and Case Presentation*. St. Louis, MO: Mosby-Year Book, Inc.; 1999.
19. McNamee C. Chapter 8—Communicating with the hard of hearing. In: *Physician–Patient Communication—Reading and Recommendation*. Henderson G, ed. Springfield, IL: Thomas; 1981.
20. Lee SJ, Back AL, Block SD, et al. Enhanced physician–patient communication. *Hematology*. 2002; 464–83.

The Patient's Health Record

"For better or worse, I have come to believe that we—patients, families, clinicians, and the health care system as a whole—would all be far better off if we professionals recalibrated our work such that we behaved with patients and families not as hosts in the care system, but as guests in their lives."
—Donald M. Berwick

CHAPTER OUTLINE

Purpose

Patient Health Information
- Consumer Empowerment
- Health Information Exchange

Conduct Issues Related to Patient Health Information
- Security, Privacy, and Confidentiality
- Corporate Policies

Patient's Health Records—The Medical Record
- Electronic Medical Record
- Electronic Health Record
- Continuity of Care Record
- Personal Health Record
- Patient Portals
- Registries

The Patient's Health Record
- Use of the Record
- Record Organization
- Record Content

Pharmacy Records
- Prescription Records—Outpatient Practice
- Medication Orders—Inpatient Practice
- The Patient's Profile—All Settings
- Pharmacists' Notes

Summary

Assessment Questions

Pharmacist–Patient Encounter with Our Four Cases
- Case 1: Lauren Smith brings a prescription to Nasir Jabr, PharmD, RPh, after seeing Dr. Miller
- Case 2: Christine Johnston, PharmD, RPh, reviews Eduardo Montanez's clinic record and laboratory findings
- Case 3: Luisa Rodriguez, PharmD, RPh, reviews Huong Tran's admission note from the physician
- Case 4: Michael Jones, MS, RPh, reviews Samuel Robinson's medical record and other sources of information

OBJECTIVES

To gain knowledge of:

1. patient health information and the impact of consumer empowerment on its management;
2. the changing form of health records from paper to electronic that exist for a patient as a result of health information technology adoption and the evolving national health information network;
3. the role of health information exchange and how it relates to the use of patient health information and the patient record;
4. definitions of various health records that exist for a patient, how these records are used, and by whom;
5. use of the patient medical record or patient profile in the provision of patient care;
6. how to act legally and ethically to safeguard the management of patient health information assuring security, privacy, and confidentiality.

PURPOSE

The purpose of this chapter is to describe the current and evolving structure and uses of the patient's health information and the patient's health records. You will review the important concepts of practice related to patient confidentiality, and review the privacy and security rights of patients about their health information and the responsibilities we have in health care to assure them. You will learn about the forms and types of patient health records, where these records are located, and how organizations, health professionals, and you as a pharmacist will use them. You will also be introduced to the personal health record, a consumer-driven patient managed health record which you will encounter when providing care to some of your patients. You may find yourself contributing information to the personal health record, transferring information from the record, or possibly participating in the co-management of this record with patients. In summary, this chapter will provide you with an understanding of health information, the patient's various health records, the pharmacy record, and how they are useful to you in care.

PATIENT HEALTH INFORMATION

Patient health information is the comprehensive set of data about the patient that is accumulated throughout a patient's life. We use relevant portions of that information to guide our approaches to patient care. Patients trust that the information about them will be kept private and confidential. Patients expect that we will share that information with other providers or organizations only when it is important to carry out health care on their behalf. Otherwise, patient health information belongs to the patient—it is private.

Consumer Empowerment

Historically, personal health information that is stored in health records has been managed and used by health professionals and health care delivery organizations—with little consideration of consumers' use of the information. However, our move from the industrial age to the technology-connected age has resulted in us being individually more empowered and able to connect with our own health information. Consumer empowerment, the investment of power or authority in those who purchase goods and services, is changing our social approaches through use of the Internet.[1] This has fostered a new generation of people known as the Net Generation. Net Generation people consider computers a natural part of their environment. By 2002, all of the college students (at least in the United States) had begun using computers and the Internet was commonplace.[2] These people are technically "savvy" and are able to negotiate the virtual environment with comfort and ease. When these people become our patients, many want to email their providers and use texting as their preferred means of communication. Communication is more interactive in this approach, with the ability of patients to say what they want, when they want it, and use social networking tools to connect and collaborate. This social change that has occurred with younger patients is having a significant impact on provider–patient relationships overall.

Value-driven health care is a key concept in consumer empowerment. A recent survey conducted in 2010 by PricewaterhouseCoopers found that 97% of government and health leaders in 20 countries agreed that patients should have some responsibility for managing their health and chronic conditions such as obesity, diabetes, and heart disease. Patients and their caregivers must be engaged in managing medications and staying true to care plans.[3] Consistent with these findings, the federal government has identified consumer empowerment as a key breakthrough area in its strategic goals for health care.[4] Value-driven health care asserts that consumers deserve to know the quality and cost of their health care. Health care transparency provides consumers with the information necessary, and the incentive, to choose health care providers based on value. This empowers consumer choice. Consumer choice creates incentives at all levels, and motivates the entire health care system to provide better care for less money. The cornerstones approach of connecting systems, standards, and support for e-health; measuring and publishing quality data; measuring and publishing price data; and creating positive incentives requires consumer empowerment to influence the health care marketplace.

Consumerism and Collaboration. Openness of information sharing through online tools is now increasingly common. Patients are actively contributing to their own care process, causing increased demands for collaboration between professionals and patients. A gradual transformation in patient roles in health care has empowered patients to be on the same level playing field as other stakeholders in care. Physicians, pharmacists, and other health professionals involved with patients are positioned together through an active partnership. Eventually, this change in role for the patient is ultimately resulting in a new collaborative approach to care between patients and their providers.[5]

Consumerism and Patient Vulnerability. There is no doubt that consumerism is driving the care delivery model to one where the patient has an equal role on the playing field of health care stakeholders. However, this also amplifies the potential conflict created between provider trust and consumer vulnerability. Patient vulnerability is ever present when patients are highly dependent on some aspects of provider care delivery.

KEY POINT

As a pharmacist, you have responsibility to be aware of what the vulnerabilities and dependencies are in each of your patient's care and consider appropriate approaches to protecting the patient while participating in consumer empowerment approaches.

Social Networking and Consumerism. The advent of social networking through the Internet has provided a means of increased participation and empowerment of patients in their own health care management. The formation of informal on-line communities, access to evidence needed for self-care, and the ability to formally connect electronically to health care providers has led to consumer demands for access to their own health information through electronic means. There are direct implications of this change to how personal health information is stored, handled, and shared. These implications are addressed as we proceed through this chapter's discussion.

Health Information Exchange

The continuity of care for a patient between providers is an important aspect to patient-centered care. To achieve this, providers need the ability to exchange relevant health information in order to assure the complete and accurate care provision for a patient. The process of electronic data sharing of the patient's health information is called health information exchange (HIE). The United States is currently engaged in a 10-year plan to develop and implement a nationwide infrastructure known as the National Health Information Network (NHIN). The primary purpose of the network is to allow authorized health professionals to participate in such an exchange to access relevant patient data securely from any location in the country at anytime. How did the NHIN come to be? Historical knowledge is valuable to understand the impact of this development on pharmacy.

The 1999 Institute of Medicine report *To Err is Human* provided evidence for the need to reduce harm in our medical care systems by implementing safety concepts and practices, including the use of medical technologies.[6] In 2001, the Patient Safety Task Force was formed as a part of the Quality Improvement Initiative for the nation.[7] The work products of this task force all pointed toward the need for exchangeable patient health information. Key evidence for which this conclusion was based on was an estimate that 1 in 7 hospitalizations are due to unavailable medical records and 1 in 5 lab tests are repeated due to unavailable results at the point of care. In 2004 a vision of developing a nationwide, interoperable health information technology infrastructure called the NHIN (**Figure 6-1**) was to make accessible to every United States citizen an interoperable electronic health record (EHR) by 2014.[8] This has caused transformative changes in the creation, storage, and sharing of patient health information. In 2005, the Office of the National Coordinator for Health Information Technology (ONCHIT) was established within Health and Human Services and the American Health Information Community, a national public–private collaboration formed to facilitate the transition to interoperable electronic health systems in a market-led approach. These two formed a Health Information Technology Standards Panel (HITSP) to harmonize the industry-wide effort. A Certification Commission for Healthcare Information Technology (CCHIT) was appointed and developed a certification process for health information technology products and health information technology professionals.[6] The NHIN will allow health care providers to not only have access to patients' health history (both within a single health system and across multiple health systems), but also real-time access to the most up-to-date patient information, including lab results and progress notes.[9,10]

The introduction of e-HIE will help pharmacists in better assisting patients to manage their own disease states and medications. This will further enhance communication between pharmacists and patients, contributing to an evolving patient–pharmacist relationship that is impacted by the increased use of HIT (e.g. EHRs, personal health records, e-prescribing, and patient-specific technologies already being used). Pharmacists are accessible resources for health care, a role that will likely be enhanced by e-HIE, and one that will continue to grow as the e-HIE movement evolves.[11,12]

CONDUCT ISSUES RELATED TO PATIENT HEALTH INFORMATION

The patient medical record is a legal document of the health services provided to the patient during care; it belongs to the care delivery organization or provider if in a solo practice. However, the information contained in the record belongs to the patient and, therefore, is private. This same arrangement is true for the patient profile and prescription records of the pharmacy. As health care providers, pharmacists have access to this information and must ensure that the patient's right to privacy is not violated.

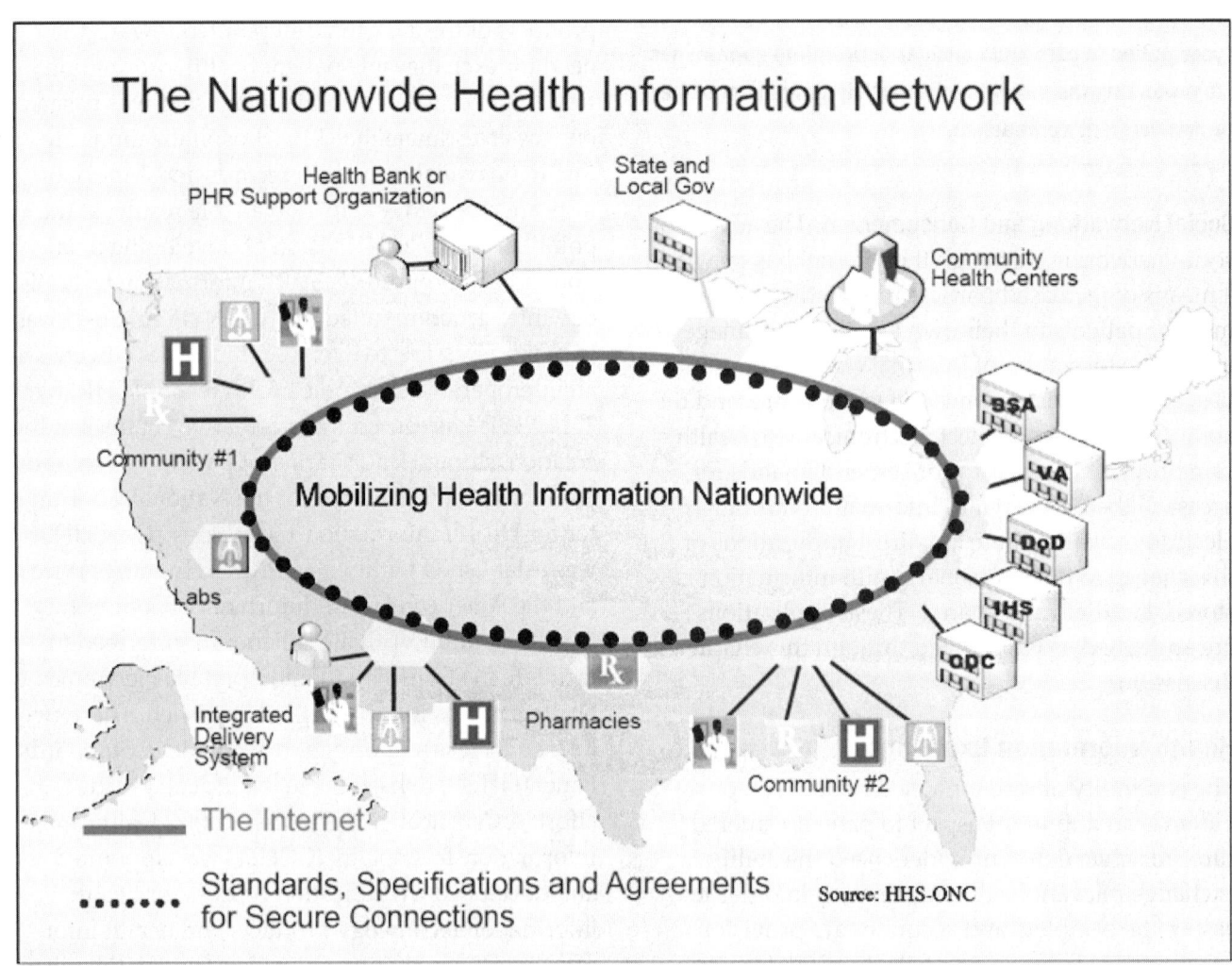

Figure 6-1. National Model for Technology Development in Health Care Service Delivery and Self Care via the National Health Information Network (NHIN)

Security, Privacy, and Confidentiality

A patient's personal health information is private, confidential, and must be held securely and treated as such by all health providers and health care delivery organizations that provide the patient with care services. Three major pieces of legislation in the United States guide the development of rules, regulations, and our practical behavior to maintain a patient's health information as secure, private, and confidential. These are the Privacy Act of 1974, the Kennedy-Kassebaum Health Insurance Portability and Accountability Act of 1996 (HIPAA), and Subtitle D of the Health Information Technology for Economic and Clinical Health Act (HITECH Act), enacted as part of the American Recovery and Reinvestment Act of 2009.

Privacy Act of 1974. In 1974, Congress passed Public Law 93-579, or the Privacy Act of 1974, to preserve an individual's right to privacy. In many hospitals, this law is used as a framework for policies on patient confidentiality. In short, the law states that any federal agency maintaining records on individuals must permit them to know what records are being kept and how the information is being used. The law gives individuals access to their records and permission to have a copy. Individuals also have the right to correct or amend the records. The Privacy Act requires that a person's data be collected for a specific purpose and if the information is to be used for other purposes, the law requires written consent by the individual. State laws and professional codes of ethics also protect patient privacy. You should be familiar with your own state's privacy legislation and the codes of the pharmacy profession.

Health Insurance Portability and Accountability Act of 1996 (HIPAA). In 1996, Congress enacted Public Law 104-191, popularly known as HIPAA. Patient confidentiality is part of the right to privacy. By designating information as confidential, the right to privacy is recognized. Patients trust that information about them will be kept private and confidential. Confidentiality gives patients the right to indicate what information will be available and to whom. In fact, patient consent must be obtained before patient information can be released to outside parties. In all health care settings, patients are asked to sign an "Authorization to Release Medical Information." This statement authorizes the health care delivery organization and providers involved in the patient's care to release information to named parties. The patient must specifically authorize release to anyone else. Title I of HIPAA protects health insurance coverage for workers and their families when they change or lose their jobs. Title II of HIPAA, known as the Administrative Simplification (AS) provisions, requires the establishment of national standards for electronic health care transactions and national identifiers for providers, health insurance plans, and employers. The Administration Simplification provisions also address the security and privacy of health data. The standards are meant to improve the efficiency and effectiveness of the nation's health care system by encouraging the widespread use of electronic data interchange in the U.S. health care system.

Electronic data interchange (EDI) is the structured transmission of data between organizations by electronic means. It is used to transfer electronic documents or business data from one computer system to another computer system without human involvement. In 1996, the National Institute of Standards and Technology defined electronic data interchange as "the computer-to-computer interchange of strictly formatted messages that represent documents other than monetary instruments. EDI can be formally defined as the transfer of structured data, by agreed message standards, from one computer system to another without human intervention.

The HIPAA Privacy Rule regulates the use and disclosure of certain information held by "covered entities" (generally, health care clearinghouses, employer-sponsored health plans, health insurers, and medical service providers that engage in certain transactions). It establishes regulations for the use and disclosure of Protected Health Information (PHI). Protected health information under HIPAA is any information about health status, provision of health care, or payment for health care that can be linked to a specific individual. This is interpreted rather broadly and includes any part of a patient's medical record or payment history that can be used to identify an individual and that was created, used, or disclosed in the course of providing a health care service such as diagnosis or treatment.

HIPAA regulations allow researchers to access and use PHI when necessary to conduct research. However, HIPAA only affects research that uses, creates, or discloses PHI that will be entered in to the medical record or will be used for health care services such as treatment, payment, or operations. For example, PHI is used in research studies involving review of existing medical records for research information such as retrospective chart review. Also, studies that create new medical information because a health care service is being performed as part of research, such as diagnosing a health condition or a new drug or device for treating a health condition, create PHI that will be entered into the medical record. For example, sponsored clinical trials that submit data to the U.S. Food and Drug Administration involve PHI and are therefore subject to HIPAA regulations. PHI that is linked based on the following list of 18 identifiers must be treated with special care according to HIPAA:

1. Names
2. All geographical subdivisions smaller than a state, including street address, city, county, precinct, zip code, and their equivalent geo codes, except for the initial three digits of a zip code, if according to the current publicly available data from the Bureau of the Census: (1) The geographic unit formed by combining all zip codes with the same three initial digits contains more than 20,000 people; and (2) The initial three digits of a zip code for all such geographic units containing 20,000 or fewer people is changed to 000.
3. Dates (other than year) for dates directly related to an individual, including birth date, admission date, discharge date, date of death; and all ages over 89 and all elements of dates (including year) indicative of such age, except that such ages and elements may be aggregated into a single category of age 90 or older.
4. Phone numbers
5. Fax numbers
6. Electronic mail addresses
7. Social Security numbers
8. Medical record numbers
9. Health plan beneficiary numbers
10. Account numbers
11. Certificate/license numbers
12. Vehicle identifiers and serial numbers, including license plate numbers
13. Device identifiers and serial numbers
14. Web Uniform Resource Locators (URLs)
15. Internet Protocol (IP) address numbers
16. Biometric identifiers, including finger, retinal, and voice prints
17. Full face photographic images and any comparable images
18. Any other unique identifying number, characteristic, or code (note this does not mean the unique code assigned by the investigator to code the data)

The Privacy Rule requires covered entities to notify individuals of uses of their PHI. Covered entities must also keep track of disclosures of PHI and document privacy policies and procedures. They must appoint a Privacy Official and a contact person responsible for receiving complaints and train all members of their workforce in procedures regarding PHI. When a covered entity discloses any PHI, it must make a reasonable effort to disclose only the minimum necessary information required to achieve its purpose. The Privacy Rule gives individuals the right to request that a covered entity correct any inaccurate PHI. It also requires covered entities to take reasonable steps to ensure the confidentiality of communications with individuals. For example, an individual can ask to be called at his or her work number, instead of home or cell phone number.

HIPAA legislation also required the establishment of security standards. The Security Rule complements the Privacy Rule. While the Privacy Rule pertains to all PHI including paper and electronic, the Security Rule deals specifically with Electronic Protected Health Information (EPHI). It lays out three types of security safeguards required for compliance: administrative, physical, and technical. For each of these types, the Rule identifies various security standards. Individual covered entities can evaluate their own situation and determine the best way to implement addressable specifications. Some privacy advocates have argued that this "flexibility" may provide too much latitude to covered entities. The administrative safeguards are policies and procedures designed to clearly show how the entity will comply with the act. The physical safeguards control physical access to protect against inappropriate access to protected data. The technical safeguards control access to computer systems and enable covered entities to protect communications, containing PHI transmitted electronically over open networks, from being intercepted by anyone other than the intended recipient.

Health Information Technology for Economic and Clinical Health Act (HITECH Act). Subtitle D of the Health Information Technology for Economic and Clinical Health Act (HITECH Act) was enacted as part of the American Recovery and Reinvestment Act of 2009. The HITECH Act addresses the privacy and security concerns associated with the electronic transmission of health information. This subtitle extends the complete Privacy and Security Provisions of HIPAA to business associates of covered entities. This includes the extension of newly updated civil and criminal penalties to business associates. These changes are also required to be included in any business associate agreements with covered entities. Another significant change brought about in Subtitle D of the HITECH Act is the new breach notification requirements. This imposes new notification requirements on covered entities, business associates, vendors of personal health records (PHR), and related entities if a breach of unsecured protected health information (PHI) occurs. The final significant change made in Subtitle D of the HITECH Act implements new rules for the accounting of disclosures of a patient's health information. It extends the current accounting for disclosure requirements to information that is used to carry out treatment, payment, and health care operations when an organization is using an electronic health record (EHR).

When EHR adoption and advancing health information exchange practices moved to the state level, issues of security and privacy moved to the forefront, and a cross-sectional study (Health Information Security and Privacy Collaboration) of issues of security and privacy in 33 states and territories was funded.[13] In 2006, the National Governors Association was also contracted by the Office of the National Coordinator for Health Information Technology to provide advisory services for health information exchanges as they developed in the various states.

The ASHP policy on nondiscriminatory pharmaceutical care states, in part, that "all patients have the right to privacy, respect, confidentiality, and high-quality pharmaceutical care" and that "pharmacists must always act in the best interest of individual patients while not placing society as a whole at risk." The American Pharmacists Association (APhA) Code of Ethics makes a similar statement: "A pharmacist should respect the confidential and personal nature of professional records; except where the best interest of the patient requires or the law demands, a pharmacist should not disclose such information to anyone without proper patient authorization."

Corporate Policies

Now that you have a general understanding of the legality and professional ethics of privacy and confidentiality, let us address the specific directives of your organized health care setting or community pharmacy. Each organization has a policy on patient confidentiality and release of information that is specific to that organization, but all policies serve the same purpose: to guarantee patients access to their own medical information while maintaining their privacy and monitoring the release of that information to other individuals. How do you orient your practice so that you use the information available with discretion and respect for a patient's rights? The basic rule is to be constantly vigilant.

CASE EXAMPLE

Confidentiality

Your responsibilities as a home care pharmacist are to coordinate the medication reconciliation process for your patient's transition in care from the hospital or nursing home setting to his home setting. You receive a phone call from your home care service nurse discharge coordinator that a patient by the name of Mr. Shoemeister, a 24-year-old white male who was discharged from St. Mary's hospital yesterday evening, will be receiving home care infusion services. You log into your electronic health record system and view the hospital discharge summary via the electronic health information exchange system serving your company. (Your company has an agreement with the hospital for shared access to view records for patients who have provided authorization via the health information exchange.) You also have received electronic prescriptions for home parenteral nutrition therapy and antiretroviral treatments. As you review the discharge history, you see there are no medications listed and no medication use history documented. It is your usual practice to contact the patient by telephone and conduct a medication history to assure the patient's safety by addressing any potential therapeutic conflicts or needs. You call, and a woman answers. You introduce yourself and explain that you wish to speak to Mr. Shoemeister. The woman introduces herself, explains that she is Mr. Shoemeister's mother, and is responsible for his care. She further explains that he is presently too tired to speak with you but she would be happy to answer your questions. While you are tempted to share with her the medical information that you have and to ask her about his current medication use and history, you realize that you cannot do that without potentially breaching this patient's rights to confidentiality. You explain to her that you would be happy to have her provide medical information to you and tell her more about his care needs; however, you must first speak with him directly and obtain his consent to do so. You further explain that these are legal rights he has that you are obliged to uphold. She understands and asks you to hold while she checks on her son's availability to speak with you.

The above example illustrates the importance of respecting each patient's rights, even when the circumstances seem innocent and it makes common sense to act in a way that actually violates these rights. It is common to be in a situation as a health care provider where you may inadvertently reveal a patient's confidences to a member of the patient's family or a close friend and do not intend to do harm by doing so. Discussion of patient information in public places, even when among appropriate health professionals, also violates patient confidentiality. Such discussions should never occur in hospital elevators, in the cafeteria, or at social gatherings. Mr. Shoemeister has the right to limit the information that anyone else may know, and you must respect that right.

In this example, failure to observe patient confidentiality occurred because personal information was released without the patient's consent. Health care professionals can never be too careful when protecting a patient's privacy and preserving confidentiality.

What consumers can do if a violation of privacy occurs:

- Contact the Privacy Officer of the provider where you believe the violation occurred to try to resolve your concern.
- If you are unable to resolve a concern locally, file a formal complaint directly to the organization, health plan, or Department of Health and Human Services' Office for Civil Rights. Web site is ww.hhs.gov/ocr/hipaa/.

Complaints to the Office for Civil Rights (OCR) must:

- Be filed in writing, either on paper or electronically, within 180 days of your knowledge of the

act or omission. (Violations must have occurred on or after April 14, 2003, for the OCR to investigate.)
- Name the provider or person whom you believe violated or failed to protect the privacy of your health information.
- Describe what occurred, as far as you know the facts.

PATIENT'S HEALTH RECORDS— THE MEDICAL RECORD

The national goal of exchangeable health data has caused the explicit development of four major electronic records: the electronic medical record (EMR), the electronic health record (EHR), the continuity of care record (CCR), and the personal health record (PHR). Most practice settings actually have what is called a "hybrid record." A hybrid record refers to a system of health records with functional components that include both paper and electronic documents and data, and use both manual and electronic processes. The hybrid record will continue to exist until all components of health information are made available through paperless media. The implications of this are that practitioners almost always need to get information from both the electronic and paper component of a patient's health records.

What constitutes a "record" is broad because the most important content varies depending on the provider; even a funeral director has official health record information. Survey research we conducted on behalf of the Nebraska Health Information Security and Privacy Committee revealed that 23 of the 24 health professionals' licensure governing boards indicate that their groups maintain some kind of patient health record.[12] In addition, some professions also have specialized records that focus on the form of practice that they maintain (e.g., pharmacists, physical therapists, optometrists). Several practitioners identified patient medications as a specific data element that they record.

Pharmacists train and usually use an electronic pharmacy record in practice. As the use of electronic records continues, it is anticipated that either all of these records will become an integrated record in the form of one entity that represents each individual patient, retrievable from any location; or that the data that is stored in these records will be readily exchangeable for use by providers and patients through a health information exchange system. There are models that are emerging for local, regional, and national health information exchange which will eventually be refined to become mechanisms for this process. The different electronic health records have emerged because of specific needs.

> **KEY POINT**
>
> It is anticipated that the electronic records will become integrated into one record of an individual patient, or that the data that is stored in each record will be readily exchangeable for use by providers and patients.

The EMR, EHR, and CCR are datasets managed by health professionals and health care organizations or entities associated with providing care. Common to all records are standards for data collection, storage, and management. These common standards are needed to make it possible for patient health data to be exchanged between systems. The American Health Information Management Association (AHIMA) represents Health Information Management professionals, generally considered the legal custodians of health records in hospitals. HIM professionals are trained to ensure the quality, privacy, and integrity of health records in any form. AHIMA members are custodians of health records for their facilities. These persons respond to requests for release of information, including to subpoenas and court orders for health records. AHIMA is a great resource about EHRs, PHRs, and HIE specifically.

Electronic Medical Record

The EMR is the set of databases (or repositories) that contains the health information for patients within a given institution or organization. Thus, an EMR contains the aggregated data sets gathered from a variety of clinical service delivery processes such as laboratory data, pharmacy data, patient registration data, radiology data, surgical procedures, clinic and inpatient notes, and others. EMRs may also contain clinical applications that can act on the data contained within this repository (e.g., clinical decision support system, computerized provider order entry system, controlled medical vocabulary, results-reporting system). If an EMR is set up at multiple organizations or institutions, an EHR can be put in place to link together these different EMRs and exchange health information data.

Electronic Health Record

Electronic health records are key to the successful establishment and successful use of the NHIN. The concept of the patient records being located only where a practitioner's practice is located has changed. The EHR extends the notion of an EMR to include the concept of cross institutional data sharing. Thus, an EHR contains data from a subset of each institution's EMR that is agreed on by the institution. An EHR may also reside "entirely within one institution" and link various affiliated practice sites together. An EHR can only be present if the participating sites all have an EMR in place that is interoperable. With the EHR, a common repository structure is developed and managed by a parent organization, most commonly referred to as a regional health information organization (RHIO). Through massive, secure data exchange management, the RHIO will also take the data from the pharmacy practice and other health care provider practices and reposit (au?) and maintain an accurate record and archive of the data.

EHRs are expected to contain comprehensive information about a patient's health, including his or her medical conditions and care received from multiple providers who have access and privileges to the patient's record. Some proposed ways that both pharmacists and patients could benefit from the introduction of an EHR into pharmacy practice are improvements in the medication reconciliation process both within health care organizations and between care settings, progression of public health initiatives, and enhancement of the patient–pharmacist relationship.[9,14] There may also be advantages to consumers. The suggested advantages include:

- Stronger privacy and security of information (access control)
- Quicker access to accurate and complete medical history data by patient and health care professional
- Increased quality of care—notes about care are easier to read and reduce risk of errors
- Efficient use of physical space—eventual elimination of paper records and charts
- Reduction in duplication of lab tests, imaging, and other services
- Improved emergency backup and recovery

The use of pharmacists to manage chronic care patients, such as through the use of collaborative practice agreements, can be enhanced through the additional patient information available in the EHR. Competency levels will need to be established for pharmacists to demonstrate the ability to obtain, utilize, and contribute to the patient information maintained in the EHR, leading to evolving privileging and credentialing of pharmacists.[15] For instance, obtaining a pharmacotherapy specialist credential or developing a collaborative practice agreement allowing pharmacists to directly manage patients' care may require a pharmacist to demonstrate an understanding of the benefits and limitations of EHRs and/or the technical skills to use the EHR.

Continuity of Care Record

The CCR is a set of health information that accompanies the patient when he or she is transferred from one institution to another, or to a different facility within the same organization. The CCR is a core dataset to be sent to the next health care provider whenever a patient is referred or transferred or otherwise uses different clinics, hospitals, or other providers. The CCR is centered on the concept of continuity of care and is complementary to the EHR and provides systematic guidance for health information exchange. Both the content and specifics of the data elements are defined by a standard entitled, "ASTM E2369-05 Standard Specification for Continuity of Care Record (CCR)." ASTM E2369 defines the core data set of most relevant administrative, demographic, and clinical information about a patient's health care. It provides a means for one health care practitioner, system, or setting to aggregate all of the pertinent data about a patient and forward it to another practitioner, system, or setting to support the continuity of care. The CCR may be prepared, displayed, or transmitted on paper or electronically. These records are now being designed so that the preparation, transmission, and viewing can occur in multiple ways—browser, secure email, PDF file, HTML file, word processing document, or as an element in an HL7 message of an HL7 CDA-compliant document.

Personal Health Record

The PHR is a computer-based patient health record intended primarily for use by consumers to maintain and manage their health information in a private, secure, and confidential environment. The PHR is a patient-controlled record that in concept will accompany the patient throughout his or her entire life, and may contain additional information that is entered by the patient that he or she perceives as important such as self-care behaviors, self-initiated treatments, and preventive care activities that are not recorded in the provider-controlled records. At the present, it is not clear whether the PHR will evolve to this central role in health care or not. Fundamental to the PHR is the concept that each individual can decide who he or she wants to share health information with.[9,16] PHRs are in development, along with all other electronic records in health care. A national goal of PHR development is to assure that PHRs are consistent with the Institute of Medicine (IOM) quality goals for a safe, effective, patient-centered, timely, efficient, and equitable health care system described in its Crossing the Quality Chasm report in 2001 and continued through the Connection for Health's Common Framework.[17,18] As such, PHRs should have the following attributes:

- Each person controls his or her own PHR
- PHRs contain information from one's entire lifetime and from all health care providers
- PHRs are accessible from any place at any time
- PHRs are private and secure
- PHRs are transparent. Individuals can see who entered each piece of data, where it was transferred from, and who has viewed it.
- PHRs permit easy exchange of information.

Networked PHRs should be supported with the following attributes:

- Care based on continuous healing relationships
- Customization based on patients' needs and values
- Patient as the source of control
- Shared knowledge and free flow of information
- Evidence-based decision-making
- Safety as a system property
- Need for transparency
- Anticipation of needs
- Continuous decrease in waste
- Cooperation among clinicians

Current forms of PHRs may or may not interface with providers' EHRs. Individuals, however, may be able to interface using, for example, Smartcard- or flash drive–stored PHRs or, alternatively, web-supported PHRs. In a recent survey of Nebraska community pharmacists, 2% indicated exchanging data through patient PHRs.[9] The use of PHRs is just beginning with consumers. Consumers believe the PHR allows ready access and use of "credible" personal health information, enabling health care providers to gain easier access to patient information and open channels of communication with other health care providers and entities.[19,20] The PHR facilitates consumers becoming active participants in their health care decisions. Patients are also interested in keeping track of their personal health data, which includes self-treatment such as over-the-counter products, nutritional supplements, and self-monitoring about health maintenance or progress.[21,22]

> **KEY POINT**
>
> **Recent studies have shown that patients demonstrated enthusiasm toward use of a PHR and were diligent in bringing them to health appointments.[23]**

Employers, government entities, health care providers, and health care organizations also desire PHR adoption for a variety of reasons. Employers desire PHR adoption because employees who keep track of their health are likely to be healthier and have decreased absenteeism. Employers also carry a great deal of the cost of providing health care coverage plans. Healthier employees should lead to lower health care costs overall. Some large employers have already set up PHRs for their own employees. Government entities view the PHR as another step toward developing health information exchange between patients and providers of health care. The Centers for Medicare and Medicaid Services and the U.S. Secretary of Health and Human Services both support the development of PHRs because of the great potential for improved safety and quality of health care overall. Currently, Veterans Administration patients are able to access their personal health records, called Personal Health Journals, through My HealthyVet, an online service linked to the Vista electronic health record system.[24]

Pharmacy organizations are beginning to take a lead with further development of PHRs, as the American Society of Health-System Pharmacists has partnered with the Robert Wood Johnson Foundation to start the Project HealthDesign program. This program "will build on and extend the range of uses offered by existing PHRs by supporting multidisciplinary teams to design and test a broad spectrum of innovations in how consumers can use information technology to better manage their health and more easily navigate the health care system."[25]

Health information management organizations such as the American Health Information Management Association (AHIMA) and the American Medical Informatics Association (AMIA) are also encouraging individuals to keep their own complete PHR, and educating them about the potential impact it could have on their health care. Pharmacists are in a strong position to develop how to engage with patients and support the use of the patient and the PHR. For years, the pharmacy profession has utilized computer-based record keeping systems, making pharmacists very technology oriented. This experience makes pharmacists uniquely prepared for the PHR movement. PHRs have the potential to restructure pharmacists' time commitments, and to increase quality interaction with the patient. As pharmacists are in a unique role to impact patient care and overall patient safety, it is important to provide pharmacists with the information necessary to do this job effectively. In 2008, major organizations in pharmacy convened a Medication List Summit to develop guidelines for a standardized medication list.[26] Early pharmacist involvement in developing a complete, accurate, and up-to-date medication list through a PHR can yield tremendous benefits on the quality of care patients receive. By helping patients set up and maintain their own PHR, it is possible to have a more thorough record of health information. This can further facilitate members of the health care team to treat the patient holistically and from a patient-centered perspective.

Patient Portals

Patient portals are the online applications that connect patients so they may interact and communicate with their health care providers, hospitals, and clinics where they receive care. The implication of a portal is that it is available to the patient around the clinic via Internet connectivity. A patient portal allows the patient to securely expose personal health information via the Internet to accomplish such things as register for appointments or health care events, request prescription refills, access personal medical records for various providers, pay for services, schedule appointments for care, and other fundamental activities required for health maintenance. Portals have developed through the private investment of health organizations or businesses interested in this product development.

Registries

Registries are increasingly becoming a part of organized health systems in hospitals, community health clinics, and for use in research. Although there are many kinds of registries, the registry organized for chronic disease management of populations with particular conditions, or groups of conditions, is becoming more commonplace. If you are involved in population disease management in practice, you will likely work with and use registries.

THE PATIENT'S HEALTH RECORD

Each patient who receives care within an organized health care institution (e.g., hospital, nursing home, or clinic) has a medical record. The record is the repository for all written information concerning that patient's care, condition, and treatment. Health professionals use it to record their assessments, diagnoses, treatment plans, and other pertinent information. In it, you will find laboratory values, test results, and descriptions of procedures you need to assess. The record is the primary mode of communication between you and other health care professionals providing treatment to a patient. Use it to obtain the data you need to make good drug therapy decisions and then communicate those decisions to the rest of the health care team.

Uses of the Record

A patient's medical record is most commonly used by health professionals during patient care. However, the record may be used by several individuals for multiple purposes:

The Clinician Who Enters Information in the Medical Record. Preparing a medical record aids in organizing and remembering information about patients, developing clinical skills, reflecting on the diagnosis and management, and planning continuing care.

Health Care Professionals within the Hospital. The record serves as the primary mode of communication of patient information among health care professionals who collaborate in the patient's care. Medical professionals such as physicians, pharmacists, and nurses use the medical record daily. Physical and occupational therapists, dieticians, respiratory therapists, and other allied health professionals also consistently refer to patient records. When your care notes are available, you potentially enhance the quality of care these professionals can provide. With the increasing use of e-mail, fax machines, and computerized medical records, your notes are readily available to other clinicians who are collaborating in the patient's care.

Patients. Patients may access the record to help them understand and review their treatment, allowing them to be more active in their self-care. They may also secure record information to provide to outpatient health care providers or other professionals such as insurance agents. Doctors' offices often request a copy of a patient's record when seeing a patient for the first time, especially if the patient has an extensive medical history.

Administrative Personnel. Hospital administrators, risk managers, medical records personnel, and ward clerks all need to access the record. Your supervisors may use the record to evaluate and guide your clinical development. Insofar as the record is an accurate account of what you observed, concluded, and did for the patient, it is one measure of your clinical performance. Similarly, record audits have been used to evaluate the quality of care, though their usefulness has been limited by discrepancies between what is recorded and what is actually done. The medical record contains data for assessing disability, mental competency, and eligibility for insurance billing, while also being used in utilization review and lawsuits.

Research Use. Patient medical records can provide data for clinical research. Personnel researching drugs and medical devices use the record to document information relevant to patient care. The information may be collected retrospectively, concurrently, or prospectively from patient records. Pharmacy schools may have a research requirement as part of their degree program, and pharmacy residency programs usually have a research project requirement. Medical records are a common source of data for such projects.

Public Health. Health agencies and registries use data from patient records to compute health statistics. The Centers for Disease Control (CDC), the Public Health Department, and the Food and Drug Administration (FDA) are a few of the many administrative offices that collect data from patient records for statistical analysis. For example, the CDC might gather data from patient records to study the long-term complications of diabetes.

Legal Use. Lawyers and other legal personnel may wish to review a patient's medical record for legal purposes. The patient's medical record then may be used as evidence against the health care professional to prove that harm was done, or it may be used as evidence in defense of the professional that proper care was provided. Malpractice suits may be filed against health care professionals for various reasons. Patients (or their families) may sue because of poor judgment of standard of care, medication or treatment errors, or negligence.

Educational Use. The education of future health care professionals is another use of the patient medical record. Students of the health professions receive valuable instruction from "real life" patient records. During didactic training, patient case presentations excerpted from records help students to integrate "book learning" and the "real world." Students get additional, hands-on training during hospital clerkships and rotations where they have direct contact with patients and see the medical record system in action. In both cases, the students become familiar with the record's contents, organization, and patient care uses.

Audit Use. Patient medical records are used in audits of patient care. Within an institution, the Quality Assurance or Continuous Quality Management Department professionals may review patient records to monitor hospital health care practices and to determine if standards for care are being met. Plans to improve patient care can be developed from the information. For example, patient records may be audited to assess the appropriateness of blood product use or to determine the necessity of a specific surgical procedure. Or drug-use evaluation studies may be conducted by gathering information from patient records on the appropriateness of medication use within a hospital. Hospital Medical Records Departments also routinely review patient records for accuracy and completeness. The review commonly includes the following:

- Is there a signed consent form for every surgical or diagnostic procedure performed?
- Is there patient identification on every page of the record?
- Have physicians signed or countersigned every order written?

These audits increase the accuracy of information and ensure that legal requirements are met. From outside the health care setting, third-party payers employ auditors to review patient records; payment or reimbursement is based on the results of these audits. Medicare/ Medicaid, Blue Cross/Blue Shield, indemnity carriers, and managed care organizations routinely audit patient records for this purpose.

Program Evaluation. Hospital administrators are interested in patient information that helps them plan for the hospital's future. Statistics gained from medical records aid administrators in budgeting and financial planning, expansion or reduction of hospital services, and personnel management.

Record Organization

Inpatient and outpatient records exist for the same purposes and are similar in content. This chapter discusses "the record" in a comprehensive way. Discussion about different aspects of the record will identify the inpatient or outpatient setting when appropriate.

The Problem-Oriented Medical Record (POMR) represents a useful attempt to systematize the recording and processing of clinical information. Many aspects of this approach have been widely adopted. Rational, orderly clinical action is facilitated by the POMR requirement of defining a list of clinical problems, identifying the database relevant to each problem, and providing an assessment and a plan for each. All records are generally organized in this way so that information retrieval can be both efficient and consistent. A typical organization scheme is as follows:

- Admitting or Initial Clinic Visit Data
- Physician Orders
- Graphic Records
- Nursing Notes
- Laboratory (lab) Data
- Diagnostic Procedures/Consults
- Operating Room (OR) or Outpatient Procedures
- History and Physical
- Progress Notes
- Medical Administration Record (MAR) or Medication List
- Miscellaneous

Records are located in common centralized areas in hospitals, clinics, nursing homes, medical offices, home health agencies, and pharmacies when they are not actively being used. However, when a patient is actively receiving care, the record is retrieved from the storage area and may be found in several places as previously discussed.

In any practice setting, the record follows the patient. For example, if a patient goes to surgery or is having a procedure performed in the endoscopy department of the hospital, the record is with that patient so it is available for reference and documentation. When the patient returns to the hospital room, the record is returned to its permanent location. If a record is not in its assigned location, it may be found with physicians, medical residents, or medical students while they are on rounds. Sometimes, other members of the health care team (e.g., nurses, pharmacists, or physical therapists) may have it. Or you may find a medical record in the transcription or dictation rooms. Often, physicians, medical residents, or medical students take the records of all their patients to a quiet place to work. When patients have been hospitalized for an extended period or have received chronic care in an office or clinic for several years, the amount of paper generated becomes too great to fit into the record binder. Then, records may be "thinned" (i.e., information rarely used from the start of the hospitalization or from earlier clinic visits is filed in a separate location). Early physician orders, MARs, and graphic sheets are often thinned. Summary type reports, such as dictated consultations and diagnostic procedures, usually are kept in the binder.

The future goal of most health-related industries is to become "paperless," by storing, exchanging, and using all information electronically. Increasingly, components of the medical record are electronic. For example, the MAR produced by a pharmacy is available on computer and printed in most health facilities. However, as facilities gradually invest in computer-based information technology infrastructures, these printed documents will be accessed "on-line" throughout the patient care facilities. Presently the U.S. Department of Veterans Affairs has most of its inpatient facilities supported with an information technology infrastructure that supports the complete electronic medical record. The information presented here will hold true whether the record is totally paper based, totally electronic, or integrated. You should expect to encounter the different methods of record information access, retrieval, and documentation and adapt in your practice setting, as required.

Record Content

We turn now to a more detailed look at what is contained in each section of the medical record. Considerable overlap and duplication exist among sections. Understanding both the routine contents of each section and the logic of this overlap and duplication will help you search efficiently for specific information. We discuss the Patient Profile commonly used in community and outpatient pharmacy settings later on in this chapter. We shall describe highlights of each section of the record. **Figure 6-2** shows common locations for specific types of clinical information in the typical medical record.

Inpatient Admitting or Initial Outpatient Visit Data. In most cases, admitting data is the first section of the patient medical record. This information is usually gathered by the admitting department when the patient enters the health care institution. Information is collected on standardized forms to ensure consistent, accurate, and complete data collection. The data usually are divided into four groups: biographical, financial/insurance, admission-related, and consent forms.

Biographical Data. Biographical data serve to identify the patient. Typical information collected may include the patient's name, address, date of birth, sex, marital status, religious affiliation, emergency contact, occupation, employer, and social security number. Most demographic information you need about a patient appears in this section.

Financial/Insurance Data. Financial and insurance data are collected so that the hospital's billing department can receive payment from the appropriate source(s). The guarantor, or party who guarantees payment, often is the patient, patient's spouse, or parent/guardian. The patient's financial status, or ability to pay, is noted as well as insurance information (i.e., insurance companies and policy numbers) and other methods of payment (e.g., self, Medicare, or worker's compensation).

Inpatient Admission-Related Data. Admission-related data apply only to the current admission. Common categories of admission-related data are name of admitting physician, date and time of admission,

Patient Data	Admission Form	Consent Form	Admit Summary	Admission Orders	Progress Notes/Transfer	Progress Notes/General	Flow Sheet	Rehab Form	Consultant Report	Procedure Requisition Form	Clinical Pathology Laboratory Report	Patient Interview	Medication Administration Record	Discharge Summary and Plan
Demographic Information	X													
Chief Complaint			X			X								X
Past Medical History			X											
Problem List			X											X
Medication History on Admission			X											
Social History			X									X		
Allergies			X									X		
Physical Examination			X	X	X	X								
Laboratory Tests											X			
Pulmonary Function Tests							X	X		X				
Arterial Blood Gasses											X			
Emergency Room Treatment Plan			X											
General Medicine Progress						X								X
Medications Used in Hospital													X	
Patient's Medication Use Behavior												X		
Medications Planned for Use at Discharge														X
Consent to be Taped/Information Shown to Others Publicly		X												

Figure 6-2. Sections of Medical Record Where Specific Information is Usually Found

admitting diagnosis for problem, room or bed number, and admission or account number.

In the initial outpatient visit data, the name of the primary care practitioner, date and time of visit, and initial problem list are generally identified.

Consent Forms. Consent forms are statements that must be read, understood, and signed by the patient or his or her guardian. The types of consent forms that you can expect to find in a patient's medical record include forms for medical treatment, tests, procedures, investigational treatments or drugs, release of information, photographs, videotapes, or films of the patient. Many of these forms are often presented to the patient at the time of the initial admission or visit. Others are presented when decisions must be made to take a particular course of action.

Physician Orders. Physician orders are directives for patient treatment written either directly by a physician or by another health care professional and then countersigned by a physician. In office or clinic records, the physician's orders are usually summarized in the progress note that describes the visit. The orders themselves are usually written on order sheets for services (e.g., laboratory or X-ray services) or prescriptions (e.g., medications, devices, other treatments).

Physician orders in hospitals are usually written on a standardized form specific to each hospital. The form usually is in three parts and preprinted with the hospital's name or logo and space for the date, time, and patient's allergies. The patient's addressograph is stamped prominently on the form. Often, there is space for the patient's height and weight; preprinted statements specific to hospital policy may be present. Clinicians in the outpatient setting write prescriptions that are usually given to the patient or transmitted to the pharmacy requested by the patient.

Computerized practitioner order entry (CPOE) may be taking place in your practice setting. This is a paperless method for clinicians to order tests and procedures, labs, or treatments using computer access. If CPOE is active in your setting, then it is highly likely the entire patient medical record is computerized. The practitioner orders may be reviewed online by viewing the patient's electronic medical record.

Written or Transcribed Orders. Orders may be written directly on the record by a physician or transcribed to the record by another health care professional after discussion with the physician. Transcription usually occurs when a physician gives orders to a registered nurse, pharmacist, or other professional over the telephone or from some place remote from the patient record. The order is then written in the record by the health care professional who signs the physician's name and his or her own name, separated from the physician's name with a slash (/) mark. A physician must countersign or initial the order within a specified time that is identified by institutional policy.

Electronic Transmission of Orders. Orders also may be transmitted from a physician's office to the hospital nursing unit, nursing home, or outpatient or clinic pharmacy using facsimile (fax) technology. Orders can be faxed prior to a patient's hospital or nursing home admission to be ready for the patient on arrival. Fax technology also is used within the hospital to speed order processing; nursing units may fax orders to the pharmacy or other departments. This process usually gets the order to its destination faster than if a courier or other transport system is used.

Pre-Printed Routine or Standard Orders. Some facilities or practices solve the poor handwriting issue and also standardize and streamline the order-writing process by pre-printing routine or standard orders. Individual physician or physician groups often write the same set of orders for every patient they admit or after a specific test or procedure is performed. To avoid writing the same order repeatedly, routine orders are typed and duplicated ahead of time. Orders that may vary, such as site of treatment, length of therapy, or drug dose, may be typed with blanks to be filled in later. Using this format, a physician can implement a set of routine orders on the order sheet by filling in the blanks, dating and signing it, and inserting it in the patient's record. Chemotherapy, pre- and postpartum procedures, pre-and postsurgical procedures, and other complex orders readily lend themselves to this format.

Clarification of Orders. What do you do when you cannot read a word or even an entire order or prescription? Sometimes, you may be able to decipher the order if it is taken in context of other orders and the patient's condition. Usually, it is not that easy. The pharmacist is generally responsible for contacting the physician who wrote the order to ask for clarification. If the handwriting makes it difficult to determine the physician's name, a nurse, ward clerk, or other pharmacist may be familiar with the physician's handwriting and "translate" the name for you. Sometimes, the physician may have discussed the order with another pharmacist who can tell you what is ordered. However, it is a poor safety practice to have an order translated secondhand. Pharmacists should always contact the prescriber when any aspect of an order is unclear.

Graphic Records. Graphic records, sometimes called flowsheets, are standardized forms that simplify data collection and retrieval. They are quantitative records of repetitive monitoring activities and are usually arranged so that trends and patterns are easy to visualize. Information suitable for graphic records includes the patient's vital signs, intake and output data, and activities of daily living. Other patient parameters that are frequently assessed or administered, such as blood glucose values, insulin doses, intravenous (IV) fluids and blood products, or neurologic checks, often are documented on graphic records. The records are printed with the word "data" and various time intervals so that the person documenting the data, usually a nurse or nurse's aide, needs only enter the information. The frequency of data collection and documentation depends on the parameters and the patient's clinical status.

Nursing Notes. The Nursing Notes section sometimes is a subsection under Progress Notes. If not, hospitals, clinics, and offices may use an integrated approach where Nursing Notes are eliminated and all health professionals make entries in the Progress Notes section. The kinds of information you may find routinely in the Nursing Notes section are described here.

- *Physical functioning.* Physical functioning is usually reported in narrative notes made by the nurse or clinician who has observed it. Vital signs are examples of data recorded about physical functioning.
- *Behavior/mental status.* Behavior and mental status descriptions are identified.
- *Clinical signs and symptoms.* A clinical description of observed signs or reported symptoms is included.
- *Nursing interventions.* Nursing interventions include P.R.N. medications administered, risk assessments, and pain assessments or interventions. Sometimes checklists rather than a narration are used to assess progress.
- *Documentation of care.* These entries record implementation of patient care directives by the nursing staff (i.e., physical restriction, tests, procedures, blood samples, and routine treatments).
- *Patient education.* Patient education may be documented on specialized custom forms or as a narrative in the progress notes or profile.
- *Additional types of educational activities that may be recorded.* This includes the patient's attendance in education classes, viewing of videotapes, and demonstration of self-care skills, such as Hickman catheter care or administration of insulin.
- *Consults.* Consults from various health care professionals, such as physicians, pharmacists, enterostomy nurses, or physical therapists, can be found in this section.
- *Nursing care plans.* Nursing staff plans describe what nursing intends to do in the care of the patient.
- *Nursing admission data.* A nursing admission database is established by nurses who interview patients.
- *Discharge plans.* Discharge planning entries are made in the Nursing Notes section of a record.

In summary, the Nursing Notes section reflects the diversity of functions performed by the nursing staff. The categorization scheme offered gives some order to this information. As you can see from the examples, these notes and sections are not categorized easily and may overlap with other sections of the patient medical record.

Laboratory Data. Lab test results are found in this section. The format of the lab report is tailored to each institution or outpatient contract laboratory, although the same basic information is found regardless of the format. The lab results are separated into several categories:

- Hematology
- Urinalysis
- Type and screen
- Chemistry
- Microbiology
- Arterial blood gases

When appropriate, the normal range is given for each test. Most lab reports highlight abnormal values in some fashion, perhaps with an asterisk (*). An "H" next to values higher than the normal range and an "L" next to values lower than the normal range are commonly found on laboratory reports. Hematologic test results include measurements of red blood cell, white blood cell, and coagulation parameters. The urinalysis section divides test results into macroscopic and microscopic categories. A section on type and screen lists the results for ABO & RH testing and antibody screening.

The chemistry–renal function category lists the BUN, creatinine, sodium, potassium, chloride, carbon dioxide, and other tests of renal function. In the chemistry–metabolic category, you will find glucose, calcium, magnesium, phosphorus, total protein, albumin, cholesterol, and triglyceride measurements. The cardiac and liver chemistries are reported next, followed by cardiac enzymes and therapeutic drug concentrations.

The microbiology section reports information on blood and other body fluids and tissue cultures. Gram stain (if performed) and culture results are given. Antibiotic susceptibility and minimum inhibitory concentration (MIC) information is usually presented. Other microbiologic results, such as spinal or joint fluid examinations, also are found here.

The final section under Lab Data is arterial blood gases. Here, information about the patient's oxygen source (i.e., room air, ventilator, and FiO_2) and blood gas results are given.

The lab reports include all lab tests performed during a patient's admission or clinic visit. In the hospital, an updated cumulative report must be printed and placed in the record daily, usually during the night. The report from the previous day can then be discarded. After discharge, a final cumulative summary is compiled and becomes a permanent part of the medical record.

Sometimes, test results are not available when the updated reports are printed. This problem often occurs for tests sent to an off-site laboratory or in outpatient clinics or pharmacies. In these cases, the updated report may list the time and date of sample collection, but a notation of "pending," "in lab," "sent out," or some other similar term appears instead of a result. Once results are known, the next updated report is corrected.

Therapeutic Drug Monitoring Test Results. Several drug therapies are used by pharmacists and other health professionals to monitor for both effectiveness and toxicity by including the collection and interpretation of serum, whole blood, saliva, or sometimes urine drug concentration samples. Examples of such drugs include phenytoin, aminoglycosides, or digoxin. Other drug therapies are monitored for effectiveness and/or toxicity by using clinical laboratory tests that are proxy indicators for effectiveness and/or toxicity. One example is the monitoring of the International Normalized Ratio (INR) as a reflection of warfarin sodium. These test results are usually reported by identifying the monitored substance, the concentration of the substance reflecting the time that the sample was collected, and the desired or target ranges of the substance.

Home Test Kits and Monitoring Devices Results. Many patients use home test kits to monitor their progress in controlling their condition [e.g., blood sugar for diabetes, total cholesterol for dyslipidemia, or blood pressure cuff (sphygmomanometer) for essential hypertension]. Others use tests to determine the status of a condition (e.g., pregnancy testing or ovulation prediction tests). These results are usually brought in by patients or their family members to share how they are doing with clinicians. Clinicians will often regard this data as "subjective" when reported by the patient and will often verify the accuracy of them through clinical laboratory testing. As testing accuracy improves and community quality laboratory standards have been set, more clinicians accept the data generated by these methods. They offer the pharmacist a unique opportunity to incorporate monitoring tools into practice in a variety of settings.

Diagnostic Procedures/Consults. The diagnostic procedure reports are presented in a standardized format as a typed narrative, either a diagram or graph. Examples of the common diagnostic procedures included in this section are X-rays, electrocardiograms (ECGs), electroencephalograms (EEGs), computed axial tomography (CT) scans, magnetic resonance imaging (MRI), arteriograms, and invasive hemodynamic monitoring.

Operating Room Procedures. This section contains information presented in a typed narrative or graphic/diagrammatic format. Some hospitals may combine the Diagnostic Procedures/Consults section with the OR Procedures. Included in this section is documentation of surgical procedures, biopsies, and other invasive procedures. The same documentation is required for outpatient or office-based procedures.

History and Physical. Information about the patient's past and present medical history and physical examination findings appears in the eighth section of the medical record. This information is presented in a standardized format and may be handwritten or dictated.

When a patient is admitted, the physician often writes a note about his or her initial findings and impressions in addition to the patient's medical history in the Progress Notes section. Then, when more information is available or when the physician has more time, a complete history and physical note are dictated. The History and Physical section documents subjective and objective information about the patient. Subjective information is open to individual interpretation (e.g., assessments of pain, comfort, and orientation). Objective information is based on replicable or quantifiable data. This type of information usually is measurable and has a numerical value (e.g., body temperature, serum drug concentrations, and urine output). Both subjective and objective information is obtained from multiple sources: the patient, the patient's family members, caregivers such as nurses and physicians, and other health care professionals such as pharmacists, dieticians, and physical therapists. The contents of the History and Physical section usually appear in the following order:

Chief Complaint. The patient's chief complaint is exactly what brought the patient to the hospital. Often, the physician will document the patient's own words to describe his or her medical problem. Chief complaints may include "My chest feels like there's an elephant standing on it," "I've been coughing up blood for 3 days now," or "I slipped and fell."

History of Present Illness. The history of the present illness chronologically outlines the events of the patient's current medical problem(s) and gives details about the characteristics of the chief complaint. If a patient's chief complaint is "My chest feels like there's an elephant standing on it," the history of present illness may say "The patient had been mowing the lawn about 9:00 this morning when, suddenly, he experienced sharp pain in the chest. He sat down to rest and took three nitroglycerin tablets with no relief. After 6 hrs of constant chest pain, the patient's wife convinced him to go to the emergency room."

Past Medical History. The past medical history describes the patient's more remote history such as past surgeries, diseases, and medical conditions. Also included are patient allergies and resulting reactions, family history, and social history (e.g., smoking and alcohol habits, prescription and over-the-counter medication use, recreational drug use, occupation, and marital history). The health history may be obtained from the patient, the patient's family, other caregivers (e.g., private nurse or nursing home personnel), the present or previous physician(s), and/or records of the patient's previous hospitalization(s).

Review of Systems. The review of systems is an attempt by the examining health professional to elicit information from the patient. The patient is systematically questioned about each organ system and its functional status. The organ systems are grouped and presented in the review of systems in a top-to-bottom order: head, eyes, ears, nose, and throat (HEENT); respiratory system; breasts; cardiovascular (CV) system; gastrointestinal (GI) system; skin, bones, joints, and muscles; endocrine system; and nervous system. Questions that a clinician may ask a patient about his or her respiratory system include the following:

- Do you have any trouble breathing?
- Do you get short of breath when climbing stairs?
- Do you wake up short of breath at night?
- Do you cough up blood?

If the answers are negative, the clinician may note that "patient denies shortness of breath, exertional shortness of breath, paroxysmal nocturnal dyspnea (PND), or hemoptysis."

Other questions that health care professionals may ask include

- Do you suffer from dizziness or lightheadedness? (cardiovascular system assessment)
- Do you have trouble urinating or pain when urinating? (genitourinary system assessment)
- Do you have trouble with diarrhea or constipation? (gastrointestinal system assessment)

Physical Examination. The physical examination can be considered physical evidence that supports and verifies the information discovered in the review of systems. This examination report describes what the health care professional saw, heard, felt, and sometimes smelled while examining the patient. Documentation of the examination may start with a short statement describing the patient's general status and a summary of the vital signs. Then, the results of the physical examination are again presented by organ system in a head-to-toe order: HEENT; neck, thorax or chest, and lungs; breasts; CV system; abdomen; extremities; lymph nodes; bones, joints, and muscles; genitals; rectum; and neurological system. Statements that you may read in a physical examination report include "pupils reactive to light," "abdomen soft, nontender, no masses or organomegaly," "fingers cyanotic with clubbing," and "regular cardiac rhythm without murmur or gallop." It is not always possible or convenient to examine every organ system. In these situations, the physician may note "deferred." Short statements may explain why a particular organ system was not examined. Examples include "unable to assess" or "patient refused."

Admission Tests. When available, results of admission tests follow the physical examination. Lab data and report of diagnostic procedures are documented. Occasionally, a patient may have had relevant lab tests or diagnostic procedures as an outpatient before being admitted to the hospital. If the information is pertinent, that data may be presented here as well.

Assessment and Plan. A description of the clinician's assessment or impression of the patient's condition is the clinician's working diagnosis. The clinician compiles all of the data presented in the History and Physical and integrates it to determine known and/or possible explanations for the patient's medical problem(s). The clinician usually concludes the History and Physical with an initial plan of therapy based on the aforementioned impressions. The plan may include medications, surgical procedures, or diagnostic tests. These plans are not final; they may change during the patient's hospitalization. Standards for good records also structure what information is collected and thus promote self-teaching and self-critique of clinical work. For instance, the standard format for a write up helps you remember what data to collect (e.g., do a family history and a stool guaiac). The format for the assessment and plan should help you ask the following sorts of questions: What problems have been identified? What is the significance of each finding? What other information has been collected (or should have been collected) that bears on this finding? What do I make of each problem? What do I intend to do to clarify my diagnosis? What treatment will I undertake for each problem? How has the patient been educated?

Progress Notes. The Progress Notes provide a running commentary on the patient's condition and treatments throughout the entire hospital stay. Progress Notes document the patient's response to treatment from admission to discharge. Events of the hospitalization and the patient's physical condition are described. These notes are a chronological log of how the patient is feeling and what is happening on a day-by-day, or even hour-by-hour, basis.

Various health care professionals write entries in the Progress Notes section. Each person who cares for the patient documents what he or she did to or for the patient; when, where, and why; and how the patient reacted or responded. As discussed previously, some institutions ask nurses to record their notes in a separate Nursing Notes section, while others integrate all health professionals' entries into a single Progress Notes section. The following are characteristics of correctly written progress notes:

- Date note is written is documented.
- Time of note is documented.
- Note is entitled, "Pharmacist Consultation" or "Pharmacist Progress Note." Each discipline identifies itself on the notes prepared for the record (e.g., Cardiology Consult for cardiologists note).
- Note is handwritten, dictated, or typed. Note is neat, legible, professional in appearance, and written in black or blue ink.
- Note is well organized using the S.O.A.P. format.
- Content is written in either outline or narrative format.

- Note is signed with a cursive signature with the name printed clearly below it.
- Errors are documented with a cross out; "error" is written above the line with the writer's initials.

Progress notes are filed in forward or reverse chronological order, depending on the preference of the institution.

Progress note entries may take one of two formats: outline or narrative. A standardized outline approach in common use is the SOAP format where the entry is divided into four sections: subjective data (S), objective data (O), assessment (A) or impression, and therapeutic plan (P) or recommendation.

To review, subjective data are open to individual interpretation, while objective data are easily duplicated or quantified. As in the Historical and Physical section, the assessment portion of a SOAP note describes the writer's interpretation of the aforementioned subjective and objective data and subsequent impressions. Finally, the writer outlines a therapeutic plan just as in the History and Physical section.

Sometimes an author may combine the subjective and objective data (S/O) and the assessment and plan portions (A/P). If no data are available for one section, the note writer may choose not to mention that section. Sometimes the data to be documented are not easily adapted to a SOAP format. This situation is especially true if there are a lot of subjective data to record with little or no objective data available.

Medication Administration Record (MAR). Most facilities produce a typed form, the MAR, which documents all of the medications that are active on a patient (see **Figures 6-3 A and B**). This record usually includes the start date, stop date, name, strength, route, and frequency of administration. It is also common to see the recommended time of administration of the medication pre-printed on the form. When the medication is actually administered to the patient, the health professional or aid initials the recommended time and records the actual time of administration. The medications are listed in groups (i.e., scheduled medications, including "one-time" orders and p.r.n. medications). The MAR is produced usually every 24 hours by the pharmacy department, disseminated to the patient care areas, and placed in the record for daily use. A similar listing of prescribed medications is usually maintained in a patient's outpatient record.

Referrals. Whenever a formal referral takes place, an order (often on a separate, pre-printed form) is generated and placed in the record. It is often kept in a separate section of the record, readily identifiable.

Self-Monitoring Forms. Many facilities have a self-care program for medications, particularly with patients who are going out of the facility "on pass," intending to return in a day or so, or learning to self-administer their medication regimen upon discharge. Patients will document their medication use in a manner similar to the MAR procedures used by health professionals.

Temporary Information. Different types of temporary information are placed in records to assist clinicians with care. Preliminary laboratory results, initial diagnoses from informal consults, and recommendations made by pharmacists to change therapy or follow a policy are all examples of temporary information that does not necessarily become a part of the permanent record. Once the permanent report or progress note is placed in the record, the temporary documents are discarded.

PHARMACY RECORDS

Pharmacists have led in the use of electronic records, as they have been an integral part of pharmacy practice and management for more than 30 years. Electronic records were first implemented to maintain billing, inventory, and purchasing records for pharmacists, organizations, and patients. Pharmacists currently use the pharmacy record as their repository for patient information relevant to medication use in nearly all health care settings—a pharmacy-specific electronic health record. The pharmacy record in the hospital, home care, nursing home, and community pharmacy typically contains information about patients' prescription medications; drug and other forms of allergies; pharmacists' care plan notes that include patient-specific

NAME OF HOSPITAL						
MEDICATION ADMINISTRATION RECORD: SCHEDULED AND PRN MEDICATIONS						

INJECTION SITE CODE

A (R)Deltoid   H (L) Upper Quad
B (L)Deltoid   I (R) Lower Quad
C (L)Lat. Thigh   J (L) Lower Quad
D (R)Lat. Thigh   K (L) Glutial
E (R)Ant. Thigh   L (R) Glutial
F (L)Ant. Thigh   M(L) Ventro-Glutial
G (R)Upper Quad   O (R) Ventro-Glutial

DIAGNOSIS:

ALLERGIES:

GENERATED:
FOR PERIOD:
THROUGH:

START	STOP	MEDICATION	ORDER#	07:01-15:00	15:01-23:00	23:01-07:00
1-5	1-12	AMPICILLIN 250 MG CAPSULES 250 MG EVERY SIX HOURS	1267904	1200	1800	2400 0600
1-5	1-12	DYAZIDE CAPSULES 1 CAPSULE AT 9AM	1267907	0900		
1-5	1-12	GLUCOTROL 2.5 MG TABLETS ONE TABLET EVERY 12 HOURS	1267908	0900	2000	

INITIALS	NAME & PROFESSIONAL DESIGNATION	INITIALS	NAME & PROFESSIONAL DESIGNATION	INITIALS	NAME & PROFESSIONAL DESIGNATION	INITIALS	NAME & PROFESSIONAL DESIGNATION

Figure 6-3A. Example of a Medication Administration Record for Scheduled and p.r.n. Medications

NAME OF HOSPITAL
INTRAVENOUS, STAT, AND ONE-TIME MEDICATION ADMINISTRATION RECORD

INJECTION SITE CODE

A (R)Deltoid	H (L) Upper Quad
B (L)Deltoid	I (R) Lower Quad
C (L)Lat. Thigh	J (L) Lower Quad
D (R)Lat. Thigh	K (L) Glutial
E (R)Ant. Thigh	L (R) Glutial
F (L)Ant. Thigh	M(L) Ventro-Glutial
G (R)Upper Quad	O (R) Ventro-Glutial

DIAGNOSIS:

ALLERGIES:

GENERATED:
FOR PERIOD:
THROUGH:

START	STOP	MEDICATION	ORDER#	07:01-15:00	15:01-23:00	23:01-07:00
1-5	1-12	DEXTROSE 5%/0.45 NORMAL SALINE I.V. INFUSE AT 125 ML/HR (1000 ML)	1267909	0800	1600	2400
1-5	1-6	WARFARIN 2.5 MG TABLETS ONE TABLET AT 5 P.M.	1267905		1700	
1-5 STAT		MORPHINE SULFATE INJECTION 10 MGS I.V. NOW FOR PAIN	1267915			

MEDICATION * DOSAGE * RT OF ADMIN.	GIVEN		NURSE INITIAL	MEDICATION * DOSAGE * RT OF ADMIN.	GIVEN		NURSE INITIAL
	DATE	TIME/SITE			DATE	TIME/SITE	

INITIALS	NAME & PROFESSIONAL DESIGNATION	INITIALS	NAME & PROFESSIONAL DESIGNATION	INITIALS	NAME & PROFESSIONAL DESIGNATION	INITIALS	NAME & PROFESSIONAL DESIGNATION

Figure 6-3B. Medication Administration Record for Intravenous, STAT, and One-Time Medication Orders

considerations (e.g. preferred medication use decisions governed by formularies); and a variety of elements included in a patient's medication use history often including over-the-counter medication and herbal supplement use. Pharmacy records are often recognized as a relatively accurate proxy for a patient's general adherence to medications.[27] The detail maintained in a pharmacy record exceeds that of the EHR maintained by other providers and settings in order to serve the needs of the patient–pharmacist relationship. Pharmacy records indicate what prescribed medications a patient has chosen to pick up for use, and may also make reference to the patient's medication use behaviors and outcome responses to prescribed therapies.[28-36]

Prescription Records—Outpatient Practice

The prescription is the primary form of communication between the pharmacist and the practitioner who is initiating treatment for the patient with prescription drugs or the use of prescription devices. It is the vehicle by which a patient chooses care when in need of prescription drug management. It is provided to the pharmacist in written form: handwritten (**Figure 6-4**), generated from a printer or fax machine, or electronically transmitted to the pharmacy. The prescription is the legal order for prescription medication or other items in the outpatient setting, including skilled nursing facilities.

Medication Orders—Inpatient Practice

When a physician or other authorizing prescriber prescribes the patient's medications while in the hospital setting, they do so on order forms usually entitled "Physicians Orders." The medication order is the legal order for prescription and over-the-counter medications prescribed in the inpatient setting.

The Patient's Profile—All Settings

The Patient's Profile is the medical record equivalent document for the pharmacist. It is maintained in all practice settings. Its purposes and uses are the medical record equivalent for the pharmacist and the pharmacy staff serving the patient. Therefore, you will see much more information than that provided by a prescription or medication order alone, depending upon the quality and breadth of pharmacy services offered. The profile may serve as the record of care provided to the patient when served by the pharmacists and technicians. Almost all pharmacy settings are computerized today. As a result, the pharmacist (or pharmacy clerk or technician depending upon both the practice model and state rules and regulations) will enter prescription or

```
Joyce Miller MD                              DEA No. AC 1269478
Don Hancock, M.D.                            DEA No. AD 3497682

                  Metropolitan General Family Medicine Clinic
                            1234 Detroit Avenue
                           Detroit, Michigan 48169
Rx




Refills: ____

_____            _____
Dispense as Written               May Substitute Generic/Therapeutic Equivalent
```

Figure 6-4. Example of a Traditional, Hand-Written Prescription Blank Commonly Used in Outpatient Settings

medication orders into the pharmacy computer system. A computer-based medication profile is created from the order entry process. Numerous settings have expanded to have both physicians and prescribers enter the prescription or medication order; however, this is not yet a standard of practice.

Most prescription records are on paper, as originally written by the prescriber. The profile is commonly observed as several computer screens reflect the range of patient data within the pharmacy computer system, the Medication Administration Record (MAR) summarizing the medication orders in the inpatient setting, or the Medication Record summarizing the prescriptions in the outpatient setting. The profile is stored in the pharmacy computer system, with supplementary medication orders or prescription records in paper files. When the profile is viewed on the computer screen, it is common for several computer windows to reflect detailed information such as medication name, strength, dose and form, route of administration, frequency of administration, and start and end dates. Additional information is displayed to assist the pharmacist with drug regimen review at the time of order entry. Two examples of this regimen review, which commonly result in follow up, may include assessment of the patient's medication order against the acceptable dosing range (minimum–maximum dose) or determining the presence of a clinically significant drug interaction. Biographical, financial/insurance data, and consent forms are also part of the profile. Throughout the cases examples of how the profile varies in content illustrate these differences.

Pharmacists' Notes

Pharmacists' Notes are similar to the section entitled Progress Notes or Nursing Notes in the medical record. This section is where problem identification, care plan development, and documentation of care provision occur. The Progress Note is typically organized as such.

Problems or Complaints.
Depending upon the clinical setting, patients may present at a scheduled or drop-in appointment with a pharmacist, or they may initiate a conversation with the pharmacist. Often patients in a retail setting initially present with clinical signs or symptoms resulting in a complaint.

Physical Functioning and Behavioral/Mental Status.
The patient's ability to function independently is an important assessment of the pharmacist. Pharmacists use specific tools, such as activities of daily living (ADLs) or the mini-mental status examination (MMSE), to assist in this assessment.

Physician Examination and Assessment.
A review of systems approach may be employed by the pharmacist to gather greater clinical insight. Pharmacists also employ limited, focused physical assessment skills to determine clinical problems and assess response to drug therapies. Pharmacists in community settings also provide blood pressure cuff devices and body temperature measurement devices to assist patients with home monitoring activities.

Laboratory Data and Assessment.
Clinical laboratory test results are sometimes ordered or requested by pharmacists who perform drug therapy monitoring and dosing adjustments. However, the consumer home testing market has made the pharmacy a central place for purchase. Individuals are now self-monitoring their diabetes through blood sugar testing strips and monitors, lipid management through cholesterol measurement, and diagnostic pregnancy testing and ovulation prediction kits. Many pharmacists have established practices to help patients select and properly use and interpret the diagnostic and monitoring tests.

Medication-Use Evaluation.
This evaluation is conducted on patients whenever they approach a pharmacist for drug therapy-related care. Chapter 8 will take us through the clinical reasoning process that both identifies drug-related problems and conducts the medication-use evaluation. These results are documented in the profile. Patients may receive brief, meaningful evaluations and feedback from the pharmacist, with a care plan successfully designed and implemented in episode of care. On the other hand, pharmacists may have multiple, scheduled visits with patients to optimize drug therapy and patient care.

Medication Adherence/Compliance History.
The prescription records provide a unique history of medication use. The pharmacist has a unique data-

set—knowing what prescription medications have been filed, when they were filled, and whether the patient has maintained a continuous refill history. Evaluation of these records provides the pharmacist with insight about the medication-use pattern of the patient.

Care Plans. The pharmacist evaluates these problems and develops an overall care plan. The plan may be limited in focus on one problem or activity or comprehensive to include multiple goals, alternative treatments with proxy outcome measures to monitor, and patient education plans to achieve goals.

- *Drug therapy problems.* Evaluation of the previous information and consultation with the patient leads the pharmacist to identify the patient's drug therapy problems. They are recorded in the patient's profile.
- *Interventions.* Some drug-related problems require recommendations to other care providers for an alteration or change in the drug therapy approach. Recommendations might include changing the drug entirely or modifying the regimen to optimize the patient's outcome individualized to the lifestyle and personal considerations of the patient.
- *Patient education.* Pharmacists' care plans usually involve a structured form of patient education. Common plans include proper drug use, monitoring devises and testing kits, and therapeutic intervention with patient re-education.

Documentation of Care. The patient profile should document all aspects of a pharmacist's care plan and provision. This documentation of care is necessary for ongoing continuity of care, determination of a patient's progress, and for reimbursement of patient care services.

Consults. If a patient is referred by another practitioner for a pharmacist consultation, you may record the assessment and findings in consultation notes in the profile.

SUMMARY

The patient's medical record or patient profile provides a key source of information in the provision of care. The record or profile represents common vehicles to document care and track the monitoring of the patient's progress. Other uses for the patient's record aid research initiatives or public health statistics. However, any use of the patient's record must be consistent with the Privacy Act of 1974, the Health Insurance Portability and Accountability Act of 1996 (HIPAA), and the HITECH Act. The care delivery models that pharmacists are uniquely capable of providing have greater potential with participation in health information exchange and use of a patient EHR along with pharmacy records. It is important for pharmacists to become knowledgeable about the use of PHRs and the potential impact they have on health care and patient safety. PHRs have potential to positively impact the patient–pharmacist relationship. Pharmacists who understand the PHR encourage patients to use a PHR, and they engage with patients using a PHR to help build a level of trust with their patients. As PHRs are patient-controlled, the patient determines who views the health information in it. Engaging and building trust with patients in this health information exchange movement will create an avenue for pharmacists to have increased access to patient health information with the expressed permission and involvement of the patient in the process. As pharmacists are the medication-use experts, obtaining the most up-to-date, accurate, and complete medication-related health and self-care information (including over-the-counter medications, herbal and dietary supplements, vitamins, home remedies, laboratory data relevant to drug therapy monitoring, and other information) will enable more effective and efficient pharmacist's care. Implications of these developments for the pharmacy profession include the following:

- The pharmacist history of medication use is valuable. The reconciliation process is of high importance to building an accurate EHR. Pharmacists should consider a business model to exchange this information with other health professions; as such a model is emerging in the profession of medicine.
- Pharmacist access to patient EHRs is a public safety imperative. Pharmacists should expect to access and exchange health information with

other health professionals electronically. This is a critical time for pharmacists and pharmacies to become engaged with private and public entities, as well as state boards, in revising practice structure and services and the laws and regulations governing the use of exchangeable health data. EHRs are still relatively new to physicians and other health disciplines.

- Pharmacists need to understand patients' views of how they believe their personal health information should be managed. Consumers believe personal health information should be shared to improve patient care; however, they lack knowledge about EHRs and health information exchange and do not understand processes used in health care to exchange information if the process does not involve them directly. Consumers also lack an understanding of how various health care providers use personal health information to improve the quality and safety of patient care within their scope of practice. Understanding remains limited regarding what consumers will participate in and how they will participate as systems for sharing personal health information continue to emerge. Pharmacists have traditionally been community resources for health care access and information, and this role should continue.

- Pharmacists will work directly with patients to "upload" and "download" medication use, therapeutic drug monitoring, and progress note data into devices that patients carry or to web sites on which patients maintain a PHR.

- Pharmacists need to engage in education and regulation review at the state level to contribute to ensuring security and privacy rights for patients and health professionals while gaining access to health information exchange.

- Pharmacists need to understand physicians' and other providers' expectations and views on sharing patient information. Health professionals indicate that they would be willing to share a patient's electronic health information with other providers if the patient gave permission. However, health professionals also acknowledge the existence of many barriers of both a professional and personal nature that must be overcome.

- Pharmacists' models of care delivery and array of services will continue to change by incorporating technology support and increasing communication-based relationships with patients. Geography will become less important and relationships more important to patients with EHR access availability.

Embracing the electronic health information movement and participating in health information exchange to advance the way we care for patients in our pharmacy practice settings will be essential to the future work models of pharmacists in patient clinical care.

ASSESSMENT QUESTIONS

1. What are the various health records in which a patient's health information is potentially stored?
2. Describe five common uses for the health record.
3. Describe the differences between subjective and objective information.
4. How does the Privacy Act protect a patient's confidentiality?
5. What action should you take as a pharmacist when a patient's medication order or prescription is difficult to read or unclear in its intent?
6. If you wanted to audit several medical records for patients to gather data about a pharmacy program's effectiveness (you do not intend to publish this), would you need to seek each patient's consent before you did it?

ASSIGNMENT

1. Contact the director of pharmacy in your community hospital. Ask the director to describe the characteristics of the medical record at his or her hospital. Is it all paper, all electronic, or a mixture of both? Do they use an electronic medication administration record (MAR)? Do pharmacists document their patient care activities in the medical records? What section?

2. Speak with a hospital pharmacist in your community. Ask about the process to transmit orders from the patient's record to the pharmacy. Describe this process.

3. Contact a pharmacist in your local community pharmacy. Ask the pharmacist to describe the characteristics of the pharmacy patient profile at his or her pharmacy. Is it all paper, all electronic, or a mixture of both? Do they document patient care activities on the pharmacy profile?

4. Speak with a community pharmacist in your community. How do orders get transmitted from the physician's office to the pharmacy? Describe the various methods.

CASE 1

Lauren Smith brings a prescription to Nasir Jabr, PharmD, RPh, after seeing Dr. Miller

Lauren Smith had followed up on Nasir Jabr's recommendation to see the physician and returns to the pharmacy to have Jabr fill her prescription for an antibiotic to treat a urinary tract infection. In the course of conversation, Lauren has other questions that lead Jabr to conduct an initial patient consultation. He sees Lauren approaching and greets her.

Nasir Jabr: "Hello Lauren. What may I do for you?"

Lauren: "Well, I wanted to thank you Nasir. Dr. Miller was very good. But I have a few problems that I was unaware of. You were right; I have a urinary tract infection. So I brought my prescription for you to fill."

(Jabr takes the prescription and hands it to Joe, the Pharmacy Technician.)

Nasir Jabr: "Joe, would you please set this up for me while I speak briefly with Ms. Smith? Thank you. Lauren, come around to this counseling area over here so that we can speak with some privacy." (She looks slightly relieved.)

(Jabr shakes her hand. He notices that it is cold to the touch and a little "clammy"—perspiring.)

Nasir Jabr: "Lauren, I have started a patient profile for you here at the pharmacy (**Figure 6-5**).

When patients come in for care and advice, we establish a record, just like in the physician's office or in the hospital. May I ask you a few more questions so that I can have a complete record? It should help both of us in the future."

Lauren: "Sure."

(While Jabr and Lauren are speaking, he notices that she appears a little tired and slightly pale.)

Nasir Jabr: "What did Dr. Miller tell you your medical problems were in addition to the urinary tract infection?"

Lauren: "Well, she really surprised me because she suspected that I have hypertension! The nurse had taken my blood pressure, and it was 148/100. I was so shocked, I didn't really say anything! Then she said something about my birth control pills and the smoking, too. I am not exactly sure. Oh, and I forgot to tell her about the Advil™."

Nasir Jabr: "I would like to ask you a few more questions, and then I would like to explain what I believe Dr. Miller was trying to let you know. Is that okay?"

Lauren: "Yes."

Nasir Jabr: "What birth control pills are you taking?"

Lauren: "Well…I am not. I am using the patch."

Pharmacy Profile					
Patient: Smith, Lauren			New Patient	Print	Close Record
Demographic	OTC / Allergy		Insurance	Diagnosis	Contacts
General Health	Care Plans	Surveys	Account Status	Current Therapy	
General Information		Illnesses	Systems Review	Vital Signs	Lab Values

---

Pharmacist's Progress Note: Date: 02-12

LS referred to Dr. Miller by NJ on 02-01 for evaluation of probable UTI. LS presented today with co-trimoxazole prescription. Upon brief history and examination the following was noted:

S: LS reports BP at physician's 148/100; using birth control patch after 2 year history of Lo-Ovral; 3–4 Advil 200 mg tablets 3–4 x per week for headaches—characterized by frontal discomfort and occasional periorbital pain; 1–2 ppd cigarettes. Denies allergy to medications.

O: BP 150/102 seated (repeated here)

A: UTI, probable essential HTN worsened by NSAID use and nicotine addiction—increased risk of thromboembolic events and elevated BP and, headaches—symptoms consistent with sinus headache—likely in need of a decongestant rather than Advil.

P: Dispensed co-trimoxazole and counseled to consume water, take to completion. Offered smoking cessation and hypertension management service. Research her question, "Does birth control patch affect BP also?" Asked her to visit in one week for follow-up.

Nasir Jabr, Pharm.D.

Figure 6-5. Computerized Pharmacy Profile for Patient Lauren Smith

---

Nasir Jabr: "How long have you been on this?"

Lauren: "Just a year. Before that I took Lo-Ovral™ for 2 years."

Nasir Jabr: "Describe how you take your Advil™."

Lauren: "I usually take three or four tablets whenever I have pain or discomfort."

Nasir Jabr: "How often do you have pain or discomfort?"

Lauren: "Well… I have three to four headaches a week… some of them are pretty bad."

Nasir Jabr: "Tell me more details about how you use the Advil™."

Lauren: "Well, I usually wait until my headaches are pretty bad before I take any of it. But it seems like I always need to take it."

Nasir Jabr: "Can you describe the headaches for me?"

Lauren: "I usually get pain in my forehead area, but sometimes it seems like it's also in my eyes."

Nasir Jabr: "Does it get worse when you lean forward?"

Lauren: "No, not really."

Nasir Jabr: "Does anything in particular seem to cause the headaches?"

Lauren: "I can't really identify anything."

Nasir Jabr: "How many packs of cigarettes do you smoke a day?"

Lauren: "Probably one or two. It just depends on how busy I am that day. I wish I never started."

Nasir Jabr: "Have you ever been told that you have any allergies?"

Lauren: "No."

Nasir Jabr: "Allergies to medications?"

Lauren: "No."

Nasir Jabr: "Is there anything else that you might want to tell me about?"

Lauren: "I can't think of anything. How do I use the medication Dr. Miller prescribed?"

Nasir Jabr: "Let me go check the prescription so that I can show it to you while I am explaining what you need to do. Could I have Joe take your blood pressure while you are waiting?"

Lauren: "Sure. I didn't know pharmacists did this sort of thing!"

Nasir Jabr: "Yes. We are developing programs in community practice to help our patients with medication management. I am very glad you wandered in to see us. It will just be a moment." (Joe, Pharmacy Technician, takes Lauren's blood pressure. It reads 150/102. Joe tells Nasir. Jabr returns to Lauren with the prescription.)

Nasir Jabr: "Lauren, this is an antibiotic; the name is 'trimethoprim–sulfamethoxazole.'"

(Jabr opens the container and shows her the oblong white tablets. He recaps the bottle and hands it to her so that she can read the instructions while he is explaining them.)

Nasir Jabr: "Lauren, you need to take two tablets right away, and then take one tablet two times a day until they are all gone. This should take 7 days. Do you have any questions so far?"

Lauren: "No. I understand."

Nasir Jabr: "It is very important for you to finish all of the tablets, even after you are feeling better. You will start experiencing less pain, and will likely be pain free within 2 days of starting the antibiotic. It is also important that you drink plenty of liquids; water is best. This will help clear the bladder of infection."

Lauren: "Okay."

Nasir Jabr: "Let's move on to the other concerns. Your blood pressure reading here is 150/102, which is high. You have multiple reasons for a high blood pressure. Birth control pills have been shown to increase blood pressure. Smoking contributes to increased blood pressure. And frequent use of medications, known as nonsteroidal anti-inflammatory drugs, also increases blood pressure. That is your Advil™. I offer a smoking cessation program and a hypertension management service in cooperation with a few of the physicians in the area. Dr. Miller is one of them. I wanted you to be informed of this option. In the meantime, I would like you to stop back in a week. We would be happy to check your blood pressure again, and you can tell me how everything is going. How does that sound?"

Lauren: "Sounds okay…I do have a question though. Does the birth control patch cause high blood pressure also? Or is it just the birth control pills?"

Nasir Jabr: "Well, that is an excellent question. Why don't I investigate the correct answer to that question and have an answer for you when you stop by next week?"

Lauren: "That would be great. Thanks for everything Nasir."

Nasir Jabr: "My pleasure. If you would check out with Joe, you will be all set. Please call or stop by if you have any other questions."

(Jabr writes a pharmacy progress note in Lauren's Pharmacy Profile.)

CASE-SPECIFIC QUESTIONS

1. Review the case details provided to you about Lauren Smith in Chapters 1–6. Establish the data needed for her patient profile by completing the details that you can to make one comprehensive pharmacist's database using the Patient's History Form–Pharmacist's Recommendations/Plan (see Figure 5-1).

CASE 2

Christine Johnston, PharmD, RPh, reviews Eduardo Montanez's clinic record and laboratory findings

Christine Johnston is preparing her professional knowledge base about her patient, Eduardo Montanez. In this brief sequence, Johnston reviews several pieces of data through retrieving this information from different sources of the patient's health record. Practice reviewing Mr. Montanez's information.

Christine Johnston reviews the clinic records of Eduardo Montanez. She focuses on a summary note about Mr. Montanez prepared by Dr. Mattis, his primary physician (see **Figure 6-6**). She also reviews the laboratory data obtained when he visited with her at the clinic (see **Figures 6-7** and **6-8**).

				Patient Identification (Stamp)
HEART OF TEXAS SYSTEM CLINICS **PROGRESS NOTES**				Name: Eduardo Montanez
	Age	**Sex**	Leukocytes _____	Reg.No. 16254
V S I I T G A N L S	Weight ____ B/P _____ Pulse _____	Height ____ Temp _____ Resp _____	Nitrite _____ ph _____ Protein _____ Glucose _____ Ketones ____ Urobilinogen ____ Bilirubin _____ Blood _____	Location: Main Clinic Date: 09/15

Hct __12__ Preg. __NA__ Hemocult _____ Strep _____ Other _____

UA Micro: WBC _____ RCB _____ WBC _____ Epis _____ Bacteria _____

Appt. __x__	Call/Walk In _____	Primary Physician __Dr. Mattis__ /Staff _____

Date: __9-15__

1:30 p.m.	EM is a 68 year old Hispanic male who is here for a routine check up for his diabetes mellitus. He presents with thirst, hunger and increased urination. PMHx: diabetes mellitus type II x 15 years known 　　　Dyslipidemia; 10 years PMI: DM, Dyslipidemia, pain and discomfort in legs – probable neuropathy 2° to long standing Diabetes SH: Lives with daughter-in-law, Maria and his son. Dependent upon son for medical coverage. EtOH- 5-6 beers a day; denies smoking PE: V.S. BP – 145/89 HR – 60 Resp 18/min. ROS: HEENT: Poor vision – no corrective lenses – refuses care. 　　　NECK: supple, no JVD, carotids 2/2. Trachea is midline 　　　CARDIAC: regular rate and rhythm, S_1 and S_2, no S_3 no S_4. 　　　ABDOMEN: no distension or organomegaly 　　　GI/GU: polydypsia, polyphagia, polyuria 　　　RECTAL: guaiac negative 　　　NEURO: alert and oriented x 3. Pedal pulses dull. LABS: Fasting Blood Sugar = 218; trace protein in urine; $HgbA_1c$ = 12 mg%, total chol = 220. MEDS: Glipizide 5 mg one po q day; metformin 500 mg one po bid; simvastatin 40 mg one tab with evening meal; vicodin ES one tab every four hours prn leg pain. IMPRESSION: EM has poorly controlled diabetes. Probable cause for elevated cholesterol. Provided home blood glucose meter and taught daughter to monitor blood sugar every day. Instructed to bring readings in next clinic visit in 3 months. Recommended optometry evaluation to EM and daughter. 　　　　　　　　　　　　　　　　　　　　　　Dr. Mattis 　　　　　　　　　　　　　　　　　　　　　　Signature
2:30 p.m.	Clinic no show on 12/22/ 　　　　　　　　　　　　　　　　　　　　　　Dr. Mattis 　　　　　　　　　　　　　　　　　　　　　　Signature

Figure 6-6. Summary of Past Medical History for Patient Eduardo Montanez

UA DIP STICK			Date Requested 06/12/		
cloudy		Color/Appearance	Chart No. 16254	Doctor: Mattis	Patient: Eduardo Montanez
	Neg.	Glucose			
	Neg.	Bilirubin			
	Neg.	Ketones			
1.020	1.003-1.030	Specific Gravity			
	Neg.	Blood			
	4.5-8.0	pH			
2++	Neg.	Protein			
	Norm.	Urobilinogen			
	Neg.	Nitrite			
	Neg.	Leukocytes			
UA MICROSCOPIC					
N/A	WBC/HPF				
N/A	RBC/HPF				
N/A	Mucus				
N/A	Renal Epith/HPF				
N/A	Squamous Epith/HPF				
N/A	Bacteria				
N/A	Crystals				
N/A	Casts/HPF				
URINE PREGNANCY					
N/A					

Figure 6-7. Urinalysis Test Results for Patient Eduardo Montanez

MISCELLANEOUS LAB RESULT – STAT REQUEST PROGRESS NOTES			Patient Identification (Stamp)
			Name: Eduardo Montanez
Hemoglobin A₁c	12.5 mg%	(normal range: 4-6 mg%)	Reg.No. 16254
			Location: Main Clinic
Blood glucose	220 mg/dL	(normal range: 80-120)	Date: 06/12/

Figure 6-8. STAT Laboratory Test Request for Patient Eduardo Montanez

CASE-SPECIFIC QUESTIONS

1. Review the case details provided to you about Eduardo Montanez in Chapters 1–5, and the clinic summary note and laboratory reports. Establish the data needed for his complete patient profile by compiling the details that you can into one comprehensive pharmacist's database using the Patient's History Form–Pharmacist's Recommendations/ Plan (Figure 5-1).

CASE 3

Luisa Rodriguez, PharmD, RPh, reviews Huong Tran's admission note from the physician

Luisa Rodriguez is establishing her professional knowledge base about Huong Tran through reviewing sources of patient data from the patient's records established on Huong at the time of admission. Practice reviewing these data sources by examining the information about Huong Tran.

Luisa Rodriquez goes to the record to review the details of Huong's admission (see **Figure 6-9**). She also looks to see what the admitting orders are from Dr. Mooris (see **Figure 6-10**).

Memorial Hospital and Health System

PROGRESS NOTES

Patient Identification (Stamp)

Name: Huong Tran

Reg.No. 2364590

Location: 5W Pediatrics

Date: 04-02

Age: 8 years old **Sex:** Male **VITAL SIGNS:**

Weight 40 kg   Height 5'   B/P 110/70   Temp 98.6°

Pulse 85   Resp. 18

4-2 Admit to 5W Pediatrics:

HT is an 8 yom who presented to the ER with moderate to severe asthma exacerbation. 3x in 2 weeks. His FEV was 60% - Was treated with two courses of - albuterol 8 puffs in 10 minutes/ repeat every 20 minutes until breathing normal. Solu-medrol 40 mg IV. Pharmacist used spacer device and assisted HT with albuterol use.

Mother and father present – non-English speaking Vietnamese descent. Only child can speak and translate English for himself and parents. No additional relatives or immediate care takers.

Will follow-up in afternoon...

Dr. Mooris
Signature

Figure 6-9. Brief Admission Note in the Progress Note Section for Patient Huong Tran

START DATE →	DATE 04-02	TIME 1500	I CERTIFY THAT THE ADMISSION OF THIS PATIENT IS MEDICALLY NECESSARY	**Memorial Hospital and Health System**
PHYSICIAN'S ORDERS:				ADDRESSOGRAPH IMPRINT HERE
Admit to hospital:				
Acute exacerbation of asthma				Name: Huong Tran Reg.No. 2364590 Location: 5W Pediatrics Date: 04-02
1. V.S. every 4 hours for 24 hours				
2. Albuterol metered dose inhaler – 2 puffs every 4 hours while awake.				
3. Pharmacist consult – medication history and education on Metered dose inhaler				
4. Solu-medrol 40 mg IV q 6 hours for remaining 24 hours – DC at 1500 on 04-03				
5. Start D5/0.25NS at 30 ml/hour starting at 1600.				
6. Labs in a.m. – CBC, chem-20, PT, PTT				
7. Social work consult – need for assistance with medical coverage And comprehensive discharge plan.				
8. Request Vietnamese interpreter for family.				
Dr. Mooris Signature/pager no 0693				
				ALLERGIES AND SENSITIVITIES: 1. **Penicillin – rash and itching** 2. *A GENERICALLY OR THERAPEUTICALLY EQUIVALENT DRUG AS APPROVED BY THE PHARMACY COMMITTEE MAY BE DISPENSED UNLESS OTHERWISE SPECIFICALLY STATED.

Figure 6-10. Hospital Admission Orders for Patient Huong Tran

---

CASE-SPECIFIC QUESTIONS

1. Review the case details provided to you about Huong Tran in Chapters 1–6. Establish the data needed for his patient profile by compiling the details that you can into one comprehensive pharmacist's database using the Patient's History Form–Pharmacist's Recommendations/Plan (Figure 5-1).

CASE 4

Michael Jones, MS, RPh, reviews Samuel Robinson's medical record and other sources of information

Michael Jones is trying to establish an accurate medication use history about Samuel Robinson. He reviews several health record documents and assesses what he learns from each. He needs to find additional information. Practice determining what other sources of data exist in the health record to gain the knowledge required for Michael Jones.

Michael Jones goes to the nursing station area where the patient's medical record and medications from home are located. (Medications brought from home are not allowed to be administered in the hospital per policy and are stored under lock and key and returned to the patient upon discharge.) He decides to first review the Nurses Admission Database and the Laboratory Test Order Form (see **Figures 6-11 and 6-12**). He knows that this form contains much of the demographic and economic information. He examines the medications in the bag from home and finds the following:

Synthroid 125 mcg orally every day

Warfarin 5 mg orally every day Monday through Saturday

Vitamin E 1,000 I.U. orally every day

Digoxin 0.25 mg orally every day

Clonidine 0.5 mg orally every day

Hydrochlorothiazide 25 mg orally every day

Dofetilide 250 mcg orally two times a day

Aspirin 81 mg orally every day

After looking at all of these sources of information, he determines that there is a discrepancy between the Nurses Admission Database and the medication container for warfarin about the daily dose. He is concerned about the dosing of warfarin that needs to be initiated in the hospital. He also notes that the vitamin E is 1,000 I.U.s—and that this is a pretty large dose. The bottle containing Synthroid is nearly full, even though the date on the medication label of the bottle is from 3 months ago.

NURSING ADMISSION DATABASE	NOTE: ENTRIES DOCUMENTED IN PENCIL ARE NOT CONSIDERED PART OF THE PERMANENT RECORD. (TRANSCRIBE IN PEN)	
A. ADMISSION INFORMATION ☐A.M. ☐P.M. ADMISSION DATE: _____ TIME: _____ ADM. FROM: _____ VIA: _____ REASON FOR ADM: Acute asthma ANTICIPATED DISCHARGE DATE: _____ CONTACT IF NECESSARY: REL. _____ PHONE (H) _____ PHONE (W) _____ REL. _____ PHONE (H) _____ PHONE (W) _____ PERSONAL BELONGINGS/HEALTH AIDES: ☐ DENTURES ☐ GLASSES ☐ PACEMAKER ☐ PROSTHESIS ☐ WALKING AIDS ☐ CONTACT LENSES ☐ HAIRPIECE ☐ HEARING AIDS PT./FAMILY INSTRUCTED: ☐ INTERCOM ☐ BATHROOM ☐ LIGHTS ☐ MEALTIMES ☐ CHAPLAINCY SVC. ☐ HELPLINE ☐ SMOKING PLICY ☐ BED CONTROLS ☐ VISITING HOURS ☐ JEWELRY (LIST INDIVIDUAL ITEMS, STATE BRAND NAMES IF APPLICABLE): ☐ MONEY (ENCOURAGE NO MORE THAN $20) AT BEDSIDE): $ _____ INFORMATION OBTAINED FROM: _____ ORGAN DONOR: Completed by R.N. Ask only adult patients admitted to adult medical/surgical Units. ARE YOU AN ORGAN DONOR? ☐ YES ☐ NO ORGAN(S) DONATED: _____ SMOKE: ☐ YES x NO HOW MUCH? _____ ALCOHOL: ☐ YES x NO HOW MUCH? _____ SUBSTANCE ABUSE: ☐ YES x NO HOW MUCH? _____ ALLERGIES/SENSITIVITIES – TYPE & REACTION: _____ **PLACE ALLERGY INFORMATION ON ARMBAND AND M.A.R.** RELIGION: _____ The above information has been explained to me. It is accurate and I understand. I also understand that I have been advised the hospital is not responsible for valuables kept at bedside. PATIENT/FAMILY SIGNATURE _____ UNIT PERSONNEL _____ RISK/FALL ASSESSMENT: ☐ NOT AT RISK ☐ AT RISK IF AT RISK, COMPLETE RISK/FALL ASSESSMENT SHEET PRE-ULCER ASSESSMENT: ☐ NOT AT RISK ☐ AT RISK IF AT RISK, COMPLETE PRE-ULCER RISK ASSESSMENT SHEET	**B. PHYSICAL PROFILE** ADMISSION VITAL SIGNS: BP _____ T _____ P _____ R _____ HEIGHT _____ WEIGHT _____ DIET: _____ MEDICATIONS: (DISPOSITION ☐ HOME ☐ PHARMACY ☐ OTHER _____ HISTORY OF PRESENT ILLNESS: PAST MEDICAL HISTORY: (MAJOR ILLNESSES, SURGERIES, OTHER TREATMENTS, FAMILY HISTORY, NEUROLOGICAL, MUSCULOSKELETAL, CARDIOVASCULAR, GI, RENAL, RESPIRATORY, AND ENDOCRINE CONDITIONS. INCLUDE DATES)	**C. DISCHARGE PLANNING CRITERIA** The following are High Risk Criteria for discharge planning, check all that apply: x AGE OVER 65 ☐ TRANSFERRED FROM A NURSING HOME ☐ FOLLOWED BY COMMUNITY AGENCY PRIOR TO ADMISSION ☐ HISTORY OF REPEATED ADMISSIONS x ELDERLY PATIENT WHO LIVES ALONE ☐ ALTERED MENTAL STATE ☐ HISTORY OF DRUG OR ALCOHOL ABUSE x NO FAMILY MEMBERS AVAILABLE TO PT. ☐ NO METHOD OF PAYMENT x FINANCIAL DIFFICULTIES REQUIRING INTERVENTION ☐ HIGH LEVEL OF ACUITY WITH POOR PROGNOSIS ☐ VICTIM OF ABUSE OR NEGLECT ☐ ADM. DIAGNOSIS OF FAILURE TO THRIVE OR LIFE-THREATENING ILLNESS ☐ NONCOMPLIACNE ☐ HISTORY OF PHYSICAL OR MENTAL ABUSE ☐ DIAGNOSIS REQUIRING FOLLOW-UP TREATMENT, TEACHING OR REFERRAL ADL'S: ☐ INDEPENDENT ☐DEPENDENT – SPECIFY: LIVES WITH: alone SUPPORTIVE FAMILY: ☐ YES ☐ NO PRIMARY CAREGIVER: neighbots ☐ NO REFERRALS NEEDED INITIAL SCREENS OBTAINED PT./FAMILY SVCS. _____ ☐ NURSING CONSULTANTS _____ ☐ PT/OT/ST _____ ☐ DIETARY _____ ☐ FINANCIAL COUNSELOR _____ ☐ ADM. NURSE SIGNATURE: _____
DATE ADMITTED	ROOM/BED	NAME: Robinson, Samuel	AGE: Born in 1928	SEX: male	M.D.

Figure 6-11. Nurses Admission Database for Samuel Robinson

| REQUIRED PATIENT INFORMATION | **Memorial Hospitals and Health Systems** |

REQUIRED PATIENT INFORMATION

Last Name: ROBINSON First Name: SAMUEL Middle Initial:

Date of Birth: 11 / 23 / 1935 Sex: X M ☐ F Patient I.D. 02946372

SSN: 680-12-3927 Phone: (901) 468-4832

Bill To: ☐ Our Account (No further information is needed).
  X Patient Insurance (The following must be completed or your account will be billed.)

Patient's Marital Status (Circle One): S M D (W)

Responsible Party
  Name:
  Address: 1362 MOCKINGBIRD LANE
  City: BILOXI State: MS Zip: 78023

  SSN: ___-___-_____ Relationship to Patient: SELF

Primary Insurance Information
  Insurance Co. Name:
  Address:
  X Medicare ☐ Medicaid ☐ Insurance No.:
  Group No.:
  Primary Care Physician (if other than ordering physician):
  Secondary Insurance Information: Attach separate sheet
  Check if this incident involves: ☐ Worker's Comp ☐ Litigation
  Are ABN's, Referrals or Waivers needed for this billing? X No ☐ Yes (Attach Copy)

Diagnosis #1 **CHF**   Diagnosis #2 **DVT prophy**   Diagnosis #3

Specimen Information
Collection Date: ___/___/____ Time: ___ ☐ PM ☐ AM
IF APPLICABLE
☐ Fasting X Therapeutic Drugs Phlebotomist's ID _____
Time of last dose: __PTAdmit__ ☐ AM ☐ PM
Handling: ☐ Room Temp ☐ Refrigerated
  ☐ Frozen ☐ Spun-Down
☐ Perform **STAT**
  ☐ Phone Results to
  ☐ Fax Results to #

	Panel Tests (Defined on Back)								
x	Basic Metabolic (S)	x	Lipid (S)		x	Hemogram (incl. plt/no diff) (L)			
x	Comprehensive (S)		Obstetrics*(R,L,S)			Hepatitis A IgM Ab(S)			
	Electrolytes (S)	x	Renal Function (S)			Hepatitis B Core Ab (HBcAb) (S)			
	Hepatic (S)					Hepatitis B Surface Ab (HBsAb) (S)			

Hemoglobin A_1C (L)

	Individual Tests
x	Albumin (S)
	Alkaline Phosphatase (S)
	ALT (SGPT) (S)
	ANA (Anti-nuclear AB) (S)
	AST (SGOT) (S)
	Bilirubin, Direct (S)
	Bilirubin, Total (S)
	BUN (S)
	Calcium (S)
	CBC (incl. hemogram/plt/diff)*(L)
	Cholesterol, HDL (S)
	Cholesterol, LDL Direct Measure (S)
	Cholesterol, Total (S)
	Creatinine (S)
	Creatinine Clearance (S, 24U)
	Digoxin (R)
	Electrophoresis (includes interpretation)
	Hemoglobin L Serum R Urine U or 24 U
	GGTP (S)
x	Glucose (S)
	Glucose Tolerance (Pregnant? Yes/No) (S)
	HCG Qualitative (S)
	HCG Quantitative (S)

Hepatitis B Surface Ag (HBsAg)* (S)
Hepatitis C AB (HCV Ab) (S)
HIV-1/HIV-2 Abs (Consent Form Required)* (S)
Lead ☐ Venous (T) ☐ Capillary (LM)
Lymph Immune Markers (1L)
Room Temp Draw M-Th: call for STAT PICK-UP
Mononucleosis Screen (S)
Occult Blood (Source)_____
Phosphorus (S)
Potassium (S)
x Prealbumin (S)
Protein, Total, Serum (S)
Protein, Total, Urine (U or 24U)
PSA (Medically Indicated) (S)
PSA (Screening) (S)
x PT (Pt. on Coumadin X Yes ☐ No) LB
PTT (Pt. on Heparin ☐ Yes ☐ No) (LB)
Rheumatoid Factor (S)
Rubella (S)
Sedimentation Rate (ESR) (L)
Sodium (S)
Syphilis Serology *(S)
Triglycerides (S)
Triple Screen [complete form]

	Acct No.	Fin Class	Specimens Rcvd	Bar Code Label
x	TSH (S)			
	Uric Acid			
	Urinalysis (w/o microscopy)* U			
	Additional Tests			

Microbiology/Virology*
(Use line provided to identify source)
AFB Culture_____
Anaerobic Culture_____
Chlamydia PCR_____
Gonorrhea PCR_____
Chlamydia Culture_____
Gonorrhea Culture_____
C. Difficile Toxin_____
Fungus Culture_____
Giardia Antigen_____
Herpes Culture_____
Influenza A Antigen_____
Ova & Parasites_____
Respiratory Culture_____
RSV Antigen_____
Stool Culture_____
Stool Rotavirus Antigen_____
Throat, Beta Strep Culture_____
Rapid Strep Screen, Throat_____
Viral Culture_____
  Agent_____
Wound Culture_____
Urine Culture_____
  Method of collection_____
Other Culture_____

Total No. of Tests Checked

L=Lavender Top Tube (EDTA)   LB=Light Blue Top Tube (Sodium Citrate)(Tube must be completely full)
LM=Lavender Top (EDTA)
R=Red Top Tub (Plain Clot)   T=Tan Top Tube (K2 EDTA 5.4 mg)
S=Spun Unopened Barrier Tube (SST)   U=Random Urine
24U = 24 HR Urine Collection

Figure 6-12. Laboratory Test Order Form for Patient Samuel Robinson

CASE-SPECIFIC QUESTIONS

1. Identify two other information sources that Michael Jones might use to determine what the correct regimen for warfarin was supposed to be just prior to Mr. Robinson's admission to the hospital.

REFERENCES

1. Ball M, Smith C, Bakalar R. Personal health records: empowering consumers. *Journal of Healthcare Information Management*. 2007; 21(1):76–86.

2. Jones S. The Internet goes to college. Pew Internet and American Life Project. Washington, DC. http://www.pewinternet.org/pdfs/PIP_College_Report.pdf. Accessed September 20, 2007.

3. Pricewaterhouse Coopers. Health reform lays ground for new era of individualized care and more patient-focused health system; 2010. Available at: http://www.prnewswire.com/news-releases/health-reform-lays-ground-for-new-era-of-individualized-care-and-more-patient-focused-health-system-says-pricewaterhousecoopers-in-new-healthcast-report-89976312.html.

4. www.hhs.gov/valuedriven/.

5. Van De Belt TH, Engelen LJ, Berben SAA, et al. Definition of health 2.0 and medicine 2.0: a systematic review. *J Med Internet Res*. 2010; 12(2):e18. Available at: http://www.jmir.org/2010/2/e18/; doi: 10.2196/jmir.1350; PMID: 20542857.

6. Institute of Medicine. To err is human: building a safer health system. Available at: http://books.nap.edu/catalog.php?record_id=9728. Accessed September 2, 2007.

7. Bates D, Deering MS, Leavitt M. E-pharmacy: improving patient care and managing risk. *J Am Pharm Assoc*. 2002; 42(suppl 1):S20–1.

8. Bush Administration: Executive order: incentives for the use of health information technology and establishing the position of the National Health Information Technology Coordinator. Available at: www.whitehouse.gov/news/releases/2004/04/20040427-4.html. Accessed September 2, 2007.

9. Downard S, Galt KA, Reel AB. Pharmacists' use of electronic health records: Silent leaders no more. *Journal of the American Pharmacists Association*. 2008; 47(6):680–92.

10. United States Department of Health and Human Services. Nationwide Health Information Network (NHIN): Overview. Available at: http://healthit.hhs.gov/portal/server.pt?open=512&mode=2&cached=true&objID=1142. Accessed June 21, 2010.

11. Berry A, Bramble J, Galt K, et al. Pharmacists' views on health care information interoperability and privacy. *Nebraska Mortar & Pestle*. 2007; 70(3):18–9.

12. Berens D, Galt KA. Report 1: survey of health/licensure/certification and facilities oversight board managers. Available at: http://chrp.creighton.edu/Documents/HISPC_Report_1.pdf. Accessed September 3, 2007.

13. Dimitropoulos LL. Interim assessment of variation: privacy and security solutions for interoperable health information exchange: RTI project no. 0209825.000.004.002. Chicago, IL: RTI International; 2006.

14. American Society of Health-System Pharmacists. ASHP long-range vision for the pharmacy work force in hospitals and health systems. *Am J Health-Syst Pharm*. 2007; 64:1320–30.

15. Galt KA. Credentialing and privileging for pharmacists. *Am J Health-Syst Pharm*. 2004; 61:661–70.

16. Lowes R. Personal health records: what's the status now? *Medical Economics*. 2006; 83(4):TCP13–4.

17. The IOM report is available at: www.nap.edu/catalog.php?record_id=10027.

18. Connection for Health's Common Framework documents are available at www.connectingforhealth.org.

19. Tang P, Ash J, Bates D, et al. Personal health records: definitions, benefits, and strategies for overcoming barriers to adoption. *J Am Med Inform Assoc*. 2006; 13:121–6.

20. Ball MJ, Smith C, Bakalar RS. Personal health records: empowering consumers. *J Health Inf Manag*. 2006; 21(1):76–86.

21. Markle Foundation Connecting for Health. Americans want benefits of personal health records. Available at: http://www.connectingforhealth.org/resources/phwg_survey_6.5.03.pdf. Accessed May 2009.

22. Harris Interactive. Two in five adults keep personal or family health records and almost everybody thinks this is a good idea. *HealthCare News*. 2004; 13(4):1–5. Available at: http://www.harrisinteractive.com/news/newsletters/healthnews/HI_HealthCareNews2004Vol4_Iss13.pdf. Accessed May 2009.

23. Albright B. Prepping for PHRs: the growing trend of consumer empowerment includes the speedy rise of personal health records. *Health Inform*. 2007; 44–6.

24. United States Department of Veterans Affairs. MyHealth eVet. Available at: http://www.myhealth.va.gov. Accessed June 2009.

25. Project HealthDesign Overview. Available at: http://www.projecthealthdesign.org/about/overview. Accessed May 2009.

26. American Society of Health-System Pharmacists. Executive summary of the continuity of care in medication use summit. *Am J Health-Syst Pharm.* 2007; 65:e3-e9.

27. Bubalo J, Clark RK Jr, Jing SS, et al. Medication adherence: pharmacist perspective. *J Am Pharm Assoc.* 2003; 50:394–406.

28. Rakel E. *Essentials of Family Practice.* Philadelphia, PA: W.B. Saunders; 1993.

29. Shepherd MF. *Module 1: Reviewing Patient Medical Records, in ASHP Clinical Skills Program—Advancing Pharmaceutical Care.* Bethesda, MD: American Society of Health-System Pharmacists; 1992.

30. Mason NA, Shimp LA. *Module 2: Building a Pharmacist's Patient Database, in ASHP Clinical Skills Program—Advancing Pharmaceutical Care.* Bethesda, MD: American Society of Health-System Pharmacists; 1993.

31. Shimp LA, Mason NA. *Module 3: Constructing a Patient's Drug Therapy Problem List, in ASHP Clinical Skills Program—Advancing Pharmaceutical Care.* Bethesda, MD: American Society of Health-System Pharmacists; 1993.

32. Jones W, Campbell S. *Module 4: Designing and Recommending a Pharmacist's Care Plan, in ASHP Clinical Skills Program—Advancing Pharmaceutical Care.* Bethesda, MD: American Society of Health-System Pharmacists; 1993.

33. Frye CB. *Module 5: Monitoring the Pharmacist's Care Plan, in ASHP Clinical Skills Program—Advancing Pharmaceutical Care.* Bethesda, MD: American Society of Health- System Pharmacists; 1993.

34. Galt KA. *Module 1: Drug Information: Analyzing and Recording a Drug Information Request, in ASHP Clinical Skills Program—Advancing Pharmaceutical Care.* Bethesda, MD: American Society of Health-System Pharmacists; 1994.

35. Smith GH, Norton LL, Ferrill MJ. *Module 2: Drug Information: Evaluating Drug Literature, in ASHP Clinical Skills Program—Advancing Pharmaceutical Care.* Bethesda, MD: American Society of Health-System Pharmacists; 1995.

36. Galt KA, Calis KA, Turcasso NM. *Module 3: Preparing a Drug Information Response, in ASHP Clinical Skills Program—Advancing Pharmaceutical Care.* Bethesda, MD: American Society of Health-System Pharmacists; 1995.

Drug Information and Evidence-Based Practice

"Science is taught as if its facts were somehow superior to the facts in other scholarly disciplines, even though every field of science is incomplete."
—Dr. Lewis Thomas

CHAPTER OUTLINE

Purpose

Evidence-Based Practice
- Origins of Drug Information Requests

Determining the Patient's Care Needs
- Gathering Background Information
- Gathering Drug Information and Published Evidence
- Evaluating the Literature for Quality and Reliability
- Gathering Expert Opinions

Incorporating Evidence in the Patient Care Plan

Summary

Assessment Questions

Pharmacist–Patient Encounter with Our Four Cases
- Case 1: Lauren Smith calls Nasir Jabr, PharmD, RPh; *Nasir Jabr seeks evidence in response to Lauren Smith's question.*
- Case 2: Christine Johnston, PharmD, RPh; *Christine Johnston investigates the evidence about the use of herbal remedies for diabetes based upon her interview with Mr. Montanez and Maria.*
- Case 3: Luisa Rodriguez, PharmD, RPh; *Luisa Rodriguez investigates the ingredients and use of Bai Guo Ye.*
- Case 4: Michael Jones, MS, RPh; *Michael Jones evaluates the literature about the significance of Mr. Robinson's vitamin E use and warfarin.*

OBJECTIVES

To gain knowledge of:

1. how to use drug information in evidence-based practice;
2. how to determine drug information needs in patient care situations;
3. how to formulate and communicate evidence-based responses in practice;
4. reliable, high-quality information sources to consult for drug information needs;
5. how to systematically search to retrieve drug information and evidence;
6. the application of clinical decision support systems to evidence-based practice;
7. the influence of health informatics on information access and retrieval; and
8. the use of expert opinion in evidence-based practice.

PURPOSE

The purpose of this chapter is to assist you in understanding and developing the evidence-based practice skills you need to provide patient care. You will be introduced to the skills needed to respond to information requests from patients and other providers, gain a working knowledge of available resources, and learn how to select information relevant to the patient's needs. Selecting high-quality, reliable, and relevant

*All of the appendixes for this chapter can be found on the web at www.ashp.org/patientcare.

information for use in a timely manner is the key to this area of practice expertise. Use of drug information resources distinguishes your professional expertise and contribution to patient care from other health professionals. Performing this skill well is one way in which you uniquely contribute to the care of patients who require medication therapy management.

EVIDENCE-BASED PRACTICE

A common professional service you provide as a pharmacist is expert information about drug therapies and treatments. To do it well, you must distinguish between serving as an expert information resource (such as a medical librarian) and providing a clinical recommendation that meets the needs of the patient. The latter is the essence of evidence-based practice. Evidence-based practice is an approach to health care practice where the clinician is aware of the evidence in support of a particular practice, the strength of that evidence, and the appropriate application of that evidence to the practice in the context of the patient's characteristics, culture, and preferences, interpreted through your prior experiences as a clinician. When you practice using evidence, you combine the use of your own clinical expertise with the best available published evidence yielded from systematic research of the literature, also referred to as a systematic review. The best available published evidence supports your decision about what treatments are effective under the specific circumstances that you are considering for the patient's needs. Your understanding of the patient's preferences and cultural needs are part of the considerations and your own prior experiences provide a framework and context for understanding the relevance of the evidence.[1,2]

Evidence-based practice was born from its predecessor, evidence-based medicine, a little over 2 decades ago. An evidence-based practitioner must be able to understand the patient's circumstances and needs; understand what knowledge remains to be attained to help the patient; frame this knowledge gap in the form of questions to be answered through a literature search, to critically appraise the research evidence; and apply that evidence to the individual patient. Two fundamental principles guide this process. The first accepts there is a hierarchy of evidence to guide clinical decision making. The second recognizes that persons who make the decisions must weigh the benefits and risks, inconvenience, and costs of alternative management strategies in the context of the patient's values.[3]

What is a systematic review? This is a review of the literature that summarizes the results of several studies that represent the highest quality and most relevant research about the question of relevance you are asking. Procedures are outlined for common use to find, evaluate, and synthesize the results of the relevant research. The procedures are designed to minimize the bias of the findings and are described in a way that they can be replicated. The review process identifies clear inclusion and exclusion criteria for the study selection, explicit searching strategy, systematic coding and analysis of the included studies, and meta-analysis when appropriate for the types of studies. A systematic review conducted in this manner is described as having a peer review process, as the literature review is generally conducted by qualified and independent researchers who are assessing the published author's methods and results during the selection and use phase of the literature review.

To effectively engage in evidence-based practice, you have to possess the ability to conduct a relevant literature search, have access to resources to do it, and have the skills to review and synthesize the findings into a relevant form for use. A strong foundation in methodological knowledge is needed to understand and conduct an appraisal of studies. Evidence is regarded as stronger or weaker and is evaluated for quality based upon the principles of sound research design and methods. Knowing how to access and use key information sites that support the technology of evidence-based practice is of great benefit to your efficiency and expertise.

> **KEY POINT**
>
> **A strong foundation in methodological knowledge is needed to understand and conduct an appraisal of studies.**

How do you search, select, and apply use of the medical literature when every few years the literature doubles in size, and you have less and less time to evaluate it for use? How do you search the literature when you have limited time? Research about searching the literature to find answers from the clinician perspective revealed three challenges: (a) inadequate time to search for information; (b) failure of the resource to address the topic; and (c) inadequate synthesis of multiple bits of evidence into a clinically useful statement.[4] The goal is to develop an approach so that each of us in practice may become fluent in use of the medical literature to access what is relevant and then assess its quality and its applicability to a specific patient. This is a young science. As it develops, tools and guides for how to do this form of practice are evolving. Social policy is continuing to mature and advance evidence-based practice through improving the infrastructure to facilitate both the quality of information and the efficiency of access.[5,6]

Scholars are continuing to improve the pragmatic approaches to use of evidence. The most widely recognized tool to aid practitioners in these skills is the Users' Guides Series in the *Journal of the American Medical Association*. A series of 33 articles published in a span of a decade set the standards internationally. The series is now in the form of a published book and continuously updated web site called "JAMA Evidence." Other popular sources include the Cochrane Collaboration focusing on medical and mental health treatments, the Campbell Collaboration emphasizing social and behavioral interventions, the Agency for Healthcare Research and Quality focusing on health care outcomes, and the National Guideline Clearinghouse offering treatment guidelines. Using an evidence-based practice approach helps you to keep your knowledge up to date and augments your clinical judgment. It can ultimately save time and improve the care of your patients.[7]

KEY POINT

Evidence-based resource web sites to assist you in practice:
- "JAMA Evidence" (http://www.jamaevidence.com/index)
- Cochrane Collaboration (www.cochrane.org)
- Campbell Collaboration (www.campbellcollaboration.org)
- Agency for Healthcare Research and Quality (www.ahrq.gov)
- National Guideline Clearinghouse (www.guideline.gov)

Origins of Drug Information Requests

Requests for information come from people with a wide range of backgrounds and in a multitude of settings. Such requests commonly originate from physicians, nurses, patients, the public, and other pharmacists. Requests also come from other health professionals such as physical or respiratory therapists, dietitians, psychologists, and social workers. When you receive a request, you should first note the date and time that you received it, who you received it from, and the route of communication by which it was received (telephone, in writing, or in person). Documentation assists you in "keeping track" of the circumstances surrounding a request and in meeting the turnaround time required for a useful response. You should obtain the name and phone or fax number of the individual requesting information. By also knowing this individual's professional background, you can sometimes determine the complexity of the information required. Be sure to ask the affiliation and title of the individual so you can reply in writing, if required. It takes a few extra minutes to gather this information; however, it may make the difference in accurately and promptly responding. The process becomes efficient once you have established professional relationships with your patient or health care colleagues.

Compared to requests from other professionals or patients, physicians often require more extensive knowledge and literature support to substantiate a response. For example, imagine that you are in the outpatient pharmacy when you receive a telephone call from a psychiatrist. He states, "I'm trying to write a discharge prescription for Mr. Cook on 3B. What is the maximum dose of propranolol I can give him?" To answer this question correctly, you will have to gather patient-specific information such as indication for use, age, concurrent diseases, and other medications being taken. Your response may include advice not only on dose but also on route, frequency of administration, duration of therapy, and caution for patients with diabetes and/or pulmonary disease. Be prepared to discuss other alternatives if your conversation results in a change in care. If your response requires multiple references, inform the physician about them.

Conversely, answers to some questions may require your existing professional knowledge without additional literature searching. Suppose that a nurse stops you in the hallway to ask, "Is it possible for patients who are on captopril to get hypotension?" The nurse further explains that an elderly black male patient was started on a regimen of captopril 25 mg taken orally every 8 hours about 5 days ago, and his blood pressure was 90/54 mm Hg this morning. You probably will not need to substantiate your response to this information request with additional expert resources. Your clinical knowledge and experience should suffice.

Pharmacy technicians often seek information from pharmacists to advance their own knowledge and to confirm the correct way to perform tasks. However, when a technician requests information for someone else, you should provide this information directly to that person, rather than through the technician as an intermediary individual. Technicians often need your assistance to determine when an information request is within their scope of practice. It is your responsibility to teach them an appropriate referral technique to make sure you interact directly with the persons seeking information.

Caution should be used when responding to requests from lawyers, journalists, or health care administrators from other organizations. Although this text is intended to develop your skills in answering patient-specific requests, there are a few valuable points to remember. You are not required to respond. It is important to assess whether you even have the right to respond to these requests with any level of disclosure. They may be seeking information that violates a patient's rights or is proprietary. You should always check with the patient or his or her representative even if you have the right to respond. Similarly, you should check with the appropriate individual in your organization if the request is of a proprietary nature. You should establish the motive for initiation of the request. In general, your primary responsibility is to protect the rights and proprietary information of the patients and/or health care organization you are serving.

The individuals to whom you commonly provide drug information and the frequency of such requests depend on your practice setting and your primary practice responsibilities. If you are a hospital staff pharmacist, you frequently respond to requests from other health professionals, administrators, and technicians. If you participate in medication history taking, discharge counseling, and drug therapy monitoring in a decentralized setting, you often answer questions from patients and caregivers directly. Pharmacists in ambulatory, home care, and extended care settings frequently respond to drug information requests from patients and caregivers as well as professional staff. Health care administrators, who may or may not have training as health care providers, frequently ask drug information questions. You need to identify the person's level of knowledge before formulating your response.

Patients usually ask questions to whoever is accessible to them. In the hospital setting they will often ask the nurse who is most frequently present and in contact with them. Frequently, patients will ask questions of pharmacists if the pharmacist is available in the patient care area and meets the patient. In the community setting the patients often approach clerical staff members that come to you for answers. Educate them to direct patient questions to you (or another pharmacist) so that you can determine the true nature of the request and your ability to answer it. Information requests from patients usually are specific to themselves or to a personal friend or relative. Patients may be asking for information only. However, patients frequently seek advice or affirmation on a directive given by another provider. In all cases, you must understand the nature of the patient's request before responding.

CASE EXAMPLE

How to Respond to a Patient's Request for Information at the Time of Hospital Discharge

You are counseling Mr. Horton, a male patient, about discharge medications. He asks, "Is it okay to take my warfarin in the morning when I come home from work instead of at 5 p.m.? I know that the doctor told me to take it at 5 p.m., but that's when I'm asleep. I start my evening shift at 9 p.m. and work until 7:30 a.m. I usually sleep from noon to 8 p.m. The physician was in such a hurry that I didn't want to interrupt her and ask about it."

To respond to this patient's request, you must evaluate his total drug therapy regimen, counsel him on all medications, and contact his physician to discuss the change in care plan away from the physicians' initial instructions. This seemingly simple question is actually a request for information and advice that on face value differs from his physician's instructions.

You respond "Mr. Horton, I believe this should be okay providing that you take the medication at the same time each day, including the days you do not work. I first must look at all of the medications you are taking to make sure we do not have any interactions that would be harmful. I also would like to contact Dr. Kucera to discuss the change. In this way, I will make sure that we have taken into consideration what she thinks we need to consider as well."

The patient replies, "Thank you for checking on this for me. It will really be a problem for me at work if I do not get a regular night's sleep and have to wake up every afternoon after falling asleep for a couple of hours. I don't think I can keep up with this medicine if that is what I need to do."

You place a call to the patient's physician to discuss the treatment plan.

Requests for information may come via telephone, in person, in writing, by facsimile, or through electronic mail. All requests, regardless of source or route, should be treated professionally and followed through to completion.

DETERMINING THE PATIENT'S CARE NEEDS

The goal in determining the patient's care needs is to learn what is relevant to the patient's situation so that you can use an organized approach to ask the right questions, record your data, and provide valuable drug information. To accomplish this task, you need expert knowledge about the various types of drug information sources and how to search them productively. These sources are described later in the chapter along with the searching strategies needed to use them effectively. The remainder of this chapter will focus on the approach itself. Our assumption is that the requestor is seeking your expert knowledge and recommendation for a patient who needs care. Chapters 7 through 10 will illustrate how to integrate the use of expert information into clinical skills for patient care.

Gathering Background Information

When researching a patient-specific request, you must obtain precise patient data to respond appropriately to the clinical circumstances. Different kinds of patient-specific data are needed for different classifications of drug information requests. Discerning what is needed will improve the efficiency of your search. A general or basic set of data about a patient is required for all of these requests. Information that you should always seek includes patient name, age, height and weight, gender, race, diagnoses, allergies/intolerances, any present and past medical history, relevant laboratory data, and the physical location of the patient. These data may be obtained through the patient encounter, use of the medical chart, pharmacy records, pharmacy patient profile, laboratory data, and professionals caring for the patient, or family members and caregivers who are not health care professionals. **Figure 7-1** is an example of a documentation form to use for drug information requests. The form may be used for training or documentation purposes. It is organized in a way to help you master the skills of providing a drug information response, based upon a search of the evidence and available resources.

The patient database you assimilate to answer this request should provide you with enough information so that you can individualize your response and determine the urgency of care. If not readily available, gather as much information as you can before making a recommendation. If you do have access and sufficient time, retrieve additional data from the available sources. **Appendix 7-1** illustrates patient-specific data to collect, depending on the classification of the request. Although these examples may not be all inclusive, they convey the types of questions you should formulate.

Framing the Question. An effective search requires you to frame the question. Framing the question involves formulating it and determining how much time you have, classifying the question to guide your reference search, developing and conducting your search strategy, and preparing and documenting your response. As you learn the outcomes of your recommendations, you will gain greater confidence in your skills.

Formulate the Question and Determine the Timeframe for the Response. Make sure you have the question right. You should accurately restate the actual drug information need and timeframe required for a response based upon your background information. It will guide the remainder of your information search. When a request is received, you might assume that the information needs are immediate. This assumption can be frustrating if the answer requires great depth. But even in this situation, you should not provide a substandard answer. Instead, you should gather sufficient background information to feel as confident as possible about your response within the amount of time available.

Classify the Question. Next, you should classify the request using your organizational or personal classification scheme and identify how to access additional information. Classification will help you to determine your information resources for collecting patient-specific background information and literature data. Although organizations may have different classification systems, use of a systematic approach helps you to be thorough and less likely to overlook relevant resources. By classifying the request, you can determine what (1) further background information or patient history to gather, (2) preliminary reference sources to search, and (3) type and complexity of response to provide.

Appendix 7-1 provides a classification scheme that is commonly used in practice. For example, imagine that a nurse asks, "Does captopril cause hypotension?" After clarifying that the question is specific to a particular patient, you could classify this request in two categories: adverse drug reaction (ADR) and drug of choice/therapeutics/pharmacology. But because your response could result in changed drug therapy, you would need to gather more background information. The more complex or general the question, the more likely that multiple categories will apply.

Develop Your Searching Strategy. Classifying a request directs you to the appropriate references to search. Sources such as the captopril product insert and a tertiary drug information text may answer the nurse's request. Since this request is patient specific, you also will need information about the time order of events, frequency and severity of the patients' presentation, and usual management approaches. Specialized information resources about adverse reactions and general therapeutics texts for management guidelines will be essential. Moreover, you may be required to consult the medical literature and then evaluate the studies or case reports. A description of drug information sources and their characteristics are provided in **Appendix 7-2**, Tertiary Literature Content Matrix of Pharmacotherapeutic Characteristics. This description provides you with a quick decision tool for selecting the appropriate drug information sources based upon your classification. If you classify a request but information in that category is insufficient or inappropriate, you should reevaluate the classification. Be sure to find the best category or categories to get the information you need.

DRUG INFORMATION WORKSHEET

Date/Time Received_____ Person Receiving_____ How Received (phone, visit, etc)_____

Requester or Source Information

Name_____
Affiliation _____
Title_____

How to Reach_____
Phone #_____
Pager#_____
Fax #_____
Address_____

Who Requested (check one)
- ☐ MD
- ☐ MD Student
- ☐ RN
- ☐ Patient
- ☐ Physical/Respiratory Therapy
- ☐ Nutrition Support
- ☐ Secretary/Ward Clerk
- ☐ Other_____

Classification of Request
- ☐ Adverse Drug Reaction (ADR)
- ☐ Availability
- ☐ Compatibility/Stability
  (Chemical, Pharmaceutical, Sorption, Solubility, etc.)
- ☐ Compounding/Formulation
- ☐ Dosage/Schedule
- ☐ Drug Interactions
  (Drug-Drug, Drug-Lab, Drug-Disease, Drug Food)
- ☐ Drug of Choice/Therapeutics/Pharmacology
- ☐ Identification
- ☐ Method of Administration
- ☐ Pharmacoeconomics
- ☐ Pharmacokinetics
- ☐ Pregnancy/Lactation/Teratogenicity
- ☐ Poisoning/Toxicology
  (Environmental, Exposure, Occupational, Mutagenicity, Carcinogenicity)
- ☐ Odd Drug Entities and OTCs
  (Investigational, Orphans, Foreign Drugs, Chemical Substances, Homeopathic Remedies, Vitamin Substances, Herbs, etc.)
- ☐ Other _____

Patient Data

Name_____ Patient ID_____ Room/Bed Number or Location_____
Age_____ years_____ months Height ____ ft ____ in Setting (e.g., inpatient or outpatient) _____
Gender ☐male ☐female Weight____ lb ____ kg
Race_____
Diagnosis _____ Allergies/Intolerances_____
Pertinent Medical History/Problem List_____

Pertinent Medication History_____

Pertinent Laboratory Values_____

Miscellaneous Information_____

The Request, Actual Drug Information Need, and Time Frame for Response

Original Questions/Notes_____
_____
_____
Clear Statement of Actual Drug Information Need _____

Figure 7-1. Sample Drug Information Worksheet to Research, Respond to, and Document the Responses to a Drug Information Request

Time Frame Required for Response_____

Record of Search/Notes

_____
_____
_____
_____
_____
_____
_____
_____
_____
_____
_____
_____

Clear Statement of Response

Clear Statement of Response_____
_____
_____
_____
_____

Response Written: ____documented in chart ____ memo   Response Oral: ____telephone follow-up ____ face to face

Outcomes

General:	Patient-Specific:
☐ More information requested	☐ More information requested
☐ Recommendation accepted	☐ Recommendation accepted
☐ Recommendation rejected	☐ Recommendation rejected
☐ Requester will call back with results/additional requests	☐ Requester will pass information on to patient
☐ Contributed to policy development	☐ Patient education provided
☐ Standard of practice (upheld or improved)	☐ Clinical Impact (+ / - / neutral)
☐ Improved efficacy	☐ Positive patient relations
☐ Improved compliance	☐ Estimated cost impact
☐ Assured safety	☐ None or
☐ Prevented potential medication error	☐ $_____; Describe:_____
☐ Prevented potential ADR	
☐ Estimated cost impact	☐ Probably life saving
☐ None or	☐ Other_____

Figure 7-1 (continued). Sample Drug Information Worksheet to Research, Respond to, and Document the Responses to a Drug Information Request

The correct order of searching for answers to questions, once classified, is to start with tertiary general references, then tertiary specialty references. If these sources do not provide adequate information, you should search secondary, then primary resources. To identify potentially relevant information sources, you usually begin a broad search of resources at the tertiary level. You evaluate the information to determine relevance to your specific information need, and focus your efforts within the tertiary sources until you are satisfied. If you determine that the information is not sufficient for your needs, you progress to secondary information sources. Once again, you start with a broad search and narrow it down to potentially relevant resources. You evaluate the content again; if it is not sufficient, move to primary sources. This systematic approach allows you to learn about the generally accepted information on a particular subject and the key vocabulary terms. By using these terms, you can search secondary sources. If abstracted information is inadequate, the primary literature can be obtained and evaluated. More details about these reference categories are provided later in this chapter.

Your primary objective is to find information that is clinically relevant to your patient. Determination of the actual drug information question, patient, and pertinent background data guide you to search selected resources. Factors that alter your searching approach include classification of the request, type of requester, and timeframe and depth of response required. Because of the numerous drug information resources, a skill you should retain is continuously learning about new sources and updates to the existing sources, and the data that each resource provides.

Keep a Record of Your Searching Strategy and What It Yields. When gathering drug information, you should keep track of your searching strategy and resources. These notes will help you to construct your final response. Furthermore, if a question arises regarding this information, you can efficiently refer to your notes. Be sure to document your personal communications with patients, caregivers, other professionals, and organization representatives (e.g., pharmaceutical company and Food and Drug Administration personnel). Record the names of the individuals you speak to and their phone numbers in case there is need for follow up.

Formulate Your Response and Document It. Be sure to record what you tell the requester, including a description of your recommendation. If your recommendations influence the requester to take a particular course of action in patient care, document it on the patient chart and/or the pharmacy profile, whichever is appropriate. If you solicit the feedback and opinion of another colleague or professional, you may also choose to document this source. It is customary to provide the actual recommendation in the patient's chart and to record it in a pharmacy documentation system maintained in many practice settings. If this is the case, you should document the route of communication you used to provide the response (verbally, in writing, or by facsimile). Also indicate if you documented the response in a progress note or patient consultation in the patient's medical chart. If your response is written, attaching a copy may be appropriate.

Outcomes. During the provision of care, you should reassess how a patient is responding as a result of your recommendations. If you are unable to observe the outcome directly, contact the original requester for follow up. You should document your observations about the patient's progress or other outcomes resulting from your recommendations.

Access to Additional Information. Patient information may be difficult to obtain if you cannot examine the patient's chart or consult the caregivers or patient. For this reason, you should try to obtain as much patient information as possible from the requester. If the patient is in your same inpatient, clinic, or home care setting, this information may be readily retrievable from current records.

In some situations, however, the patient information you may need is not known or documented. You may be asked, for example, to evaluate whether a patient has developed amiodarone-induced hepatotoxicity. If baseline liver function tests were never performed, you may be unable to determine the time order of events. If history of use of both alcohol and over-the-counter medication is unknown, you cannot rule out these factors. Furthermore, if the requester is unable to supply you with this information or it is inaccessible, this question cannot be answered satisfactorily.

In your response, therefore, you should explain that you are unable to answer this request but will provide as much information as possible. You also may need to classify this request as non-patient specific. After the reclassification, you can provide information from the literature about the usual presentation of amiodarone-induced hepatotoxicity without concluding that this patient experienced it. Furthermore, you may offer information about its management. A determination would be made after discussion with the requester about your limited information. If you decide that the patient should be treated as a "probably" case (patient probably has hepatotoxicity), you should restate the information request and reclassify it. This reclassification will enable you to design a new searching strategy.

Communication Skills for Identifying the Actual Question. Requesters often do not ask for the information they really want or need. Your task then—to search and identify the actual request—is not always straightforward. You must ask questions and listen carefully to learn what you need to know.

Questioning Strategies. Keep in mind that your goal is to clarify the actual question being asked. To assess its context, you must gather sufficient information. You can accomplish this task by using the different questioning techniques interchangeably discussed in Chapter 5: open-ended versus close-ended questioning, direct versus indirect questioning, and probing.

The amount of trust a person places in you will be established not only by the quality of your information but also by your professionalism, interest, and approach when responding to a request. If you solicit the necessary background information but then provide an answer "whenever you get around to it," your attitude will leave a bad impression and overshadow your hard work.

All of these questioning techniques may be used whether you are communicating with someone in person or over the telephone. However, with phone exchange, you lose most components of nonverbal communication except voice quality. Detailed conversations illustrating these techniques are in the cases at the end of this chapter. Let's examine some representative example questions and the interchange between the pharmacist and the requestor.

A pharmacist who works in inpatient care area 5D receives a telephone call from a physician. As illustrated in the following example, questions are asked in an illogical order resulting in inefficiency (i.e., details about the patient's characteristics are obtained before demographic information; information relevant to who provides patient care services).

Physician: "What is the dose of gentamicin?"

Pharmacist: "Is this question about a patient?"

Physician: "Yes."

Pharmacist: "How old is the patient?"

Physician: "He's a 59-year-old male."

Pharmacist: "How is his renal function?"

Physician: "His renal function is fine; no problems."

Pharmacist: "To determine a dose, I need to know renal function stability and his most recent serum creatinine, BUN, and weight."

Physician: "His renal function has been stable since he was hospitalized 5 days ago. I believe his serum creatinine was 1.2 yesterday, and his blood urea nitrogen was 15. He weighs about 73 kg."

Pharmacist: "Well, if his renal function is stable, I estimate his creatinine clearance to be around 68 ml/min. Has he been started on gentamicin yet or will this dose be his first?"

Physician: "He hasn't been started yet. I'd like to start him as soon as possible."

Pharmacist: "What is this patient's name and room number? I'll review his record and recommend a dose in his chart, if you like."

Physician: "Would you? Great. The patient's name is Mr. Martin, and he's in room 252 on unit 2D."

Pharmacist: "Oh, I didn't realize that the patient was on the second floor. Another pharmacist handles those patients; let me give you his name and pager number. In the meantime, I will contact him and review what we just discussed. He'll handle it from there. If you have any questions, you can page him."

In this case, the pharmacist gathered useful information by asking specific questions and probing for the facts to calculate a gentamicin dose. However, the questions were asked in an illogical order. This patient's location, for example, should have been determined at the beginning. Only after the pharmacist spent considerable time collecting information did he learn that the patient was not in his area of responsibility.

Now let us see what happens when a pharmacist does not adequately probe for information.

Physician: "What is the dose of gentamicin?"

Pharmacist: "Is this question about a specific patient?"

Physician: "Yes. I want to start him on gentamicin as soon as possible."

Pharmacist: "How much does he weigh?"

Physician: "About 75 kilos."

Pharmacist: "The usual loading dose for a man this size is 1.5–2 mg/kg, if you think he is close to his ideal body weight. His loading dose would be 110–150 mg. You would see a peak serum concentration of 4–10 mcg/ml. Have you calculated his creatinine clearance?"

Physician: "No. I haven't done that yet. But his renal function is stable."

Pharmacist: "His maintenance dose and schedule should be adjusted based on his creatinine clearance. I'll calculate them if you know his serum creatinine. How old is he?"

In this example, the pharmacist again did not establish the actual question. He assumed that the physician wanted him to recommend a dose of gentamicin for this patient. Instead, the pharmacist should have asked probing questions to decide if this patient should actually receive gentamicin. As a result, a dose of gentamicin was recommended. The dose also was not specific to achieve a particular peak/trough concentration based on an infectious disease indication.

Now, look at this same gentamicin dosing question from the perspective of a pharmacist who is inquisitive about its true purpose. The pharmacist demonstrates how to identify the actual question.

Physician: "What is the dose of gentamicin?"

Pharmacist: "Is this question for a specific patient?"

Physician: "Yes. The patient is Mr. Martin in room 252, up here on unit 2D."

Pharmacist: "What type of infection are you treating?"

Physician: "Well, the patient has most likely developed pneumonia. He came in with a pretty rapid onset of symptoms."

Pharmacist: "From what type of setting was the patient admitted? Do you think that he has a community-acquired infection or was he in a nursing home?"

Physician: "Right. He was at his own home. We think the most likely causative organism is strep. His sputum showed many gram-positive cocci in pairs and chains. The culture and sensitivity results are pending for blood culture; however, we want to start treatment empirically."

Pharmacist: "Well, if you truly suspect a community-acquired strep pneumonia, you should start with penicillin. How severe is the infection?"

Physician: "Oh, I'd describe it as moderately severe but progressing. We need to start treatment."

Pharmacist: "Under these circumstances, it is probably best to start with cephalosporin plus a macrolide or mono-therapy with a quinolone antibiotic. Is the patient allergic to penicillins or cephalosporins?"

Physician: "No, there's no documented allergy, and he denies it on history."

Pharmacist: "Based on this background information, what do you intend to treat with?"

Physician: "I will start empirically with a quinolone. What do you recommend?"

Pharmacist: "At this point I would like to have the pharmacist assigned to this patient care area prepare a recommendation for you. I will contact him and explain the situation. He will contact you shortly and request your countersignature on treatment orders."

In this example, the pharmacist asked pertinent questions to determine why the original request was being made. Moreover, key inquiries about the infection and its origins helped to determine that the original question was not needed. Gentamicin was clearly not the drug of choice in these circumstances, so the pharmacist could recommend more appropriate empiric therapy (i.e., quinolone).

Now, let us evaluate an example of a common occurrence in drug therapy communication. In this example, pharmacokinetic information is needed but not just drug dosing.

Physician: "What is the dose of gentamicin?"

Pharmacist: "Is this question about a specific patient?"

Physician: "Yes. The patient is Mr. Martin in room 252, up here on unit 2D."

Pharmacist: "What kind of infection are you treating?"

Physician: "We've isolated *Pseudomonas aeruginosa* in Mr. Martin's cerebrospinal fluid."

Pharmacist: "Is the patient already receiving gentamicin?"

Physician: "Yes, we've had him on high doses of gentamicin and cefepime parenterally for 48 hr with minimal response. We're confused because the culture and sensitivity results show that *Pseudomonas* is highly sensitive to gentamicin and cefepime. Does gentamicin get into the CSF very well?"

Pharmacist: "No. The problem is that the concentration of aminoglycosides in CSF, whether the meninges are inflamed or not, is low and unpredictable. If the patient needs to achieve therapeutic levels of gentamicin in the CSF, the drug should be administered intraventricularly."

Physician: "I've never been involved in a case where we've had to give a drug intraventricularly. How much does its administration change the dose of gentamicin?"

Pharmacist: "To be honest, it has been a while since I've dosed gentamicin intraventricularly. I know intraventricular administration changes the gentamicin dose, but I don't remember by how much. I'll do some checking, review the patient's records, and then make a recommendation in Mr. Martin's chart, if you'd like."

Physician: "Great. In fact, why don't you page me when you get everything? Since I'm not familiar with this area, I'd like you to go over it with me."

Pharmacist: "Sure, doctor. I'll do it right away and page you when I'm done. Could you please give me the patient's name and birth date? I'll make sure that the chart and additional patient data are available."

The pharmacist listened to the needs of the requester in this brief but effective discussion. With the first three questions, the pharmacist concluded that the request was patient specific, that the indication for the drug was appropriate, and that the patient had already started gentamicin therapy. By asking the third question, the pharmacist implied, "Why are you calling about dosing information for a patient already receiving the drug?" As a result, the requester offered detailed background information.

The next example again illustrates that the actual question is not expressed in the original request.

Physician: "What is the dose of gentamicin?"

Pharmacist: "Is this question about a specific patient?"

Physician: "Yes. Mr. Martin in room 252 on unit 2D."

Pharmacist: "Why do you need to know the dose of gentamicin?"

Physician: "I may have Mr. Martin on too high a dose. Yesterday's urinalysis had casts, and he's starting to dump protein. His urinary output has really dropped off over the last 2 days. Do you think this decrease is related to his gentamicin?"

Pharmacist: "It's likely. Patients on gentamicin, especially if they are dehydrated, are more susceptible to nephrotoxicity. Nephrotoxicity associated with gentamicin, actually all aminoglycosides, may present as tubular necrosis or increases in serum creatinine and blood urea nitrogen with a drop in the creatinine clearance. The urinary output can drop and protein, cells, and casts may be found in the urine. However, a drop in the urinary output is rarer than nonoliguric elevations in blood urea nitrogen."

Physician: "I guess I should discontinue the gentamicin. I have alternatives."

Pharmacist: "A reduction in dosage or discontinuation of therapy usually is recommended. It seems wise to discontinue therapy with reduction in urinary output. If you tell me what alternatives you're considering, I'll recommend one for this patient."

By asking an open-ended versus a direct question ("Why do you need to know the dose of gentamicin?"), the pharmacist encouraged the physician to offer more background information. The pharmacist then determined that an adverse drug reaction required a change in the management of this patient. Both the patient and physician were better served through this in-depth approach to identify the actual information need.

Gathering Drug Information and Published Evidence

Drug information sources are the cornerstone to your pharmacy practice. You are known for your expertise in information provision and its application to patient care as much as for your oversight of the medication-use process. Information sources warranting lifelong familiarity include those used by health care providers as well as those accessed by your patients—commonly referred to as consumer drug information sources.

Characteristics of Drug Information Sources for Health Care Providers. Traditionally, information sources used by health professionals have been classified as primary, secondary, or tertiary, based upon function and format. Having this knowledge of a source governs our searching strategies. With the information technology explosion, other sources have emerged for daily use (e.g., web-based search engines, online retrieval and handheld computer sources). These forms of information should not result in altering your searching approach, as we will describe in greater detail below. However, they should broaden your scope of inclusion in obtaining up-to-date information. **Figure 7-2** provides a visual explanation of how a research idea *should* become information that is relevant for use and how it migrates through the various peer-review and publisher-based resources as points of access for dissemination.

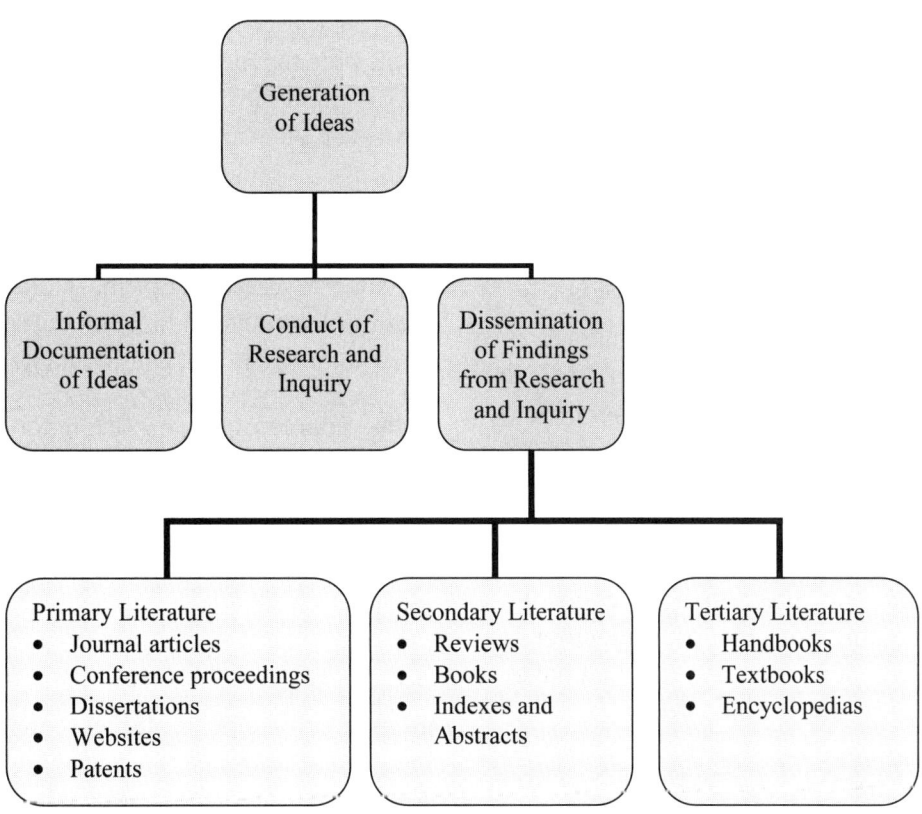

Figure 7-2. Scientific Information: The Process from Generation to Dissemination Starts with the Generation of an Idea, Discussion with Colleagues, or Presentations at Seminars or Forums with Eventual Documentation. A Journal Publication (Primary Literature) Is Usually Produced and Is Soon Reviewed and Abstracted, Summarized, and Indexed (Secondary Literature). Eventually the Literature Is Summarized and Included in Textbooks or Handbooks Once There Is Wide Spread Acceptance.

> **KEY POINT**
>
> With the information technology explosion, other sources have emerged for daily use (e.g., web-based search engines, online retrieval and handheld computer sources). These forms of information should not result in altering your searching approach, as we will describe in greater detail below.

Tertiary Sources. Frequently labeled general references, tertiary information sources highlight the widely accepted data from primary literature, evaluate this information, and publish the results. Tertiary sources include textbooks, reference books, handbooks and manuals, compendia, and pharmacopoeias. Commonly used general references are found in pharmacies; while a broad range of general references have traditionally been available only in drug information centers or health sciences libraries. Tertiary information sources are more limited yet practical for most information needs. One of the growing tertiary resource types is known as systematic reviews. The best known in that category is the Cochrane Collaboration. This international collaboration conducts systematic reviews of health care interventions and publishes them electronically. It is an example of a resource that is not likely to be detected through traditional searching strategies but may provide great utility depending upon your needs.

Another tertiary resource that has emerged as a result of the evidence-based movement in care is the clinical practice guideline. These guidelines provide steps to diagnosing or managing medical problems by integrating evidence with clinical experience. They are typically produced through consensus and published for wider use. Guidelines are usually produced under the direction of professional associations or organizations that come together to provide guidance on approaches to care that have the potential to be relatively standard.

Secondary Sources. Secondary information sources are frequently used to access the primary literature and usually consist of review articles or bibliographic citations. Most sources identify citations through a computer or "online" searching process. However, some do exist in print form. They are available as abstracting services, citations, indexes with and without full text, and directories. Secondary sources expedite the retrieval of information in the primary literature but are less current than primary literature. One of the biggest problems in drug information searching is the concept of "time lag." In recent years, the publication rate of primary literature has shortened, and the abstracting and cataloging of the literature into secondary searching sources has shortened considerably. The time lag for most secondary sources is now 4–8 weeks after primary resource publication. This shortened timeline substantially reduces the need to search primary information sources that are indexed in these secondary sources.

Primary Sources. Primary information sources are original published or unpublished works that introduce new knowledge or enhance existing knowledge on a subject. They include research results and case reports as well as evaluative and descriptive studies. Moreover, these sources are the foundation for secondary and tertiary literature. Primary sources provide the most accurate information because they contain the original communication of ideas. However, you cannot efficiently search for specific data, as you must go to each primary source for the needed information. It is important to note that not all primary sources are catalogued into secondary sources. Searching primary literature directly requires high-level skill when the secondary source does not provide sufficient, reliable information.

Online Sources. Online information sources are increasing in quantity and accessible via the Internet.[8] The Internet greatly increases the accessibility of online information sources and the rapidity of retrieval. However, searching online introduces less reliability of the information sources, depending upon the point of access. Points of access may be thought of as either general Internet searching engines or professional Internet searching engines. Using general Internet searching engines (e.g., Yahoo!, Alta Vista, Google, others) usually results in many sources that are not reviewed using traditional peer or editorial review processes associated with reputable information sources. Therefore, online searching may produce far more *unreliable* sources of information, requiring you to spend substantially more time distinguishing what is useful. If the point of access is through a professional secondary online source (e.g., Google Scholar, PubMed, Science Citation Index, Toxline, others), you will focus your access on the professional scholarly publications that are usually peer-reviewed and vetted for quality. It is important to keep in mind that there are many proprietary medical resources and databases. These resources are not accessible to search through the use of any search engines available on the Internet unless you purchase access through a subscription. A search engine can index only the material that it has access to and that it can search through and process.

Because databases have different characteristics, you must attain competency using each database individually to conduct your searches. This is true whether you are considering the general Internet or professional Internet resources. Common to all databases is 1) the use of the Boolean operator terms "and, or and not"; 2) the use of filters that limit the identification of resources based upon the criteria you select; and 3) a controlled vocabulary. All databases have a hierarchy of terms indexed; some provide a thesaurus for these terms and others do not. It is important that you become skilled at using these features for each database.

Your choice of using one search engine over another depends on the information you are looking for and the strengths and weaknesses of the search engines you are considering. The general Internet search engines of Google and Yahoo! include the contents of PubMed and other scholarly publishers as well as general public information sources. As a result, you have a mixture of sources to sort through in your search yield. PubMed confines its scope to the life sciences scholarly papers, and Google Scholar confines its scope to scholarly papers from all research fields published. Google Scholar and PubMed are the most used search engines of the professional Internet resources.

Google Scholar is one of over 150 domains within the Google search engine. Google is a corporation that makes information access to all free while supporting itself financially through investors and advertisements. The searching features of the Google domains are referred to as universal search technology, combining search results of different sources of information such as videos, images, maps, patents, and news articles along with scholarly works into one query. Google Scholar works with publishers of scholarly information to index peer-reviewed papers, preprints, abstracts, and technical reports from all disciplines of research to make them searchable. Google Scholar orders the results based upon an algorithm that assesses the relevance of the citations found to the query you have posed. This algorithm includes searching the full text of the article, the author, the publication in which it appeared, and how often it is cited in other published scholarly works. You can narrow your search in Google Scholar by using specific search terms rather than general terms as narrow as the author's name, publication dates, or specific publication name. Google Scholar also has an application that links a paper you have found to other papers that have cited it. A disadvantage of Google Scholar is that the product does not maintain a listing of sources that it has indexed. As a result, you cannot know what is not indexed or missing from a Google Scholar search.

PubMed is a free resource that is developed and maintained by the National Center for Biotechnology Information (NCBI) at the U.S. National Library of Medicine (NLM), located at the National Institutes of Health (NIH). Publishers of journals can submit their citations to NCBI and then provide access to the full text of articles at journal web sites. PubMed comprises over 20 million citations for biomedical literature from MEDLINE, life science journals, and online books. The information includes the fields of medicine, nursing, dentistry, veterinary medicine, the health care system, preclinical sciences, and web sites and links to the other NCBI molecular biology resources. PubMed is organized so you can limit your search by type of information you are seeking (such as human studies of therapy, diagnosis, etiology or prognosis) or types of research methods (such as clinical trials, quasi-experimental studies, meta-analyses or reviews).

Web Sites. What are these non-reviewed information sources? The emergence of web sites is one of the largest growing forms of information. Web sites commonly used by health professionals include those maintained by professional associations, pharmaceutical companies, and special interest groups. Appendix 7-2 provides a listing of many of these web sites that are relevant to patient-centered, evidence-based practice.

Availability of Journals Online. Publishing of traditional biomedical journals electronically in a paperless format is emerging as a common format. Costs associated with publishing and housing printed articles are becoming prohibitive for libraries and individuals. As a result, most major medical publishers are providing biomedical journal literature electronically. The format, appearance, and accessibility methods are affected by this medium. Potentially, increased access by individual users is tremendous. But there are no agreed-upon standards or methods to providing these publications electronically, thus most publishers are producing both electronic and print versions. Paperless publishing will become the primary, if not the sole, method for publishing in the near future.

Another emerging source that has rapidly diffused into practice is the availability of information resources via handheld computers. Appendix 7-2 also provides a listing of currently available products. Access to these information sources requires that a handheld device have connectivity to a host computer (connectivity can be accomplished through hot syncing or wireless transmission). Almost all sources are provided on a subscription basis to individuals. However, medical libraries are also sources if you have them in your community and have privileges to use the facilities. The most common form of these products are tertiary references that provide most of the core, basic practice information needed, replacing pocket books and what some call "peripheral brains." They will continue to be popular and diffuse as a standard method for accessing needed core information. The handheld device, when loaded with the appropriate software applications, can also serve as a point-of-care computer to receive primary literature sources and graphical information from secondary sources such as the National Library of Medicine PubMed product and others. Becoming comfortable with the handheld device is a good choice to continue advancing your skills in accessing needed information for routine practice. Increasingly, handheld devices are also being used to access patient information in some settings.

If we select and use information that has not gone through the peer review and publisher vetting processes, we greatly increase our risk of selecting research findings that have not been validated or determined reliable for the patient-specific need we are fulfilling. Or in other words, we may mis-apply evidence. It is this process that provides us with confidence in selection and use of the findings. It is now the case that the ready availability of tertiary, secondary, and primary sources at the point of care occurs simultaneously. This makes it very easy to by-pass the searching process that should be followed.

Consumer Drug Information Sources. Similar to health professionals, consumers are being bombarded with information via such resources as web sites, computer-based commercials, and direct-to-consumer advertising through all media. But the online global movement has made rapid access to all forms of information possible for consumers just as it has been for health professionals. A 2010 survey entitled, "The Pew Internet & American Life Project" surveyed American adults and found that 85% of adults use a cell phone; 17% have used their phone to look up health or medical information; 29% ages 18–29 have done such searches; and 15% of those ages 18–29 have software applications or "apps" on their phones that help them track or manage their health.[9] The ability of consumers to rapidly access information is changing the dynamics of the relationship between health professionals and patients.[10] Consumers access both the publicly available worldwide web as well as proprietary networks. In sum, you must be prepared to deal with the "informed" consumer through these new sources of information.

Evaluating the Literature for Quality and Reliability

The skills associated with both determining the quality and reliability of published information is commonly known as critical literature evaluation. A large body of literature exists that describes the skills necessary to evaluate and use published literature.[11-31] Several textbooks are published on this specific subject.[10,32-35] This chapter focuses on how to identify and retrieve the relevant information needed based upon the patient's needs and the information resource characteristics. However, representative tools to assist you with the skills of critical literature appraisal are presented in **Appendix 7-3**, Drug Information Tools and Checklists.

Reliability of Information—Relationship to Source.

A reliable source provides valid, truthful information. Reliability is a concern in both people and in published resources. In the case of persons, reliability varies with the expertise, knowledge, memory, trustworthiness, and motivation of a source. Reliability in published literature is dependent upon these same characteristics. However, an additional quality standard known as peer review is intended to capture questionable reliability. Peer review is a process that depends upon colleagues who have knowledge, training, and experience to critique and recommend inclusion and exclusion of materials and information to ensure accuracy, reliability, and quality. By considering both the source of your data and the circumstance of the relationship, you may assess the value and biases of your information.

Online information sources are of great concern when evaluated for reliability. You must use the same degree of care and concern when evaluating the quality of an Internet-based information source as you would if it were published in a reliable print source. However, this can be difficult, particularly when you must sort through the large number of resources usually identified. An organization known as Health on the Net Foundation was formed as an approval body to determine the reliability and credibility of information accessed on the Internet that is located through web sites. The organization publishing the web site applies for this approval and is able to post a symbol indicating they have received it. However, this is not a requirement of a web site.

Navigating Unreliable Information from Consumer/Patient Information Sources.

Some information obtained by consumers or patients is inaccurate. Increasingly, individuals are accessing a wide range of resources that do not have the quality assurances built in like professional resources. Nonetheless, consumers and patients bring this information to you to ask for your advice. You're in a good position to assess the information and make your expert recommendation. Patients are likely very receptive since they were seeking your assistance in the first place. However, if you are approached by a patient who clearly has decided that the information is going to guide his or her behaviors, then you can only advise the patient optimally with your current knowledge and expertise. Other things may be important and helpful to the patient, in addition to the course of action chosen. If you believe harm may come to the individual, you have an ethical obligation to educate the patient with your knowledge and inform him or her of the possible outcomes. The patient will ultimately decide. However, you will have provided essential information to prevent harm from occurring.

Gathering Expert Opinions

At times, published information is unavailable to help you answer the questions you have. Experts become a valuable resource to you in these situations. Expert resources are used frequently in the provision of patient care. There is tacit knowledge that we gain through the development of practice expertise. This knowledge is often not transcribed to paper and provided for general use. Experts provide an opinion about the likelihood of an event, or a likely best course of action based upon context and circumstances. When you contact an expert for advice, be prepared to provide as much detail as you possibly can, and inform the expert of the attempts you have already made in your systematic search process for information. These individuals are usually well versed in the published literature, and may be able to point you toward a published source that is valuable, in addition to offering expertise.

When you have exhausted your resources and still need additional information or expertise, you should consult your network of alternative resources. This network may consist of experienced colleagues, local experts, or a specialized practitioner. Additional sources may also include

- Poison control centers
- Drug information centers
- Medical librarians and searching services
- Other health care professionals
- Pharmaceutical manufacturers

- Professional associations
- Government agencies

You are always responsible for information that you provide, regardless of the source. Therefore, you must ensure the accuracy of your information. If circumstances allow, you should always request written documentation of any information received orally.

INCORPORATING EVIDENCE IN THE PATIENT CARE PLAN

It is important to document the evidence you use to affect the decisions in care. If you are providing a recommendation to another care provider, provision of a brief written response with the source citations used to support your recommendation is the optimal professional approach. If you are the care provider, then incorporating this documentation within the patient care plan is the optimal approach. Inclusion of the relevant data or findings from the evidence base should be incorporated into the assessment portion of the care plan and then the application of the findings explicitly described. This information becomes a part of the patient's database and health care record.

SUMMARY

Your skills as a drug information provider directly relate to the development of your practice expertise. Mastering these skills and continuing your competency development with the changing landscape of drug information products and services is an essential lifelong commitment you *must* make to be an outstanding care provider.

ASSESSMENT QUESTIONS

1. Why is it important to "classify" the subject matter of a drug information question?
2. Once you have classified the question, what is the correct searching strategy? Describe the types of references and order of searching that is generally pursued.
3. What is the purpose of a clinical practice guideline? By what process is it usually developed?
4. What advantages do drug information sources offer when made available on handheld devices?
5. What is the nature of reliable drug information?
6. Explain why experts hold a unique body of knowledge.

ASSIGNMENT

1. Visit a local hospital pharmacy department. Work with a pharmacist to show you the drug information references in the pharmacy department. Include computer-based and handheld references.
2. Identify five key references warranting immediate access in your daily practice. Describe the rationale for these choices.
3. Go to the Google Scholar search engine (http://scholar.google.com/). Then select the link "About Google Scholar" (http://scholar.google.com/intl/en/scholar/about.html) and review the quality and criteria guidelines for Google Scholar. Then do a search for a topic of interest to you. Save your search strategy and your search results.
4. Go to the National Library of Medicine PubMed search engine (www.nlm.gov). Complete the tutorial on how to conduct an online search. Be sure to become familiar with the following terms: (a) MeSH Terms; (b) Boolean Operators; (c) Field Descriptions; (d) Search limit; (e) Field tags or qualifiers; (f) Automatic explosion (explode); (g) ISSN (International Standard Serial Numbers). Repeat the search for the same topic of interest you did with Google Scholar. Save your search strategy and your search results.
5. Compare the search strategy and search results you obtained between Google Scholar and PubMed. What similarities and differences do you find?

CASE 1

Nasir Jabr seeks evidence in response to Lauren Smith's question

Lauren returns to the pharmacy 1 week later for a follow-up blood pressure check and a response to her question.

Nasir Jabr: "Hello Lauren; how are you today?"

Lauren: "Well, I'm feeling quite a bit better. That prescription really worked. Thanks for all of your help. Did you find anything out about the smoking and birth control patch?"

Nasir Jabr: "Yes…I was able to evaluate the literature about this medication. As it turns out, the cardiovascular risks are considered the same whether you take birth control pills or use this patch."

Lauren: "What do you mean 'risk?'"

Nasir Jabr: "If you smoke while using either of these forms of birth control, your chances of having a clot form in your bloodstream causing a stroke, heart attack, or problems with your circulation are higher than when you do not smoke."

Lauren: "Well…what is the best thing for me to do?"

Jabr researches the subject and documents his work on the Drug Information Sheet and in his Progress Note (see Figures 7-3 **and** 7-4**).**

DRUG INFORMATION WORKSHEET

Date/Time Received 02/12 3 p.m. Person Receiving __N. Jabr__ How Received (phone, visit, etc) __Visit__

Requester or Source Information

Name **Lauren Smith**
Affiliation **patient**
Title _____

How to Reach **will return in one week**
Phone # _____
Pager# _____
Fax # _____
Address _____

Who Requested (check one)
- ☐ MD
- ☐ MD Student
- ☐ RN
- **X** Patient
- ☐ Physical/Respiratory Therapy
- ☐ Nutrition Support
- ☐ Secretary/Ward Clerk
- ☐ Other _____

Classification of Request

- **X** Adverse Drug Reaction (ADR)
- ☐ Availability
- ☐ Compatibility/Stability
  (Chemical, Pharmaceutical, Sorption, Solubility, etc)
- ☐ Compounding/Formulation
- ☐ Dosage/Schedule
  - ☐ Drug Interactions

  (Drug-Drug, Drug-Lab, Drug-Disease, Drug-Food)

- ☐ Drug of Choice/Therapeutics/Pharmacology
- ☐ Identification
- ☐ Method of Administration

- ☐ Pharmacoeconomics
- ☐ Pharmacokinetics
- ☐ Pregnancy/Lactation/Teratogenicity
- ☐ Poisoning/Toxicology
  (Environmental, Exposure, Occupational, Mutagenicity, Carcinogenicity)
- ☐ Odd Drug Entities and OTCs
  (Investigational, Orphans, Foreign Drugs, Chemical Substances, Homeopathic Remedies, Vitamin Substances, Herbs, etc.)
- ☐ Other _____

Patient Data

Name **Lauren Smith** Patient ID _____ Room/Bed Number or Location _____
Age **23** years _____ months Height ___ ft ___ in Setting (e.g., inpatient or outpatient) _____
Gender ☐ male **X** female Weight ___ lb ___ kg
Race **Caucasian**
Diagnosis **UTI, probable HTN, Headaches** Allergies/Intolerances _____
Pertinent Medical History/Problem List **smokes, elevated BP – underevaluation for essential HTN**

Pertinent Medication History **Uses Ortho-Evra; past use of oral BCP x 2 years; Advil use 3-4x/week; actively using co-trimoxazole starts today for 10 days.**
Pertinent Laboratory Values _____

Miscellaneous Information _____

The Request, Actual Drug Information Need, and Time Frame for Response

Original Questions/Notes **Does birth control patch cause high BP also—or is it just the birth control pills?**

Clear Statement of Actual Drug Information Need **What are the cardiovascular risks associated with the use of Ortho Evra? Does Lauren have other risk factors for negative cardiovascular events as well?**

Time Frame Required for Response **patient will return in one week**

Figure 7-3. Drug Information Worksheet Prepared by Pharmacist Nasir Jabr to Research and Respond to Lauren Smith's Request

Record of Search/Notes

Package insert: Ortho Evra contains norelgestromin and ethinyl estradiol–delivered topically and administered once a week. The use of combination hormonal contraceptives is associated with increased risks of several serious conditions including myocardial infarction, thromboembolism, stroke, hepatic neoplasia, and gallbladder disease, although the risk of serious morbidity and mortality is very small in health women without underlying risk factors. The risk of morbidity and mortality increases significantly in the presence of other underlying risk factors such as hypertension, hyperlipidemias, obesity and diabetes. **AS A BLACK BOX WARNING:** Cigarette smoking increases the risk of serious cardiovascular side effects from hormonal contraceptive use. This risk increases with age and with heavy smoking (15 or more cigarettes per day) and is quite marked in women over 35 years of age. Women who use hormonal contraceptives including Ortho Evra–should be strongly advised not to smoke.

Micromedex: Women on combination oral contraceptives may experience a modest yet statistically significant increase in blood pressure which returns to normal in 1 to 6 months after cessation (AMA 1991;Woods,1988). The risk of developing hypertension is also reported to bed 3 to 6 times greater in oral contraceptive users than non users (AMA,1991).

Clear Statement of Response

Clear that she is at risk because of smoking using the patch. Needs to discontinue smoking.

Response Written: ____ documented in chart ____ memo   Response Oral: ____ telephone follow-up ____ face to face

Outcomes

General:	Patient-Specific:
☐ More information requested	☐ More information requested
☐ Recommendation accepted	☐ Recommendation accepted
☐ Recommendation rejected	☐ Recommendation rejected
☐ Requester will call back with results / additional requests	☐ Requester will pass information on to patient
☐ Contributed to policy development	☐ Patient education provided
☐ Standard of practice (upheld or improved)	☐ Clinical Impact (+ / - / neutral)
☐ Improved efficacy	☐ Positive patient relations
☐ Improved compliance	☐ Estimated cost impact
☐ Assured safety	☐ None or
☐ Prevented potential medication error	☐ $_____; Describe:_____
☐ Prevented potential ADR	
☐ Estimated cost impact	☐ Probably life saving
☐ None or	☐ Other_____
☐ $	

Figure 7-3 (continued). Drug Information Worksheet Prepared by Pharmacist Nasir Jabr to Research and Respond to Lauren Smith's Request

Pharmacy Profile for:					
Patient: Smith, Lauren			New Patient	Print	Close Record
Demographic	OTC / Allergy		Insurance	Diagnosis	Contacts
General Health	Care Plans	Surveys	Account Status		Current Therapy
General Information	Illnesses	Systems Review	Vital Signs		Lab Values

Pharmacist's Progress Note: Date: 02-12

LS referred to Dr. Miller by NJ on 02-01 for evaluation of probable UTI. LS presented today with co-trimoxazole prescription. Upon brief history and examination the following was noted:

S: LS reports BP at physician's 148/100; using birth control patch after 2 year history of Lo-Ovral; 3-4 Advil 200 mg tablets 3-4 x per week for headaches – characterized by frontal discomfort and occasional periorbital pain; 1-2 ppd cigarettes. Denies allergy to medications.

O: BP 150/102 seated (repeated here)

A: UTI, probable essential HTN worsened by NSAID use and nicotine addiction - increased risk of thromboembolic events and elevated BP and , headaches – symptoms consistent with sinus headache – likely in need of a decongestant rather than Advil.

P: Dispensed co-trimoxazole and counseled to consume water, take to completion. Offered smoking cessation and hypertension management service. Research her question, "Does birth control patch affect BP also?" Asked her to visit in one week for follow-up.

                    Nasir Jabr, Pharm.D.

Drug Information Search   Date: 02-03

Figure 7-4. Pharmacy Profile for Lauren Smith

CASE 1: SPECIFIC QUESTIONS

Use the Drug Information Worksheet completed by Nasir Jabr and the Pharmacy Profile for Lauren Smith (see **Figures 7-3** and **7-4**) to answer the case-specific questions.

1. Did Jabr restate Lauren's question accurately?
2. Were the resources he used appropriate choices in which to find information?

CASE 2

Christine Johnston investigates the evidence about the use of herbal remedies for diabetes based upon her interview with Mr. Montanez and Maria

Christine Johnston now has a better understanding of Mr. Montanez. She decides to investigate whether cactus flowers (prickly pear cactus) and yucca root have any effect in diabetic patients. She researches the subject and documents her work on the Drug Information Sheet (**Figure 7-5**).

DRUG INFORMATION WORKSHEET

Date/Time Received_____ Person Receiving_____ How Received (phone, visit, etc)_____

Requester or Source Information

Name **My own background question**   How to Reach_____
Affiliation _____ Phone #_____
Title_____ Pager#_____
 Fax #_____
 Address_____

Who Requested (check one)
❏ MD ❏ MD Student ❏ RN ❏ Patient
❏ Physical/Respiratory Therapy ❏ Nutrition Support ❏ Secretary/Ward Clerk ❏ Other_____

Classification of Request

X Adverse Drug Reaction (ADR) ❏ Pharmacoeconomics
❏ Availability ❏ Pharmacokinetics
❏ Compatibility/Stability ❏ Pregnancy/Lactation/Teratogenicity
  (Chemical, Pharmaceutical, Sorption, Solubility, etc) ❏ Poisoning/Toxicology
❏ Compounding/Formulation   (Environmental, Exposure, Occupational, Mutagenicity,
X Dosage/Schedule   Carcinogenicity)
X Drug Interactions ❏ Odd Drug Entities and OTCs
  (Drug-Drug, Drug-Lab, Drug-Disease, Drug-Food)   (Investigational, Orphans, Foreign Drugs, Chemical
X Drug of Choice/Therapeutics/Pharmacology Substances
❏ Identification   Homeopathic Remedies, Vitamin Substances, Herbs, etc.)
X Method of Administration ❏ Other _____

Patient Data

Name **Eduardo Montanez**   Patient ID_____ Room/Bed Number or Location_____
Age **68** years_____ months Height ____ ft ____ in Setting (e.g., inpatient or outpatient) _____
Gender X male ❏ female Weight____ lb ____ kg Race____ **Hispanic**
Diagnosis **Diabetes, dyslipidemia** Allergies/Intolerances_____ **codeine**
Pertinent Medical History/Problem List_____
_____
Pertinent Medication History_____
_____
Pertinent Laboratory Values_____
_____
Miscellaneous Information_____
_____

The Request, Actual Drug Information Need, and Time Frame for Response

Original Questions/Notes_____ See actual below_____
_____
Clear Statement of Actual Drug Information Need: **Do cactus flowers (prickly pear cactus) and yucca root have any effect in patients with diabetes?**
Time Frame Required for Response_____

Figure 7-5. Drug Information Worksheet Prepared by Pharmacist Christine Johnston to Research and Respond to Mr. Montanez's Request

Record of Search/Notes

1. Micromedex–negative, no information available
2. www.naturaldatabase.com–paydirt! Pricky pear cactus used orally for diabetes. May be possibly effective in the short-term to reduce blood glucose levels in patients with type 2 diabetes. Single doses can decrease blood glucose levels by 17-46% in some patients. Not known if daily use will consistently lower blood glucose levels and decrease HbA1c levels. Only the broiled stems of the species Opuntia streptacantha seem to be beneficial. Raw or crude stems don't seem to decrease glucose levels. Some species decrease lipid levels too (I need to investgate this further). Drug interaction cited with chlorpropamide! Ref cited is: Meckes-Lozyoa M, Roman-Ramos R. Opuntia streptacantha; a coadjutor in the treatment of diabetes mellitus. Am J Chin Med 1986;14(3-4):116-18. They warn of hypoglycemia being enhanced–caution probably an oral antidiabetic agent problem in general. Dosing discussed is broiling stems of 100-500 grams daily is typically used. Wonder how person knows what is 100-500 gms? Will check further. Comment is made that prickly pear cactus is primarily used in Mexican and Mexican-American cultures as part of diet and as a treatment for type 2 diabetes. It is the immature form of the cactus that is used.

Clear Statement of Response

Clear Statement of Response_____**Will discuss this with Maria and Mr Montanez…need to evaluate frequency and quantity of consumption at next clinic visit.**

Response Written: ____documented in chart ____ memo   Response Oral: ____telephone follow-up ____ face to face

Outcomes

General:
☐ More information requested
☐ Recommendation accepted
☐ Recommendation rejected

☐ Requester will call back with results / additional requests
☐ Contributed to policy development
☐ Standard of practice (upheld or improved)
  ☐ Improved efficacy
  ☐ Improved compliance
  ☐ Assured safety
☐ Prevented potential medication error
☐ Prevented potential ADR
☐ Estimated cost impact
  ☐ None or
  ☐ $_____; Describe:_____
☐ Other_____

Patient-Specific:
☐ More information requested
☐ Recommendation accepted
☐ Recommendation rejected

☐ Requester will pass information on to patient
☐ Patient education provided
☐ Clinical Impact (+ / - / neutral)
☐ Positive patient relations
☐ Estimated cost impact
  ☐ None or
  ☐ $_____; Describe:_____

☐ Probably life saving
☐ Other_____

Figure 7-5 (continued). Drug Information Worksheet Prepared by Pharmacist Christine Johnston to Research and Respond to Mr. Montanez's Request

CASE 2: SPECIFIC QUESTIONS

Use the Drug Information Worksheet completed by Christine Johnston on pages 178 and 179 to answer the case-specific questions.

1. Did Christine Johnston restate the correct questions? Would you have stated them differently?
2. Do you agree with how she categorized this request? How might you have done it differently?
3. Do you agree with the choice of references she selected in her search strategy? What are some of the other choices that might also have worked?

CASE 3

Luisa Rodriguez investigates the ingredients and use of Bai Guo Ye

Rodriguez feels uncomfortable with the remedy that Huong has told her about and does not have many references available about foreign drugs, natural products, or herbs and remedies. She starts her search as shown on the Drug Information Sheet in **Figure 7-6**.

DRUG INFORMATION WORKSHEET

Date/Time Received_____ Person Receiving_____ How Received (phone, visit, etc)_____

Requester or Source Information

Name **My own background question**
Affiliation _____
Title _____

How to Reach_____
Phone #_____
Pager#_____
Fax #_____
Address_____

Who Requested (check one)
❏ MD ❏ MD Student ❏ RN ❏ Patient
❏ Physical/Respiratory Therapy ❏ Nutrition Support ❏ Secretary/Ward Clerk ❏ Other_____

Classification of Request
❏ Adverse Drug Reaction (ADR)
❏ Availability
❏ Compatibility/Stability
  (Chemical, Pharmaceutical, Sorption, Solubility, etc)
❏ Compounding/Formulation
❏ Dosage/Schedule
❏ Drug Interactions
  (Drug-Drug, Drug-Lab, Drug-Disease, Drug-Food)
❏ Drug of Choice/Therapeutics/Pharmacology
❏ Identification
❏ Method of Administration

❏ Pharmacoeconomics
❏ Pharmacokinetics
❏ Pregnancy/Lactation/Teratogenicity
❏ Poisoning/Toxicology
  (Environmental, Exposure, Occupational, Mutagenicity, Carcinogenicity)
X Odd Drug Entities and OTCs
  (Investigational, Orphans, Foreign Drugs, Chemical Substances, Homeopathic Remedies, Vitamin Substances, Herbs, etc.)
❏ Other _____

Patient Data

Name **Huong Tran**   Patient ID_____   Room/Bed Number or Location **Peds Med**
Age __8__ years____ months Height ____ ft ____in   Setting (e.g., inpatient or outpatient) _____
Gender **X** male ❏female   Weight____ lb ____ kg
Race **Vietnamese**
Diagnosis **uncontrolled asthma**   Allergies/Intolerances_____**penicillin**_____
Pertinent Medical History/Problem List_____
_____
Pertinent Medication History_____
_____
Pertinent Laboratory Values_____
_____
Miscellaneous Information_____

The Request, Actual Drug Information Need, and Time Frame for Response

Original Questions/Notes_____
_____

Clear Statement of Actual Drug Information Need _____What is Bai Guo Ye? Has it been used in the treatment of asthma? What are the effects of this substance on an 8 year old boy?_____

Time Frame Required for Response   **need information today**_____

Figure 7-6. Drug Information Worksheet Prepared by Pharmacist Luisa Rodriguez to Research Her Need in Managing Huong Tran's Case

Record of Search/Notes

1. Lexi-Drugs on PDA – negative info 2. Pub med – negative info 3. IPA – negative info
4. Micromedex–negative info 5. www.naturaldatabase.com– bai guo ye is ginkgo extract. Using ginkgo for asthma and bronchitis was described in the first pharmacopoeia, Chen Noung Pen T'sao, dating to 2600 BC. Reference cited is: Diamond BJ, Shiflett SC, Feiwel N, et al. Ginkgo biloba extract: mechanisms and clinical indications. Arch Phys Med Rehabil 2000;81:668-78. Specific dosing not clear to me.

Clear Statement of Response

Clear Statement of Response_____

Response Written: ____documented in chart ____ memo   Response Oral: ____telephone follow-up ____ face to face

Outcomes

General:	Patient-Specific:
☐ More information requested	☐ More information requested
☐ Recommendation accepted	☐ Recommendation accepted
☐ Recommendation rejected	☐ Recommendation rejected
☐ Requester will call back with results / additional requests	☐ Requester will pass information on to patient
☐ Contributed to policy development	☐ Patient education provided
☐ Standard of practice (upheld or improved)	☐ Clinical Impact (+ / - / neutral)
☐ Improved efficacy	☐ Positive patient relations
☐ Improved compliance	☐ Estimated cost impact
☐ Assured safety	☐ None or
☐ Prevented potential medication error	☐ $_____; Describe:_____
☐ Prevented potential ADR	
☐ Estimated cost impact	☐ Probably life saving
☐ None or	☐ Other_____
☐ $_____; Describe:_____	
☐ Other_____	

Figure 7-6 (continued). Drug Information Worksheet Prepared by Pharmacist Luisa Rodriguez to Research Her Need in Managing Huong Tran's Case

CASE 3: SPECIFIC QUESTIONS

Use the Drug Information Worksheet completed by Luisa Rodriguez on pages 181 and 182 to answer the case-specific questions.

1. Do you agree with the choice of references she selected in her search strategy?
2. How might experts play a role in helping her find this information?

CASE 4

Michael Jones evaluates the literature about the significance of Mr. Robinson's vitamin E use and warfarin

Michael Jones checks the Anticoagulation Assessment Guidelines for Pharmacists used in his hospital and identifies the possibility of an interaction with warfarin and vitamin E (see guidelines in case presentation in Chapter 5). When he looks at the guidelines, he notices several other medications of concern, including synthroid and nonsteroidal anti-inflammatory agents such as aspirin and ibuprofen (Advil). He decides to research them to determine what is appropriate to do in the care of Mr. Robinson. He uses the Drug Information Worksheet (see **Figure 7-7**) to guide him through the process of searching for answers to these questions.

DRUG INFORMATION WORKSHEET

Date/Time Received_____ Person Receiving_____ How Received (phone, visit, etc)_____

Requester or Source Information

Name **background search for myself**_____ How to Reach_____
Affiliation _____ Phone #_____
Title_____ Pager#_____
                                                                                                          Fax #_____
                                                                                                          Address_____

Who Requested (check one)
❏ MD   ❏ MD Student   ❏ RN   ❏ Patient
❏ Physical/Respiratory Therapy   ❏ Nutrition Support   ❏ Secretary/Ward Clerk   ❏ Other_____

Classification of Request

❏ Adverse Drug Reaction (ADR)   ❏ Pharmacoeconomics
❏ Availability   ❏ Pharmacokinetics
❏ Compatibility/Stability   ❏ Pregnancy/Lactation/Teratogenicity
   (Chemical, Pharmaceutical, Sorption, Solubility, etc) ❏ Poisoning/Toxicology
❏ Compounding/Formulation   (Environmental, Exposure, Occupational, Mutagenicity,
❏ Dosage/Schedule   Carcinogenicity)
        ☒ Drug Interactions   ❏ Odd Drug Entities and OTCs
                                                             (Investigational, Orphans, Foreign Drugs, Chemical
   (Drug-Drug, Drug-Lab, Drug-Disease, Drug-Food)   Substances, Homeopathic Remedies, Vitamin Substances,
                                                             Herbs, etc.)
❏ Drug of Choice/Therapeutics/Pharmacology   ❏ Other _____
❏ Identification
❏ Method of Administration

Patient Data

Name **Samuel Robinson**_____   Patient ID_____   Room/Bed Number or Location   **347 - 1**
Age **76 years**   ___ months   Height ____ ft ____ in   Setting (e.g., inpatient or outpatient) **INPT**
Gender ☒ male ❏ female   Weight ____ lb ____ kg
Race_____ **African American**
Diagnosis **CHF, AF, hypothyroid, HTN, dyslipidemia**   Allergies/Intolerances_____
Pertinent Medical History/Problem List_____

Pertinent Medication History_____

Pertinent Laboratory Values_____

Miscellaneous Information_____

The Request, Actual Drug Information Need, and Time Frame for Response

Original Questions/Notes_____

Clear Statement of Actual Drug Information Need _____ Patient is taking vitamin E while on warfarin, also has thyroid replacement and baby aspirin. What are the interactions between these agents and the use of warfarin in this elderly man?

Time Frame Required for Response_____ need in 1 hour

Figure 7-7. Drug Information Worksheet Prepared by Pharmacist Michael Jones to Research His Need in Managing Mr. Robinson's Case

Record of Search/Notes

1. Micromedex–Warfarin Monograph–large doses of Vitamin E interfere with vitamin K dependent clotting factors and may lead to enhanced risk of bleeding. Monitor INR closely. Large doses of Vitamin E considered greater than 300 IUs per day. Thyroid replacement in a hypothyroid patient may increase metabolism of clotting factors, thus increasing the anticoagulant effects of warfarin itself. Low dose aspirin in patients on warfarin provokes no more bleeding than with warfarin alone—another study in Micromedex said that there was a 27% increase in major bleeding episodes after an average of 2.5 years when aspirin around 100 mg per day was used.

Clear Statement of Response

Clear Statement of Response___ Need to get detailed history from Mr. Robinson. IF he is using the vitamin E a few times a week….probably not a problem. But if it's every day…is a problem. He may also not be taking his thyroid …in that case not a problem yet, but will be when he starts back up. Aspirin is okay.

Response Written: ____documented in chart ____ memo   Response Oral: ____telephone follow-up ____ face to face

Outcomes

General:
- ☐ More information requested
- ☐ Recommendation accepted
- ☐ Recommendation rejected

- ☐ Requester will call back with results / additional requests
- ☐ Contributed to policy development
- ☐ Standard of practice (upheld or improved)
  - ☐ Improved efficacy
  - ☐ Improved compliance
  - ☐ Assured safety
- ☐ Prevented potential medication error
- ☐ Prevented potential ADR
- ☐ Estimated cost impact
  - ☐ None or
  - ☐ $_____; Describe:_____
- ☐ Other_____

Patient-Specific:
- ☐ More information requested
- ☐ Recommendation accepted
- ☐ Recommendation rejected

- ☐ Requester will pass information on to patient
- ☐ Patient education provided
- ☐ Clinical Impact (+ / - / neutral)
- ☐ Positive patient relations
- ☐ Estimated cost impact
  - ☐ None or
  - ☐ $_____; Describe:_____
- ☐ Probably life saving
- ☐ Other_____

Figure 7-7 (continued). Drug Information Worksheet Prepared by Pharmacist Michael Jones to Research His Need in Managing Mr. Robinson's Case

CASE 4: SPECIFIC QUESTIONS

Use the Drug Information Worksheet completed by Michael Jones on pages 184 and 185 to answer the case-specific questions.

1. Evaluate the conclusion that Jones has drawn about the significance of using vitamin E while taking warfarin. Do you agree with his conclusion? Why or why not?

REFERENCES

1. Gilgun J. The four cornerstones of qualitative research. *Qualitative Health Research*. 2006; 16(3):436–43.

2. American Psychological Association. Evidence based practice in psychology—APA presidential task force on evidence based practice. *American Psychologist*. 2006; 61(4): 271–85. DOI: 10.1037/0003-066X.61.4.271.

3. Guyatt G, Rennie D, Meade M, et al. *Users' Guides to the Medical Literature: A Manual for Evidence-Based Clinical Practice*. 2nd ed. New York, NY: The McGraw-Hill Companies, Inc.; 2008.

4. Ely JW, Osheroff JA, Evell MH, et al. Obstacles to answering doctors' questions about patient care with evidence: qualitative study. *BMJ*. 2002; 324:1–7.

5. Bloomrosen M, Detmer DE. Informatics, evidence-based care, and research; implications for national policy: a report of an American Medical Informatics Association health policy conference. *J Am Med Inform Assoc*. 2010; 17:115–23. DOI: 10.1136/jamia.2009.001370.

6. IOM (Institute of Medicine). *Digital Infrastructure for the Learning Health System: The Foundation for Continuous Improvement in Health and Health Care: Workshop Series Summary*. Washington, DC: The National Academies Press; 2011.

7. Montori VM, Guyatt GH. Progress in evidence-based medicine. *JAMA*. 2008; 300(15):1814–6.

8. Steinbrook R. Searching for the right search—reaching the medical literature. *N Engl J Med*. 2006; 354(1):4–7.

9. Fox S. Mobile Health 2010. Available at: http://pewinternet.org/Reports/2010/Mobile-Health-2010.aspx. Accessed February 2011.

10. Nash DB, Manfredi MP, Bozarth B, et al. *Connecting with the New Healthcare Consumer—Defining Your Strategy*. New York, NY: McGraw-Hill Companies; 2000.

11. Osman AD, Sackett DL, Guyatt GH, for the Evidence-Based Medicine Working Group. Users' guides to the medical literature—I. How to get started. *JAMA*. 1993; 270(17):2093–5.

12. Guyatt GH, Sackett DL, Cook DJ, for the Evidence-Based Medicine Working Group. Users' guides to the medical literature—II. How to use an article about therapy or prevention. Are the results of the study valid? *JAMA*. 1993; 270(21):2598–601.

13. Guyatt GH, Sackett DL, Cook DJ, for the Evidence-Based Medicine Working Group. Users' guides to the medical literature—II. How to use an article about therapy or prevention B. What were the results and will they help me in caring for my patients? *JAMA*. 1994; 271(1):59–63.

14. Jaeschke R, Guyatt G, Sackett DL, for the Evidence-Based Medicine Working Group. Users' guides to the medical literature—III. How to use an article about a diagnostic test. A. Are the results of the study valid? *JAMA*. 1994; 271(5):389–91.

15. Jaeschke R, Guyatt G, Sackett DL, for the Evidence-Based Medicine Working Group. Users' guides to the medical literature—III. How to use an article about a diagnostic test. B. What were the results and will they help me in caring for my patients? *JAMA*. 1994; 271(9):703–7.

16. Levine M, Walter S, Lee H, et al., for the Evidence-Based Medicine Working Group. Users' guides to the medical literature—IV. How to use an article about harm. *JAMA*. 1994; 271(20):1615–9.

17. Laupacis A, Wells G, Richardson S, et al. for the Evidence-Based Medicine Working Group. Users' guides to the medical literature—V. How to use an article about prognosis. *JAMA*. 1994; 272(3):234–7.

18. Oxman AD, Cook DJ, Guyatt GH, for the Evidence-Based Medicine Working Group. Users' guides to the medical literature—VI. How to use an overview. *JAMA*. 1994; 272(17):1367–71.

19. Richardson WS, Detsky AS, for the Evidence-Based Medicine Working Group. Users' guides to the medical literature—VII. How to use a clinical decision analysis. A. Are the results of the study valid? *JAMA*. 1995; 273(16):1292–5.

20. Richardson WS, Detsky AS, for the Evidence-Based Medicine Working Group. Users' guides to the medical literature—VII. How to use a clinical decision analysis. B. What are the results and will they help me in caring for my patients? *JAMA*. 1995; 273(20):1610–3.

21. Hayward RSA, Wilson MC, Tunis SR, et al., for the Evidence-Based Medicine Working Group. Users' guides to the medical literature—VIII. How to use clinical practice guidelines. A. Are the recommendations valid? *JAMA*. 1995; 274(7):570–4.

22. Wilson MC, Hayward RSA, Tunis SR, et al., for the Evidence-Based Medicine Working Group. Users' guides to the medical literature—VIII. How to use a clinical decision analysis. B. What are the recommendations and will they help you in caring for your patients? *JAMA*. 1995; 274(20):1630–2.

23. Guyatt GH, Sackett DL, Sinclair JC, et al., for the Evidence-Based Medicine Working Group. IX. A method for grading health care recommendations. *JAMA*. 1995; 274(22):1800–4.

24. Naylor CD, Guyatt GH, for the Evidence-Based Medicine Working Group. X. How to use an article reporting variations in the outcomes of health services. *JAMA*. 1996; 275(7):554–8.

25. Naylor CD, Guyatt GH, for the Evidence-Based Medicine Working Group. XI. How to use an article about a clinical utilization review. *JAMA*. 1996; 275(18):1435–9.

26. Guyatt GH, Naylor D, Juniper E, et al., for the Evidence-Based Medicine Working Group. XII. How to use ar-

ticles about health related quality of life. *JAMA*. 1997; 277(15):1232–7.

27. Drummond MF, Richardson WS, O'Brien BJ, et al., for the Evidence-Based Medicine Working Group. XIII. How to use an article on economic analysis of clinical practice. *JAMA*. 1997; 277(19):1552–7.

28. Dans AL, Dans LF, Guyatt GH, et al., for the Evidence-Based Medicine Working Group. XIV. How to decide on the applicability of clinical trial results to your patient. *JAMA*. 1998; 279(7):545–9.

29. Richardson WS, Wilson MC, Guyatt GH, et al., for the Evidence-Based Medicine Working Group. Users' guide to the medical literature. XV. How to use an article about disease probability for differential diagnosis. *JAMA*. 1999; 281(13):1214–9.

30. Guyatt GH, Sinclair J, Cook DJ, et al., for the Evidence-Based Medicine Working Group and the Cochrane Applicability Methods Working Group. XVI. How to use a treatment recommendation. *JAMA*. 1999; 281(19):1836–43.

31. Barratt A, Irwig L, Glasziou P, et al, for the Evidence-Based Medicine Working Group. Users' guide to the medical literature. XVII. How to use guidelines and recommendations about screening. *JAMA*. 1999; 281(21):2029–34.

32. Watanabe AS, Connor CS. *Principles of Drug Information Services—A Syllabus of Systematic Concepts.* Hamilton, IL: Drug Intelligence Publications, Inc.; 1978.

33. Slaughter RL, Edwards DJ. *Evaluating Drug Literature—A Statistical Approach.* New York, NY: McGraw-Hill Medical Publishing Division; 2001.

34. Khan KS, Kunz R, Kleijnen J, et al. *Systematic Reviews to Support Evidence-Based Medicine.* Lake Forest, IL: The Royal Society of Medicine Press Limited; 2003.

35. Garrard J. *Health Sciences Literature Review Made Easy.* Gaithersburg, MD: Aspen Publishers, Inc.; 1999.

APPENDIX 7-1. REPRESENTATIVE QUESTIONS TO ASK FOR EACH REQUEST CLASSIFICATION

Classification and Additional Patient-Specific Data

Adverse Drug Reaction (ADR)

To determine the likelihood of an adverse drug reaction, you must reconstruct facts about the events. You must include subjective and objective clinical information along with a specific description of events, including time sequence, to evaluate the onset and severity. You also must review management approaches to provide appropriate advice for the patient's care.

Representative questions:

- What are signs and symptoms of possible reaction?
- What is severity of reaction? (provide specific description)
- What is temporal relationship between drug administration and reaction?
- What is current medical status of patient?
- What is management plan for patient?
- Was patient exposed to similar or identical substance? (document clinical result)

Availability

Frequently, medications that prescribers want to use are not readily available in your institution. Reasons for this restriction may include a controlled formulary management system and budgetary constraints. If alternative therapy is needed, the indication for treatment provides you with recommendations. You probably have available agents within the pharmacologic class that are equally efficacious and have an acceptable side effect profile. For example, you may suggest ranitidine (a "representative H2 blocker") on your formulary to a physician who wants cimetidine.

Representative question:

- What is indication for treatment? (provide alternatives, if more readily available)

Compatibility/Stability

Many patients are both fluid and electrolyte restricted. These patients may be unable to tolerate exposure to amounts of fluid recommended by usual compatibility and stability guidelines. Sometimes, alternative routes of administration are needed. You must know if the patients are limited, particularly those who are managing complex drug therapy at home. Commonly, home chemotherapy patients require evaluation of their parenteral drug therapy and appropriate combinations of medication to allow administration through one access site. This procedure eliminates multiple intravenous punctures.

Representative questions:

- What are fluid volume and electrolyte restrictions?
- What are available routes of administration?
- What is indication for treatment?
- Is drug self-administered in home?

Compounding/Formulation

Prescribers often are unaware that commercial products are available for older, popular formulations. If a patient has tried a commercial formulation and had a bad experience, you should determine if a compounded product has the same offending substance. This practice is common in dermatology preparations. For example, many patients are allergic or sensitive to wool fat-based products (e.g., lanolin).

Representative questions:

- Are agents available in commercial formulation?
- Did patient use agent? What was result?

Dosage/Schedule

The dose range of a drug depends on its indication for treatment. However, new indications for medications may require a different dose and schedule than the original indication. For example, amitriptyline as an antidepressant is dosed at 50–300 mg/day. When it is used for intermittent nocturia, amitriptyline usually is dosed at 10 mg/day.

A specific dose within the range often depends on a patient's ideal body weight or actual body weight (if significantly different from ideal). Other factors include whether the drug is plasma protein bound and whether the dose is affected by organ dysfunction. By determining the extent of renal or hepatic impairment, you usually can recommend a dosage adjustment to suit the patient's needs.

A patient's medication compliance with multiple daily doses can be severely hampered by cognitive as well as non-cognitive impairments. Therefore, you should determine the extent of a patient's reading, hearing, and vision damage.

Individual lifestyles also influence recommended times for drug therapy administration, so the dosage schedule should be compatible with your patient's needs.

Representative questions:

- What is indication for treatment?
- What is body weight relative to ideal? (provide lean estimate)
- What is protein or albumin status pertinent to plasma protein-bound drugs?
- Are cognitive impairments limiting compliance?
- Is lifestyle affecting ideal dosing schedule?

Drug Interactions

Medicine and pharmacy have volumes of literature on drug interactions and interferences. Each patient case requires evaluation of individual circumstances surrounding the suspected interaction. To determine the likelihood of an interaction, you should identify the patient's exposure to all medications or substances. You also must determine if the size of the doses and sequence of events were within a time period likely to support an interaction.

Many variables, such as drug–disease, drug–food, and drug–laboratory interferences, may contribute to a drug–drug interaction and its significance.

Representative questions:

- What is suspected interaction?
- What are respective doses, durations, and time courses of administration of drugs?
- Is drug interference suspected?
- Is lab interference suspected? (identify specific assay method for laboratory procedure)
- Is disease interference suspected? (document temporal relationship)
- Is food interference suspected? (document temporal relationship between food and medication consumption)

Drug of Choice/Therapeutics/Pharmacology

Treatment recommendations must be based on knowledge of the drug's medical indication and determination of the desired therapeutic endpoints. By also knowing concurrent treatments and medical problems, you can refine your recommendations.

Representative questions:

- What is indication for treatment?
- What are current hepatic and renal functions?
- What is current medication regimen?
- What are current medical problems that may be affected by drug in specific class?

Identification

Seemingly simple identification questions usually are intended to determine what medications a patient is taking and then what the patient should be taking. Reasons for these questions include

- A patient mixed up medications in one container, and the physician or nurse is unable to identify them without labels.
- A patient ingested a large quantity of medication, and the physician must identify the substances.
- A patient wants to take a foreign drug product.
- You should know the source, size, shape, and any markings of a product without an identifying name. To identify the drug, you can use a specific reference (e.g., Identidex component of Micromedex) or photographs in the Physicians' Desk Reference. If the product is foreign, its name and country of origin allow you to search foreign product compendiums.

Representative questions:

- What is reason for inquiry? Large amount ingested? Foreign product—need equivalent?
- What are dosage form and appearance characteristics (e.g., size, shape, identifying marks, letters, and numbers)?

Method of Administration

By anticipating limitations that patients may have to a route of administration, you can recommend alternatives. Patients in the home setting, for example, may be better at managing their drug therapy preparation and administration by a particular route.

Representative questions:

- Are any routes of administration prohibitive because of patient-specific limitations?
- Is patient receiving product in home?

Pharmacoeconomics

Often, prescribers are unaware of alternative agents that are efficacious but more cost effective. A more readily available alternative may be acceptable if the original treatment request is about a nonformulary drug. For antibiotic use in organized health care settings, the least expensive regimen usually is recommended.

Representative question:

- Is cost-effective alternative available based on patient-specific data?

Pharmacokinetics

A question initially posed as a pharmacokinetics request frequently leads to a clinical decision about altering drug therapy. Therefore, you must gather pertinent information about how to interpret specific pharmacokinetic data in your patient. To evaluate the data, you should determine the temporal relationship between the dose administered and the drug concentration. Dosage form and frequency of dosing also may affect your interpretation. To assess the peak serum concentration of a drug, you must select the appropriate time interval when the dose is administered. If a drug is administered more frequently, the trough concentration is likely to be higher. A prescriber who asks for the half-life of Dilantin probably wants to alter dosing for uncontrolled seizures.

Representative questions:

- What are possible routes of drug administration for patient?
- What is organ function in patient?
- What are single and multiple doses in patient?
- What are body fluid drug levels in relationship to dosage form administered and time since last dose?

Pregnancy

To prevent complications to both a mother and fetus, you should try to avoid the administration of drugs during pregnancy. However, many women consume drugs during the initial phases of pregnancy when they may be unaware of their condition. You should determine how many weeks, or in which trimester, the drug was consumed so you can accurately evaluate teratogenicity data. In many clinical circumstances, administration of a drug is desirable or even necessary during pregnancy. If consumption has occurred, you should document the amount of drug and duration of use to determine the significance of exposure to the mother and fetus.

Questions regarding lactation can be asked for the following reasons:

- Because a baby might have been exposed to a substance through breast milk.
- Because a decision to breastfeed is or is not being made.

As a pharmacist, you need to identify the reason. If an exposure has occurred, you should obtain as much information as possible about clinical presentation.

Representative questions:

- Did patient take drug? (describe dose, route, frequency, and duration)
- In what trimester of pregnancy is patient?
- Are nondrug alternatives available? (if patient has not consumed drug)

Lactation

- Is patient breastfeeding?
- Was baby exposed?
- What are clinical manifestations, if any, in breast-fed baby?
- What are time course and sequence of events?

Teratogenicity

- Was fetus exposed?
- Did drug probably cause deformity or abnormality in child?

- What are dose, frequency, route, and duration of therapy?
- What are clinical manifestations?
- What are time course and sequence of events?

Poisoning/Toxicology

The appropriate management of a poisoning requires a good history. The ingested substance provides information about the toxicity of the agent, whereas age and weight indicate the potential severity of an exposure. Moreover, the amount ingested and time passed since ingestion provides information about the symptoms to expect and their management. Ingestion of multiple medications is common and can make management more complex. Sometimes, antidotes and remedies that are administered by well-meaning individuals result in further complications. A patient's clinical presentation, explained in an interview, determines your management of the case.

Representative questions:

- What is accurate identification of drug or substance?
- What was amount of substance ingested? What was package size?
- Were other medications ingested?
- When was substance ingested?
- Were other substances ingested, including alcohol or attempted remedies?
- What was route of administration or exposure?
- Does system history indicate if signs or symptoms are developing?
- What was done to treat patient?

Odd Drug Entities and OTCs

Uncommon drug products include medications made in foreign countries, investigational medications, and herbal preparations sold at health food stores. To answer questions about either common or uncommon and prescription or nonprescription products, you must gather specific information about the particular medication. Information for such requests may require specialized information resources and drug literature searches.

Representative questions:

- Is substance commercially available in the United States? A foreign country? Which ones?
- Was substance obtained through participation in a research study? Special request from the government?
- Was product obtained in a health food or natural products store? Herbal market? Chinese apothecary? Homeopathic pharmacy or doctor's office?
- Is substance from a plant source?
- What are other names for substance (if any)?
- Is substance a vitamin?
- Was product obtained by prescription?

APPENDIX 7-2. TERTIARY LITERATURE CONTENT MATRIX OF PHARMACOTHERAPEUTIC CHARACTERISTICS

Reference Title, Author and Publisher	Adverse drug reaction	Product availability	Compatibility/stability	Compounding/formulation	Dosage/schedule	Drug–drug interactions	Drug–lab interactions	Drug–disease interactions	Drug–food interactions	Drug of choice	Identification	Method of administration	Investigational agents	Foreign products	Pharmacokinetics	Pharmacology	Pregnancy/lactation	Therapeutics	Toxicology/poisoning
AHFS DI Essentials; McEvoy GK, ed. American Society of Health-System Pharmacists	•		•		•	•	•	•	•	•		•			•	•	•	•	•
American Drug Index; Billups NF, Billups SM. Facts and Comparisons		•	•	•							•								
American Hospital Formulary Service Drug Information; McEvoy GK, ed. American Society of Health-System Pharmacists	•				•	•	•	•	•	•		•			•	•	•	•	•
Applied Pharmacokinetic: Principles of Therapeutic Drug Monitoring; Evans WE, Schentag JJ, Jusko WT. Applied Therapeutics, Inc.															•				
Applied Therapeutics: The Clinical Use of Drugs; Koda-Kimble MA, Young LL, Kradjan WA, et al. Applied Therapeutics, Inc.	•				•	•	•	•	•	•		•				•		•	•
Basic Clinical Pharmacokinetics; Winter M. Applied Therapeutics, Inc.									•						•				
Basic Skills in Interpreting Laboratory Data; Lee M. American Society of Health-System Pharmacists															•				
Clinical Pharmacokinetics, 5th ed.; Murphy J. American Society of Health-System Pharmacists					•							•			•				
Clinical Toxicology of Commercial Products: Acute Poisoning; Gosselin RE. Lippincott, Williams, & Wilkins	•	•									•						•		
Diccionario de Especialidades Farmaceuticas; Medical Economics Company		•										•		•		•			
Drug Facts and Comparisons; Facts and Comparisons	•				•	•			•		•	•	•		•	•		•	•

Reference Title, Author and Publisher	Adverse drug reaction	Product availability	Compatibility/stability	Compounding/formulation	Dosage/schedule	Drug-drug interactions	Drug-lab interactions	Drug-disease interactions	Drug-food interactions	Drug of choice	Identification	Method of administration	Investigational agents	Foreign products	Pharmacokinetics	Pharmacology	Pregnancy/lactation	Therapeutics	Toxicology/poisoning
Drugs in Pregnancy and Lactation: A Reference Guide to Fetal and Neonatal Risk; Briggs GG, Freeman RK, Yaffe SJ. Lippincott, Williams, & Wilkins	•						•										•		•
Drug Interaction Facts; Tatro DS. Facts and Comparisons	•				•	•	•	•	•			•			•	•		•	•
Drug Interaction Handbook with International Trade Names Index; Lacy CF. Lexicomp, Inc.	•				•	•	•	•	•							•		•	
European Drug Index; Muller NF, Dessing RP. American Pharmaceutical Association											•			•					
Pocket Guide to Evaluation of Drug Interactions; Zuchero FJ, Hogan MJ, Sommer CD, et al. American Pharmaceutical Association						•	•	•	•										
Goodman and Gilman's Pharmacological Basis of Therapeutics; Hardman JG, Limbird LE, Gilman AG. McGraw-Hill Professional	•									•				•	•	•	•	•	•
Guide to Parenteral Admixtures; King JC, Catania PN. King Guide Publications, Inc.			•	•								•							
Handbook of Clinical Drug Data; Smith K, Henyan NN, Riche D. McGraw-Hill Medical	•				•	•				•		•			•	•	•	•	•
Handbook of Nonprescription Drugs; Berardi R, DeSimone EM. American Pharmaceutical Association		•			•				•	•		•				•	•	•	•
Driesbach's Handbook of Poisoning: Prevention, Diagnosis, and Treatment; True BL, Driesbach RH. CRC Press – Parthinon Publishers	•																		•
DrDrug – Drug Guide for Physicians www.skyscape.com; FA Davis Company	•				•					•		•						•	
ePocrates www.epocrates.com; ePocrates, Inc.	•				•	•				•	•				•	•		•	

APPENDIX 7-2. TERTIARY LITERATURE CONTENT MATRIX OF PHARMACOTHERAPEUTIC CHARACTERISTICS (continued)

Reference Title, Author and Publisher	Adverse drug reaction	Product availability	Compatibility/stability	Compounding/formulation	Dosage/schedule	Drug–drug interactions	Drug–lab interactions	Drug–disease interactions	Drug–food interactions	Drug of choice	Identification	Method of administration	Investigational agents	Foreign products	Pharmacokinetics	Pharmacology	Pregnancy/lactation	Therapeutics	Toxicology/poisoning
Handbook on Injectable Drugs, 16th ed.; Trissel LA. American Society of Health-System Pharmacists	•		•		•	•						•	•						
Drug Interactions Analysis and Management; Hansten PD, Horn JR. Lippincott Williams, & Wilkins	•					•	•	•	•										
The Harriet Lane Handbook: Mobile Medicine Series; Expert Consult: Online and Print Mosby			•	•	•							•				•	•	•	
iFacts www.skyscape.com; Facts and Comparisons						•	•	•	•										
Imprex; Collier WA, ed. American Pharmaceutical Association		•									•	•		•					
Index Nominum By Swiss Pharmaceutical Society - CRC-Press				•						•	•	•			•				
Lexi-Complete www.lexi.com; Lexi-comp, Inc.	•				•	•	•	•	•	•	•	•			•	•	•	•	•
Martindale: The Complete Drug Reference; Sweetman S. Pharmaceutical Press	•	•	•	•	•	•	•	•	•	•		•			•	•	•	•	
Handbook of Antimicrobial Therapy; Abramowicz M. The Medical Letter, Inc.					•			•		•		•						•	
Ellenhorn's Medical Toxicology: Diagnosis and Treatment of Human Poisoning; Hathwani B, Ellenhorn MJ. Lippincott, Williams, & Wilkins	•														•	•		•	•
Merck Index; O'Neil MJ. Merck		•									•		•	•	•	•			•
Meyler's Side Effects of Drugs: An Encyclopedia of Adverse Reactions and Interactions; Aronson JK, Dittman D, Dukes MN. Elsevier Health Sciences, Inc.	•				•	•	•	•	•			•			•	•	•	•	•
Micromedex–Drugdex® www.micromedex.com; Micromedex, Inc.	•	•	•	•	•	•	•	•	•	•	•			•	•	•	•	•	•

Reference Title, Author and Publisher	Adverse drug reaction	Product availability	Compatibility/stability	Compounding/formulation	Dosage/schedule	Drug–drug interactions	Drug–lab interactions	Drug–disease interactions	Drug–food interactions	Drug of choice	Identification	Method of administration	Investigational agents	Foreign products	Pharmacokinetics	Pharmacology	Pregnancy/lactation	Therapeutics	Toxicology/poisoning
Micromedex–Identidex www.micromedex.com; Micromedex, Inc.		•									•		•	•					
Micromedex–Poisondex www.micromedex.com; Micromedex, Inc.	•				•						•	•	•	•				•	•
Pediatric Dosage Handbook with International Trade Names Index; Takemato CK. Lexicomp, Inc.	•			•	•							•		•	•	•	•	•	
Pediatric Drug Formulations; Nahata MC, Pai VB. Harvey Whitney Books Company				•															
Pharmacotherapy: A Pathophysiological Approach DiPiro JT, Talbert RL, Yee GC, et al. McGraw-Hill Medical	•	•		•	•	•	•	•	•	•		•			•	•		•	•
Physician's Desk Reference www.franklin.com; Thomson Healthcare, Inc.	•		•	•	•	•	•	•	•		•	•				•		•	
Pocketbook of Pediatric Antimicrobial Therapy; Bradley JS, Nelson JD. American Academy of Pediatrics	•				•	•				•		•				•		•	•
Remington: The Science and Practice of Pharmacy Gennaro AR. Lippincott, Williams, & Wilkins	•		•	•	•					•	•	•				•		•	
Tarascon ePharmacopoeia www.tarascon.com; Tarascon Publishing				•	•														
USP Dictionary of USAN and International Drug Names; USP Committee of Revision United States Pharmacopeial Convention, Inc.											•		•	•					
USP DI, Volume 1 Drug Information for the Healthcare Professional Medical Economics	•				•	•	•	•		•		•			•	•		•	•

APPENDIX 7-2. TERTIARY LITERATURE CONTENT MATRIX OF PHARMACOTHERAPEUTIC CHARACTERISTICS (continued)

Reference Title, Author and Publisher	Adverse drug reaction	Product availability	Compatibility/stability	Compounding/formulation	Dosage/schedule	Drug–drug interactions	Drug–lab interactions	Drug–disease interactions	Drug–food interactions	Drug of choice	Identification	Method of administration	Investigational agents	Foreign products	Pharmacokinetics	Pharmacology	Pregnancy/lactation	Therapeutics	Toxicology/poisoning
USP DI, Volume 2: Advice for the Patient – Drug Information in Lay Language. Medical Economics		•									•			•					
USP DI, Volume 3: Approved Drug Products and Legal Requirements. Medical Economics		•		•							•		•						

APPENDIX 7-3. DRUG INFORMATION TOOLS AND CHECKLISTS FOR CRITICAL LITERATURE APPRAISAL

Several tools are provided here to assist you with learning how to critically evaluate the quality of information sources. Tools provided include:

Appendix 7-3.1   Evaluation of tertiary reference sources

Appendix 7-3.2   Evaluation of primary reference sources

Appendix 7-3.3   Checklist of items to include when reporting a randomized trial based upon the Consolidated Standards of Reporting Trials (CONSORT)

Appendix 7-3.4   Checklist of items to evaluate the quality of reports of meta-analysis of randomized controlled trials (QUOROM)

Appendix 7-3.5   Web sites and resources useful for evidence-based practice

Appendix 7-3.1

Evaluation of Tertiary or General References

_____ Author credibility. The authors are reputable, suggesting they are likely to publish more accurate, complete, and contemporary information.

_____ There is a minimal timeframe gap between the coverage of the subject matter and new developments.

_____ Current edition is being used.

_____ There is a bibliography or reference list. The references appear up to date.

_____ The information is easily found and accessible in the general reference.

_____ The indexes and table of contents facilitate rapid discovery of information.

Appendix 7-3.2

Critical Evaluation Checklist for General Primary Literature

_____ The journal in which the article appears is considered to be a reputable one.

_____ The title is consistent with the scope of the "summary."

_____ The investigators are considered to be reliable, and the study was conducted in a reputable medical center or university teaching hospital.

_____ The location was adequate for the application of good scientific experimental methods.

_____ The objectives and/or hypothesis (i.e., purpose) of the study was well-defined.

_____ Appropriate scientific methods of experimental design were employed for this type of study.

_____ The population sample size was adequate.

_____ The population sample was described adequately.

_____ The subjects were chosen by appropriate means.

_____ Adequate methods and experimental design were used to ensure that the results obtained were valid and free from bias.

_____ The trial was prospective or retrospective.

_____ There were adequate controls established.

_____ Drug and control treatments were allocated to the subjects in a random manner.

_____ Adequate blinding techniques were utilized.

_____ Appropriate considerations for the proper use of the drug were made.

_____ Drug doses and regimens were within the therapeutic range.

_____ The duration of the trial was adequate.

_____ Drugs were used concurrently and were accounted for.

_____ Appropriate considerations were made for the correct measurement of the established parameters of therapeutic efficacy.

_____ Appropriate considerations were made for the correct number and type of observers.

_____ Appropriate considerations were made for the methods of collection.

_____ The measurable parameters were indicative of therapeutic effectiveness.

_____ Factors are known that may influence the parameters measured.

_____ The characteristics of the test methods are used to assess these parameters, and factors may influence the accuracy of the test methods.

_____ Standard measurements are used and are reproducible.

_____ The results are reported accurately.

_____ Side effects were reported, including the nature and incidence of the reactions.

_____ Dropouts were reported, and the precise reasons for their dismissal were given.

_____ There was missing or irreconcilable data.

_____ Appropriate statistical methods were utilized.

_____ Valid conclusions were drawn, i.e., the conclusions of the study were actually supported by the results.

_____ The article does provide a reference list or bibliography to verify footnoted citations.

Adapted from: Watanabe AS, Conner CS. Principles of Drug Information Services: A Syllabus and Concepts. *Hamilton, IL: Drug Intelligence Publications, Inc.; 1978.*

Appendix 7-3.3

Checklist of items to include when reporting a randomized trial based upon the Consolidated Standards of Reporting Trials (CONSORT)

CONSORT 2010 checklist of information to include when reporting a randomised trial*

Section/Topic	Item No	Checklist item	Reported on page No
Title and abstract			
	1a	Identification as a randomised trial in the title	
	1b	Structured summary of trial design, methods, results, and conclusions (for specific guidance see CONSORT for abstracts)	
Introduction			
Background and objectives	2a	Scientific background and explanation of rationale	
	2b	Specific objectives or hypotheses	
Methods			
Trial design	3a	Description of trial design (such as parallel, factorial), including allocation ratio	
	3b	Important changes to methods after trial commencement (such as eligibility criteria), with reasons	
Participants	4a	Eligibility criteria for participants	
	4b	Settings and locations where the data were collected	
Interventions	5	The interventions for each group with sufficient details to allow replication, including how and when they were actually administered	
Outcomes	6a	Completely defined pre-specified primary and secondary outcome measures, including how and when they were assessed	
	6b	Any changes to trial outcomes after the trial commenced, with reasons	
Sample size	7a	How sample size was determined	
	7b	When applicable, explanation of any interim analyses and stopping guidelines	
Randomisation:			
Sequence generation	8a	Method used to generate the random allocation sequence	
	8b	Type of randomisation; details of any restriction (such as blocking and block size)	
Allocation concealment mechanism	9	Mechanism used to implement the random allocation sequence (such as sequentially numbered containers), describing any steps taken to conceal the sequence until interventions were assigned	
Implementation	10	Who generated the random allocation sequence, who enrolled participants, and who assigned participants to interventions	
Blinding	11a	If done, who was blinded after assignment to interventions (for example, participants, care providers, those assessing outcomes) and how	
	11b	If relevant, description of the similarity of interventions	

Statistical methods	12a	Statistical methods used to compare groups for primary and secondary outcomes	_____
	12b	Methods for additional analyses, such as subgroup analyses and adjusted analyses	_____

Results

Participant flow (a diagram is strongly recommended)	13a	For each group, the numbers of participants who were randomly assigned, received intended treatment, and were analysed for the primary outcome	_____
	13b	For each group, losses and exclusions after randomisation, together with reasons	_____
Recruitment	14a	Dates defining the periods of recruitment and follow-up	_____
	14b	Why the trial ended or was stopped	
Baseline data	15	A table showing baseline demographic and clinical characteristics for each group	_____
Numbers analysed	16	For each group, number of participants (denominator) included in each analysis and whether the analysis was by original assigned groups	_____
Outcomes and estimation	17a	For each primary and secondary outcome, results for each group, and the estimated effect size and its precision (such as 95% confidence interval)	
	17b	For binary outcomes, presentation of both absolute and relative effect sizes is recommended	_____
Ancillary analyses	18	Results of any other analyses performed, including subgroup analyses and adjusted analyses, distinguishing pre-specified from exploratory	_____
Harms	19	All important harms or unintended effects in each group (for specific guidance see CONSORT for harms)	_____

Discussion

Limitations	20	Trial limitations, addressing sources of potential bias, imprecision, and, if relevant, multiplicity of analyses	_____
Generalisability	21	Generalisability (external validity, applicability) of the trial findings	_____
Interpretation	22	Interpretation consistent with results, balancing benefits and harms, and considering other relevant evidence	_____

Other information

Registration	23	Registration number and name of trial registry	_____
Protocol	24	Where the full trial protocol can be accessed, if available	_____
Funding	25	Sources of funding and other support (such as supply of drugs), role of funders	

*We strongly recommend reading this statement in conjunction with the CONSORT 2010 Explanation and Elaboration for important clarifications on all the items. If relevant, we also recommend reading CONSORT extensions for cluster randomised trials, non-inferiority and equivalence trials, non-pharmacological treatments, herbal interventions, and pragmatic trials. Additional extensions are forthcoming: for those and for up-to-date references relevant to this checklist, see www.consort-statement.org.

The CONSORT Statement and the CONSORT Explanation and Elaboration Document are distributed under the terms of the Creative Commons Attribution License, which permits use, distribution, and reproduction in any medium provided the original author and source are credited.

Appendix 7-3.4

Checklist of items to evaluate the quality of reports of meta-analysis of randomized controlled trials (QUOROM)

Heading	Subheading	Descriptor	Reported? (Y/N)	Page number
Title		Identify the report as a meta-analysis [or systematic review] of RCTs[26]		
Abstract		Use a structured format[27]		
		Describe		
	Objectives	The clinical question explicitly		
	Data sources	The databases (i.e., list) and other information sources		
	Review methods	The selection criteria (i.e., population, intervention, outcome, and study design); methods for validity assessment, data abstraction, and study characteristics, and quantitative data synthesis in sufficient detail to permit replication		
	Results	Characteristics of the RCTs included and excluded; qualitative and quantitative findings (i.e., point estimates and confidence intervals); and subgroup analyses		
	Conclusion	The main results		
		Describe		
Introduction		The explicit clinical problem, biological rationale for the intervention, and rationale for review		
Methods	Searching	The information sources, in detail[28] (e.g., databases, registers, personal files, expert informants, agencies, hand-searching), and any restrictions (years considered, publication status,[29] language of publication[30,31])		
	Selection	The inclusion and exclusion criteria (defining population, intervention, principal outcomes, and study design)[32]		
	Validity assessment	The criteria and process used (e.g., masked conditions, quality assessment, and their findings[33–36])		
	Data abstraction	The process or processes used (e.g., completed independently, in duplicate)[35,36]		

Heading	Subheading	Descriptor	Reported? (Y/N)	Page number
	Study characteristics	The type of study design, participants' characteristics, details of intervention, outcome definitions, &c,[37] and how clinical heterogeneity was assessed		
	Quantitative data synthesis	The principal measures of effect (e.g., relative risk), method of combining results (statistical testing and confidence intervals), handling of missing data; how statistical heterogeneity was assessed;[38] a rationale for any a-priori sensitivity and subgroup analyses; and any assessment of publication bias[39]		
Results	Trial flow	Provide a meta-analysis profile summarising trial flow (see figure)		
	Study characteristics	Present descriptive data for each trial (e.g., age, sample size, intervention, dose, duration, follow-up period)		
	Quantitative data synthesis	Report agreement on the selection and validity assessment; present simple summary results (for each treatment group in each trial, for each primary outcome); present data needed to calculate effect sizes and confidence intervals in intention-to-treat analyses (e.g., 232 tables of counts, means and SDs, proportions)		
Discussion		Summarise key findings; discuss clinical inferences based on internal and external validity; interpret the results in light of the totality of available evidence; describe potential biases in the review process (e.g., publication bias); and suggest a future research agenda		

Reprinted with permission from Mohler D, Cook DJ, Eastwood S, et al., for the QUORUM Group. Improving the quality of reports of meta-analysis of randomized controlled trials: the QUORUM statement. Lancet. *1999; 354:1896–900.*

Improving the quality of reports of meta-analyses of randomised controlled trials: the QUOROM statement flow diagram

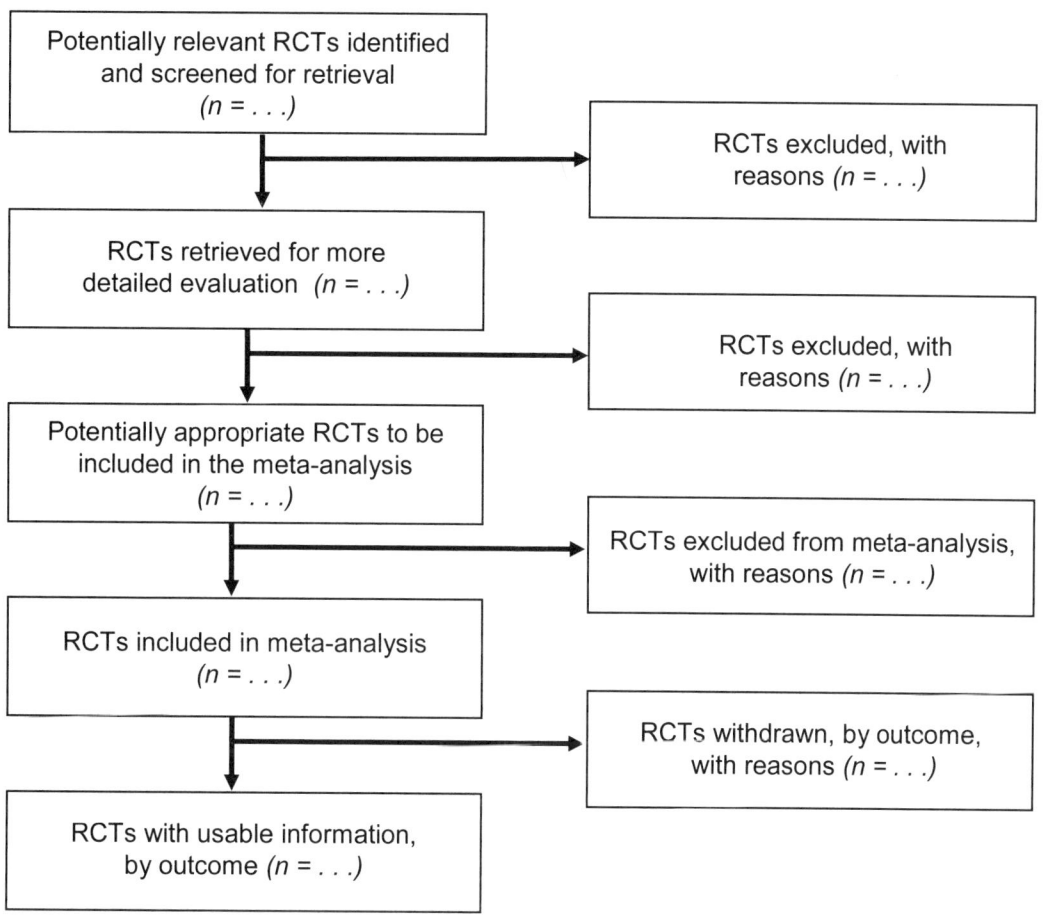

*The *Lancet* is happy for readers to make copies of the checklist and flow diagram. Permission need not be obtained from the journal for reproduction of these items.

Appendix 7-3.5

Web Sites and Resources Useful for Evidence-Based Practice

References	Site Address
National Organizations	
U.S. Food and Drug Administration	www.fda.gov
U.S. National Library of Medicine	www.nlm.nih.gov
Centers for Disease Control and Prevention	www.cdc.gov
National Institutes of Health	www.nih.gov
Professional Organizations	
American Society of Health-System Pharmacists	www.ashp.org
American Pharmaceutical Association	www.pharmacist.com
American College of Clinical Pharmacy	www.accp.com
American Association of Colleges of Pharmacy	www.aacp.org
American Heart Association	www.heart.org
American Diabetes Association	www.diabetes.org
American Cancer Society	www.cancer.org
Representative Pharmaceutical Companies	
Abbott	www.abbott.com
Bristol-Myers Squibb	www.bms.com
Eli Lilly	www.lilly.com
GlaxoSmithKline	www.gsk.com
Merck	www.merck.com
Novartis	www.novartis.com
Pfizer	www.pfizer.com
Professional Practice Resources	
Avicenna	www.avicenna.com
BIDS Embase	www.bids.ac.uk
Biosis	http://science.thomsonreuters.com/ and access http://thomsonreuters.com/products_services/science/science_products/a-z/biosis/
CenterWatch	www.centerwatch.com
Clinical Pharmacology on Line	http://www.clinicalpharmacology.com
CMA Infobase: Clinical Practice Guidelines	www.cma.ca/cpgs
Current Contents	http://science.thomsonreuters.com/ and access http://thomsonreuters.com/products_services/science/science_products/a-z/current_contents/
Docnet Journals	http://www.docnet.org.uk/
DoseCalcOnLine	http://www.meds.com/DoseCalc/DoseCalc.html
Guidelines and Guidelines Practice	www.eguidelines.co.uk

References	Site Address
Harrison's Online	http://harrisons.accessmedicine.com/ (This site requires a password to gain access)
Health Services/Technology Assessment Text (HSTAT)	http://www.ncbi.nlm.nih.gov/books/NBK16710/
Lexi-Comp On-Line	http://www.crlonline.com/crlsql/servlet/crlonline
Health on the Net Foundation	http://www.hon.ch/HONsearch/Patients/medhunt.html
Medical Matrix	http://www.medmatrix.org/index.asp
MedicineNet Medical Dictionary	http://www.medicinenet.com/diseases_and_conditions/article.htm
Healthtouch Online	http://www.healthtouch.com/level1/p_dri.htm
Medscape	http://www.medscape.com/
Merck Manual of Diagnosis and Therapy	http://www.merck.com/
Merck Manual of Geriatrics	http://www.merck.com/
Merck Manual of Medical Information – Home Edition	http://www.merck.com/
MyOptumHealth	http://www.myoptumhealth.com/portal/
National Institute for Health and Clinical Excellence	http://www.nice.org.uk/
Natural Medicines Comprehensive Database	http://naturaldatabase.therapeuticresearch.com/home.aspx?cs=schoolnopl&s=ND&AspxAutoDetectCookieSupport=1
PharmWeb	http://www.pharmweb.net/
Physicians' Online (POL)	http://www.medscape.com/public/help/pol
PubMed	http://www.ncbi.nlm.nih.gov/pubmed/
RxList The Internet Drug Index	http://www.rxlist.com
SIGN Guidelines	http://www.sign.ac.uk/guidelines/development/index.html
StatRef search engine (applied to textbooks)	http://online.statref.com (This site requires a password to gain access)
Turning Research Into Practice (TRIP Database – Clinical Search Engine)	http://www.tripdatabase.com/

Application of Clinical Reasoning

"A medical student asked his attending physician how one acquires clinical judgment. The response was 'from experience.' Then the student asked how to acquire experience. The response was 'from bad clinical judgment.'"

—Neal Whitman

CHAPTER OUTLINE

Purpose

Clinical Reasoning
- Skills Needed to Perform Clinical Reasoning
- Heuristics for Clinical Reasoning
- Assessing Meaning from Information Using Evidence-Based Clinical Reasoning

Clinical Reasoning for Medication Use Assessment
- Individualized Assessment
- Systems of Care Issues Related to Medication Use

Summary

Assessment Questions

Pharmacist–Patient Encounter with Our Four Cases
- Case 1: Lauren Smith calls Nasir Jabr, PharmD, RPh; *Jabr engages Lauren about her values and preferences in care.*
- Case 2: Christine Johnston, PharmD, RPh; *Johnston reevaluates the challenge of guiding care after obtaining information about cactus flowers as a treatment.*
- Case 3: Luisa Rodriguez, PharmD, RPh; *Rodriguez tailors Huong's problem list based upon his needs and prepares a progress note reflecting it.*
- Case 4: Michael Jones, MS, RPh; *Jones analyzes his data sources and determines additional evidence is needed before making his care decisions.*

OBJECTIVES

To gain knowledge of:

1. the skills needed to do clinical reasoning;
2. how empathy, metacognition, genuineness, respectfulness, self-directedness, and experience contribute to becoming an expert clinical reasoner;
3. how to incorporate the use of evidence into clinical reasoning;
4. how to adopt the skills of life-long, self-directed learning to be an expert clinical reasoner;
5. how to apply clinical reasoning skills for the purposes of patient-centered medication use assessment; and
6. how to apply clinical reasoning skills to address system of care issues related to medication use.

PURPOSE

The purpose of this chapter is to discuss in-depth the skills you will need to perform critical thinking, reflection, and self-directed learning to conduct evidence-based clinical reasoning for your patients. This chapter will focus on the use of these evidence-based clinical reasoning skills in the pharmaceutical care process to provide patient-centered care.

*Appendix 8-1 can be also be found on the web at www.ashp.org/patientcare.

CLINICAL REASONING

Clinical reasoning is central to delivering professional care to patients. Your ability to use the clinical reasoning process for each patient is what distinguishes you as a professional. Without the use of this reasoning, you become someone who is limited to delivering technically competent service only. Technical competence does not address the moral or empathic needs of the patient in relationship to the pharmaceutical care services that you have a responsibility to provide. If these services are missing, then your purpose as a pharmacist is limited to ensuring technically correct product preparation and dispensing; in other words, only a portion of your professional responsibilities and value to the patient are fulfilled.

Clinical reasoning is a major component of expert clinical problem solving. It is a dynamic, cyclic, reiterative process in which observation, analysis, synthesis, deduction, induction, hypothesis generation and testing, inquiry-strategy design, and the skills of examination are all interrelated.[1] Expert clinical performance is effective problem solving. It is accomplished by combining clinical reasoning with accurate knowledge of background information and evidence. Clinical reasoning involves the application of knowledge and experience to identify patient problems and to direct clinical judgments and actions that result in positive patient outcomes. These skills can be cultivated.[2] The use of clinical reasoning skills continues throughout each step in the care process. Your ability to use clinical reasoning skills is critical to preparing a patient's care plan incorporating both the individual's health care needs and his or her values with the optimal practices and evidence available. These skills help you determine the best approach that is specific to the patient's needs. Your approach will vary with each patient based upon the values and specific concerns for that person.

▶ KEY POINT

The general steps to evidence-based clinical reasoning are:

1. **be aware of the stage of the clinical reasoning process you are in. These stages may be identified as data acquisition, problem recognition, interpretation, or hypothesis generation.**
2. **integrate information from the patient encounter to define the problem(s) with which you are assisting the patient.**
3. **search for additional data and evidence to refine the problem and develop preferred and alternative solutions.**
4. **recognize there are usually multiple reasoning strategies and approaches to tailor your solutions to the complexity and context for each patient.**

What are the consequences of not using clinical reasoning to develop a patient care plan? Without the development of evidence-based reasoning skills, you are likely to use other approaches such as delaying an important decision with negative implications for the patient's progress, deferring to someone else, continuing with the current approach that is not working well, or trying something new for which no reflection or evidence has been sought. All of these approaches are suboptimal, likely ineffective, and may be an invitation for harm and injury.

Chapter 8 helps us to gain a greater knowledge about the skill and application of clinical reasoning. Figure 2-3 in Chapter 2 shows a representation of the clinical reasoning process. This reasoning, combined with use of evidence, defines your expertise in practice. Here we will focus on the clinical reasoning skills needed in the pharmaceutical care process. Being able to think critically provides you with the power to meet the patients' needs in their own context and preferences, confronting uncertainty by considering alternatives and evaluating them. Important attributes that support your ability to perform clinical reasoning include moral reasoning, metacognition, and empathy as well as display of genuineness in your work and respect for others. Core to these skills is the presence of a desire in you to be self-directed, self-disciplined, self-monitored, and self-corrective in your thinking. You must develop rigorous habits of critical thinking, situated in the structures of the clinical traditions and practices of the profession.[3] Experience provides the on-going learning needed to practice competently and responsively to patients.

Skills Needed to Perform Clinical Reasoning

The following discussion will address what skills you can demonstrate that are consistent with these attributes when delivering care to your patient.

Moral Reasoning. Pharmacists who demonstrate clinical reasoning use moral reasoning skills.[4] What are moral reasoning skills? They are the processes that an individual undergoes to arrive at decisions based upon a concept of right and wrong. The theory that describes moral reasoning in the context of development is Kohlberg's stages of moral development (refer to Table 2-2). Moral reasoning is a significant determinant of how pharmacists behave; pharmacists with higher moral reasoning skills demonstrate better clinical performance. Research has already demonstrated that when a person in the health professions has more advanced moral reasoning skills, that individual is most assuredly a high clinical performer.[5,6] These individuals work at being competent and effective as a standard of practice behavior.[7,8] Your moral reasoning skills help you to identify acceptable solutions for a patient.

What moral reasoning skills would you employ? These skills include being aware of your own motivations, abilities, competence, and limitations in order to act on behalf of the patient. Your approach to care requires a commitment to using evidence on behalf of the patient and a commitment to continuing care for that patient. You should get to know as much as you can about the patient in order to understand his or her needs. Maintaining confidentiality about your patient and what you learn in the patient–pharmacist relationship is essential. You have an obligation to inform the patient about what you are going to do or plan to do, while helping him or her reach decisions that are appropriate for the illness and for life. These basic moral skills make you a sound clinical performer.

Metacognition. Metacognition refers to deliberation and reflection during problem solving. It is the self-monitoring function that tells you how well you are doing in thinking through the patient's problems and possible solutions to consider. It is this ability that is the hallmark of an expert clinician.

KEY POINT

Metacognition is the main skill in the clinical reasoning process that you must employ to grow and develop professionally. It is the "how" in "how do you clinically problem solve?"

Donald Schon has described the metacognitive reasoning process as reflection-in-action.[9] This descriptive phrase sums up metacognition. Well developed metacognitive skills are observed in expert clinicians. This set of skills is recognized within yourself when you are purposefully positing questions, gathering information iteratively, and testing hypotheses. Metacognition is the constant engagement in this process that makes you aware of the inconsistencies in the patient information or story, the importance of missing data that is not yet understood or sense of a problem not yet solved, creating in you a feeling of discomfort until resolved. Metacognition is the constant use of reflective skills, which you are aware of, through an iterative experience. You use these skills to develop and consider information, discern its relevance, and then make decisions. It is the cumulative experience of the professional that continually builds and develops with each case, contributing to the ongoing development of these metacognitive skills in each of us. We must purposefully develop our expertise using this approach in order to become better at what we do.

Intuition is not the same as metacognition. Knowing intuitively is to have a direct understanding without reasoning. Intuition can be attributed to the recollection of forgotten facts, to automatic thinking, or to the unconscious processing of a difficult problem. These experiences are not reflective or systematic. Metacognition is a skill set that you work at developing.

Empathy. The core of caring behavior in the pharmacist–patient relationship is empathy. Empathy is a reflexive understanding of patient and self.[10] In essence, the ability to empathize is to be able to put yourself in someone else's place, sometimes referred to as being able to "walk in someone else's shoes." Empathy is an important ability to draw upon at every stage of clinical reasoning. Without the use of empathic reasoning, you cannot identify what the patient views as a problem and how a patient feels about or accepts the possible solutions (or course of action) that you recommend. It is important to understand empathy as a skill set that is used to understand and learn what the patient is experiencing and needs. Empathy itself is not the emotional state of sympathizing; rather, it is understanding what exactly is being told to you through all forms of communication.

Empathy includes listening and responding skills. Listening involves hearing what is said and observing what is demonstrated in nonverbal behaviors. Listening involves interpreting the emotions of the patient. Responding involves determining the most appropriate response to what your listening reveals in order to maximize what you learn from the patient about his or her concerns and needs.[11] Coulehan and Block have identified levels of responding to help describe optimal responses to gain the full understanding of what the patient is trying to communicate. The first two levels are ignoring and minimizing. Ignoring is when you act like you didn't hear the patient and provide no acknowledgment about what the patient has told you. Minimizing is when you respond to what the patient has told you but you respond by indicating that things are less important or serious than what the patient has implied. Both forms of response result in the patient interpreting you as not listening—or being a poor listener, interpreting inaccurately what has just been communicated.

The two levels of response that are desired in empathic communication are known as interchangeable or additive. An interchangeable response is one that recognizes the feelings and symptoms expressed by the patient at an accurate level of intensity and provided back to the patient indicating that you have identified the feelings and experiences and the intensity accurately. An additive response takes this skill one step further. You not only understand what the patient is expressing, but you can relate to what is being felt but not expressed in any way. Your response articulates these feelings back to the patient in words that indicate you understand. Additive responses become possible as you gain experiences over time with patients who have had similar problems. As their stories unfold, you assimilate a body of experiential knowledge that allows you to substitute words for the unspoken. This is an expert skill. We will examine empathic communication and levels of responding in the patient cases in this chapter.

The ways in which you use verbal and nonverbal language will influence your ability to be empathic. Patients do not use medical terminology to express the presence of or degree of intensity of their symptoms. Patients use words that express how they feel about their symptoms as well as what symptoms they are having. It becomes your job to translate what the patient is saying in patient language into the professional language you use.[12] **Table 8-1** shows a listing of words that describe levels of feelings to help you interpret both the quantity and intensity of what the patient is discussing with you. This may be useful generally in understanding patient communications during the patient–pharmacist encounter. You may find this useful to build upon the knowledge gained through completing the work in Chapter 5. Specifically, this table provides language cues in order for you to construct an appropriate empathic response.

Nonverbal communication involves the way a person uses his or her body—including personal and social space and paralinguistics—the "how" of speech. The body language of both you and your patient become important to empathic reasoning. You must act interested, make eye contact, and stay focused on the patient. Otherwise, the patient is likely to interpret your actions as disinterest and you will not learn what you need to know. The distance between you and the patient can also make a difference. For example, if you are trying to discuss a delicate and private aspect of the patient's condition, the patient is less likely to respond if he or she has to speak loudly in order for you to hear. Characteristics of the boundaries of space between you and the patient in any interaction are shown in **Table 8-2**. Consider using an appropriate distance from the patient for the type of interaction you expect to have.

The most subtle aspects of the communication exchange are probably the paralinguistic characteristics of the patient's speech. When we hear the words a patient is saying, we are also influenced by the rate of speech, pauses, tone or voice quality,

TABLE 8-1.

Descriptive Words for Levels of Feelings

Intensity	Anger	Joy	Anxiety or Fear	Depression
Weak	Annoyed	Pleased	Uneasy	Sad
	Upset	Glad	Uncertain	Down
	Irritated	Happy	Apprehensive	Blue
Medium	Angry	Turned on	Worried	Gloomy
	Testy	Joyful	Troubled	Sorrowful
	Quarrelsome	Delighted	Afraid	Miserable
Strong	Infuriated	Marvelous	Tormented	Distraught
	Spiteful	Jubilant	Frantic	Overwhelmed
	Enraged	Ecstatic	Terrified	Devastated

Adapted from Coulehan JL, Block MR. The Medical Interview: A Primer for Students of the Art. Philadelphia, PA: F.A. Davis Company.

TABLE 8-2.

Space Boundaries in Patient Interactions

Interaction	Distance between You and Patient	Body Contact	Eye Contact	Vocalization
Intimate	0–1.5 feet	Expected (e.g., exam)	Not possible; restricted to small area	Low and frequent
Personal	1.5–4 feet	Close contact likely	May see whole face	Moderate
Social	4–12 feet	Out of reach	Eye contact important	Louder
Public	12–25 feet	No	Individuality lost	Louder; the pronunciation exaggerated

Adapted from Forsyth DM. Looking good to communicate better with patients. Nursing. 1983; July:34–7.

pitch, volume, and word choice. These characteristics, combined with the words stated, tell us the patient's emotions, feelings, and sincerity. Learning the nuances of paralinguistics is a communication skill that develops through formal study and your accumulated experience in working with a wide range of patients. Overall, your main goal with the patient should be to assess the consistency between what is being said and the physical behavior. When there is consistency, the communication is likely to be accurate. When there is inconsistency, you should probe further to determine why.

Genuineness. Genuineness means being "you," both professionally and personally. It requires you to express your feelings within the boundaries of your professional relationships. This means that you must be able to distinguish your personal self from your professional self. But this is where it gets more difficult for many people. You may have personal feelings in response to information provided or the behavior of a patient with whom you work; however, these feelings are inappropriate to act on. Your professional feelings must govern your response to these situations. The skill of being genuine requires that you restrict your responses to those that you think will help the patient therapeutically. It may be appropriate to confirm a patient's feelings through sharing a reflection of a personal nature, but only after you have evaluated it through a professional frame of reference and determined that it has therapeutic value to your relationship with the patient.

Respect for Others. Respect is about valuing the patient's traits and beliefs rather than considering your own feelings first. You must see the patient's attitudes, beliefs, and behaviors as a legitimate representation or extension of illness or problems. This means that you are personally nonjudgmental about the patient, and are able to serve the patient professionally with all of these factors taken into consideration. The skill of respect requires you to stay focused on what is needed to care for the patient and to help the patient improve. Follow the communication tips noted below to demonstrate your respect for the patient:

1. Introduce yourself and communicate specifically why you are there. You should address the patient by his or her proper last name when you first meet. The patient should be the one who invites you to use a first name in conversation.

2. Ask the patient how you might improve his or her comfort. Consider this response throughout your interaction.

3. Use proper communication skills for the specific situation.

4. Warn the patient when you are going to say something that may induce emotional harm or when you will do something that might be unexpectedly painful.

5. Always acknowledge through your response that you have heard what the patient has said.

Self-correction. Self correction is the process of acting to improve your applied knowledge through reflection and action. As we gain clinical reasoning skills, we are gaining clinical knowledge. As you become an expert, you transform the way you recall information for use from data to patterns, i.e., patterns in the form of similar cases and an array of relevant knowledge. You continue to make judgment errors as you become an expert, i.e., you are not error free in your thinking. When you encounter something new, the most common type of error is to misidentify the problem you are seeing. As you become expert, this type of error continues, however, you are less likely to identify this as an error because of gained confidence and reinforced case patterns. This is a fundamental reason why self-correction

through reflection and action is essential. You must continue to actively monitor for the quality and soundness of the clinical reasoning process you follow and attend to the resultant outcomes. The stronger your critical thinking skills and willingness to self-correct, the higher your level of expertise will become. This is a long-term process yielding excellent clinical care results.

▶ **KEY POINT** ••••••••••••••••••••••

The identification and management of common and familiar clinical problems are often addressed through the external development of clinical guidelines and protocols. These are tools that provide you assistance with patient care. While helpful, it is still important for you to reflect when using protocols to assure the application of the protocols is contextually appropriate for the patient you are serving.

Experience. Experience provides the on-going learning in order to develop competence in the actual clinical situations for care provision. Transitioning from an early beginner practitioner to a competent practitioner occurs as a result of gaining experience with the particular area of interest and employing self-correction through reflection gained from this experience. Experiential learning requires you to be ready and open to that which evolves in the patient care situation. Practicing your profession requires experiential learning supported by knowledge in the form of evidence, and the use of the evidence in a way relevant to the patient's situation.[13]

HEURISTICS FOR CLINICAL REASONING

Occasionally, you may encounter a very difficult problem that is not solvable using your systematic methods. How does one clinically reason through these complex or messy problems? Heuristics are techniques we use as people to solve such problems. We rely on the use of heuristics to address high stakes problems that are ambiguous to us even after reflective thought or when we do not have adequate time to think through solutions.[15] We each adopt different heuristic approaches to solving them. Here is a summary of some possible approaches:[9]

- Consider the most common problems first.
- Consider more seriously those problems for which effective therapeutic options are available; if you failed to initiate treatment, it would be harmful to the patient.
- Make sure that both history taking and the physical examination are branching procedures.
- Strive for the degree of precision or reliability at hand.
- Form a reasoned plan to test your hypotheses, because there should be a reason for every piece of data you intend to gather.
- Seek out and evaluate evidence that tends to rule out any hypothesis or alternative.
- Consider the possibility that a patient with multiple symptoms or complaints may have more than one problem.

Assessing Meaning from Information Using Evidence-Based Clinical Reasoning

The subjective and objective data gathered through various sources must be interpreted for its significance to the patient's case. As you gain skills in clinical reasoning, it becomes clear that interpreting the language of the patient is a critical aspect of selecting relevant subjective information. As you gain technical knowledge about the conditions, effective treatments, and methods of management, it becomes clear that you must integrate this information with what you know to be significant to the patient. Both forms of knowledge are critical to expert clinical care. Use of these combined forms of knowledge as the framework for applying the components of clinical reasoning is evidence-based clinical reasoning. Research has been conducted on this subject with family physicians. The findings revealed that family physicians think about evidence during patient interactions but do so in the context of their patients and their communities. They appreciated evidence that had been appraised, summarized, and published as a guideline by an independent national organization. Evidence is an important part of clinical practice and was considered along with many other factors in their practices. This work accurately summarized the place for evidence in clinical reasoning.[14]

CLINICAL REASONING FOR MEDICATION USE ASSESSMENT

Individualized Assessment

Clinical reasoning is all about individualizing the patient's care plan to best meet the patient's needs.

Identifying the Patient's Health Care Needs. To identify the patient's health care needs, you must evaluate the information in the patient database, and assess the needs and preferences as perceived by the patient. Anticipating the most common problems before beginning your detailed evaluation is a proactive approach to patient assessment—and one that is strongly tied to the concept of patient-centered care. This approach is preferred to a reactive technique where you only perform an assessment and provide advice for existing problems noted by other people or for problems recognized by scanning the patient data only after they occur. The proactive approach evaluates the overall patient and his or her needs. You will likely identify therapeutic issues not recognized by others. You are able to identify and document "significant negatives" (i.e., the absence of problems) and "significant positives" (i.e., the presence of problems), improving the ability for yourself and others to monitor and assist the patient with his or her progress. Screening for problems that may not have manifested or been recognized increases your opportunity to prevent problems or resultant undesired outcomes. Your personal method for conducting the assessment should suit your personal style and experience level. However, the method should incorporate the following characteristics:

1. Anticipate and discuss if the most common potential problems encountered with patients are present or absent with this patient.
2. Be consistent between patients about the basic evaluation you conduct.
3. Individualize the depth and scope of the evaluation beyond the basic assessment provided to all.
4. Document the complete assessment (i.e., both significant positives and significant negatives).

The more effective your clinical reasoning process, the better you will be at identifying all of the potential problems.

Identifying the Patient's Medical Needs. Once you have established an initial impression of the patient's overall health care needs, you narrow your assessment to determining the patient's actual medical needs. Specifically, the patient has some history to share with you and an accompanying list of medical problems or active conditions. Other sources of information (e.g., medical chart, pharmacy profile) may be accessible to you to provide this detail.

Identifying the Patient's Medication-Related Needs. This level identifies all of the patient's medication-related needs. This list of needs must be prioritized by the most important or significant problems to be addressed to meet the patient's goals. The development of this list requires your clinical reasoning skills. For many of these needs, identifying those that must be addressed also requires the shared decision making of the patient. Upon completion of your initial assessment of the patient, you will have a "picture" of the patient—the patient's story. This story leads you to an initial problem list that both you and the patient share. You must further discern the pharmaceutical care aspects of this problem list that require your attention. To identify the patient's drug therapy problems and needs, you should use a systematic process that meets your personal style but addresses the core practice and care considerations of the patient and his or her drug therapy care. The problem list contains everything that you should consider when setting pharmacotherapeutic goals.

CASE EXAMPLE

Pharmacist's Initial Establishment of a Problem List from Existing Data—Part 1

A 78-year-old woman, Mavis Paschal, comes to your once-a-month brown bag session at the hospital that is open to the local community to attend. Ms. Paschal had been discharged from the hospital 2 weeks ago after being admitted for a suspected stroke. She has difficulty hearing and has partially corrected vision with eye glasses, rendering her unable to read clearly. During her hospitalization, she was diagnosed with early onset heart failure and coronary artery disease. Her adult daughter, June Paschal, has been living with her in her home as an in-home caregiver since being discharged. June says her mother has "mild occasional dizziness, forgetfulness, and difficulty 'doing what she usually does.'" June brought her mother to the brown bag session, bringing all of her medications in a bag. You have June and Mavis empty out the bag and find the following:

1. *Bayer® aspirin 81 mg tablets*
2. *PreserVision® Soft Gels with Lutein*
3. *B vitamin complex capsule*
4. *Excedrin PM® capsules*
5. *Hydrochlorothiazide 25 mg tablets*
6. *Zyrtec® 10 mg tablets*
7. *Ranitidine 150 mg tablets*
8. *Ginkgo biloba tablets*
9. *Digoxin 0.25 mg tablets*
10. *Prevacid® 30 mg capsules*
11. *Lipitor® 20 mg tablets*
12. *Oscal-D® 250 mg tablets*
13. *Vitamin D 2,000 International Unit capsules*
14. *Warfarin 5 mg tablets*

You examine the different medications, reflect briefly on the initial information that June and Mavis have provided, and form an initial impression that includes a preliminary list of potential medication-related issues.

Initial Impressions:

- *Visual impairment and hearing impairment need to be addressed in the home setting to assure general safety.*
- *Visual impairment and hearing impairment need to be considered when determining the counseling strategies with Mavis.*
- *June needs to be included in the counseling activities related to Mavis's medications.*
- *Assess drug–drug interactions particularly related to over-the-counter and herbal medication use.*
- *Consider opportunity for medication regimen streamlining and elimination of duplicate or unnecessary medications.*

Individualized Assessment Based Upon the Patient's Preferences and Needs. By answering these basic questions, you are able to identify areas that require further individualized attention in your care planning for each patient:

1. What are the ethnic, cultural, religious, and personal beliefs that are affecting the patient's behaviors related to health overall and medication use?
2. What are the patient's beliefs about health and the value and worth of the medication?
3. How is the patient taking the medication? Is it consistent with what was prescribed?
4. Is the chosen medication(s) cost effective? Does the cost of medication pose a financial barrier to the patient adhering to use?
5. Does the patient understand the purpose of his or her medication(s), how to take it, and the potential side effects of therapy?
6. What educational tools would the patient benefit from (e.g., written patient education sheets, wallet cards, and reminder packaging)?
7. What are the clinical outcomes from the medication use plan?
8. What are the economic outcomes associated with the medication use plan? What are the quality-of-life outcomes experienced by the patient that are directly related to the medication use plan?
9. Are there any other factors to be considered regarding this patient's use of medications?

Individualized Medication Use Assessment. The assessment of medications currently being used involves remembering the patients' health needs and medical problems as you evaluate their medication use. To conduct a basic medication use assessment, you should first identify all of the medications that a patient is actively taking. This process is done in different ways depending on the care environment. In the hospital setting, you may be the professional conducting a medication history on admission. On the other hand, this process may routinely be handled by the nurse and you may need to supplement or augment it. In many settings, you will be able to ask the patient to show you all of the medications that are being taken. Some pharmacists conduct "brown bag" medication reviews. This review occurs when the patient brings a bag containing all of the medication containers he or she is using. The pharmacist then interviews the patient based upon this information as an initial starting point.

Patients and their caretakers may also maintain written lists of active medications. This source is often the one that reflects what the patient is supposed to be doing presently with the medications. However, you may need to use your drug information inquiry skills. For example, you may need to check information resources for tablet or capsule identification based upon a physical description of a drug you are shown. You might also have to contact the patient's pharmacy(ies) or other providers to reconstruct what the patient is supposed to be doing. After the medications are identified, then you should assess the patient's current use of them.

Several routine questions should be asked of every patient in order to understand what he or she is presently doing related to medication use. As you are assessing the medications used, incorporate your technical knowledge of evidence. Knowledge of best clinical practices, evidence-based evaluations, and other methods of scientific support for optimal therapeutic management become critical to serving your patient. Key questions suggested for the basic medication use assessment are shown here:

1. Appropriateness of medication selection. Are the medications chosen for this patient optimal? Do these medications have the greatest relative safety? Have the medications selected been tailored to this individual patient's health and medical needs?

2. Appropriateness of drug regimen. Are the prescribed dose and dosing frequency appropriate—within the usual therapeutic range and/or modified for patient factors?

   Is use as needed appropriate for those medications either prescribed or taken that way?

   Is the route/dosage form/mode of administration appropriate, considering efficacy, safety, convenience, patient limitations, cost, patient preferences, and needs? Are doses scheduled to maximize therapeutic effect and compliance and to minimize adverse effects, drug interactions, and regimen complexity? Is the length or course of therapy appropriate?

3. Presence of therapeutic omission. Have any conditions or problems gone untreated?

4. Presence of therapeutic duplication. Are there any therapeutic duplicates?

5. Existence of allergy or intolerance to medications. Is the patient allergic to or intolerant of any treatments currently being taken or considered? If the patient has an allergy or intolerance, is he or she using any method to alert health care providers of the allergy/intolerance (emergency bracelet, wallet card)?

6. Potential for or actual adverse drug event. Are any symptoms or medical problems possibly drug induced? What is the likelihood that the problem is drug related?

7. Presence of clinically important interactions: drug, disease, nutrient, or laboratory. Are there interactions? Are they clinically significant?

8. Are any medications contraindicated (relatively or absolutely) given patient characteristics, beliefs and preferences, and conditions?

9. Relationship of social or recreational drug use to medical management with drug therapy.

   Is the patient's current use of social drugs problematic?

   What is the patient's usual consumption of alcohol as a social or recreational drug? Could the sudden decrease or discontinuation of social drugs be related to patient symptoms (e.g., withdrawal)?

CASE EXAMPLE

Modifying a Patient's Problem List due to Religious, Economic, or Personal Values—Part 2

After a brief encounter during a free brown bag session, Mavis Paschal discloses that she has no prescription medication insurance. She mentions that her next door neighbor is a nurse and occasionally obtains samples from her work. Her neighbor also assists her with medication decisions, including ordering medications on the Internet on her behalf. Ms. Paschal does not have a regular pharmacist and trusts her next door neighbor with her health care decisions. June Paschal appreciates the help from her neighbor, but questions if these decisions are in the best interest of her mother.

You carefully consider the additional information provided by June and Mavis. You modify the problem list based on economic and personal values expressed by the patient and primary caregiver. You offer to arrange follow-up care.

Modified Problem list:

- *Visual impairment and hearing impairment needs to be addressed in the home setting to assure general safety.*
- *Visual impairment and hearing impairment need to be considered when determining the counseling strategies with Mavis.*
- *Include June and the next door neighbor in the counseling and medication management activities related to Mavis's medications.*
- *Refer Mavis to pharmacist-managed Medication Management Clinic provided by the local public health clinic for significant drug-related problems including multiple drug interactions, duplicate medications, medication regimen streamlining, and medication resources for Mavis.*

Systems of Care Issues Related to Medication Use

Your role as a clinician is to optimize the patient's care experience using evidence-based clinical reasoning to problem solve and determine appropriate care, and to implement that care with the patient. Sometimes, aspects of the larger systems of health care influence this beyond your control. For example, payers may not cover the costs associated with medications determined to be optimal for this patient's use. Or errors are made, and the patient does not receive the intended medication in the way you have intended. These barriers will confront you and your patient. It is essential that you identify these obstacles in the reasoning process and work through possible solutions with the patient.

One barrier that may prevent modifying the drug regimen after your evaluation and assessment is the practical issue of prescribing authority. In the inpatient setting, a medication order may be rewritten by a pharmacist as a verbal order and countersigned by the physician. The pharmacist may also have authority through a collaborative practice agreement to change the medication order or prescription through a practice guideline that indicates the authority that the pharmacist has to make medication regimen changes without the physician's countersignature. In many states, it is possible for the pharmacist to initiate or modify prescription medications in the outpatient setting by being delegated this authority by a physician. In some states, these agreements are not recognized as a legal vehicle to accomplish this goal. In these states, the pharmacist must contact the prescriber ahead of time and recommend a change. The prescriber will then initiate a prescription change and either fax the prescription to the pharmacist or require that the patient pick up the new prescription and have the changes made by the pharmacist.

SUMMARY

Clinical reasoning is applied throughout the care process with the patient. As we progress through the care steps, clinical reasoning is used to determine the problems and the therapeutic options, design the care plan (including the goals and therapeutic regimen), design the monitoring plan, and determine the care behaviors supportive of achieving the goals. You will continue to use clinical reasoning as you implement the plan, assess a patient's response, and use this skill to redesign the plan.

ASSESSMENT QUESTIONS

1. Can someone have sound clinical reasoning skills without having content expertise in the subject matter of concern? Explain the rationale for your answer.
2. Differentiate the characteristics of empathy from sympathy.
3. How do metacognition and intuition differ?
4. Why do experts continue to make problem misidentification errors?
5. Identify five circumstances that a patient might have that would contribute to your clinical reasoning on behalf of that patient.

ASSIGNMENT

1. Identify a family member or friend to interview about his or her general health, medical needs, and medication-related needs. During the interview, practice the skills of empathy, genuineness, respect for others, and clinical reasoning. List this person's health needs, medical needs, and medication-related needs. Prioritize them based upon your own opinion of priority. Then reprioritize them based upon the priorities of the individual. How do they compare? How do you account for the differences?
2. Practice the space boundaries during your interactions with other people and in various settings. Can you perceive the difference in how you feel toward others based upon these geographic space guidelines?
3. Identify situations in your life where you have employed the skills of self-correction to become increasingly expert at something. How did you personally incorporate self-correction skills to become expert?

CASE 1

Jabr engages Lauren about her values and preferences in care

Nasir Jabr and Lauren continue with Lauren's return visit to the pharmacy 1 week later for a follow-up blood pressure check and a response to her question—refer back to Chapter 7. Jabr answers Lauren's question and establishes a collaborative drug therapy management service with her and her physician.

Nasir Jabr (responds to her question): "The best thing for you to do will depend upon what is most important to you and what you believe you can change about your own behaviors. Your health choices depend on it."

(Lauren looks somewhat troubled.)

Nasir Jabr: "You look troubled Lauren. What can I do to help you?"

Lauren: "You mentioned before that you offer a smoking cessation program."

Nasir Jabr: "Yes, and also blood pressure management."

Lauren (expressing herself with lack of confidence)**:** "Is it possible for me to consider this as an option? You know… having this service?"

Nasir Jabr (detects her lack of confidence)**:** "Yes it is. It would be my pleasure to provide this care for you. You are an excellent candidate for benefiting from these services. However, I would like to inform you of a few things before we both agree that this is the best choice for you."

Lauren (looks somewhat relieved)**:** "Okay. I would like to hear more."

Nasir Jabr: "Your physician refers you to me for these services. Your physician and I have agreed to a relationship that is called 'delegated authority.' This means that your physician and I have agreed that I can make decisions about this area of your care, including writing prescriptions and ordering monitoring tests that are needed to provide you with this care."

Lauren (interrupts)**:** "You mean that you are doing something that isn't legal?"

Nasir Jabr (acknowledging her concerns)**:** "Not at all. This is the legal way in which you, your physician, and I will handle helping you with your care. This is also a method of assuring that you will receive quality services from me, and that your physician will be informed of our progress so that everyone involved in your care can be supportive. How does this sound so far?"

Lauren: "I think I understand. It sounds okay. Is there a charge for this service?"

Nasir Jabr: "Yes there is. The charges are established based upon the community standard; if you have insurance, I will bill them with your permission."

Lauren (looking depressed)**:** "I do not have insurance; my parents have been paying for everything."

Nasir Jabr (sensing her reaction)**:** "I have worked with many patients who do not have insurance. I have permission from the pharmacy to work out special payment programs and options for individuals in your situation. Joe (pharmacy technician) has a written explanation of how we can do this. If you think you would still like to pursue this, I will transfer the financial parts of this over to Joe. I will work on your care, and he will work with you to achieve a financial arrangement that meets your situation. I have not encountered a patient situation that Joe hasn't been able to work with yet."

Lauren (relieved)**:** "That sounds good, Nasir. How do we proceed?"

Nasir Jabr: "I would like to share my collaborative practice agreement with you that Dr. Miller and I have prepared (see **Appendix 8-1**). I also have to send a document to the state that indicates I have this arrangement. It is yours to keep and review. You will need to contact Dr. Miller and indicate that I have offered these services and that you would like to receive them. Her office will follow up with me after that. In the meantime, we will need to set up an evaluation and assessment appointment to establish your overall care plan and how we will go about implementing it. Joe will set this up for you too."

Lauren (looking grateful)**:** "Thank you so much, Nasir. I will call Dr. Miller's office."

Nasir Jabr: "Great. Joe can facilitate that if you like. Just let him know if you want his help."

[Nasir updates Lauren's patient profile (see **Figure 8-1**).]

Pharmacy Profile for:					
Patient: Smith, Lauren			New Patient	Print	Close Record
Demographic	OTC / Allergy		Insurance	Diagnosis	Contacts
General Health	Care Plans	Surveys	Account Status	Current Therapy	
General Information	Illnesses	Systems Review	Vital Signs	Lab Values	

Pharmacist's Progress Note: Date: 02-02

LS referred to Dr. Miller by NJ on 02-01 for evaluation of probable UTI. LS presented today with co-trimoxazole prescription. Upon brief history and examination the following was noted:

S: LS reports BP at physician's 148/100; using birth control patch after 2 year history of Lo-Ovral; 3-4 Advil 200 mg tablets 3-4 x per week for headaches – characterized by frontal discomfort and occasional periorbital pain; 1-2 ppd cigarettes. Denies allergy to medications.

O: BP 150/102 seated (repeated here)

A: UTI, probable essential HTN worsened by NSAID use and nicotine addiction - increased risk of thromboembolic events and elevated BP and headaches – symptoms consistent with sinus headache – likely in need of a decongestant rather than Advil.

P: Dispensed co-trimoxazole and counseled to consume water, take to completion. Offered smoking cessation and hypertension management service. Research her question, "Does birth control patch affect BP also?" Asked her to visit in one week for follow-up.

Nasir Jabr, Pharm.D.

Drug Information Search Date: 02-03

Figure 8-1. Pharmacy Profile for Lauren Smith Updated by Pharmacist Nasir Jabr

CASE 1: SPECIFIC QUESTIONS

1. What were some examples of nonverbal communication demonstrated by Lauren?
2. Describe some examples of empathic responses observed in Jabr. At what level of response would you categorize them?
3. Did Jabr demonstrate any moral reasoning skills? If so, identify them in this case.
4. What questions did Lauren ask that suggests she has a trusting relationship with Jabr?

CASE 2

Christine Johnston reevaluates the challenge of guiding care after obtaining information about cactus flowers as a treatment

Christine Johnston evaluates the sources of information she has available to help Mr. Montanez. After learning that there is a clinical hypoglycemic effect with cactus flowers when prepared as Mr. Montanez's family prepares them, Johnston reevaluates the challenge she faces.

Johnston reviews the clinic chart, laboratory data, progress notes, information and impressions from the patient interview, and the biomedical literature-based evidence about alternative product use. In addition, she reviews the biomedical literature for evidence and clinical guidelines for dyslipidemia management, diabetes management, and hypertension management. She prepares a priority list of problems that she thinks require attention. She takes notes to prepare herself for her next meeting with Mr. Montanez and Maria to discuss his perceptions of the problems that need to be addressed. She will work with him and Maria to establish these issues.

Johnston then reprioritizes her notes based upon the priorities she anticipates from Mr. Montanez. These priorities are different than her own, but she thinks that she will make more progress in their relationship by demonstrating this respect for Mr. Montanez's beliefs. She knows that she is at a disadvantage by not understanding the alternative care of his family. She wants him to know that this is a limitation but that she will learn more and work with him in both areas.

Johnston's personal notes in preparation for next visit:

General health problems:

1. Poor vision needs correction.
2. Daily alcohol consumption is excessive.
3. His beliefs about the cause of his diabetes that may not facilitate traditional care. Need to further evaluate this issue with his daughter Maria.
4. Are his immunizations up to date? Recommendations of the American Diabetes Association "Standards of Medical Care in Diabetes." Diabetes Care 2004;27(1):S15–35.
5. Why isn't he on preventive aspirin therapy? He meets the criteria recommended in "Aspirin Therapy in Diabetes." Diabetes Care 2004;27(1):S72.

Medical problems:

1. Diabetes mellitus not controlled based upon blood glucose, HgbA1c, urinary protein, and signs and symptoms.
2. Neurologic pain in legs secondary to diabetes of 15 years.
3. Dyslipidemia borderline—total cholesterol 220; LDL cholesterol not evaluated. Need to determine this – will order LDL for next visit. Recommendations of the Third Report of the National Cholesterol Education Program Expert Panel on Detection, Evaluation, and Treatment of High Blood Cholesterol in Adults (Adult Treatment Panel III) NIH publication no. 01-3670.
4. May have stage 1 hypertension based upon last progress note in chart—needs evaluation. Recommendations of the Seventh Report of the Joint National Committee on Prevention, Detection, Evaluation and Treatment of High Blood Pressure (JNC 7) NIH publication no. 03-5233.
5. Evaluate for retinopathy secondary to diabetes based upon guidelines, "Retinopathy in Diabetes." Diabetes Care 2004;27(1):S84–87.

Medication-related problems:

1. His use of oral diabetes agents is unclear to me. I will discuss with him further the use of these medicines. Confirm that he uses 1 tablet per day of glipizide 5 mg and 1 tablet twice per day of metformin 500 mg.
2. His use of cactus flowers and yucca is sporadic. We need to decide if he will continue to use them. There is a drug interaction between his use of the cactus flowers and his oral hypoglycemics. However, it is difficult to assess if this is a manageable interaction for which he can continue both types of treatment. If so, then we

need to agree on how this will be done. This may be difficult to work out with him.

3. He uses 1 tablet per day of simvastatin 40 mg. Does he take this with an evening meal or at bedtime to maximize its effect?

4. Need to evaluate use of hydrocodone/acetaminophen and drinking. Concerned about dizziness and falls related to this combination, as much as the diabetes. Need to sort this out.

5. Mr. Montanez does not have a contraindication to codeine use—he needs to be re-educated. This is based upon the opioid decision tree departmental guideline.

6. Not sure if Mr. Montanez relates his poor vision, leg pain, frequency of urination, thirst, and hunger to his diabetes—need to discuss and assess.

7. Not sure if Mr. Montanez's beliefs will be compatible with educational effort and adherence to plan recommendations.

CASE 2: SPECIFIC QUESTIONS

1. How does Johnston show genuineness in this description of her clinical reasoning?
2. How does Johnston demonstrate respect for Mr. Montanez in this situation?
3. Identify two examples in this case where Johnston uses evidence-based clinical reasoning.

CASE 3

Luisa Rodriguez tailors Huong's problem list based upon his needs and prepares a progress note reflecting it

Luisa Rodriquez evaluates and prioritizes Huong Tran's health, medical, and medication-related needs.

Rodriguez reviews Huong Tran's admission progress note to pediatrics 5W, the Admitting Physician's Orders by Dr. Morris, her own medication history notes, and the drug information documentation she has collected thus far. She identifies all of Huong's health, medical, and medication-related needs, then prioritizes them. Since several other health professionals would benefit from knowing Rodriguez's analysis of Huong's case, she decides to write a Pharmacist's Progress Note identifying Huong's needs. Her personal notes are as follows:

Problems

1. Medically indigent patient with no personal resources for health care.
2. Without English-speaking parents or caretakers—no translator.
3. Without a primary physician to advocate/ provide care.
4. Uncontrolled asthma—moderate to severe.
5. Alternative medical treatment—acupuncturist, ginkgo (Bai Guo Ye).
6. Uses albuterol to control asthma; school nurse provides sample supply—not dependable or continuous.
7. Without spacer device for albuterol.
8. Needs resources to support discharge medications and followup.

Rodriguez prepares a Pharmacist's Progress Note to communicate her findings (see **Figure 8-2**).

Memorial Hospital and Health System

PROGRESS NOTES

Patient Identification (Stamp)
Name: Huong Tran
Reg.No. 2364590
Location: 5W Pediatrics
Date: 04-02

Age: 8 years old   Sex: Male   VITAL SIGNS:

Weight 40 kg   Height 5'   B/P 109/72   Temp 98.6°
Pulse 82   Resp. 16

Date: 04/02

Pharmacist's Progress Note:
HT is an 8 yo male admitted to 5W Pediatrics from the ER $2°$ to 3rd exacerbation of asthma in 2 weeks. Admitting pharmacist history reveals the following problems:

#1 Medically indigent patient
#2 Non-English speaking Vietnamese parents - no other caretakers
#3 No primary provider
#4 Uncontrolled asthma – exacerbations are moderate to severe
#5 Alternative medical treatment pursued by family – acupuncture and Bai Guo Ye (gingko) – no evidence of effectiveness of gingko in asthma.
#6 Albuterol samples only medication source – provided by sporadically by the school nurse.
#7 Benefits from spacer-device albuterol administration – does not have one.
#8 Needs resources/support for discharge medications and follow up.
A: Child will continue to have uncontrolled asthma episodes without resource support, primary provider, and continuous medication supply with pharmacist's care. Will discuss acceptable solutions with family and social work. Need the interpreter to make progress with parents! I will wait to discuss solutions with family until interpreter is made available.

Luisa Rodriguez
Signature

Figure 8-2. Pharmacist Luisa Rodriguez Prepares a Progress Note to Update Everyone on the Health Care Team about the Patient's Medication-Related Problems and Assessments

CASE 3: SPECIFIC QUESTIONS

1. Which of the clinical reasoning skills dominates Rodriguez's prioritization of Huong's problems in this case? Explain why you identified this particular one.

2. What piece of technical knowledge did Rodriguez have that improved Huong's ability to respond to medication during his acute asthma exacerbation?

CASE 4

Michael Jones analyzes his data sources and determines additional evidence is needed before making his care decisions

Jones reflects on the information he has available from his various data sources. He takes time to think about what he knows to determine the best course of action.

Jones stops to reflect on the information he now knows from his various data sources. It becomes a bit overwhelming, so he decides to extract the meaningful findings he has learned and update Samuel Robinson's Patient History Form—Pharmacist's Recommendations/Plans (see **Figure 8-3**). While he is updating this form, Charlotte (the nurse) conducts an Instrumental Activities of Daily Living (IADL) (see **Figure 8-4**) on Mr. Robinson. Just then, Mr. Robinson's two lady friends, Althea Jones and Dorothy Roberts, stop by to see him. Charlotte briefly interviews them and documents their responses in the IADL. She brings this form to show Jones. He assesses Mr. Robinson's health, medical, and medication-related problems (see **Figure 8-5**). His overall problem list includes:

1. Essential need for in home assistance with ADLs, including medication administration.
2. Anticoagulation management
3. Congestive heart failure management
4. Atrial fibrillation management
5. Thyroid management
6. Evaluate drug–drug interactions:

    warfarin—vitamin E

    warfarin—non-steroidal anti-inflammatory drug and aspirin

7. Evaluate drug–disease interactions: warfarin thyroid disease/synthroid
8. Evaluate possible clonidine-induced hypotensive episodes
9. Evaluate duplication in drug therapy: aspirin

Jones decides to wait for laboratory data before making a dosing recommendation about warfarin.

Demographic and Administrative Information:	Room No.	ID No. 02946372	
Date: 09-25	Gender: M	Primary Language: ENGLISH	
Name: SAMUEL ROBINSON	DOB: 11-23-35	Height:	Weight:
Street Address: 1362 MOCKINGDALE LANE	BP: 156/102	Temp:	Pulse: 110R
City, State, Zip BILOXI, MISSISSIPPI 78023	Race/Ethnicity: AF-AMER	Religion: Baptist	
Home Phone #: (901) 468-4832	MD/Phone No. Dr. Rangert/Dr. Friedland		
Work Phone #: N/A	Pharmacist/Phone No. Joe Daly		
Occupation: RETIRED - Farming	Insurance: MEDICARE		
Family Members/Care Givers: WIFE DECEASED – Friends: Dorothy Roberts, Althea Jones			

Problem List:	Pharmacist's Recommendations/Plan:
1.	
2.	
3.	
4.	
5.	
6.	
7.	
8.	
9.	
10.	

Pharmacist's Name: Michael Jones   Date: _____   Phone/Pager #: _____

Chief Complaint/History of Present Illness: "Hard time breathing – was gonna suffocate" became dizzy - started to faint – called 911.
Past Medical History/Surgery/Genetics: S/P myocardial infarction
Family and Social History (significant relationship/co-habitants): wife died 1 year ago. Friends visit almost daily however medication use is not managed appropriately
Physical Examination/Review of Systems: (-) S + Sx of bleeding or bruising; (-) bleeding gums; (-) blood in urine or stool. Sleeps 2 pillow orthopnea.
ADL: see evaluation
Lifestyle/Diet/Exercise:

Acute and Chronic Medical Problems/Associated Symptoms:	
1. Congestive heart failure	6. Poorly managed drug regimen
2. Hypertension (type unknown)	7.
3. Atrial fibrillation	8.
4. Hypothyroidism	9.
5. Status post myocardial infarction	10.
Describe Patient's Health Beliefs and Values:	

Does Patient Receive Assistance in Medication Administration? Describe: No – friends pick up and take him to Daly's pharmacy

Figure 8-3. Samuel Robinson's Patient History Form

Allergies/Intolerances: (√) No Known Drug Allergies		
Allergen:	Reaction:	Treatment:
Allergen:	Reaction:	Treatment:
Allergen:	Reaction:	Treatment:

Social Drug Use: Alcohol: ∅ Caffeine: ---- Tobacco: 1 ppd-3ppd Other:

Current Drug Therapy (prescription and over the counter, vitamins, remedies, alternative treatment):

Drug Name Strength/Route	Problem Number	Usual Schedule	Describe PRN Use	Does Med Work?	Side Effects or Concerns	Compliance Issues
1. Blood thinner/warfarin 5 mg		Qday			(pt. interview)	He can't
2. Heart pills x3/Digoxin 0.25 mg		Qday				remember-
3. Clonidine 0.5 mg		Qday				problems -
4. Hydrochlorothiazide 25 mg		Qday				reports using
5. Synthroid 125 mcg		Qday				warfarin and
6. Multivitamin		Qday				vitamin E qd
7. Advil			1-2x /wk			
8. Vitamin E 1,000 I.U.'s		Qday				
9. Dofetilide 250 mcg		2x /day				
10. Aspirin (baby) 81 mg		qday			(bottle label)	
11. Warfarin 5 mg		qod			(nurse admit)	
12. Warfarin		Mon-Sat			(bottle label)	
13. Aspirin tab 1 tab		qday			(nurse admit)	
14.						
15.						

Past Drug Therapy:

Time Line: Circle administration times and record appropriate medications and meals below:

Patient's Actual Use:
6 7 8 9 10 11 12 1 2 3 4 5 6 7 8 9 10 11 12 1 2 3 4 5
am   noon   pm   Midnight   am

Prescribed Schedule:
6 7 8 9 10 11 12 1 2 3 4 5 6 7 8 9 10 11 12 1 2 3 4 5
am   noon   pm   midnight   am

Costs of Meds/Month:	$	Insurance:	( ) Yes	( ) No
	Co-pay:	Medicaid:		Annual Income:

Completed by: _____ **Date:** _____

Figure 8-3 (continued). Samuel Robinson's Patient History Form

Instrumental Activities of Daily Living (IADL)

Patient's Name: ____S. Robinson_____ Date:_____

I = *Independent*   *A* = *Assistance Required*   *D* = *Dependent*

Obtained from Patient	Obtained from Informant	Activity	Guidelines for Assessment
(I) A D	I (A) D	Using Telephone	I = Able to look up numbers, dial, receive and make calls without help A = Able to answer phone or dial operator in an emergency but needs special phone or help in getting number, dialing D = Unable to use telephone
I (A) D	I A (D) "we take him everywhere"	Traveling	I = Able to drive own car or travel alone on buses, taxis A = Able to travel but needs someone to travel with D = Unable to travel
(I) A D	I (A) D	Shopping	I = Able to take care of all food/clothes A = Able to shop but needs someone to shop with D = Unable to shop
I (A) D	I (A) D	Preparing Meals	I = Able to plan and cook full meals A = Able to prepare light foods but unable to cook full meals alone D = Unable to prepare any meals
I (A) D	I (A) D	Housework	I = Able to do heavy housework, i.e., scrub floors A = Able to do light housework, but needs help with heavy tasks D = Unable to do any housework
I (A) D	I A (D) If we don't do it for him it doesn't get done	Taking Medicine	I = Able to prepare/take medications in the right dose at the right time A = Able to take medications, but needs reminding or someone to prepare them D = Unable to take medications
(I) A D	I A D	Managing Money	I = Able to manage buying needs, i.e., write checks, pay bills A = Able to manage daily buying needs but needs help managing checkbook, paying bills D = Unable to handle money

Adapted from Lawton M.P. and Brody E.M. Assessment of older people: self-maintaining and instrumental activities of daily living. Gerontologist 1969; 9:179-186.

Figure 8-4. Instrumental Activities of Daily Living (IADL) for Mr. Robinson

ANTICOAGULATION ASSESSMENT RECORD   Patient's Name **Samuel Robinson**   Age **76**   Date of Birth **11-23-35**   Race **B**

Home Telephone (**901**) **468-4832**   Alternate Telephone ( )   Doctor   Emergency Contact Person **None**   Telephone( )

Habits (describe pattern of use): Smoking **1-3** ppd   Alcohol **∅**   Drugs **∅**

Indication for Anticoagulation	Check One	INR Goal
Prophylaxis of DVT		2-3
Treatment of Venous Thrombosis		2-3
Treatment of PE		2-3
Prevention of systemic embolism		2-3
Tissue heart valves		2-3
Acute MI		2-3
Valvular heart disease		2-3
Bileaflet mechanical valve/aortic position		2-3
Mechanical prosthetic valve		2.5-3.5
Antiphospholipid syndrome		2.5-3.5
Acute MI (prevent recurrence)	√	2.5-3.5

Bleeding History/Risk Factors for Bleeding

Factor	Check if present
Hospital admission for bleed	
Falls	
Oral bleed	
Vaginal bleed	
Lower GI bleed	
Upper GI bleed	
Rectal bleed	
Guaiac + - √ ND	
Hemorrhoids/ulcer	
Seizure	
Urinary bleed	
Hct <30%	
Hematuria	

Conditions Requiring Dose Adjustment

Condition	Dose Change
ETOH Acute	No change
ETOH Chronic	Inc dose
Advanced renal disease	Dec dose
> 65 years old	(Dec dose)
Liver disease	Dec dose
Congestive heart failure	(Dec dose)
Thyroid disease	(Dec dose)
Baseline Hematology	
Hemoglobin	
Hematocrit	
Platelets	
WBCs	
Stool Guaiac	

Vitamin K Food Intake History (Foods High in Vitamin K)

Food Source	Amount	Consumption Qty	Food Source	Amount	Consumption Qty
Fats and Dressings			Green Scallion - raw	2/3 cup	
Mayonnaise	7 tbsp		Kale - raw	3/4 cup	
Oils: Cannola, Salad, Soybean	7 tbsp		Lettuce - raw bib, red leaf	1-3/4 cup	
Vegetables			Mustard greens - raw	1-1/2 cup	
Broccoli	1/2 cup		Parsley - chopped	1-1/2 cups	
Brussel Sprouts	5 sprouts		Spinach - raw leaf	1-1/2 cups	
Cabbage	1-1/2 cups		Turnip greens - raw	1-1/2 cups	
Collard greens	1/2 cup		Watercress - raw chopped	3 cups	
Endive - raw	2 cups				

Figure 8-5. Anticoagulation Assessment Record for Samuel Robinson Prepared by Pharmacist Michael Jones

ANTICOAGULATION ASSESSMENT RECORD (page 2)

Concurrent Medications Known to Interact with Warfarin (Prescriptions and OTC—name, dose, frequency):

Drug	Using	Action to be Taken	Drug	Using	Action to be Taken
Acetaminophen–large dose>1week (OTC)	Yes	None	Dicloxacillin		Inc W dose
Alcohol–acute ingestion	NO	Redraw INR in 24 hrs	Diflunisal		DecW dose
Alcohol–chronic ingestion	NO	Inc W dose–stop ETOH	Disulfiram		DecW dose
Allopurinol		?Inc W dose	Fluconazole		DecW dose
Aminoglutethimide		Inc W dose	Griseofulvin		Inc W dose
Aminoglycosides		?DecW dose	Isoniazid		DecW dose
Amiodarone		DecW dose–delayed effect	Ketoconazole		DecW dose
>500 mg₃/day ascorbic acid		?Inc W dose	Lovastatin		DecW dose
Azathioprine		?Inc W dose	Metronidazole		DecW dose
Azithromycin		?DecW dose	Miconazole		DecW dose
Barbiturates		Inc W dose	Multivitamin with Vit K	Yes	
Carbamazepine		Inc W dose	NSAIDs–varies with each agent (OTC)	Yes	Inc/DecW dose
Cephalosporins		?DecW dose	Omeprazole–slight increase in INR		DecW dose
Cholestyramine		Inc W dose/displace time of administration	Phenytoin		Inc/Dec W dose
Chloramphenicol		DecW dose	Quinidine		DecW dose
Cimetidine (OTC)		?DecW dose	Simvastatin		DecW dose
Ciprofloxacin		?DecW dose	Sulfinpyrazone		DecW dose
Clofibrate/Gemfibrozil		DecW dose	Tamoxifen		DecW dose
Colestipol		Inc W dose/displace time of administration	Thyroid hormones		DecW dose
Corticosteroids		Unpredictable	Tricyclic Antidepressants		?DecW dose
Cyclophosphamide		Inc W dose	TMP-SMX		DecW dose by 1/3
Cyclosporine		IncW dose	Vitamin E (OTC)	Yes	DecW dose
Danazol		DecW dose	Valproic Acid		DecW dose
			Zafirleukast		DecW dose

Considerations for dosage determination:
Indication for anticoagulation   Concurrent conditions requiring dosage adjustment
Target INR   Bleeding history/risk factors for bleeding
Initial dose recommendation taking into consideration all factors:

Date	Dose	INR	RP Initials	Comments

Drug Interactions
Dietary/alternative sources of Vitamin K

Date	Dose	INR	RP Initials	Comments

Figure 8-5 (continued). Anticoagulation Assessment Record for Samuel Robinson Prepared by Pharmacist Michael Jones

CASE 4: SPECIFIC QUESTIONS

1. How are Jones' metacognitive skills observed in this case?
2. Which of the problems identified by Jones are solved predominantly with evidence-based clinical reasoning?

REFERENCES

1. Bezold C, Halperin HA, Ashbaugh RR, et al., eds. *Pharmacy for the 21st century—Planning for an Uncertain Future.* City, state: publisher?; 1984.
2. Paul R. *Critical Thinking: What Every Person Needs in a Rapidly Changing World.* Santa Rosa, CA: Foundation for Critical Thinking; 1993.
3. Scriven M, Paul R. Defining critical thinking. 2006. Available at: http://www.critical-thinking.org/ University/univclass/Defining.html. Accessed April 20, 2006.
4. Latif DA. The link between moral reasoning scores, social desirability, and patient care performance scores: empirical evidence from the retail pharmacy setting. *Journal of Business Ethics.* 2000; 25:255–69.
5. Benor DE, Notzer N, Sheehan TJ, et al. Moral reasoning as a criterion for admission to medical school. *Med Educ.* 1984; Nov 18(6):423–8.
6. Newell KJ, Young LJ, Yamoor CM. Moral reasoning in dental hygiene students. *J Dent Educ.* 1985; Feb 49(2):79–84.
7. Sheehan TJ, Husted SD, Candee D, et al. Moral judgment as a predictor of clinical performance. *Evaluation and the Health Professions.* 1980; 8:379–400.
8. Baldwin DC, Adamson E, Self DJ, et al. Moral reasoning and malpractice: a study of orthopedic surgeons. *Am J Ortho.* 1996; 25(7):481–4.
9. Schon DA. *Educating the Reflective Practitioner.* San Francisco, CA: Josey-Bass, Inc.; 1990.
10. More ES. Empathy as hermeneutic practice. *Theor Med.* 1996; 17(3):243–54.
11. Coulehan JL, Block MR. *The Medical Interview: A Primer for Students of the Art.* Philadelphia, PA: F.A. Davis Company; 1987.
12. Brennan PF, Strombom I. Improving health care by understanding patient preferences: the role of computer technology. *J Am Med Inform Assoc.* 1998; May Jun 5(3):257–62.
13. Benner, P, Ronda G, Sutphen M. Chapter 6. Clinical Reasoning, Decision Making and Action: Thinking Critically and Clinically. Pages 1-23. Accessed on March 25, 2011 at: http://www.ahrq.gov/qual/nurseshdbk/docs/bennerp_crda.pdf
14. Putnam W, Twohig PL, Burge FI, et al. A qualitative study of evidence in primary care: what the practitioners are saying. *CMAJ.* 2002; Jun 11 166(12):1525–30.
15. Gilovic T, Griffin D, Kahneman D. *Heuristics and Biases: The Psychology of Intuitive Judgment.* Cambridge, UK: Cambridge University Press; 2002.

APPENDIX 8-1.

Pharmacist Collaborative Practice Application

Application

STATE OF <u>MICHIGAN</u>

DIVISION OF LICENSING

BOARD OF PHARMACY

PHARMACIST COLLABORATIVE PRACTICE APPLICATION

Instructions: Complete this application form and submit, along with the written protocol, to the above address for approval by the board. For hospitals with protocols approved by the hospital pharmacy and therapeutics committee, an "umbrella protocol" may be accepted by the board.

Title of Protocol: <u>Therapeutic Drug Management Services</u>

Principal Pharmacist:

<u>   Nasir Jabr   </u> License # <u>   16492   </u>
Name

For protocols involving multiple pharmacists, list participating pharmacists and license numbers, or identify by description those participating (i.e.; all pharmacists employed by XYZ Pharmacy):

<u>   All pharmacists employed by Werbert's Pharmacy   </u>

Practice Site:

<u>Werbert's Pharmacy   </u> License # <u>   9001   </u>
Pharmacy Name

<u>6907 Detroit Avenue   </u>
Street Address

<u>Detroit, MI 48169   </u> Telephone Number: <u>(712) 501-4279</u>
City/State/Zip Code

Principal Authorizing Prescriber:

Type of License: <u>Doctor of Medicine</u>

<u>Joyce Miller, M.D.   </u> License # <u>1269478</u>
Name

For protocols involving multiple prescribing practitioners, list participating practitioners and license numbers, or identify by description those participating (i.e., all staff physicians at XYZ Hospital): _____

All physicians participating at Metropolitan General Family Medicine Clinic

Practice Site: Metropolitan General Family Medicine Clinic

1234 Detroit Ave.
Street Address

Detroit, MI 48169   Telephone Number: (712) 493-8560
City/State/Zip Code

Required in accordance with pharmacy practice rules and regulations

		Yes	No
1.	Does the protocol contain an agreement in which practitioners authorized to prescribe legend drugs in this state authorize pharmacists licenses in this state to administer or dispense in accordance with that written protocol?		
2.	Does the protocol contain a statement identifying the practitioners authorized to prescribe and the pharmacists who are party to the agreement?		
3.	Is a time period for the protocol specified (may not exceed 2 years)		
4.	Does the protocol include the types of collaborative authority decisions that the pharmacists are authorized to make, including a. types of diseases, drugs, or drug categories involved and the type of collaborative authority authorized in each case? b. procedures, decision criteria, or plans the pharmacists are to follow when making therapeutic decisions, particularly when modification or initiation of drug therapy is involved?		
5.	Does the protocol include the activities that pharmacists are to follow in the course of exercising collaborative authority, including documentation of decisions made and a plan for communication and feedback to the authorizing practitioners concerning the specific decisions made?		
6.	Does the protocol contain a list of the specific types of patients eligible to receive services under the written protocol?		
7.	Does the protocol include a plan for the authorizing practitioners to review the decisions made by he pharmacist at least once every 3 months?		
8.	Does the protocol include a plan for providing the authorizing practitioners with each patient record created under the written protocol?		
9.	Are the authorizing practitioners in active practice, and is the prescriptive authority within the scope of the practitioners' practice?		
10.	Does the protocol specify and require completion of additional training, if required, for the procedures authorized under the protocol?		

Also please note:

- Documentation related to the written protocol must be maintained for at least 2 years.
- The written protocol may be terminated upon written notice by the authorizing practitioners or pharmacists. The pharmacists shall notify the board in writing within 30 days after a written protocol is terminated.
- Any modification to the written protocol must be approved by the board as required by this section for a new written protocol.

_____ _____
Signature of Principal Pharmacist   Signature of Principal Prescriber

_____ _____
Date   Date

COLLABORATIVE PRACTICE REGULATIONS

PHARMACIST COLLABORATIVE PRACTICE AUTHORITY

a. A pharmacist planning to exercise collaborative practice authority in the pharmacist's practice by initiating or modifying drug therapy in accordance with a written protocol established and approved for the pharmacist's practice by a practitioner authorized to prescribe drugs must submit the completed written protocol to the board and be approved by the board before implementation.

b. A written protocol must include

1. an agreement in which practitioners authorized to prescribe legend drugs in this state authorize pharmacists licensed in this state to administer or dispense in accordance with that written protocol;

2. a statement identifying the practitioners authorized to prescribe and the pharmacists who are party to the agreement;

3. the time period during which the written protocol will be in effect, not to exceed 2 years;

4. the types of collaborative authority decisions that the pharmacists are authorized to make, including

    A. types of diseases, drugs, or drug categories involved and the type of collaborative authorized in each case;

    B. procedures, decision criteria, or plans the pharmacists are to follow when making therapeutic decisions, particularly when modification or initiation of drug therapy is involved;

5. activities the pharmacists are to follow in the course of exercising collaborative authority, including documentation of decisions made, and a plan for communication and feedback to the authorizing practitioners concerning specific decisions made;

6. a list of the specific types of patients eligible to receive services under the written protocol;

7. a plan for the authorizing practitioners to review the decisions made by the pharmacists at least once every 3 months; and

8. a plan for providing the authorizing practitioners with each patient record created under the written protocol

c. To enter into a written protocol under this section, practitioners authorized to prescribe must be in active practice, and the authority granted must be within the scope of the practitioners' practice.

d. Unless the board is satisfied that the pharmacist has been adequately trained in the procedures outlined in the written protocol, the board will specify and require completion of additional training that covers those procedures before issuing approval of the protocol.

e. Documentation related to the written protocol must be maintained for at least 2 years.

f. The written protocol may be terminated upon written notice by the authorizing practitioners or pharmacists. The pharmacists shall notify the board in writing within 30 days after a written protocol is terminated.

g. Any modification to the written protocol must be approved by the board as required by this section for a new written protocol.

DEFINITIONS

c. "monitoring of drug therapy" means a review of the drug therapy regimen of patients by a pharmacist for the purpose of evaluating and rendering advice to the prescribing practitioner regarding adjustment of the regimen. "Monitoring of drug therapy" includes

1. collecting and reviewing records of patient drug use histories;

2. measuring and reviewing routine patient vital signs, including pulse, temperature, blood pressure, and respiration; and

3. ordering and evaluating the results of laboratory tests relating to drug therapy, including blood chemistries and cell counts, drug levels in blood, urine, tissue, or other body fluids, and culture and sensitivity tests that are performed in accordance with a written protocol.

COLLABORATIVE PRACTICE AGREEMENT

DEFINITIONS

Collaborative Practice Agreement refers to the written agreement identifying the collaborating professionals and delineating jointly agreed upon parameters for the delivery of health care services, by which the collaborating individuals agree to function in practice.

Collaborating Professionals refers to Dr. Joyce Miller and Nasir Jabr, RPh, Pharm.D. respectively physician and pharmacist, which have entered into collaborative practice.

Clinical Practice Guidelines refers to written documents, jointly agreed upon by the collaborating professionals that describe a specific plan, arrangement, or sequence of orders, steps, or procedures to be followed or carried out in providing patient care in various clinical situations.

HIERARCHY

Nasir Jabr is a pharmacist employed at Werbert's Pharmacy. Dr. Joyce Miller is employed at Metropolitan General Family Medicine Clinic.

1. **Methods of Patient Care**— Nasir Jabr is authorized to provide professional services within the scope of a general pharmacist practitioner within collaborative practice guidelines agreed upon by the collaborative parties.

    The parameters of this practice include initial or follow-up assessment, history taking, physical examination of patients, utilization of differential diagnosis, appropriate interventions, consultation, and referral as indicated. Emergency treatment and stabilization are also authorized.

2. **Clinical Practice Guidelines** agreed upon within this collaborative arrangement are meant to provide guidelines for safe and effective care and will:

    — Be mutually agreed upon by the decision of the collaborating professionals.

    — Be specific to a variety of clinical situations and to the practice setting.

    — Describe a general plan, arrangement, or sequence of orders, steps, or procedures to be followed in providing patient care in various clinical situations, including medications and referral procedures.

    — Be adjusted on an on-going basis to fulfill individual patient's needs/situations and to accommodate ongoing research and changing standards.

    — Be maintained on site and readily available in the clinic to the collaborating professionals.

    — Be reviewed and signed yearly or more frequently, as appropriately by both parties.

    Responsibilities of the pharmacist are to see patients in a timely manner, follow practice guidelines, and consult collaborating physician as needed. All documentation is to be completed within 48 hours.

    Responsibilities of the collaborating physician are to be available for collaboration during clinic hours, review selected charts weekly, and provide call coverage for all patients.

3. **Chart Notes and Co-Signatures**—Documentation of active medical records such as the SOAP format will be utilized. Medical documentation will include subjective data, objective data, assessment, and recommendations for treatment, referral, and/or follow-up. Documentation will indicate cases discussed in the clinical setting. In the instances of cases not discussed in the clinical setting, a selection of those charts will be reviewed periodically, as agreed upon between collaborating practitioners.

4. **Diagnostic/Lab Requests**—Diagnostic tests and/or laboratory tests will be ordered by the pharmacist according to mutually agreed upon office evaluation and management practice guidelines. If results are abnormal, the pharmacist will follow practice guidelines utilizing appropriate consultation, treatment, and/or referral as indicated.

5. **Medications/Prescriptions**—The distribution or administration of medications by the pharmacist within the collaborative practice agreement shall comply with current state and federal law. The physician will initiate pharmacological intervention not addressed by current practice guidelines only after appropriate consultation with the collaborating physician or directly.

6. **Radiology Requests**—Ordering of all radiological exams will be guided by practice guidelines. Radiological testing not addressed by current practice guidelines will be initiated only after appropriate consultation with the collaborating physician or by the physician directly. The radiologist will do final evaluation of all radiological examinations.

7. **Specialty Consults**—Specialty consultations/referrals will be completed according to practice guidelines. If need falls outside of practice guidelines, consultation with the physician will be completed prior to specialty consultation or referral.

8. **Hospital Admissions and Privileges**—All patients who need hospital admission will be registered under the collaborating physician. The pharmacist will cooperate with the hospital pharmacists in continuing to provide information relevant to the care for the patients admitted.

9. **Emergency Absences**—One of the collaborating physicians will manage the pharmacist's patients if the pharmacist is absent. Back-up physician and pharmacist to manage MDs patients if MD absent.

10. **After Clinic Hours Coverage**—The collaborating physician, or designee covers all hospitalized patients and manages "on call" coverage. In the event that a patient contacts the pharmacist outside of pharmacy hours, that patient will be referred to the on-call physician or the emergency center, as deemed appropriate for the circumstance.

11. **Cancellation of Collaborative Arrangement**—Collaborating parties individually retain the right to terminate the collaborative arrangement with written notification of both parties with a timeline of sixty (60) days.

12. **Availability of the Collaborating Physician**—Be available for immediate consultation to the pharmacist at all times, either personally or via telecommunications. The collaborating physician will visit the practice site periodically to:

A. Review patient histories with the pharmacist.

B. Verify that treatment and acts of limited prescriptive authority are in accordance with the clinical practice guidelines.

13. **Pharmacist's Professional Liability Insurance**—$1,000,000.00 each claim up to $5,000,000.00 aggregate professional liability coverage renewed yearly.

Signature:_____   _____16492_____

       PLEASE TYPE NAME UNDER SIGNATURE   License Number

       Nasir Jabr, RPh, Pharm.D.

       Collaborating Pharmacist

Signature:_____   _____1269478_____

       PLEASE TYPE NAME UNDER SIGNATURE   License Number

       Dr. Joyce Miller

Signature:_____   _____1279326_____

       PLEASE TYPE NAME UNDER SIGNATURE   License Number

       Dr. Mark Campos

Designing the Patient-Centered Care Plan

"If you treat an individual as if he were what he ought to be and could be, he will become what he ought to be and could be."

—Johann Wolfgang von Goethe

CHAPTER OUTLINE

Purpose

Specifying Care Goals
- Determine the Patient's Health, Medical, and Medication-Related Goals
- Prioritize the Patient's Health Care Goals
- Determine the Role of Your Care in Addressing Patient Needs

Designing the Pharmacotherapeutic Regimen
- Determine Therapeutic Regimen Options
- Select the Optimal Pharmacotherapeutic Regimen

Designing the Monitoring Plan
- Determine Proxy Outcome Indicators to Maximize Efficacy and Minimize Toxicity of Drug Therapy
- Determine Frequency of Monitoring
- Establish Desired Endpoints of Indicators
- Determine a Follow-up Plan to Evaluate Findings

Determining the Support Needed by Patients
- Advocacy Behaviors Required to Achieve Optimal Therapeutic Regimen
- Educational Needs to Be Addressed and Appropriate Audiences to Target

Document the Patient Care Plan

Summary

Assessment Questions

Assignments

Designing the Patient-Centered Care Plan for Our Patients
- Case 1: Lauren Smith has her first formal pharmacist's consultation and care visit at Werbert's Pharmacy.
- Case 2: Christine Johnston visits with Mr. Montanez and Maria to develop a care plan.
- Case 3: Luisa Rodriguez develops a care plan with Huong Tran.
- Case 4: Michael Jones develops a care plan for Mr. Robinson.

OBJECTIVES

To gain knowledge of:

1. how to construct a patient's drug therapy problem list;
2. how to establish pharmacotherapeutic goals based on a patient's health care needs;
3. how to design a drug therapy plan for achieving desired pharmacotherapeutic goals;
4. the effects of various drug product characteristics, routes of administration, dosage schedules, lengths of treatment, and modes of administration on achieving your desired pharmacotherapeutic goals;
5. how to design a monitoring plan measuring the achievement of the desired pharmacotherapeutic endpoints;
6. determining pharmacotherapeutic parameters and endpoints for a patient's drug therapy;
7. documenting a pharmacist's care plan; and
8. establishing the pharmacist's relationship to other health care professionals in the patient's care plan.

PURPOSE

This chapter integrates the knowledge and skills developed in the previous chapters to show you how to design and document a patient care plan that is individualized for each patient. A patient

*Some of the figures in this chapter can also be found on the web at www.ashp.org/patientcare.

care plan is the roadmap you create to achieve the desired outcomes agreeable to both you and the patient. It is an action plan, and it is dynamic. This means that once you and the patient have established an initial starting point, you implement the plan and monitor progress. If the results (outcomes) do not meet expectations, you modify the plan of action and re-monitor. If you think about delivering your care from this perspective, the need for a relationship with the patient built upon trust and ongoing communication becomes apparent. However, one of the most common problems in pharmaceutical care is the lack of a starting plan. Your ability to assist the patient is compromised without it. This chapter focuses on the design of the initial care plan and the documentation to support your actions. Let's look at the initial care plan in greater depth.

SPECIFYING CARE GOALS

You will design a care plan that synthesizes all of the data you have gathered using your expertise as a pharmacist. You must first define the patient's health care needs and then specify care goals. After these goals are established, you can design a therapeutic regimen and develop a monitoring plan. Your design of the care plan should take both the initial care plan as well as the monitoring and redesign of the care plan, based upon patient progress, into consideration. Application of your clinical reasoning skills will guide you through a constant reevaluation and updating of the plan based upon the patient's progress.

Determine the Patient's Health, Medical, and Medication-Related Goals

You are now ready to begin the first phase of a pharmacist's care plan: identifying the patient's health care needs. Pharmaceutical care emphasizes that you are dealing with a "whole" person whose care is entrusted to a team of health professionals, including you as the pharmacist. A patient's health care needs are elements of care required to improve or prevent deterioration of health and well being. Each health care need focuses on the elements of care required to improve or prevent deterioration of health and well being. At this point, you should understand how the health care needs relate to the pharmaceutical care concept. Therefore, your plan of action must also include both the patient's medication related and total health concerns and the goals of other team members who serve the patient when relevant. Probably the most important influence on successful care is the personal relationship between you and the patient. Your relationship provides the way to learn from the patient what he or she believes those needs to be. It is *this* relationship that facilitates a genuine exchange between you both.

The second phase of a pharmacist's care plan is to establish pharmacotherapeutic goals. You must set goals to meet each health care need. To determine these goals, you must integrate various influences: disease characteristics, goals of other health professionals, drug therapy problems, and non-disease factors. Patients may possess characteristics that interfere with the achievement of desired therapeutic outcomes. Patients may be noncompliant with prescribed medication use regimens, or there may be unpredictable variations in a patient's biological responses. Thus, in an imperfect world, intended outcomes from medication-related therapy are not always achievable.

> **KEY POINT**
>
> Your relationship with the patient will dictate the degree and amount of information that he or she will share with you. Your ability to help is related to the extent to which the patient is open to sharing and disclosing information, including values and beliefs.

Concurrent Disease Characteristics. The patient's disease dictates the drug therapy regimen and monitoring plan. When you identify pharmacotherapeutic goals for treating a disease, you must understand both the normal physiology of the system involved and the pathophysiology of the disease. The goal of treatment is to approach normal physiology as much as possible. By understanding where you are and where you would like to be, the pharmacotherapeutic goals for a given disease become clear. Your expert knowledge about conditions and their management provides the patient with the greatest number of care management options.

Previously Identified Health Care Goals by Other Health Professionals. The advantage of the team approach is that many people with different expertise levels and viewpoints contribute to a patient's care. You can ultimately develop a plan that will take the priorities of the team into consideration in order to provide optimal patient care.

Previously Identified Health Care Goals by Patient. Patients have often formed their own concepts about what is possible to achieve with their health. You must know this so that you can incorporate goals that are healthy and realistic, providing you with the information needed to establish a care plan with a greater chance of success. It also allows you to work with the patient to establish new goals or modify those that are not realistic or appropriate.

Current Drug Therapy Problems. Most of your work begins after the patient has had care initiated by another provider. You often inherit patients and drug therapy problems that they are already experiencing. Frequently, patients do not understand that they are experiencing problems *because* of their drug therapy plan, rather than solving their health problems *with* their drug therapy plan. Trust must be established in order for the patient to be receptive to the primary care provider not optimizing this aspect of care, and to allow you to work on it on his or her behalf. Patients also develop many drug therapy problems by self-diagnosis, self-treatment practices, and the solicitations of multiple advisors to their health who may not have adequate expertise in the management of drug therapy.

Social, Financial, Cultural, and System Factors. Many non-disease factors can influence pharmacotherapeutic goals. If a patient is elderly or has diminished renal or hepatic function, for example, the pharmacokinetics of drugs may be altered. Drug dosing, then, will need to be adjusted or an alternative drug chosen. Or, if penicillin is the drug of choice for treating an infection but the patient is allergic to it, a second-line agent is indicated. Likewise, if you would select a calcium channel-blocker for the treatment of hypertension but the patient cannot afford it, you must recommend a less expensive agent. Such non-disease factors will influence your pharmacotherapeutic goals and your clinical decision making.

Prioritize the Patient's Health Care Goals

After identifying the care problems and goals that need to be addressed, your next step is to determine what to address first. Your clinical reasoning skills should guide you through these decisions. In matters of urgency, you are expected to take action immediately. In less urgent situations, you must express to the patient and other team members (when appropriate) what you believe are the foremost concerns. Evaluate the disease characteristics and/or drug therapy problems related to the pharmacotherapeutic goals. Consider both the possible risks and onset of toxicity. Rank your corresponding pharmacotherapeutic goals by their importance. Then the prioritized list of problems and goals will guide you and your patient in care.

Determine the Role of Your Care in Addressing Patient Needs

The pharmacist's care plan documents a strategy to provide care that helps the patient achieve goals. Based on patient-, disease-, and drug-specific data, your plan states (1) pharmacotherapeutic goals, (2) a strategy to achieve them, and (3) a means to measure or evaluate their achievement. This plan also serves as a reference when you recommend therapy to the patient, the patient's family, and other health care providers. Although all patients are different, they should all be evaluated in the same way.

DESIGNING THE PHARMACOTHERAPEUTIC REGIMEN

Determine Therapeutic Regimen Options

The first step in the development of your drug therapy plan involves optimizing drug selection. Three factors to consider in your choice are the patient's problems, drug-related characteristics, and the patient-related characteristics. You should combine information on appropriate therapy with patient-specific data. Remember the factors noted above that are used to select an optimal drug. Based upon the patient's prioritized problems, you may be recommending discontinuation of therapy, modifications in existing therapy, or new therapies to consider.

Patient's Problems. Identification of the patient's problems establishes the boundary around the pharmacotherapeutic and treatment choices available. At this point in your care plan development you have established as best you can what conditions, diseases, and other patient-specific problems are being considered in your treatment plan. For example, you may have a patient who has type II diabetes mellitus. You should have the professional knowledge of all of the major pharmacotherapeutic treatment options to manage a patient with this condition. If a patient has medication adherence problems, you should have knowledge of key strategies that may be considered to aid the patient with achieving adherence.

Drug-Related Characteristics: Dose, Frequency, Form, Method, Route, and Duration of Administration. For each medication to be ordered, you should know the usual dosing regimen for both dose and frequency and then determine the most appropriate dose based upon patient characteristics. Medications with multiple therapeutic indications may be dosed differently for each indication. For example, the maximum daily dose for propranolol is 240 mg for vascular headaches, 320 mg for angina, or 640 mg for hypertension. Other factors such as age, height, weight, and concomitant disease states or drug therapy may affect the usual dosing regimen. Renal or liver function impairments are especially important when selecting a dose. For example, a digoxin dose should be modified for age, reduced renal function, and concomitant quinidine or verapamil therapy. In addition, medications with narrow therapeutic indices should be dosed pharmacokinetically when feasible to optimize efficacy and reduce toxicity.

Various dosage forms also may present safety considerations. While both oral and inhaled steroids can often improve asthma, a patient should use the oral product *only if* symptoms cannot be controlled with the inhaled medication. Finally, you should consider the length of therapy when evaluating a medication's safety. For example, buspirone may be acceptable for a patient needing long-term anxiolytic therapy, while a benzodiazepine such as lorazepam may be better for short-term therapy needs.

Many medications can be administered by multiple routes. For example, nitroglycerin can be administered orally, topically (either via patch or ointment), sublingually, or intravenously. The advantages and disadvantages of administration routes should be considered for a particular medication and medical symptom/problem. The mode of drug administration is important for reasons of safety and/or patient tolerance. Some drugs cause serious adverse effects when administered by rapid IV push and must be given more slowly. Phenytoin has been reported to cause hypotension when administered rapidly. Opiates administered by the IV or subcutaneous route may be more appropriate than intramuscular injection in patients with decreased muscle mass or poor circulation. Another example is the use of tetracycline for acne. Both oral and topical tetracyclines are effective for acne. The severity of the condition and the likelihood of toxicity, along with patient preference, may determine the best route for treatment.

Standard references provide information about preferred routes for a particular drug. Some drugs can be administered intravenously but cause tissue damage when given intramuscularly. Other drugs are designed to be administered intramuscularly because rapid administration causes adverse effects. Alternative routes of administration often are chosen for patients who cannot tolerate oral therapy or for enhanced efficacy and delivery. For example, intravenous antibiotics are used to treat serious infections because higher doses can be administered and drug delivery to the bloodstream is certain. However, parenteral therapy is almost always more expensive than oral. In these situations, it is common for the pharmacist to recommend switching from an intravenous to an oral dosage form to reduce the cost impact of long-term parenteral therapy. In some cases, side effects may be more prevalent with one dosage form than another (e.g., clonidine topical patch is often better tolerated than the oral form).

Dosage form considerations are similar to those for administration route. Liquid medications and chewable tablets often are selected for pediatric patients and elderly patients. Furthermore, various dosage forms of a medication may have different advantages and disadvantages. Cortisporin Otic® suspension or solution can be used to treat external otitis. Although the solution may cause stinging (due to propylene glycol), it allows visual reexamination of the ear canal that would be obscured by the suspension. Dosing adjustments must always be considered with different dosage forms. Switching from levothyroxine tablets to the injectable formulation requires a 50% dose reduction. In contrast, switching from the oral antibiotic levofloxacin to injectable requires no dose adjustment.

Scheduling of medication doses throughout the day can be a concern for both inpatients and outpatients. The goal is to select dosing times that optimize therapeutic benefits and compliance and minimize the potential for adverse effects, drug interactions, and regimen complexity. For example, antiarrhythmics and antihypertensive agents should be administered at equally spaced intervals for optimal efficacy, whereas nonsteroidal anti-inflammatory drugs (NSAIDs) (e.g., ibuprofen and naproxen) should be given with meals to minimize GI intolerance. To increase adherence in the outpatient setting, you might link drug administration with the patient's regular daily schedule and try to reduce total dosing times per day that cause a patient to have to remember to interrupt his or her daily activities throughout the day.

Finally, you must determine the length of therapy for each drug. Appropriate length of therapy can vary from a single dose to lifelong administration, depending on the condition. One problem is drug use exceeding the course of therapy. A common example is the use of proton pump inhibitors like pantoprazole longer than the recommended 6 weeks for duodenal ulcer. Conversely, length of treatment could be shorter than recommended such as a patient with thrombosis, whereby beginning comcomitant warfarin/heparin therapy may allow the heparin to be stopped several days earlier. Another common example would be failure to complete a full 10-day course of antibiotics.

Patient-Related Characteristics. In earlier chapters we emphasized the various personal characteristics and factors individualized in patients that should be considered as part of our patient database for decision making. Here we will emphasize the factors of (a) age, (b) gender, (c) pregnancy and lactation, (d) religion and occupation, (e) ethnic background, (f) cognitive impairments, (g) sensory and physical limitation, (h) patient preference and behavior, (i) factors influencing drug therapy adherence, and (j) simplicity and cost.

Age. You should consider a patient's age primarily in the *dosing* of drugs and occasionally as it influences *selection*. For example, tetracyclines and the sulfa antibiotics are contraindicated for some pediatric *age* groups. Age also may be a factor that indicates the potential for adverse effects. For example, with some drugs such as digoxin and antipsychotics, doses for elderly patients are lower than the usual adult dosage due to the likelihood for adverse reactions. This "sensitivity" to certain medications may be linked to physiologic changes associated with aging (e.g., decreased renal clearance). Age also may determine the route or dosage form used for a medication. Both young and elderly patients, for example, may have difficulty with dexterity, being unable to properly use a metered-dose inhaler. Therefore, you may need to treat these patients with either another drug or another form of the same medication.

Gender. Gender, as a factor in drug selection, is important for dosing certain drug classes (e.g., hormonal drugs) where some adverse effects are gender specific. Gender also is important in dosing if the illness presents differently in men than women. For example, men are not treated with a single dose of antibiotic for an uncomplicated urinary tract infection, but women may be. Gender also might be considered in prescribing for women of childbearing age. Gender also plays a role in dosing drugs that are cleared renally or when dosing is based on the calculation of the creatinine clearance. In some cases, the most efficacious therapy for women is not clearly defined, given the lack of clinical trial data.

Pregnancy and Lactation. Pregnancy and lactation are two special health states that you should consider when selecting drug therapy. During pregnancy and lactation, the welfare of two individuals is at stake. For example, while warfarin therapy—if indicated—would be safe for a pregnant woman, heparin or low molecular weight heparin is universally prescribed because of warfarin's potential to harm the fetus. The prudent clinician should not only consider if a patient is pregnant but also inquire about the intent to become pregnant. Standard references often are not useful for answering questions about fetal/child safety or maternal drug use. Therefore, you should consult specialty references when selecting either prescription or nonprescription medications for a pregnant or lactating patient. Excellent professional sources for this information need are listed in Chapter 7.

Religion and Occupation. Religion and occupation are other demographic characteristics that may occasionally influence drug selection. A well known area of religious conflict with use of treatment is the administration of blood products. Use of blood products is in conflict with the religious practices of persons who declare the faith of Jehovah Witnesses, even in life-threatening situations. Persons of the Islamic faith participate in fasting as a religious form of worship. During these fasting periods, some medications are forbidden. Airline pilots must avoid sedating medications while active/on duty.

Ethnic/Racial Background. Although ethnic background is rarely considered in drug selection, studies suggest some differences in both efficacy and toxicity of medications in various ethnic groups. As more data become available, pharmacists can select appropriate therapy depending on a patient's genetic background. For example, ethnic differences in response to therapy have been noted with hypertension. The different hemodynamic profiles of Caucasian and African-American patients may influence the selection and/or dosing of antihypertensive medications used for them. Therapy decisions must be modified to initiate dosing regimens appropriately. Evidence from published studies should be sought and applied clinically in each patient case. Ethnic background plays an important role in the types of products that individuals may use to self-treat as well as their beliefs about illness and what will actually work in their treatment.

Cognitive Impairments. Cognitive impairments may influence dosing frequency or route/dosage form in your therapy recommendation. For example, a transdermal patch (e.g., nitroglycerin or clonidine) or medication requiring infrequent administration (e.g. celecoxib versus ibuprofen) may be preferential for an elderly or incapacitated patient who relies on a working adult caregiver. This caregiver could then administer the medication during time at home.

Sensory and Physical Limitations. Sensory and physical limitations also may affect drug selection. For example, insulin is a commonly used medication. For a visually impaired patient, special education or devices to assist this patient population may be incorporated into the pharmacist's counseling practice. Without these aids, it may be inappropriate to use this medication because of the increased risk for clinically significant errors in a visually impaired patient. Similarly, a physical limitation such as poor grip strength may eliminate the selection of an inhaler for an asthma patient.

Patient Preference and Behavior. Finally, you should consider a patient's preference and behavior when selecting therapy. Some preferences are assumed and, therefore, selected—once-a-day dosing is preferred to multiple daily doses and oral medication is preferred to a parenteral drug. At other times, you should ask the patient about a preference. Patients may also be asked for their preference about the mode of drug administration. For example, a patient admitted for elective surgery may be asked to decide between scheduled and patient-controlled administration of a narcotic analgesic for postsurgical pain. Occasionally, the patient will prefer a certain dosage form based on convenience (e.g., lozenges versus cough syrup for a working adult). Economic status or health insurance frequently impact a patient's choice on brand of medication, dosage form, or route.

Factors Influencing Drug Therapy Adherence. You should use your knowledge of the patient's medication adherence to evaluate the suitability of a drug. A patient who cannot remember to take a nonsteroidal anti-inflammatory drug (NSAID) three or four times daily should be prescribed a once-a-day product. A patient's ability to manage a certain regimen may influence its suitability. For capable patients, a combination of long-acting insulin with variable doses of regular insulin (depending on blood glucose) is appropriate. But for a less capable or motivated patient, a once-a-day combination of long- and short-acting insulin may be better.

Simplicity and Cost. The simplicity and cost of the drug therapy regimen influence medication adherence. It is well established that a patient's adherence to a drug regimen improves when there are fewer drug treatment episodes a day. Patients on once- or twice-a-day treatment adhere to a greater degree than patients who need to take medications three or more times a day.

Select the Optimal Pharmacotherapeutic Regimen

Comparative Efficacy and Safety of Drug Regimens. To determine comparative efficacy, you should consider the severity of the patient's problem. For example, although many medications have analgesic properties, product selection should depend on the severity of pain. Acetaminophen or a NSAID may be acceptable for moderate chronic pain, while a narcotic analgesic is better for acute postsurgical pain.

Safety is usually evaluated in terms of potential adverse effects. When you assess a drug, consider both the likely side effects and the uncommon but serious adverse effects. Serious adverse effects can obviously threaten a patient's health. Common side effects, regarded as nuisance events, also may have more serious sequelae—therapeutic failure if compliance is compromised. If additional therapy is prescribed to manage these side effects, the patient may be at risk for adverse drug reactions, drug–drug interactions, and even increased therapy costs. In certain situations, you may want to consider the safety of a drug with an overdosage and/or in an unsupervised situation (e.g., patient with suicidal ideas or elderly patient with mild dementia).

Ultimately you establish the relevant knowledge you have gained through the considerations of the problem or conditions, patient characteristics, and pharmaceutical characteristics. Now that you have determined these considerations, you reason through the patient's preferences and goals and match the pharmacotherapeutic regimen considerations to these patient considerations. You will choose among the options available based upon your reasoned consideration to establish the optimal pharmacotherapeutic regimen.

DESIGNING THE MONITORING PLAN

The starting point in a monitoring plan is the selection of parameters, both quantitative and qualitative, that help to determine whether the desired pharmacotherapeutic goals or drug therapy outcomes are met. Quantitative monitoring provides specific measures that are useful to choosing and monitoring therapeutic interventions and determining effectiveness. Quantitative parameters include measurements such as blood pressure, pulse, temperature, weight, and serum glucose. Qualitative monitoring provides us information about the patient's perceived response to interventions and their effectiveness. Relief of pain, patient reports of decreased swelling or feelings of bloating or discomfort, or resolution of gastrointestinal distress and nausea are examples of *qualitative* parameters.

When selecting parameters, you should consider the following:

- Drug characteristics.
- Therapeutic efficacy and adverse effects of regimen.
- Physiological changes in the patient.
- Practicality, availability, and cost of monitoring.
- Patient's willingness to participate.

We use both quantitative and qualitative information to monitor a patient's response to therapy and determine its effectiveness.

Determine Proxy Outcome Indicators to Maximize Efficacy and Minimize Toxicity of Drug Therapy

Many conditions for which you manage drug treatments can only be monitored using proxy outcome indicators. They are indicators of the likelihood of the patient's outcome based upon his or her response to therapy, rather than the outcome itself. They are predictors of the outcome for the patient. To illustrate this, we can examine the condition of hypertension. If a patient continued to live with essential hypertension for many years and it went untreated, the patient would likely experience a stroke, renal failure, or blindness; all are undesirable outcomes. The indicator that predicts the likelihood of these outcomes is the patient's blood pressure, both systolic and diastolic, at rest. When the patient is treated with antihypertensive therapy, you monitor the blood pressure. The blood pressure is a proxy indicator for actual clinical outcomes. If it is well controlled, the likelihood of blindness, stroke, or renal failure is low. If it is not well controlled, the likelihood of these outcomes increases. Other examples of proxy indicators include $HgbA_1c$ for blood glucose control in diabetes mellitus, FEV_1 for asthma management, or pulse and rhythm for management of atrial fibrillation. ($HgbA_1c$ is a laboratory measure of blood glucose control over time; FEV_1 is the forced expiratory volume over 1 second—a measure of lung capacity.)

Determine Frequency of Monitoring

In the design of your monitoring plan, the final step is determining the frequency of monitoring. Factors that will influence monitoring frequency include

- Specific needs and willingness of the patient to participate.
- Details of the drug therapy.
- Specific physiologic effects of the drug therapy (drug characteristics).
- Cost and practicality of monitoring.
- Desires of other health professionals.

Your first consideration should be patient-specific needs such as a person's problems, conditions, disease state, or socioeconomic state. Patients may require more frequent monitoring early in the course of therapy (or, conversely, later). You should also consider cost and practicality when determining the frequency of monitoring. Measurement of serum drug concentrations can be useful if performed correctly, but various studies have shown that many serum drug levels are poorly utilized. If a serum drug concentration is measured too soon after the dose or prior to steady state, the information is probably not useful. Also, serum drug concentrations that are not obtained at the correct times may result in re-measurement or incorrect therapeutic decisions. In both cases, resources are wasted and patients may be exposed to toxicity or ineffectiveness. Hospitalized patients can be monitored frequently, but they may have to be monitored less frequently as outpatients. When developing your monitoring plan, review the monitoring parameters, desired endpoints, and monitoring frequency for each pharmacotherapeutic goal *before* you obtain measurements. In this way, you can minimize unnecessary monitoring, discomfort or nuisance for the patient, and expense.

Establish Desired Endpoints of Indicators

An endpoint signifies the achievement of a goal or completion of a process. The next step in your monitoring plan is the determination of desired endpoints—either measurable or observable—for each parameter.

A *measurable* endpoint for a patient receiving quinidine for atrial fibrillation is a serum quinidine concentration of 2–5 mcg/ml or achieving hemoglobin levels of 10–12 g/dl while receiving epoetin alpha. Another measurable endpoint might be the heart rate, heart rhythm, or the pulse. Other examples might include a 10% weight loss for a patient with both hypercholesterolemia and hypertension and an absolute neutrophil count less than 1,200/mm^3 for a patient receiving ticlopidine. Examples of *observable* endpoints include elimination of pain in a cancer patient receiving opioids and elimination of dyspnea in an asthma patient.

When determining desired endpoints, you should consider

- Patient-specific factors
- Drug characteristics
- Efficacy and toxicity

Factors such as age and concurrent illness will influence your desired endpoints of therapy. Drug characteristics will also impact your therapeutic endpoints. You must consider the medication's ability to affect the disease being treated. The availability of various dosage forms, routes of administration, and modes of administration will also influence your desired endpoints. Finally, when setting endpoints, you must consider the drug's efficacy and toxicity.

Determine a Follow-up Plan to Evaluate Findings

A follow-up plan to evaluation the findings is needed. Monitoring plans are designed to measure the achievement of pharmacotherapeutic goals established with the patient. The follow up should be with the patient and may need to involve the patient's family or caretaker if relevant. The plan should also specify the other health care providers with whom you will communicate. You should begin by determining what parameters can be monitored (either quantitatively or qualitatively) as valid indicators that a given goal has or has not been achieved. Next, you should establish desired endpoints for these parameters to indicate that the goal has actually been achieved. These endpoints can be observable or measurable. Finally, you must determine how frequently to monitor each parameter.

Some factors that will influence your monitoring plan include the needs of the patient and other professionals caring for the patient, characteristics of the drug, and policies of the health care setting. Additionally, your assessment process requires documentation that conveys your thought process to other health professionals caring for the patient.

CASE EXAMPLE

Designing a Monitoring Plan

A 78-year-old woman is discharged from the hospital to home health services on intravenous vancomycin every 12 hours for osteomyelitis for approximately 6 weeks. The physician orders' visiting nurse services 3 times a week initially and then once weekly for central line dressing changes, blood draws, and for teaching home infusion to the patient. In addition, the physician requests the pharmacist to manage vancomycin dosing. The patient is completing the 2nd day of vancomycin treatment in the hospital. You are the home infusion pharmacist who is responsible for managing this patient's home care after receiving notification that she is being discharged from the hospital. You design a monitoring plan for long-term vancomycin treatment in the home setting.

You review the discharge summary and laboratory reports sent from the hospital. You contact the home nursing service and determine the patient's spouse will be administering the intravenous medications. You contact the prescriber to obtain the desired vancomycin trough range. You are also concerned with the potential for renal and/or ototoxicity with vancomycin. You identity quantitative monitoring parameters including vancomycin trough levels, complete metabolic profile (CMP), complete blood count with differential (CBC), erythromycin sedimentation rate (ESR), and C-reactive protein (CRP). Since the majority of care will be provided by the spouse or patient, you also determine key qualitative monitoring parameters that you can assess from outside the home by discussing these observations made through the patient/caregiver. For potential renal toxicity, you will ask the patient/caregiver about 1) frequency of urination, 2) darkening of the urine, and 3) new or worsening lower extremity edema. For potential auditory/CNS toxicity, you list 1) difficulty hearing/muffled voices, 2) ringing in the ears, 3) feeling dizzy/vertigo, and 4) nausea/vomiting. You will also ask about any fever or chills, itching, and redness around the face, neck, and/or upper chest area.

After evaluating the patient's pharmacokinetic parameters, you do not believe the patient has reached steady state with vancomycin before discharge. You request the home nurse to schedule her first visit before the morning dose of vancomycin and draw a vancomycin serum trough level and CMP and then to repeat CMP, CBC, CRP, ESR, and vancomycin trough level on each weekly visit. You schedule a weekly telephone conference with the patient and caregiver to obtain qualitative monitoring data. You also request the visiting home nurse to report any issues or adverse events to you directly. You document your monitoring plan in the home care chart.

DETERMINING THE SUPPORT NEEDED BY PATIENTS

Your care behaviors influence the success that a patient experiences in attaining positive outcomes as a result of therapy. You can use empathy skills to relate to how a patient is feeling and your expertise to know what the best options are for treatment. However, what you do with this set of skills is what will make a difference for the patient.

Advocacy Behaviors Required to Achieve Optimal Therapeutic Regimen

The pharmacist–patient relationship requires you to sometimes serve as an advocate for the patient. An advocate, in this context, is someone who helps the patient obtain information to make decisions about health care. The advocate discusses with the patient and the family/caregivers the patient's preferences and represents his or her views to other members of the health care team. Working with other team members who agree with you most of the time is less challenging than when they don't agree with you. If you know a patient's preferences and they differ from those of other health care team members, it is your obligation to advocate on behalf of the patient. Your expertise, experience, and confidence in your recommendations is needed to feel assertive about the care plan to be adopted. As a health professional yourself, it is reasonable to expect other health professionals to listen and respect your recommendations. As you practice, you will gain comfort in displaying advocacy behaviors for your patient.

Educational Needs to Be Addressed and Appropriate Audiences to Target

Patients vary greatly in their educational needs to achieve the desired outcomes. You should not assume that the most highly educated patient has adequate and appropriate knowledge to participate effectively in achieving desired care outcomes. Patients require health-focused education to achieve desired outcomes. The term defining a patient's level of health knowledge is *health literacy*. Health literacy is a comprehensive concept, which means having the knowledge, values, and attitudes required to become and stay healthy. As you work with patients, you are assisting them with their health literacy. As you gain more experience, you come to realize how uncomfortable many patients are in the health care setting. This further blunts their response to your efforts to educate and inform. It is worsened when we encounter cultures alternative to our own or language barriers. Your training as a health professional centers your thinking about the health concerns and needs of the patient, often without adequate consideration for the context of the world in which patients live.

Many patient education resources are available to improve a patient's health literacy related to medication use. **Table 9-1** provides several key consumer or patient-centered web sites that can be recommended to patients who have access to and aptitude for using computer-based resources. However, many patients do not have computers available to them and are not able to assist themselves with these resources. Part of your care plan should address this need.

DOCUMENT THE PATIENT CARE PLAN

Chapter 4 provides an overview about the elements of documenting your care plan and its progress. Maintaining a sound documentation system is integral to your ability to deliver, monitor, and modify care based upon the patient's outcomes. Documentation in a permanent record provides you with the history to assess patient progress. If you share care of a patient with other colleagues, it creates a vehicle for all of you to access the history and keep each other informed. Documentation offers other advantages. It is a legal record showing the evidence of care provided and the resultant outcomes for the patient. It may be important to payors as you develop a billing system for providing care to patients. But the heart of it all is the ongoing tracking tool that documentation provides to facilitate your quality of care.

This chapter emphasizes the skills for documenting care using traditional paper and pencil methods. Integrated computerized clinical record systems are emerging to support pharmacist's documentation of clinical care. As billing for cognitive services becomes a common practice in pharmacy, the computerized systems will improve, become less costly, and be more readily available. The skills you acquire about what to record and how to record will remain important, no matter what media is used in the future.

Figure 9-1 provides a worksheet to think through plan development for each problem or patient priority. It is only intended to be helpful for focusing your thoughts on plan development. **Figure 9-2** provides a template for documenting the pharmacists' comprehensive initial care plan. It

TABLE 9-1
Databases for Patient Education and Consumer Health

Reading Level	Database Name and Developer or Sponsor/Web Site/and Description	Languages English	Spanish
4th – 6th grade	Micromedex Care Notes System™—Micromedex, Inc.	●	●
	Web site: http://healthcarescience.thomsonreuters.com/patienteducationsolutions/carenotes/		
	Description: Patient education and drug leaflet documents provide a patient-oriented overview of common conditions and frequently prescribed drugs. This is a system accessible by health care providers whose organizations have purchased it. It is not designed for direct use by patients.		
Varies	Consumers and Patients – Agency for Healthcare Research and Quality	●	●
	Web site: http://www.ahrq.gov/		
	Description: A comprehensive web access site about a wide range of health topics. The site provides information about helping patients choose providers wisely, health conditions/risks, consumer versions of clinical practice guidelines, health plans, prescriptions, prevention and wellness, quality of care, surgery, and specific conditions such as cardiac rehabilitation, pressure sores, and smoking cessation.		
Varies	Consumer and Patient Health Information Section (CAPHIS) Top 100 List – Medical Library Association	●	●
	Web site: www.caphis.mlanet.org/consumer/index.html		
	Description: This site links consumers to over 100 evaluated consumer health sites. The Medical Library Association and CAPHIS endorse the criteria for assessing the Quality of Health Information on the Internet of the Health Summit Working Group. Their symbol denotes consumer web sites that have met their quality standards based upon the following criteria: credibility, sponsorship, authorship, controls, authors, currency, disclosure, purpose, links, design, interactivity, and disclaimers.		
Varies	MedlinePlus™—National Library of Medicine	●	●
	Web site: http://www.nlm.nih.gov/medlineplus/		
	Description: MedlinePlus provides over 650 English and 600 Spanish health topic pages representing information from 850 organizations. There are over 15,000 links to authoritative health information.		
	Drug information is provided from two sources: Medmaster—a product of the American Society of Health-System Pharmacists and Drug Information—Advice for the Patient, published by the United States Pharmacopoeia.		

is representative of a chart note format commonly used in the inpatient or clinic setting. However, the elements for inclusion are universal for any patient care setting. **Figure 9-3** provides guidance about how to prepare an excellent progress note. You will focus your skill development on creating and documenting patient care plans in the patient case section of this chapter.

Health Care Need 1:
Pharmacotherapeutic Goal:
Recommendations for Therapy:
Monitoring Parameter(s) and Frequency:
Expected Outcomes:
Health Care Need 2:
Pharmacotherapeutic Goal:
Recommendations for Therapy:
Monitoring Parameter(s) and Frequency:
Expected Outcomes:
Health Care Need 3:
Pharmacotherapeutic Goal:
Recommendations for Therapy:
Monitoring Parameter(s) and Frequency:
Expected Outcomes:
Health Care Need 4:
Pharmacotherapeutic Goal:
Recommendations for Therapy:
Monitoring Parameter(s) and Frequency:
Expected Outcomes:
When to Reassess:

Figure 9-1. Worksheet to Identify Core Elements to Patient Care Plan

PROGRESS NOTES

Patient Identification (Stamp)

Name
Reg. No.
Location
Date

PHARMACIST CONSULTATION NOTE

Time: [patient's initials] _____ is a [years] _____ yo [gender] _____ who presents to clinic today with: [patient's initials] _____ history includes:

- chief complaint (cc)
- history of present illness (hpi)
- past medical history (pmh)
- review of systems (ros)
- physical examination (pe)
- laboratory values (labs)
- social history (sh)
- past/present medications
- over-the-counter medication use (otc)
- other treatments (vitamins, natural products, home remedies)

After interviewing the patient, the following problems were identified:

PROBLEM #1 [problem label or diagnosis]

Subjective (S): Interval history, subjective complaints, adherence to program/care plan, ability to adhere.

Objective (O): Physical findings, labs, x-ray, other tests, mini-mental status exam (MMSE) results, cognitive assessment.

Assessment (A): Appraisal of progress, interpretation of new findings, determine likelihood of progress. Assessment of severity/status and relevant etiologies/risk factors of active **problems**. Assessment of current non drug and drug **therapy** and patient **compliance**. **Rationale** for changes/additions in drug therapy/health maintenance.

Plan (P):

Key patient specific, goals and endpoints (i.e., needed to titrate or discontinue therapy):

Diagnostic (either referral to physician or pharmacy-based diagnostics that need to be done).

Non-drug therapy:

Therapeutic (any recommendations modifying the drug therapy-related care plan).

New / current drug therapy and health maintenance (continue/discontinue, drug/dose/route/frequency/duration):

Patient education/adherence: Document what's done during visit. Document what is long-term educational plan.

Monitoring parameters for efficacy and toxicity (include monitor(s) and interval/frequency):

Follow-up: Describe plans for follow-up, e.g., telephone follow-up, return to clinic (when), contact physician or other providers, etc.

Pharmacist Name/Signature _____ Date/Pager No. _____

Figure 9-2. Format for Pharmacist Consultation Note: Initial Care Plan Development

General guidelines for a properly prepared patient chart note include:

- *Write in ink, not in pencil. Notes are permanent.*
- *If a correction is needed, cross through the statement with a single line and place your initials next to it.*
- *Black ink is conventional. It is a requirement of some research-related agencies that records be kept in black ink.*
- *The note should be written in brief, straightforward, concise sentences or statements.*
- *The note should be complete.*
- *Dates, times, content, and spelling must be accurate.*
- *The note must be legible. Practice handwriting to eliminate interpretation errors.*
- *You should print your name and then place your signature next to or below this.*
- *Some method to communicate back to you should be identified by your name (e.g., pharmacy department phone extension 1234, or pager number 1234).*
- *Abbreviations of any kind should not be used.*
- *The patient should be identifiable by at least two demographic characteristics on the note, e.g., name and age, or name and birth date.*

The following might serve useful in self- or peer-quality assessment of a pharmacy chart note:

Meets Criteria	Criteria
	Consistent with SOAP format/accepted medical conventions. Includes **key data** necessary to support assessment. Identifies **complete problem list** and **health maintenance/compliance** issues. **Assesses** each **problem** and current **therapy**. **Assessment** of disease and therapy is **complete, specific, correct, and clear**. Provides **correct, specific rationale** for **all changes/additions** in therapy. **Plan** is **complete, clear, correct, and specific** and can be carried out by another professional. Is **neat, legible, concise**, and correctly **spelled**. Wording is **appropriate** for health care professionals and for medical record.

Figure 9-3. Characteristics of Proper Documentation—Criteria for Quality of Patient Chart Notes

SUMMARY

Designing the patient care plan requires a systematic approach. An initial assessment of care goals, followed by designing the specific therapeutic regimen and monitoring plan, require you to synthesize all of the patient-specific information with your clinical knowledge. Once the plan is developed, you further determine what care behaviors you should employ to accomplish the care plan. Documentation is essential to ensure continuity of care and progress assessment.

ASSESSMENT QUESTIONS

1. Why is it important to write a care plan and document it?
2. What is the name of the section of the care plan that describes your evaluation of the patient's condition and the rationale for this evaluation?
3. Describe how to prioritize the patient's problems.

ASSIGNMENTS

1. Identify a neighborhood health clinic or community health center that is in a cultural community different than your own. Alternatively, attend a church and the social time surrounding worship that is different from your own religious practice. Use this experience to understand what it is like for someone from a different background to navigate his or her health care. To facilitate this assignment, do the following:

    1. Introduce yourself to some individuals. Ask the following questions after explaining your purpose of understanding the difficulties encountered in the health system:
        - Tell me how you feel about going to the doctor's office? The pharmacist? The hospital?
        - Do you believe the health professionals that care for you understand your needs and preferences?
        - What would you like to see done in the pharmacy service area to improve your experience in receiving care?

        Reflect upon the answers.

CASE 1

Lauren Smith has her first formal pharmacist's consultation and care visit at Werbert's Pharmacy

One week later, Lauren returns for her first appointment with Nasir Jabr. Jabr has already contacted Dr. Miller and had her most recent outpatient records (patient information/clinic admission form—see **Figure 9-4**) faxed over to the pharmacy to establish written support for his pharmacy profile information.

Nasir Jabr: "Welcome Lauren. Let's go to the private counseling area. I am going to gather the needed materials for this initial visit. While I am doing this, please complete the history form in front of you." (There is a self-administered medical history questionnaire on the desk surface where Lauren sits.)

Lauren: "What is it you will need?"

Nasir Jabr: "Today, we will be checking your baseline blood pressure, so I will need a cuff. I will also be performing a quick ophthalmic check to make sure that there are no signs of advancing hypertension. And I will be using the

Metropolitan General Family Medicine Clinic
1234 Detroit Avenue
Detroit, Michigan 48169
PATIENT INFORMATION/CLINIC ADMISSION FORM

Allergies, Adverse Drug Reactions

Prob. No.	Entry Date	Problems/Diagnosis	Medications	Renew	Start Date	Stop Date
1		Urinary Tract Infection	Co-trimoxazole		02-02	02-10
2		Headaches	Over the counter NSAIDs			
3		Essential Hypertension	Pharmacist collaborative practice referral			
4		Smoking	No treatment at this time. Pharmacist smoking cessation program under evaluation by patient			
5		Birth Control/ CV Risk	Patch with 2 years Lo Ovral			

Risk Factors: family illnesses, occupation, alcohol, drug and tobacco use, lifestyle, etc.

Entry date	Entry date		
	Smokes 2ppd		

Patient Information

Patient Name: Smith, Lauren

Birthdate: 10/13/88

Sex: F

Chart Number: 13614

Figure 9-4. Faxed Copy of Lauren Smith's Clinic Admission Form

Clinical Practice Guidelines for Hypertension Management and Smoking Cessation."

(Lauren completes the self-administered history form. Jabr reviews Lauren's history form for any new information or inconsistencies. He determines there is no additional follow-up required.)

Nasir Jabr: "Thank you, Lauren. I don't see any new or additional complaints or concerns based upon this history form. Is there anything you would like to mention that is not here?"

Lauren: "No Nasir. I think we have discussed most things in passing."

Nasir Jabr: "Good. Let's establish your care plan together then. What I see based upon the records I keep in the pharmacy, the copy of records I requested from Dr. Miller's office, and our conversations suggests that there are five health care needs to address: a recent urinary tract infection, headaches, hypertension, smoking, and your method of birth control as it relates to cardiovascular risk."

Lauren: "I would agree. However, I think the urinary tract infection is gone."

Nasir Jabr: "Have you taken the antibiotic that was in the prescription bottle until it was completely gone?"

Lauren: "Yes, and I have not had any burning or discomfort for several days now."

Nasir Jabr: "Terrific. Let's work on the other issues then. First, I will take your blood pressure and check your pulse. (Lauren is seated. Jabr places the cuff around her upper arm and rests her arm on the table while inviting her to relax.) Your blood pressure at rest is 148/98. A little high (he records it on a note). Lauren, do you find it difficult not to smoke in situations where you would normally do so?"[1]

Lauren: "Yes, I do find it difficult."

Nasir Jabr: "Have you tried quitting smoking for good in the past but found that you could not?"

Lauren: "Yes, again. I need help."

Nasir Jabr: "Do you want to stop smoking for good?"

Lauren: "Yes, that would be wonderful. I really hate this habit."

Nasir Jabr: "Are you interested in making a serious attempt to stop in the near future?"

Lauren: "Yes, I want to start now."

Nasir Jabr: "Are you interested in receiving help with your attempt to quit?"

Lauren: "Well yes, I am here, aren't I?" (Lauren becomes a little impatient.)

Nasir Jabr: "Yes you are. I would like you to complete the following questionnaire. It will only take a minute. This is called the Fagerstrom Test (see **Figure 9-5**)."

Nasir Jabr: [He evaluates the results realizing that she is at the "attempting to stop" phase of her effort to stop smoking (see **Figure 9-6**)]. "This test helps you and I understand the depth of your dependence on nicotine, Lauren. As it turns out, your score of 5 out of 10 indicates you are moderately dependent upon nicotine. This means that you are likely to fail at quitting a few times before finally achieving it. It also means that you may do better with medication or focused counseling, as opposed to trying on your own without either of these approaches.[1,2]"

Q1. How many cigarettes per day do you usually smoke? (Write a number in the box and circle one response)	☐ 10 or less 11 to 20 21 to 30 31 or more	0 1 2 3
Q2. How soon after you wake up do you smoke your first cigarette? (Circle one response)	Within 5 minutes 6–30 minutes 31 or more	3 2 0
Q3. Do you find it difficult to stop smoking in non-smoking areas? (Circle one response)	No Yes	0 1
Q4. Which cigarette would you most hate to give up? (Circle one response)	First of the morning Other	0 1
Q5. Do you smoke more frequently in the first hours after waking than the rest of the day? (Circle one response)	No Yes	0 1
Q6. Do you smoke if you are so ill that you are in bed most of the day? (Circle one response)	No Yes	0 1

The Fagerstrom test for nicotine dependence: a quantitative index of dependence. The numbers in the gray shaded column corresponding to the smoker's responses are added together to produce a single score on scale of 0 (low dependence) to 10 (high dependence). Adapted from Heatherton et al. Br J Addict. 1991;86:1119-27.

Figure 9-5. Lauren's Response to the Fagerstrom Test

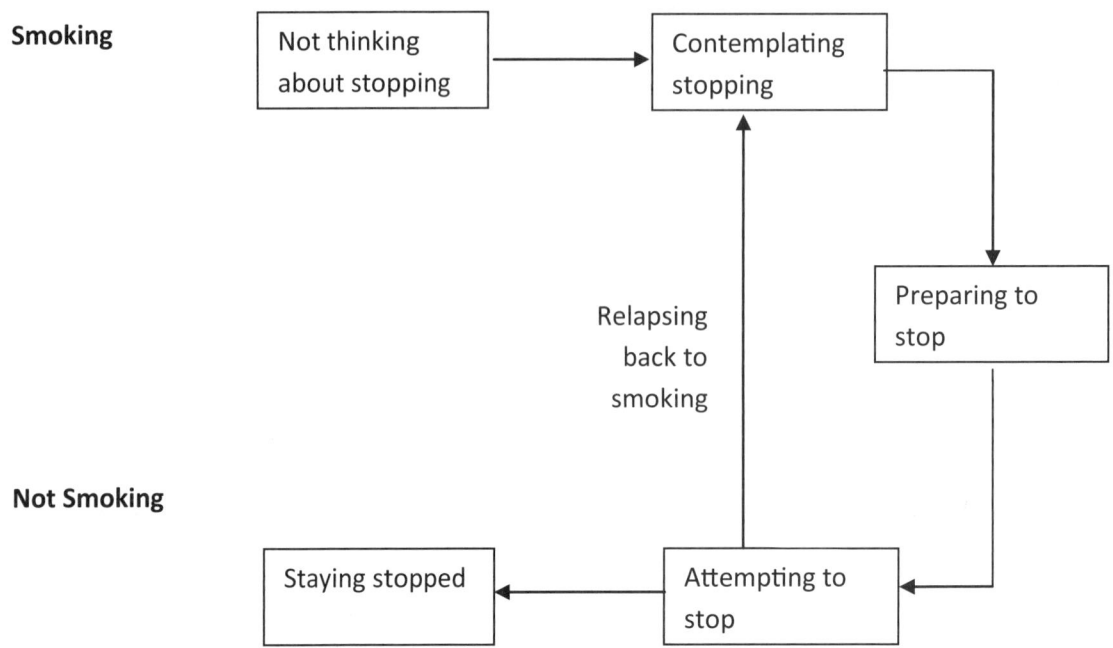

Figure 9-6. Stages of Change in the Process of Stopping Smoking. Adapted from Prochaska et al. Clin Chest Med. *1991; 12:727-35.*

Lauren: "What do you recommend?"

Nasir Jabr: "Have you ever tried the nicotine gum programs?"

Lauren: "No."

Nasir Jabr: "Why don't we start with this approach? There are other alternatives to consider if this does not achieve success."

Lauren: "Okay. I would like to try that."

Nasir Jabr: "If you can quit smoking, your hypertension is likely to resolve. However, it is not appropriate to let this go without treatment. Your blood pressure readings suggest that you are in stage I hypertension. The national guidelines for managing stage I hypertension suggest that we should start you on a medication—a thiazide-type diuretic. I believe this is appropriate for now, until we have a better understanding of how successful you will be with smoking cessation in the short term."

Lauren: "What if I can quit right away? Will being on the medicine be a problem for me?"

Nasir Jabr: "No. A person of your age is not likely to develop hypotension in response to a low-dose thiazide diuretic. And as we monitor your blood pressure, we will be able to determine if you need to continue drug treatment. I believe this is a relatively short-term need; hopefully, it will resolve when you quit smoking."

Lauren: "We haven't talked about Advil or birth control."

Nasir Jabr: "Well, we have spoken about the concerns before now. Advil, if used frequently, will cause additional fluid retention that may lead to an elevation of your blood pressure. This makes it more difficult for you to control your blood pressure. And when it is more difficult to control this, then it is more difficult to control your hypertension. Since your headaches may be related to smoking, getting control over the smoking is likely to be the solution. But in the meantime, why not use acetaminophen, for example, Tylenol?" (Lauren nods her head affirmatively.)

"The birth control is a bigger issue. Although uncommon, you are definitely at a greater risk for a stroke by taking birth control pills while smoking and having hypertension. I would urge you to consider switching to barrier birth control protection until we get this resolved. This is a choice that you will have to make. If there was a better alternative, I would suggest it. But there is not. (Lauren looks thoughtful with a resigned expression on her face.) Is there more you want to discuss about this?"

Lauren: "Well, not today. I understand what you are telling me."

CASE 1: SPECIFIC QUESTIONS

1. Evaluate the pharmacotherapeutic regimen that was designed for Lauren by Jabr. Was the clinical reasoning applied to develop the pharmacotherapeutic regimen appropriate based upon Lauren's characteristics as a patient? Describe why you believe it is.

2. Was Jabr patient centered in his approach to Lauren? What is the evidence that supports your opinion about this?

3. How likely is Lauren to follow Jabr's recommendations? Describe why or why not (support your answer).

CASE 2

Christine Johnston visits with Mr. Montanez and Maria to develop a care plan[3,4]

Johnston reviews her personal notes and sets her priorities for what she wishes to accomplish in her relationship with Señor Montanez and Maria. She realizes that she must learn more about their beliefs, provide education back, and determine what the optimal set of priorities is for managing Señor Montanez with Maria's help.

Johnston: "Buenos dias Señor Montanez and Maria. It is nice to see you once again. Thank you for returning to discuss your medicine needs with me."

Mr Montanez and Maria (simultaneously): "Buenos dias, Señora Johnston."

Johnston: "Well Mr. Montanez, overall you are doing pretty well. What do you think?"

Mr. Montanez: "Sí, yes, overall I think so. But sometimes I just don't feel so good."

Johnston: "Yes…I can understand that. I think there are few things that are starting to show up in you because you have had diabetes for a long time. But you know, diabetes does not have to be a problem like it has been. There is no shame in having it. This is a medical problem that you can manage very well. And if you manage it well, those leg pains are not likely to worsen and may improve, and it is possible that your eyesight will not worsen as well. You may notice that you feel quite a bit better. What I would like to do is decide with you what we think is important to do…and to also agree on what is realistic for you. Can we discuss this and come to a decision together?"

Mr. Montanez: "Yes Señora Johnston. This would be a good thing to do."

Johnston: "Okay. Let's start with what you think is your most important need."

Mr. Montanez: "Well…I don't like my blurry vision. I feel so dependent on Maria and others sometimes. They are great, but I should be able to read myself."

Johnston (writes down poor vision in her progress note): "Okay, what is next?"

Mr. Montanez: "Well…my leg pains keep me awake in the afternoon when I want to siesta and sometimes at night."

Johnston: "Does having to use the bathroom at night bother you too?"

Mr. Montanez: "Well yes, but not as much as the leg pains. I have gotten used to getting up to use the bathroom."

Johnston: "We can work on all of these issues at once by working on managing the diabetes. Are you interested in discussing how to do this in more detail?"

Mr. Montanez: "Yes, I am very much interested." (Maria looks a little surprised at her father-in-law's reaction, then smiles and nods her head yes in agreement.)

Johnston: "Good! Let's start with the cactus flowers and yucca plant. If I told you that the cactus flower makes the other diabetes medicine not work as well, would that surprise you?"

Mr. Montanez: "Yes! Really? That is what my family has always done."

Johnston: "I understand ...and it is not a bad thing to do by itself. But, the medicine that is more powerful and more effective that we are giving you does not work as well when it is put together. So, I want to know if you think you can accept stopping the use of the cactus flowers."

Mr. Montanez (looks at Maria who nods her head affirmatively)**:** "I will try this...wouldn't that be something else."

Johnston: "Yes it would. I think we are off to a good start, Mr. Montanez. Let's work through the other concerns and get a good plan set up. Okay?"

Mr. Montanez: "Yes. Okay. I want you to know how much I appreciate you taking this time."

(Johnston continues the discussion with Mr. Montanez and Maria, and she develops a care plan and progress note as shown in **Figure 9-7**.)

CASE 2: SPECIFIC QUESTIONS

1. Was Johnston patient centered in her approach to Mr. Montanez? What is the evidence that supports your opinion about this?
2. Was Johnston correct to focus her attention toward Mr. Montanez, and not to both Maria and Mr. Montanez? Why?
3. Do you agree with the problems and priorities that are displayed in the progress note prepared about Mr. Montanez's care? Do you have any suggestions or alternative approaches you might consider using in his case that was not demonstrated by Johnston?

CASE 3

Luisa Rodriguez develops a care plan with Huong Tran

Luisa Rodriguez visits with Huong and his family after developing her progress note and placing it in the chart. She knows that she needs to implement the social service aspects of care that Huong needs and also educate his family about basic asthma care before Huong goes home. She is concerned that there is no continuity of care plan but believes she can ask the social worker to be an ongoing advocate to interface Huong with a regular care provider or service. One thought is to interface Huong with a community health center in his vicinity. However, a problem to overcome is that no interpreter is available who speaks Huong's language. The hospital is willing to contract with someone in the community; however, they make one visit, and that visit must be well planned to accomplish the goals of the meeting. Rodriguez decides to try to make more progress on her own, considering use of the interpreter as a last step in the process (if necessary).

Rodriguez: "Hello Huong, Mr. and Mrs. Tran. You are looking much better, Huong. Your breathing seems to have returned to normal and your facial skin color looks very good. How are you feeling?"

Huong: "I am feeling much better, thank you."

Rodriguez: "Huong, I would like to speak with you about having a social worker check on you at home periodically. I know this is not something that you or your family has experienced previously, but I think that it would be a good way to get the medical help you need so that you are less likely to have asthma attacks requiring hospitalization. Could you communicate our conversation to your parents,

HEART OF TEXAS SYSTEM CLINICS		Patient Identification (Stamp)
PROGRESS NOTES		Name: Eduardo Montanez

			Leukocytes _____	
	Age	Sex		Reg.No. 16254
V S	Weight ____	Height ____	Nitrite _____ ph _____	
I I			Protein ____ Glucose _____	Location: Main Clinic
T G	B/P _____	Temp _____		
A N			Ketones ____ Urobilinogen ____	
L S	Pulse _____	Resp. _____		Date: 06/19
			Bilirubin ____ Blood	

Hct __ __ Preg. __ __ Hemocult _____ Strep ____ Other _____
UA Micro: WBC ____ RCB ____ WBC ____ Epis ____ Bacteria _____
Appt. _____ Call/Walk In _____ Primary Physician ____ _____ /Staff _____

Date: _6-19___

3:30 p.m.
EM is a 68 year old Hispanic male who presents to clinic today upon referral of Dr. Mattis. EM's history is well described in Dr. Mattis's clinical progress note of 9/15. I discussed and confirmed the accuracy of EM's history in the note. Discussed the problems identified with EM and prioritized plan of care. EM indicates that his vision, leg pain, and nocturia are most troublesome to his comfort.

#1 vision
S: does not like blurriness
O: possible retinopathy secondary to diabetes (as noted in Dr. Mattis's note)
A: vision impairment likely secondary to diabetes. Needs evaluation for retinopathy.
P: refer for visual assessment, evaluation of retinopathy, visual correction

#2 diabetes neuropathy in legs
S: EM dislikes leg pain
A: likely 2ndary to diabetes.
P: Control diabetes.

#3 Nocturia
S: has had nocturia so long is 'used to it'.
O: HgbA$_1$c = increased from 12 to 12.5 mg%, Fasting Blood Sugar = 220 mg%
A: 2ndary to poor blood sugar control
P: Control diabetes

#4 Diabetes poorly controlled
S: problems 1-3. Self treats with cactus flowers and yucca plant. Has alternative health belief of 'susto'. Confirmed that he uses 1 tablet a day of glipizide 5mg and metformin 500mg twice a day. Uses alcohol socially and frequently. Also uses Vicodin ES for pain.
O: slightly cloudy urine - proteinuria consistent with Diabetes Mellitus. HgbA$_1$c = increased from 12 to 12.5 mg% in past 6 months, Fasting Blood Sugar = 220 mg%.
A: EM is non-compliant with his diabetes care plan. He self treats and uses alcohol excessively. Evaluation is complicated by possible drug interaction with cactus flower plant consumption.
P: Educate EM about: a) the relationship between controlling blood sugar and his symptoms, b) the interaction with cactus flowers and his diabetes medication, c) educate to stop using the cactus flower treatment, d) educate to stop alcohol consumption, e) reinforce proper self administration of glipizide and metformin, f) schedule follow up for blood sugar and urine protein in two weeks.

#5 Other problems
A: May have hypertension and dyslipidemia, not sure if immunizations up to date. Not on preventive aspirin. Has an incorrect belief that he is allergic to opioids.
P: Although these all need to be corrected, will plan to work on these at next visit, if progress made on problems of primary concern to EM. Take resting blood pressure and obtain Total Cholesterol and Low Density Lipoprotein at end of visit.

Pharmacist's Signature/Pager: *Christine Johnston, PharmD*   Date: _06-19_

Figure 9-7. Progress Note Documenting Care Plan for Mr. Montanez Prepared by Pharmacist Christine Johnston

while we are speaking, so that I might understand their concerns and wishes and answer any questions they have?"

Huong (turns to his parents and explains Rodriguez's request; they nod their heads affirmatively)**:** "I would be most happy to do this. Please go on."

Rodriguez: "To keep you from coming to the hospital, we need to make sure that you see someone at least once a month or so about your asthma and that you always have medicine available to take regularly. This means that you should have enough so you do not run out." (Huong translates to his parents—they nod affirmatively.)

Rodriguez: "I think one way to do this will be to ask if a social worker could be assigned to assist you and your family with this once you leave the hospital."

(Huong translates for his parents who in turn ask: What is a social worker?)

Rodriguez: "This is a person who is paid by our community government to assist families, especially those who have children or elderly parents to care for. These people know about the programs and services available in the community. They would make sure Huong had a doctor that would accept him as a patient, and make sure that he received his medicines without interruption."

(Huong translates for his parents, who in turn ask: How do they do this?)

Rodriguez: "They come to your home by making an appointment with you. In your family's case, we will need to make sure that Huong is home with you to speak comfortably with the social worker."

[Huong and his parents briefly discuss this issue. His parents accept it and indicate that they are willing to try this, although they do not yet understand how this will work. Rodriguez records another care note to detail this discussion and request a social work consult (see **Figure 9-8**).]

CASE 3: SPECIFIC QUESTIONS

1. Was Rodriguez patient centered in her approach to Huong and his parents? What is the evidence that supports your opinion?
2. Was Rodriguez correct to focus her attention toward all of the family members? Why?
3. Do you agree with the problems and priorities that are displayed in the progress note prepared about Huong's care? Do you have any suggestions or alternative approaches you might consider using in his case that was not demonstrated by Rodriguez?

CASE 4

Michael Jones develops a care plan for Mr. Robinson

Michael Jones knows that as soon as Mr. Robinson is determined to be medically stable, he will be discharged from the hospital. This usually means that the anticoagulation therapy is not stabilized to the ideal dose before the patient is discharged. He decides to speak with his physician about problem areas he sees to determine if there is support for some care plan actions he will recommend.

Jones: "Dr. Rangert, I had a chance to review Mr. Robinson's coagulation needs as well as how they relate to his other medications and health care needs. You may not have had a chance to see this yet, but Charlotte administered the IADL and found that Mr. Robinson needs in-home assistance in order to use his medications safely. I think that his hospitalization is a direct result of his inability to safely self-medicate."

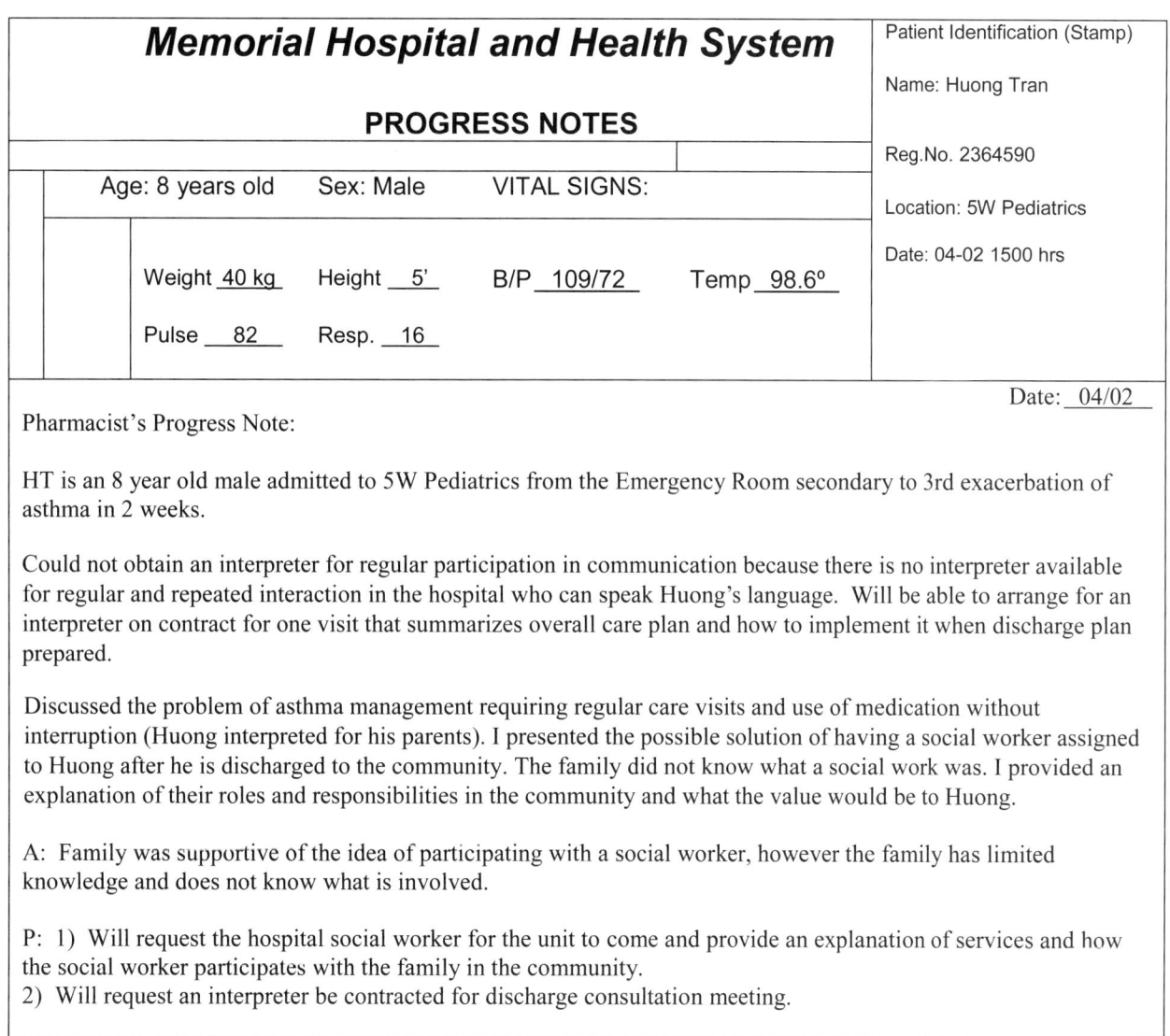

Figure 9-8. Progress Note Documenting Care Plan for Huong Tran Prepared by Pharmacist Luisa Rodriguez

Dr. Rangert: "I appreciate what you are doing Michael, but I didn't ask for a comprehensive evaluation about him…I need him stabilized and out (looking a little frustrated)."

Jones: "I understand. Actually Charlotte and I are doing what we always do in response to a request for anticoagulation consultation and management. The evidence is clear that if we don't address his needs comprehensively, he is much more likely to be re-hospitalized within the next 30 days because of anticoagulation failure or toxicity. I would like to adjust his anticoagulant dose in response to how he answers my questions about use of vitamin E (doses greater than 300 International Units per day interfere with vitamin K dependent factors leading to increased risk of bleeding), his use of thyroid replacement (increases effect of anticoagulant if used regularly), and his use of non-steroidal anti-inflammatory drugs and aspirin. I would also like to participate in the discharge planning process with the unit and make sure that in-home medication assistance is planned for him in some way. If you countersign a consult that I write, including these recommendations, I will then be authorized to handle these specific actions. I know you are very busy—I am qualified to do these things and just need your countersignature. It should not cause you more work at all."

Dr. Rangert: "All right."

Jones: "Thanks, Dr. Rangert. I will place the progress note in the chart after I speak with Mr. Robinson."

(Now that Jones has a better sense of what Dr. Rangert is thinking and will support, he discusses his thoughts and recommendations with Mr. Robinson. He picks up the home medication bag so he can clarify Mr. Robinson's medication-taking behavior.)

Jones: "Hi, Mr. Robinson."

Mr. Robinson: Hi, Michael. How ya' doin'?

Jones: "Okay sir, thanks for asking. I just spoke with Dr. Rangert, and we discussed a few ideas about your care that I want to talk with you about further. Can I take a few minutes?"

Mr. Robinson: "Sure, I'm not going anywhere!"

Jones: "Okay. I want you to tell me about this medicine (he holds up vitamin E). How much of this do you take, sir?"

Mr. Robinson: "I take one of those a day. I don't miss those because my wife told me these were most important for my heart. So I do it."

Jones: "Okay. And how about these (holds up his Synthroid)?"

Mr. Robinson: "Well, I haven't been taking too much of those."

Jones: "Why not?"

Mr. Robinson: "I haven't known what they're for, really. Just decided they probably weren't that important."

Jones: "Now tell me about these pills, Mr. Robinson (he holds up the warfarin)."

Mr. Robinson: "Oh those...well I take one of those every day."

Jones: "Do you skip Sundays, or do you skip every other day?"

Mr. Robinson: "Well, not usually. Only if I forget."

Jones: "Okay. Thanks Mr. Robinson."

[Michael Jones prepares a progress note summarizing his impressions and plan based upon his discussion with Mr. Robinson (see **Figure 9-9**).]

CASE 4: SPECIFIC QUESTIONS

1. Did Jones take the best approach in establishing Mr. Robinson's care plan by speaking with Dr. Rangert first? Why do you think so?
2. What additional questions would you ask of Mr. Robinson to further refine his care plan?

Madison Hospitals and Health Systems	Patient Identification (Stamp)
	Name: Samuel Robinson
	Reg. No. 02946372
PROGRESS NOTES	Location: INPT 347-1
	Date: 09 -02

Anticoagulation Care Consult by Pharmacist

1:45 p.m. SR is a 76 year old African American male who was referred to this service to initiate warfarin therapy for prophylaxis for atrial fibrillation Dr. Rangert has determined the target INR (International Normalized Ratio) goal range to be 2.0–3.0. Upon initial assessment of the patient, the following is noted:

#1 Atrial fibrillation – poorly controlled
#2 congestive heart failure
#3 hypothyroidism
#4 hypertension
#5 s/p myocardial infarction
#6 unable to self-manage drug therapy regimen
#7 poorly controlled anticoagulation therapy

S: After a brief interview, the patient does not report any bleeding history. Risk factors include dizziness and falling at home. Patient reports symptoms concurrent with congestive heart failure and hypothyroidism, reports use of over-the-counter use of acetaminophen, Advil (NSAIDs) and vitamin E (1,000 IUs) at home.
O: There are no signs or symptoms observed in the patient to suggest a greater bleeding risk. Baseline hematology (Hemoglobin, Hematocrit, platelets, prothrombin time) and stool guaiac have not been done.
A: The patient is an acceptable candidate for warfarin therapy, pending acceptable baseline hematology results and a care plan at home that includes assistance with medication use from a regular care provider. Dose modification likely needed based upon age > 65 years, concurrent congestive heart failure and hypothyroidism, over-the-counter use of acetaminophen, Advil (NSAIDs) and vitamin E (1,000 IUs).
P: Order hemoglobin, hematocrit, platelets, prothrombin time and INR from laboratory as soon as possible. Perform stool guaiac test. Will review results and recommend initial dose and monitoring plan. If acceptable, plan to dose warfarin at 4 mg po qday at 5 p.m. on 9/02. Obtain Prothrombin Time/INR at 9 a.m.

Michael Jones, RPh. X 4269
Pharmacist's Signature/phone extension or pager

Figure 9-9. Progress Note Documenting Care Plan for Samuel Robinson Prepared by Pharmacist Michael Jones

REFERENCES

1. West R. ABC of smoking cessation. Assessment of dependence and motivation to stop smoking. *BMJ*. 2004; 328:338–9.
2. Heatherton TF, Kozlowski LT, Frecker RC, et al. The Fagerstrom Test for Nicotine Dependence: a revision of the Fagerstrom Tolerance Questionnaire. *British Journal of Addiction*. 1991; 86:1119–27.
3. Lawson KL, Horneffer KJ. Roots and wings: a pilot of a mind-body-spirit program. *Journal of Holistic Nursing*. 2002 Sep; 20(3):250–63.
4. Bradley C. Health beliefs and knowledge of patients and doctors in clinical practice and research. *Patient-Educ-Couns*. 1995 Sep; 26(1-3):99–106.

Implementing the Patient-Centered Care Plan

"Don't let what you cannot do interfere with what you can do."
—*Anon*

CHAPTER OUTLINE

Purpose

Delivering Care to the Patient
- Recommending the Care Plan
- Influences on Your Approach
- Implementing the Care Plan
- Documenting Care Provided in the Patient's Record

Modifying Care through Patient Assessment
- Evaluate the Results and Outcomes from Implementation of the Care Plan
- Assess the Reliability and Validity of Monitoring Data Collected from the Patient
- Assess the Patient Progress Made Toward the Expected Outcomes
- Determine Changes to the Care Plan That You Would Recommend
- Document Recommended Changes to the Patient's Care Plan
- Implement the Revised Care Plan

Patient Resources

Summary

Assessment Questions

Assignment

Implementing the Patient-Centered Care Plan for Our Patients
- Case 1: Lauren Smith continues her first formal pharmacist's consultation and care visit at Werbert's Pharmacy to implement the care plan with Nasir and returns for a follow-up visit.
- Case 2: Christine Johnston implements the care plan with Mr. Montanez and Maria and conducts a care visit for monitoring and follow up.
- Case 3: Luisa implements the care plan for Huong Tran and has him return for counseling and follow up 1 month later.
- Case 4: Michael Jones implements a care plan for Mr. Robinson in the hospital, and prepares him for medication management post-discharge.

OBJECTIVES

To gain knowledge of:

1. how to recommend a pharmacist's care plan;
2. how to confirm the care plan for the patient with pertinent members of the patient care team;
3. how to advocate for the patient's health and well-being;
4. how to use patient education techniques with both patients and caregivers;
5. how to determine if the desired outcome has been achieved;
6. how to change the care goals, care plan, implementation, or monitoring plan in response to the patient's progress; and
7. how to document your care plan and the patient's progress in the patient's health record.

PURPOSE

The purpose of this chapter is for you to learn how to implement the different aspects of the patient's care plan, reassess the patient's response, and revise the plan to continue to improve the patient's care. Progress as well as outcomes assessment is needed with patients because responses are so individual. Implementing the care plan for the patient is one of the most challenging aspects of providing clinical care. To be successful, you may need to use a variety of communication approaches and follow-through techniques. For

---

*Appendixes 10-1 through 10-3 can also be found on the web at www.ashp.org/patientcare.

most patients, an optimal response is not observed easily; non-adherence is the most common problem associated with medication use. Several factors contribute to this problem, with prescription medicine misuse identified by the National Council on Patient Information and Education (NCPIE) as "America's other drug problem."[1] The quantity of prescription drugs used is overwhelming. The total number of retail prescriptions sold in 2009 in the United States was over 3.6 billion according to the Kaiser Permanente State Health Facts database.[2] The most common therapeutic service of physicians in office practice is prescribing, and 65.1% of visits conclude with prescriptions being written. More than 36% end with two or more prescriptions being written, and 10% of visits end in four or more prescriptions being written.[3] Despite this, providers lack accurate knowledge about their patients' medication use. One research project determined that a 76% discrepancy rate exists between the medicines a patient actually takes (self-reported) from the medicines that were prescribed. Over half of these discrepancies were related to a lack of accurate and up to date provider care records.[4]

When should a follow-up visit be scheduled with the patient? If a follow-up visit is scheduled by you, then you will want to decide the earliest timeframe required to meet the first monitoring event in the care plan. For acute condition management, you may have cause to follow up the same day or within a 24-hour period, for example. On the other hand, multiple medication management, complex conditions, complex medication administration technologies, and chronic disease management approaches will require multiple follow-up visits to improve the patient's response to therapy through outcome assessment and redesign of the care plan. Sometimes you are advocating for the patient's needs in addition to the challenge of designing the optimal plan. You must be prepared to modify the plan in response to rejection of your recommendations. All in all, this step requires you to keep the patient as the central focus of your efforts.

DELIVERING CARE TO THE PATIENT

In advocating for the care plan you are implementing, you must identify your role in order to know what actions you must take and with whom. There are three likely roles: 1) recommending a care plan to the patient's primary medical care provider that you initiate; 2) recommending a care plan to the patient's primary medical care provider or other health professional in response to a formal consult request; or 3) recommending a care plan directly to the patient. When you are in the first role—recommending a care plan to another provider that you initiate, then you will also follow up with the patient—taking on the third role.

Recommending the Care Plan

In all three roles, you must select the components from the pharmacist's care plan that should be included in your recommendation. Once you know what they are, consider alternative approaches to communicating those recommendations. Communication can take place by several methods: 1) face-to-face conversation, 2) telephone communication, and 3) written documentation left in the patient's health record, faxed, or emailed to the relevant care provider. Finally, you will learn about two formats for recording your recommendation to health care providers: the formal consult and the progress note.

Recommendations require selecting the appropriate information to convey. You should consider including four components in any recommendation: (a) the patient's health care need; (b) pharmacotherapeutic goals; (c) recommended therapy; and (d) a monitoring plan. Remember that the health care needs you identified for your patient are based primarily on subjective data. The second integral component of your recommendation, pharmacotherapeutic goals, can be viewed as objective in some ways. Since these goals are developed from issues such as drug response and disease process, you can make clear, measurable observations (objective information). However, your pharmacotherapeutic goals also have some relationship to your assessment of the patient. The third component of your recommendation should be your treatment suggestions, both an assessment and a plan of action. You will assess the potential for the therapies that you are recommending to achieve the pharmacotherapeutic goals and discuss plans to reach them. Your recommendation should include clear instructions for other members of the health care team about how to follow this plan. Here, you will outline your monitoring parameters, desired endpoints, and monitoring frequency.

Influences on Your Approach

Although you can follow a general systematic approach to recommending your care plan, four factors may influence your approach: (a) practice setting considerations, (b) site-specific policies, (c) practice standards, and (d) professionalism.

You should first consider your practice setting (e.g., home care, outpatient clinic, inpatient unit, or skilled nursing facility). Your approach to relaying a recommendation in the inpatient unit of a hospital, where the patient is examined many times daily, may differ from your approach in a home care setting. You may have many opportunities for face-to-face communication. You may also write your recommendations in the chart, having a reasonable degree of confidence that your recommendations will be reviewed by all relevant health professionals who, in turn, can respond and follow up. In contrast, the home care setting does not provide you the privilege of high-frequency communication opportunities. You may not see a patient's chart for several days nor see another care provider involved with that patient, possibly ever. Therefore, verbal communication over the telephone and written recommendations transmitted via facsimile or e-mail may be more appropriate.

Next, you must consider site-specific policies when making recommendations. A written recommendation in the patient chart may be preferable, but some sites have restrictions on who is allowed to do it. If restrictions exist, it is usually because of concerns about the volume of entries into the medical chart (hospitals are typically most concerned with this) or litigation fears (organizational philosophy driven). Even though some settings or site-specific policies may influence your approach, the accepted standards of practice developed by the pharmacy profession should guide your behavior. If your practice setting does not allow pharmacists to record information in the chart, you should advocate for updating the hospital's policies.

Professionals display the concepts of mutual respect when communicating about their work. To achieve acceptance of your recommendations, it is important that you adopt this approach. Many professionals appreciate being contacted prior to any written documentation taking place no matter what the circumstances. Being considerate of the other professionals' viewpoint will go a long way in having your recommendations accepted. Failure to achieve getting your recommendations accepted by other providers may result in failure to deliver some pharmaceutical care you know will improve the patient care. Therefore, use proper judgment when selecting an approach to deliver your recommendation initially.

> **KEY POINT**
>
> Displaying mutual respect to other professionals when communicating about their work and being considerate of their viewpoints will go a long way in having your patient care recommendations accepted.

Pharmacist-Initiated Recommendations to the Primary Care Provider. When your primary role is to make recommendations to improve a patient's care that were *not solicited* by the primary care provider, you should speak directly to the primary care provider on behalf of the patient. Your success at accomplishing this will depend upon practical issues. If you are working in a community pharmacy, you may not be able to implement a change via telephone at the point of care with the patient. Other providers are in the same situation. They have ongoing work and may not be able to interrupt it in order to resolve the situation. You may have to schedule a return time with the patient to initiate the changes needed. On the other hand, in the hospital setting, you may be using an informal chart note system requesting the prescriber make the changes you are recommending. The prescriber can rewrite orders to meet the request. Alternatively, you may page the care provider and take a verbal order via the telephone, transcribing the order to an order sheet for prescriber countersignature at a later time.

Recommendations for drug therapy regimens, by their nature, allow the prescriber the option of rejecting the recommendation. However, phrases such as "I would consider" or "I would recommend" allow the prescriber to contemplate the recommendation. Being too forceful can result in failure to have your recommendations accepted. The exception is when your recommendation can offset a life-threatening or substantially harmful situation. You may have to choose to be more aggressive about your communication to effect the change necessary. The prescriber may have other information to consider that you do not have. However, your communication should include an evidence-based approach to your recommendation, including risks to the patient if the recommendations are not accepted and the benefits to the patient if they are accepted. If you are helping the prescriber to make the best decision, it is highly unlikely that your recommendation will be rejected. You are advocating for the patient in this role in the most challenging situation you can encounter—uninvited. This is a unique privilege when caring for a patient, and it requires an understanding of the communication challenges.

Use clinical reasoning to decide whether you should inform the patient about your intention to contact the prescriber beforehand. Discussing the options and your intention with the patient is generally the right thing to do. However, in the event of a life threatening, or very high-risk situation, you have a responsibility to protect the patient. Therefore, you cannot ask for permission to contact a prescriber because it gives the patient an option to say "no." You have a duty to contact the prescriber. It is appropriate to take charge and contact the prescriber, offer the recommended solution to the problem, and inform the patient about it once completed.

Pharmacist Recommendations in Response to a Formal Consult. When a request for your services has been initiated formally, the need to make your recommendations through conversation first is less apparent. It is typical in this form of care to prepare your written consultation and send it directly to the requesting provider or place it in the chart (setting appropriate). If practical, you should briefly meet the patient if you have not done so already, and inform him or her that you have been requested to provide this consultation. It provides the patient with an opportunity to give you information, ask questions, and realize that your expertise is valuable. It is also important to tell the professional who requested your consult that you intend to communicate directly with the patient. Anything you learn that is relevant to the consultation for this patient should be included in the written summary.

Pharmacist Recommendations Provided Directly to the Patient. In many practice settings (particularly outpatient and community), it is most common for you to provide recommendations directly to the patient. A wide range of patient needs can be met through your direct consultation and advice. Direct consultation occurs less frequently in the inpatient setting, although the improved practices of both medication history taking on admission and discharge care planning involving medications has increased direct consultation with the patient during a hospitalization. It is also far more common to directly consult with the patient in decentralized pharmacist service models in the hospital setting. Your direct interaction with the patient will continue to be a substantially more important aspect of work with the models of care delivery moving to interprofessional approaches.

> **KEY POINT**
>
> A wide range of patient needs are met through your direct consultation and advice. Your direct interaction will continue to become more important with the models of care delivery moving toward interprofessional approaches.

Implementing the Care Plan

Successful implementation of the care plan is dependent upon follow up with the recommendations so actions and changes are made promptly. Part of your role is to identify and eliminate barriers to implementation. The following areas of discussion emphasize what you should do as a pharmacist to eliminate or minimize barriers and optimize everyone's opportunity, especially the patient's, to successfully implement the plan.

Ensure that Medication Orders and/or Prescriptions Are Written to Facilitate Care and Monitoring of the Patient. Medication orders and prescriptions are the customary vehicles that initiate treatment for the patient by other providers. These are legal terms, with the word "prescription" indicating an outpatient dispensing act associated with the product. *Inpatient medication orders* are orders written within the hospital, skilled nursing facility, or other institutional setting that are intended to have the medication administered to the patient there. Similarly, *outpatient medication orders* are orders written in a physician office, clinic, or other outpatient setting that are intended to be administered in the care setting before the patient leaves. In neither case is there dispensing of a prescription to the patient — even though the patient is administered the drug. In contrast, *discharge or outpatient prescriptions* are written by individuals having legal authority to prescribe with the intention that the prescribed treatment or device will be used outside of the facility and generally under the control of the patient once it has been dispensed by the pharmacist. And finally, when patients transfer to different care environments, either within the hospital to different units or from one care facility to another, *transfer of medication orders* are written. This process occurs to ensure that accurate and continuous medication therapy occurs when a patient changes physical facilities or locations within the same facility. The reason for overtly discussing this terminology is to be accurate in our discussion about how authorization of medications occurs for patients in different care circumstances. However, the overarching concepts emphasized in this chapter do not depend upon the legal definitions of these terms. The important point is that the proper writing of medication orders and prescriptions is essential to facilitate optimal care and monitoring of a patient's response to therapy.

It is the pharmacist's responsibility to make sure a medication order is complete, including identification of the correct patient with both the patient's name and at least another identifier (age or birth date), drug name, dose, route, frequency and instructions for use, intended duration, and indication for use. The indication for the drug provides the pharmacist with knowledge of its intended use. This information is important for advising other health care providers involved in the medication management of the patient, for monitoring the drug's effectiveness toward its intended use, and for counseling patients optimally.[5] It is particularly important for medications that are ordered for nonscheduled, or "p.r.n. use" to specify the indication so that correct patient instructions may be provided based upon intended use of the medication.

Whenever a treatment is being considered and eventually is either committed to a medication order or prescription, the natural thought processes of the prescriber move to monitoring the effectiveness. But most often, there is not a corollary order for monitoring that identifies key proxy outcomes or monitoring parameters and when they should be evaluated. If basic monitoring activities are required to assess a patient's response to treatment, you should take the initiative to contact the prescriber and have them ordered if the action of the prescriber is required (e.g., order laboratory monitoring test). If legal orders are not required, you may recommend a monitoring plan described in the patient's medical record or pharmacy profile that you can employ to assess the patient's response to therapy.

Transfer of Orders between Facilities or Setting. When patients transfer to different care environments, either within the hospital to different units or from one care facility to another, *transfer of medication orders* are written. This is a particularly error-prone time for patient care. Transfer orders typically must be rewritten as either required by standards in policy or by regulations in many states. The value of rewriting transfer orders is to ensure that the prescriber evaluates the need, safety, and effectiveness of the treatments ordered at the time of transfer (i.e., a natural time to evaluate effectiveness and safety). However, any time an order is rewritten, it creates the opportunity to omit or commit an error in transcription. Determining safety and effectiveness is your responsibility as a pharmacist prior to exposing the patient to a treatment. Evaluation of transfer orders is a "red flag" area for you. The problems are so well known at the time of transferring a patient that a process called "medication reconciliation" is becoming a standard of care to be provided by health care providers at these times. Similarly, prescription transfers in the outpatient pharmacy setting are common. This often takes place between pharmacies, from hospital outpatient discharge pharmacies to community pharmacies, or from clinic pharmacies to outpatient community pharmacies. The same assessment issues that are discussed above in the order transfer considerations apply here too.

Medication Reconciliation. Medication reconciliation is a common name for the process to ensure that an accurate and correct medication regimen is transmitted to the care providers and facilities on behalf of the patient whenever a change in care site takes place. Medication reconciliation must take place at admission, within facility transfers (hospital floors or services), and at discharge. Increasingly you will find that facilities that commonly serve the same patient are creating a common transfer form to directly facilitate the reconciliation process within the community. The process also should include a plan of care and instructions at discharge sent to the admitting facility or to the patient for home referral. An example of a Medication Reconciliation form used during the hospital admission process is shown in **Appendix 10-1**.

Because medication errors and adverse events are so common during and after a hospitalization, The Joint Commission put forth medication reconciliation as National Patient Safety Goal (NPSG) No. 8 in 2005 in an effort to minimize adverse events caused during these types of care transitions. However, the meaningful and systematic implementation of medication reconciliation, as expressed through NPSG No. 8, proved to be extraordinarily difficult for U.S. health care institutions. This resulted in the Society of Hospital Medicine convening a stakeholder conference in 2009. The overarching principle derived at the conference is that medication reconciliation must, first and foremost, be recognized as an important element of patient safety. The focus of the conference was oriented toward medication reconciliation for a hospitalized patient population; many of the themes and concepts derived would also apply to other care settings. The conference goals addressed key barriers to implementing medication reconciliation, identification of best practices, the role of partnerships, and metrics for measuring success. The conference produced key principles for achieving a successful medication reconciliation process for all patients in all settings:

1. Clear definition. There is need for a uniformly acceptable and accepted definition of what constitutes a medication and what processes are encompassed by reconciliation. Clarifying these terms is critical to ensuring more uniform impact of medication reconciliation.

2. Clarify roles and responsibilities. The varying roles of the multidisciplinary participants in the reconciliation process must be clearly defined. These role definitions should include those of the patient and family/caregiver and must occur locally, taking into account the need for flexibility in design given the varying structures and resources at health care sites.

3. Develop measurement tools. Measures of the reconciliation processes must be clinically meaningful (i.e., of defined benefit to the patient) and derived through consultation with stakeholder groups. Those measures to be reported for national benchmarking and accreditation should be limited in number and clinically meaningful.

4. Phased implementation. While a comprehensive reconciliation system is needed across the continuum of care, a phased approach to implementation, allowing it to start slowly and be tailored to local organizational structures and work flows, will increase the chances of successful organizational uptake.

5. Develop risk stratification systems. Developing mechanisms for prospectively and proactively identifying patients at risk for medication-related adverse events and failed reconciliation is needed. Such an alert system would help maintain vigilance toward these patient safety issues and help focus additional resources on high-risk patients.

6. Study interventions and processes. Given the diversity in medication reconciliation practices, research aimed at identifying effective processes is important and should be funded with national resources. Funding should include varying sites of care (e.g., urban and rural, academic and nonacademic, etc.).

7. Disseminate successes. Strategies for medication reconciliation—both successes and key lessons learned from unsuccessful efforts—should be widely disseminated.

8. Promote the personal health record. A personal health record that is integrated and easily transferable between sites of care is needed to facilitate successful medication reconciliation.

9. Promote partnerships. Partnerships between health care organizations and community-based organizations create opportunities to reinforce medication safety principles outside the traditional clinician–patient relationship. Leveraging the influence of these organizations and other social networking platforms may augment population-based understanding of their importance and role in medication safety.

10. Align financial incentives with newly developed regulatory and accreditation requirements. Aligning health care payment structures with medication safety goals is critical to ensure allocation of adequate resources to design and implement effective medication reconciliation processes.

These principles emphasize that while you as an individual pharmacist should and will do your part in the reconciliation process, full success is interdependent upon the patient and others. In this context, you must remain vigilant about assuring the accuracy of the medication use and behaviors of your patients throughout your care delivery.[6]

KEY POINT

You must remain vigilant about assuring the accuracy of the medication use and behaviors of your patient because maintaining an accurate and up-to-date list of your patient's medications is an interdependent process involving other providers and settings.

Ensure Patient Receives Medications and Supportive Technologies. Implementing a successful care plan with medications poses many challenges: 1) many prescriptions for medications are never turned in to a pharmacy to be filled by a pharmacist; 2) many are turned in but never picked up; and 3) many are initially filled, but subsequent refills are not requested by the patient. There are multiple reasons that this may occur. One study designed to evaluate why patients' chronic medication prescription refills were not picked up reveals the following reasons provided by patients:[7]

- Patient went to a different pharmacy for refills than the original pharmacy that filled the prescription. The pharmacist thinks that the patient is not compliant, but the patient is using multiple pharmacy providers, leading to lack of continuity in medication refill records.
- Medication was discontinued by the prescriber before refill was needed.
- Medication samples were provided by the physician, replacing the prescription.
- The dosage was changed—prescription was no longer valid and a new prescription was issued.
- Patient already had the medication at home—did not need more at the scheduled time. This often happens because patients are "partially compliant" (i.e., they take medication some of the time as they are supposed to).
- Medication was used on an as-needed basis; didn't need the refill yet.
- Self-reported noncompliance with medication—"I just don't take it."
- Patient denies noncompliance—just didn't pick it up.
- Patient had an adverse event from medication and no longer wanted to continue it.
- Patient did not understand that he or she was supposed to continue medication.
- Patient did not believe the medication works and decided not to continue.
- Patient was unable to afford the medication prescribed.
- Patient felt he or she had a self-limited need/short-term use despite the duration and refill status of the prescribed medication.
- Patient was unable to pick up medication on time because of an illness or hospitalization.

The process of electronic prescribing, or *e-prescribing*, is expected to improve some aspects of adherence and also reduce opportunities for errors that occur during prescribing and dispensing. Errors still do occur with e-prescribing. Dosing/dosage errors, incorrectly selected medications at the time of filling a prescription, and incorrect use instructions remain errors that can occur. Sometimes e-prescriptions are incorrectly sent to the wrong pharmacy, i.e., a different pharmacy than the one requested by the patient. More accountability is placed on patients in this process to make sure that they are getting the medication that the prescriber discussed with them, and in the regimen that is designed for them individually. Patients should continue to be advised to discuss all medications, both over-the-counter and prescription, with both the prescriber and the pharmacist to ensure that the medications they are receiving are accurate for the regimen that is planned.

Ensure Patient Takes Medication Once It Has Been Obtained. Even after obtaining the medication, a patient may not take it or may not take it incorrectly. There are social, economic, health, and other factors that contribute to this problem. Many causes can be addressed through your advocacy to initially get the patient started on the medications. You must interact enough with the patient to know whether he or she has taken the first step—obtained and started the medication! A comprehensive list of factors associated with nonadherence to care is provided in **Appendix 10-2**. These factors have been identified in prior research and should be considered by you when evaluating whether a patient is inclined to comply with proper medication use. If you can link the presence of one of more of these characteristics with the patient, you can then determine what to address if the patient's behavior is non-adherent to the medication regimens determined in the care plan.

To learn about the influence of these factors on your patient's behavior, you must communicate with him or her in order to follow up for clinical monitoring and provide encouragement and support. Three common approaches to use include:

- *Make follow-up telephone calls that you initiate* within a specified time period after visiting with a patient when seen in a community pharmacy, outpatient clinic practice, or home care visit. These calls can be reassuring to the patient, further enhancing your relationship. Your genuine concern to assist the patient may result in offering solutions you might not have known about in your patient interactions.

- *Make follow-up monitoring visits that you initiate at the time of care plan development and each subsequent visit* in order to assess your patient's response to therapy. At these visits, focus on communication about barriers and successes to care approaches in order to identify early on what might not be working and why.

- *Invite and encourage the patient to call you for assistance* when encountering any difficulties or barriers to implementing the care plan.

Conduct Counseling Relevant to the Care Plan. Effective counseling starts with involving the patient in treatment decisions. When you individualize the medication management plan by considering the patient's age, culture, gender, and attitudes, you eliminate many barriers that reduce the effectiveness of counseling.

Working with other health professionals and health care organizations to develop interdisciplinary compliance programs further improves the effectiveness of your counseling. The National Council for Patient Information and Education (NCPIE) has made several recommendations to health care organizations and hospitals that, when combined with the individual efforts of professionals such as the pharmacist, are likely to result in true improvement in patient adherence to care plans. These suggestions include

- Use existing databases to determine the extent of medicine noncompliance among patients.

- Develop and implement programs for patient compliance support (e.g., group support programs, educational interventions, monitoring clinics, compliance packaging aids, and multiple medicine reviews). Keep health care providers informed about these programs so they can refer appropriate patients as part of an individualized compliance regimen.

- Develop and implement innovative programs that teach patients responsibility for and involvement in their health care.

- Identify, implement, evaluate, and encourage successful compliance-promoting organizational practices and policies.

- Review drug use policies, such as formulary policy guidelines, from a patient compliance perspective. Revise policies accordingly to facilitate compliance.

- Develop and implement computerized systems that allow departments to share clinical patient information electronically.

Methods of Counseling to Optimize Patient Adherence. Your patient needs to know why you think a treatment plan is most appropriate for him or her. However, to determine this, you must have an understanding of the patient's values—what is personally important. If you can link the value of taking the medication (because of expected outcomes) to what is important to the person, you are likely to achieve adherence.

You conduct counseling in an environment that enhances your chance of success with the patient. You are more likely to engage the patient and hold his or her attention by communicating in an atmosphere that protects patient privacy and confidentiality. If your facilities are inadequate, work with pharmacy management to redesign them to increase pharmacist/patient contact and provide a private counseling area. Uninterrupted adjustments in operational flow may be necessary. Efficient use of supportive personnel to facilitate this important responsibility is needed.

Patients must also be advised to become active participants in their own treatment decisions and work to overcome potential barriers that prevent proper medicine use. You should counsel your patients to ask questions and to offer information without being prompted by you as it relates to all of their medicine use. You should expect the patient to carry out his or her responsibilities that are required to succeed at the treatment regimen. Your expectation of the patient is held in high regard by patients and is likely to be taken seriously. This will reinforce your effectiveness.

Counseling should be provided orally. One approach is to ask the patient questions that stimulate a conversation. Engage the patient in a conversation about the care plans and have him or her tell you (back) what approach will be used to adhere to the plan.

You should also provide written support materials at the appropriate educational level and other media that provide additional information about the medications and their proper use or monitoring skills so the patient can comply with the care plan. Use written materials to reinforce oral counseling, not as a substitute or replacement for it. Use educational brochures, patient education leaflets, books, lists of web sites, videos and CDs, and access to specialized classes, if appropriate, for the patient and his or her needs.

Educate Patients about How to Contact You and Other Health Professionals. As you implement the patient's care plan, you will coordinate the medication regimens with other health professionals who provide services to the patient. In some cases, this coordination may require you to communicate with a visiting nurse representative, physician assistant or nurse practitioner, other pharmacists who are involved in caring for the patient, or family members or other caretakers. Use a business card that provides contact information for you and your backup contacts. Make sure to have 24-hour emergency contact information.

Ensure Patient Follow Up Is Scheduled. A key to successful care plan implementation is improving adherence by scheduling follow up and monitoring with the patient. With chronic medications, you may be asking the patient to change the daily behaviors he or she has become accustomed to for a substantial time. Success with a patient adhering to a care plan at this point is largely education, assessment through monitoring, and feedback to the patient regarding his or her progress. The traditional model of care—development of a plan with no scheduled follow up—is an ineffective model of care.

To complete each visit successfully, consider using a "checklist" to assure you have provided all of the care steps needed. This is shown in **Appendix 10-3**.

CASE EXAMPLE

How to Communicate Your Care Recommendations to Another Provider on Behalf of the Patient When the Patient Is Being Discharged from the Hospital

Mabel is an 83-year-old female who is completing post-op day 4 following a right hip fracture repair. Per the orthopedic surgeon's request, you have been managing the anticoagulation therapy for this patient. The case manager has notified the surgeon that the patient must be discharged from the hospital based on insurance criteria. Social services and the family have identified a suitable skilled nursing facility in a small rural town 150 miles from the hospital. Medical management of the patient will be transferred to their home town internist, Dr. Schmidt.

You prepare the discharge plan for 6 weeks of anticoagulation. Mabel was started on enoxaparin 40mg daily on post-op day 1. Mabel was started then on warfarin 4mg daily at 5pm on post-op day 2. Her INR this morning was 1.4. Your discharge note in the hospital medical record summarizes your assessment for continuing anticoagulation for Mabel. You outline Mabel's risk factors including age, low body weight, and numerous drug–drug interactions with warfarin. Your plan includes continuing to bridge warfarin therapy with enoxaparin until the INR reaches 1.8. Your plan suggests doses less than 5mg per day due to risk factors. You write the following discharge orders:

1. *Warfarin 4mg PO at 5PM today and tomorrow.*
2. *Enoxaparin 40mg SQ daily until INR is > 1.8, then discontinue.*
3. *Obtain PT and INR in AM.*
4. *Call laboratory results to Dr Schmidt. Contact Dr. Schmidt for further warfarin and laboratory orders.*

You contact Dr. Schmidt and introduce yourself as the clinical pharmacist managing the inpatient anticoagulation for Mabel on request of the orthopedic surgeon. You verify that Dr. Schmidt will be managing Mabel's medical needs and your purpose for the telephone call is to ensure a smooth transition related to her anticoagulation. You provide a brief assessment as outlined in your discharge notes. You offer your opinion that the INR may climb quickly after 4–5 days of therapy due to her risk factors. You also share your concern for possible changes in anticoagulation when Mabel completes her 10-day course of levofloxacin for a UTI. After reviewing your discharge plan with Dr. Schmidt, you obtain agreement or modification of the plan. You conclude with a positive affirmation that Dr Schmidt will be accepting the transition in care. You provide Dr. Schmidt a written copy of your discharge plan and history of warfarin doses with corresponding INR results. Finally, you provide Dr. Schmidt a contact for the hospital pharmacy anticoagulation service. You stop by Mabel's room and discuss the plan for transition of her care with Mabel or concerned family members. You contact the orthopedic surgeon to advise him of the successful transition to Dr. Schmidt for anticoagulation management.

Documenting Care Provided in the Patient's Record

Oral communication with a written follow up is the usual and common way in which most documentation will occur. When you prepare the initial assessment and plan, you usually record it as a progress note using the "S.O.A.P." format. This format follows the development of a pharmacist's care plan discussed previously. Subjective information, what the patient relates to you, correlates to the health care need on your pharmacist's care plan. Objective data, which are quantitative, observable, or measurable, partially correlate to the information obtained from the pharmacist's patient database. The third part of the SOAP note, assessment, correlates to the information on your drug therapy problem list and/or the pharmacotherapeutic goals listed on your pharmacist's care plan. Finally, the recommendations for therapy and monitoring information on your pharmacist's care plan correlate to the fourth part of the SOAP note: the plan.

A narrative recommendation may not be labeled as clearly as the SOAP note. This format uses the same parts as the SOAP note but combines subjective and objective information into one paragraph. All information relayed by a patient, not just related to symptoms, could be documented in a "history" category. Sometimes, both subjective and objective information will come from a patient.

Either format can be used. The vast majority of physicians are accustomed to reading SOAP notes. Use the most effective and appropriate format for your practice setting. Remember to record the data and time when you write a patient's progress notes. Misinterpretation may arise if these items are missing.

Patient/Caregiver Response to Care Plan. The ways that both the patient and caregiver respond to a care plan are key subjective indicators of their intentions to support it. The reaction and responses of the patient and care provider should be captured and documented in the record. You will find it helpful to keep track of the responses that you perceive from the patient and caregiver in order to better understand why the plan is succeeding or failing. These impressions may be captured in the subjective and assessment areas of your notes.

Types of Notes Documented in the Patient Record. Several variations on the documentation notes used in charts are predominantly based on purpose. The *admission note* summarizes the data and initial assessment and plan as you prepare for the patient upon admission to the hospital. These notes usually follow a more formal format, using the chief complaint, history of present illness, past medical history, and other headings that provide a thorough representation of the impression on admission. The *progress note* is written to keep everyone up-to-date after each care provider has supplied some care and assessed the patient's response. *Medication history notes* are prepared specifically to communicate medications active on admission or to establish prior medication use history on the patient for the pharmacist in all practice settings. *Consultation notes* reflect your expert professional opinion, when requested by others, and communicate this opinion for their use. There are notes related to changes in the patient service location or provider. The *transfer note* is written to officially move a patient from one service to another and from one setting to another. A professional will leave a *sign-off note* when leaving the direct care of the patient. Sometimes professionals will write these notes at time of shift change for the benefit of the next group of professionals covering care in the hospital or long-term care setting. Finally, the notes sometimes summarize the *discharge* care plans for the patient.

MODIFYING CARE THROUGH PATIENT ASSESSMENT

Evaluate the Results and Outcomes from Implementation of the Care Plan

It is time for the patient to return for a visit. Alternatively, the patient places a follow-up phone call to tell you how things have gone. You discuss how he or she has responded to the care plan that you both developed. Did it work? This step seems straightforward and simple. But this is not necessarily the case. Between the time you and the patient developed a plan, much has often happened. The patient may have decided to not fill or not take the medication as planned. New problems may emerge since the last encounter. The patient's condition may change or drug therapy might be altered by a different provider. Likewise, when a medication is added, you may have to reconsider your assessment of several therapeutic issues. Finally, with time or additional information, your perception of the patient's situation or behavior may alter your previous assessment. Your perception of the information may change if the patient is diagnosed with a new medical problem or the severity of a medical problem changes. Because such modifications occur, you must regularly ascertain any changes using your clinical reasoning skills. **Figure 10-1** represents the dynamic nature of medication management and patient adherence.

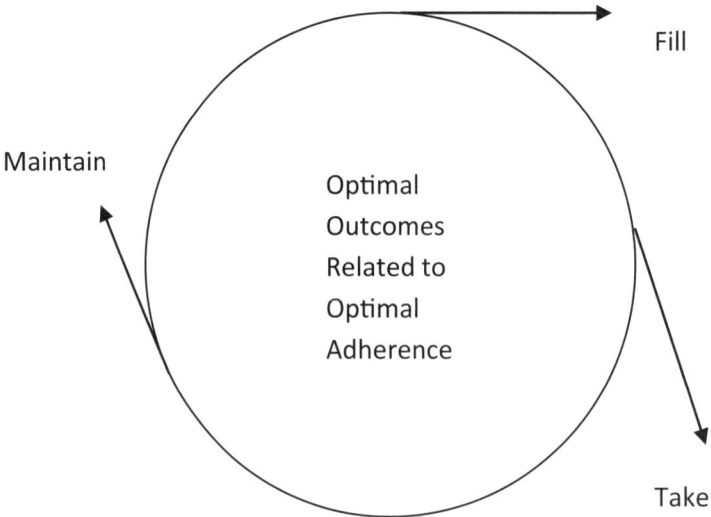

Figure 10-1. Adherence Cycle Studied—Theoretical Framework

Assess Patient Status and Condition. As new information emerges, you evaluate changes by comparing the baseline data from the various sources to current data. You should talk with the patient whenever it is practical to determine any changes. After completing this step, you should keep the general list of patient health needs up to date.

Assess Achievement of Desired Endpoints. Outcome success should be defined as responding as well as expected to the agreed upon treatment preferences of the patient. Assessing this response includes both interviewing and listening to the patient to determine the subjective and objective information needed to compare the expected monitoring endpoints to the original care plan goals. You should monitor adherence with the prescribed treatment at every patient visit. Following up outside of scheduled visits is appropriate. It is important to respect a patient's right to confidentiality when sharing medication-use experience with the patient's other health care providers, including nurses, pharmacists, physicians, and physician assistants. One method to assess patient adherence is using a monitoring form that can be incorporated into the patient's record you maintain. It is clear that implementation of systems to help you understand the patient's behavior will provide essential information to assist the patient in overcoming barriers and improving outcomes.

Assess the Reliability and Validity of Monitoring Data Collected from the Patient

Some monitoring data that you collect from the patient will be reliable (i.e., you can depend on the accuracy of that data each time you collect it). For example, you may have a patient that conducts home blood pressure monitoring using a cuff that keeps track of blood pressure readings and prints out a report or stores it for retrieval via computer. With proper education and training, the patient can use the device and obtain results that are repeatable over time, make sense, and reflect the experience of the patient. On the other hand, you may have a patient who is having more than one person take the blood pressure readings using a manual cuff. Variation in technique and skill can result in less reliable readings. Knowing the method and quality characteristics of the outcomes data being provided will help you assess reliability. You have the expertise to advise the patient about how to achieve reliable monitoring data.

Validity relates to the appropriateness of the data being gathered to reflect what you want to measure or monitor in the first place. Some professionals suggest that monitoring refills of medications from the pharmacy are a valid measure of adherence. However, as we have learned in Chapter 10, there are many legitimate reasons why a person might not fill the prescription and then obtain the refill from the same pharmacy location. Someone may erroneously conclude that monitoring medication refills is always a valid measure of adherence. This is a measure that lacks specificity and is, therefore, not necessarily a valid reflection of adherence.

Assess the Patient Progress Made Toward the Expected Outcomes

Evaluate Reasons for Success or Failure in Achievement of Desired Endpoints. Communication is the key to assessing success or failure in achievement of desired endpoints. Your skills in conducting an in-depth interview of the patient to determine progress will be instrumental in the quality and accuracy of your evaluation. A recent survey of older adults indicated that only 12% of respondents said they used "information sheets from pharmacists," and only 14% used "instructions from a doctor or nurse" to help them increase medicine compliance.[48] Today's new consumer is armed with health care information. However, your patients must tell you about all the medicines they're taking, and be truthful about their lifestyle and about their medicine compliance. It is this personal history and exchange that will reveal much of what you really need to know. You, in turn, cannot depend upon written education to influence the patient's behavior alone. Your ongoing relationship, which involves promoting counseling and continuous communication, is essential.

Assess Need for Additional or Missing Information/Data. Your care plan should serve as a guide for determining the missing information or data you need to assess patient progress. For example, if the patient has diabetes, the plan should include identification of indicators such as fasting blood glucose, $HgbA_1c$, results of ophthalmologic exams, and other items identified for monitoring at follow-up visits. An increasing number of medical conditions have practice guidelines or standards of care that should be met by all care providers. Guidelines for asthma, diabetes, dyslipidemia, congestive heart failure, and other conditions have been developed. These guidelines provide recommended monitoring parameters to follow, and the timeframe and frequency with which to measure them. The return visits for monitoring are more focused on these important aspects of patient care and less on a global assessment of health. The return visit can be efficient and is used to provide patient feedback. This visit is not to suggest that you no longer pay attention to the patient's overall health needs. A balance should be achieved of these two aspects, with the focus adjusted to correspond with the status of the patient's health.

Document the Patient Progress and Outcomes in the Record. Documentation of progress and outcomes takes place following the same guidelines for preparing written progress notes presented earlier in the chapters. However, all of the information that comprehensively describes the progress and plan does not need to be repeated. Rather, documentation should reflect the impact of the therapeutic plan on the subjective and objective data included in your monitoring parameters. At this point, you are documenting progress to make decisions to either maintain or alter the plan.

Determine Changes to the Care Plan That You Would Recommend

Care plan changes emerge when your monitoring data indicate that the plan is not working in a desirable way. Changes are likely most of the time, as it often takes several visits involving assessment to determine what needs to be changed in order to achieve the desired outcomes. Changes are required when a patient experiences adverse effects or reactions, suboptimal therapeutic responses, treatments that are incompatible with lifestyle, or is non-adherent. You must evaluate each problem and how you will change the care plan. You must also anticipate what the impact will be on all other patient concerns when you decide the changes that you will recommend. Each change must be evaluated and its impact determined. In complex patient cases, you will find that you must systematically make changes in increments that allow you to determine the impact of the change by evaluating specific monitoring parameters at each point. It may take four or more visits with a patient to first conduct an initial comprehensive assessment and then implement incremental changes with monitoring parameters.

Document Recommended Changes to the Patient's Care Plan

Documentation requires expressing enough fundamental information in each note that you will be able to discern the importance of your observations without a comprehensive review of the chart. At a minimum, you should identify the problem that the note is addressing, the monitoring parameter, the outcome observed, and the revision to the plan. The revision should include a description of the modification to the treatment and the monitoring parameters that will be followed to assess response.

Implement the Revised Care Plan

Revised care plans place a greater emphasis on monitoring. It is the "tweaking" stage of care. Or, in other words, tweaking implies that you are trying to modify rather than take large leaps in changing care. Your goal is to optimize the response that a patient has to treatment approaches rather than starting over with very different approaches. The monitoring plan developed should be reasonable for the patient, pharmacist, and primary care provider, when necessary. The checklist used to implement the care plan also includes the reassessment steps and is included here for your use.

CASE EXAMPLE

A Comprehensive Counseling Plan for a Patient Who Has Returned for Your Care After Therapeutic Drug Monitoring Results in a Change to the Care Plan

Mark Morrey is a 38-year-old steel worker who has been attending your outpatient anticoagulation clinic for the past 12 weeks. He has been stabilized on a weekly regimen of warfarin 6mg on Monday, Wednesday, and Friday, and on 4mg on Tuesday, Thursday, Saturday, and Sunday for atrial fibrillation. He has achieved the desired goal of an INR value 2–3 except for the past 3 weeks where the Tuesday INR has been significantly greater than 3. When re-tested on Fridays, the INR is back to goal. You contact Mr. Morrey and inform him of your concern with the recent erratic INR values. You ask if there have been any medication or diet changes. Mr. Morrey denies any recent changes, but does describe occasional nose bleeds that are difficult to stop. You request an extended time block for his next visit to discuss these recent changes. You ask him to bring his medication bottle and dose calendar with him to clinic.

Mr. Morrey reports to clinic on Tuesday morning as scheduled. His INR is 3.4. You review his calendar and note that he has missing entries during the weekends. You also check his prescription vial and verify the correct medication/strength; however, the date of refill and the number of 4mg tablets remaining is not consistent. You ask Mr. Morrey to tell you how he currently doses his warfarin. He repeats the correct dose schedule, but recalls occasionally missing a dose during the weekend which he tries to make up the next day. You ask about OTC, herbal, and alcohol use. Mr. Morrey denies using any of these substances. You request Mr. Morrey to describe his past two weekend activities in detail. He describes a typical weekend, but comments that he has joined a Saturday night poker club with some buddies from work. You probe further and learn that Mr. Morrey has been drinking excessive amounts of alcohol during poker night—sometimes to the point that he cannot remember whether he took his doses of warfarin or not. You believe the high INR values may be related to binge drinking and/or non-compliant self medication. You review the hazards of alcohol and warfarin. You review the importance of keeping an accurate dose calendar. You ask Mr. Morrey to also record the number of alcoholic drinks consumed each day on the same calendar. You ask if Mr. Morrey's spouse can attend the next outpatient clinic visit. You emphasize the extreme importance of following the care plan outlined for his safety. You gain Mr. Morrey's consent to the plan verbally and in writing. You make a note for yourself to call Mr. Morrey on Friday afternoon to remind him of the treatment plan.

PATIENT RESOURCES

An increasing number of resources are available to facilitate the patients' shared responsibility for ensuring the most appropriate care is taking place. The National Council on Patient Information and Education (NCPIE) has some useful safe medication tips for distribution to your patients at www.talkaboutrx.org. The Agency for Healthcare Research and Quality has produced a Patient Fact Sheet entitled, "From the Source: 20 Tips to Help Prevent Medical Errors" and is found at http://www.ahrq.gov/consumer/20tips.htm. The agency also offers a guide to assist the patient with a safe transition out of the hospital to home or to another care location without gaps in care. This guide is entitled, "Taking Care of Myself: A Guide to When I Leave the Hospital" and is found at http://www.ahrq.gov/qual/goinghomeguide.pdf. Both the American Society of Health-System Pharmacists and the American Pharmacists Association have web site access to medication information for consumers and patients at www.safemedication.org and www.pharmacyandyou.org, respectively.

SUMMARY

Implementing the care plan is one of the most challenging aspects of providing clinical care as a pharmacist. You must attend to the patient-centered approach by advocating for the patients' needs with others when recommending care. You must also directly monitor patient progress and needs by removing barriers to adherence. You will need to keep abreast of structural issues, such as workplace environment and work flow and technical support, to allow you to focus uninterrupted time and attention on the patient. With these actions at the core of your efforts, you will be successful in supporting your patients with implementation of care plans. Progress and outcomes assessment is a critical component to achieving health improvements through use of pharmaceuticals and your supportive services to patients. Even in the ideal situation, not all patients experience the desired or expected outcomes from the medication and use plan. An individualized approach to understanding the patient's behavior is needed in order to assist him or her to achieve health improvement. No other care professional has access to both the product and the patient. Therefore, this situation creates a powerful opportunity for you to achieve success on behalf of the patient.

ASSESSMENT QUESTIONS

1. There are many reasons why a patient may be non adherent to a medication plan. Interview a close friend, neighbor, relative, or another classmate who has had a need to take medications. Question this individual about the medication-taking behavior. What were challenges to adhering for this individual? How do they match what you have learned in this chapter?
2. What are tools you might use to assist the patient with carrying out the care plan you develop?
3. Why is it necessary to reassess the patient's general health and condition each time you visit with him or her to follow up on the care plan progress?
4. What are some things that following a monitoring parameter in a patient can inform you about?
5. What type of responses to a care plan would prompt a referral to the primary care provider?

ASSIGNMENT

1. Visit a pharmacist who maintains a clinical practice site. Shadow the pharmacist to observe how he or she reassesses the progress of the patients.
2. Discuss the way in which the pharmacist monitors the patient and uses the information observed to alter the care plan.

a. Does the pharmacist have conversations with the patients, other health professionals, family members, or caregivers?

b. What are the advantages and limitations with each type of relationship? How can you overcome the limitations?

3. What do you do when there is a substantial mismatch between what you think is optimal treatment and what the patient tells you is optimal? This is a difficult situation that requires strength on your part to remain true to the relationship you have with the patient. Interview another pharmacist in your community about this subject to learn about the approach he or she uses in this situation.

4. There are different systems to document patient care. Visit a pharmacy to observe the system that the pharmacists use. Evaluate the system to determine what you are able to document and not document on that particular product. Discuss what you observe with the pharmacist.

CASE 1

Lauren Smith continues her first formal pharmacist's consultation and care visit at Werbert's Pharmacy to implement the care plan with Nasir Jabr and returns for a follow-up visit.

Lauren Smith continues with her first appointment with Nasir Jabr. He reviews the care plan and how it will be implemented with Lauren.

Jabr: "It would seem we have a fairly clear idea of the care steps we should take. I would like to go over each one briefly so that you can tell me if we are on track."

(Jabr describes the following assessment from his progress note.)

Jabr: "I will send a summary of this visit to Dr. Miller's office so she is aware of our progress. If she has any questions, she will contact me for clarification. Here are two prescriptions to start out treatment (**Figure 10-2**). The first one is hydrochlorothiazide for managing your hypertension. The second one is Nicorette gum to start decreasing your dependence upon nicotine.

You need to take one tablet of hydrochlorothiazide every day. You need to use the Nicorette gum, tapering it according to the schedule I will discuss with you. These directions are also provided in the packages. After you receive the medications, you may have questions—just call me so I can answer them."

Jabr: "Let's concentrate on smoking cessation now. Here is information about smoking cessation to help you with this process, Lauren. I am providing printed material to review (see **Figure 10-3**). I am also providing a questionnaire and would like you to return with the answers to these questions on our next visit (see **Figure 10-4**). Today, I will concentrate on the correct way to use the chewing gum so that you can get the most benefit from it." (Jabr counsels Lauren on the specifics of how to use the chewing gum and answers her questions.)

Lauren: "Thanks so much, Nasir. I will make an appointment for follow up with Joe at the checkout area."

Jabr: "Good. I will see you again in 3 weeks or so. I look forward to it."

Nasir Jabr completes the documentation in the pharmacy profile for Lauren and also emails the summary to Dr. Miller's office (see Figure 10-5**).**

Jabr: "You are welcome, Lauren. I have included a return visit approximately 3 weeks from now. We can reassess your progress and determine if there are changes needed in the approach we have chosen here."

Lauren: "Sounds good." Jabr provides a business card with scheduled appointment (see **Figure 10-6**).

Lauren Smith returns to the pharmacist's consultation and care visit for monitoring and follow up with Jabr 3 weeks later.

```
          Joyce Miller MD                              DEA No. AC 1269478
          Don Hancock, M.D.                            DEA No. AD 3497682

                    Metropolitan General Family Medicine Clinic
                              1234 Detroit Avenue
                             Detroit, Michigan 48169

  Date: 02/10
  Rx:       Hydrochlorothiazide 25 mg tablets
  Quantity: 30 tablets
  Sig:      Take one tablet by mouth every day in the morning.

  Refills:   6
                                    Nasir Jabr, Pharm.D./Joyce Miller, M.D.

  _____    _____
  Dispense as Written               May Substitute Generic/Therapeutic Equivalent
```

```
          Joyce Miller MD                              DEA No. AC 1269478
          Don Hancock, M.D.                            DEA No. AD 3497682

                    Metropolitan General Family Medicine Clinic
                              1234 Detroit Avenue
                             Detroit, Michigan 48169

  Date: 02/10
  Rx:       Nicorette gum 2 mg
  Quantity: 108
  Sig:      Chew 1 piece q 1-2 hours or when you have the urge to smoke. Follow plan of
  pharmacist after initiation.

  Refills:   2
                                    Nasir Jabr, Pharm.D./Joyce Miller, M.D.

  _____    _____
  Dispense as Written               May Substitute Generic/Therapeutic Equivalent
```

Figure 10-2. Prescriptions Prepared by Pharmacist under Collaborative Practice Authority Agreement

Jabr: "It's great to see you, Lauren. Why don't we go through and see how you have been doing with this care plan?"

Lauren: "Good."

Jabr: "Have you had a return of any of your symptoms for the urinary tract infection?"

Lauren: "No. I have been drinking the water and haven't had any problems since."

Jabr: "Excellent. Tell me about the headaches."

Lauren: "Well, I have had three since I last saw you. I tried acetaminophen, and it seems to help. The headaches go away pretty quickly and are less intense. I haven't tried anything else."

Jabr: "Do you believe that acetaminophen is an adequate treatment for this problem for the time being?"

Lauren: "I think so. I would like to quit smoking first and see how it goes."

Jabr: (He takes Lauren's blood pressure while they sit and talk.) "How have you done with taking the hydrochlorothiazide?"

Ideas to Help You Quit

Do you smoke? Do you want to quit? Here are some ideas to help you kick the habit. Check with your family physician on the best way for you to stop smoking.

Want to Quit?

You promised yourself that you would finally quit smoking.

> It isn't easy giving up something that is so much a part of what you do every day.

> But you are not alone. Over 1 million people each year decide to quit and are successful.

Tried Quitting Before?

Maybe once, maybe more...

> You started out feeling the time was right but, for whatever reason, you're smoking again. Now, you're asking whether it's worth it to try quitting again. You bet it is!

Quitting Is Hard, but Don't Give Up!

Some smokers try a number of times before they quit for good. Studies show that each time you try to quit, the more likely you will be to eventually succeed. With each try, you are better able to know what helps and what hurts. Any attempt to quit is a step in a healthier direction.

Pregnant?

There's no better time to quit.

And for two very good reasons:

- You.
- Your baby.

Even if someone you know smoked during pregnancy and had a problem-free delivery, smoking puts your baby's health at risk. Quitting at any time during pregnancy is still the best chance for you and your baby to get a fresh start.

It is also important to remember that infants and children exposed to second-hand smoke are more likely to develop health problems such as chronic ear infections and asthma. Helping to eliminate these health risks is another good reason to quit.

How Do I Start?

Make a Plan

- You may want to consult a health care professional to choose a quit smoking plan that is best for you.
- Set a quit date and stick to it.
- Get the support and understanding of your family, friends, and co-workers.
- Get rid of all tobacco products and ashtrays.

Get Support and Encouragement

U.S. Public Health Service (PHS)-funded research shows the more support you have, the greater your chance for success.

Join a quit smoking program or start your own quit smoking group. Check with your health care professional, local hospitals, the American Cancer Society, American Lung Association, or American Heart Association for schedules for existing groups.

Learn How to Handle the Urge to Smoke

Be aware of the things that may cause you to smoke, such as:

- Other smokers.
- Stress.
- Depression.
- Alcohol.

Figure 10-3. Case 1 Counseling Materials

What Works?

Current Treatments

There are no magic solutions for quitting smoking. But, if you are ready to quit, effective treatments are available that can help reduce the urge to smoke.

Studies show that almost everyone can benefit from these nicotine and non-nicotine replacement therapies.

Nicotine Replacement Therapy

- Nicotine patch.
- Nicotine gum.
- Nicotine nasal spray.*
- Nicotine inhaler.*

Non-Nicotine Therapy

- Bupropion.*

*Available only by prescription.

You can get these therapies through your pharmacy or health care provider.

More Resources

Additional free materials on quitting smoking from the U.S. Public Health Service may be requested:

Publications Clearinghouse

P.O. Box 8547

Silver Spring, MD 20907-8547

Or call toll-free in the United States at 800-358-9295 (outside the United States, please call 410-381-3150). Electronic requests may be made to: ahrqpubs @ahrq.gov.

Also, you can access and download materials from the Surgeon General's web site at: www.surgeongeneral.gov/ tobacco/default.htm

These materials include the consumer guide: *You Can Quit Smoking* (PDF File, 280 KB).

The Surgeon General's Report for Kids about Smoking is an excellent resource for children, parents, and teachers to discourage tobacco use and encourage youth to quit smoking.

Internet Citation: "Help for Smokers: Ideas to Help You Quit. Based on the U.S. Public Health Service Tobacco Cessation Guideline, June 2000. Agency for Healthcare Research and Quality, Rockville, MD. www.ahrq.gov/consumer/helpsmok.htm Current as of June 2000

Figure 10-3 (continued). Case 1 Counseling Materials

Lauren: "I have done very well. I have the medicine in the kitchen and, when I get my morning coffee, I take one."

Jabr: "Well, your blood pressure is lower...looks very good at 126/82. I think we have a good solution for this for the time being." (Lauren looks very pleased.) "You have done a good job, Lauren."

Lauren: "Thanks so much, Nasir. I really appreciate your support and feedback."

Jabr: "Now the really tough one. How is the stop smoking effort going?"

Lauren (beaming again)**:** "I have not had a cigarette for 12 days straight. This is one of the toughest things I have done. I filled out the questionnaire for you."

Jabr: "This is great, Lauren. There is one trigger area to pay attention to—being around smoke."

Nasir Jabr looks it over and finds a couple of trouble or trigger areas to pay attention to. He immediately counsels Lauren to pay attention to this and concentrate on avoiding it.

Jabr: "The gum, if working properly, should eventually be tapered. Have you started the taper schedule?"

Lauren: "Yes. I haven't gone quite as quickly as is written on the instruction, but I am decreasing the quantity."

Jabr: "Terrific! As long as you are headed in the right direction, this should work!"

> **You Can Quit Smoking 5-Day Countdown**
>
> **FOLLOW THIS 5-DAY COUNTDOWN TO YOUR QUIT DATE**
>
> **5 Days Before Your Quit Date**
> - Think about your reasons for quitting.
> - Tell your friends and family you are planning to quit.
> - Stop buying cigarettes.
>
> **4 Days Before Your Quit Date**
> - Pay attention to when and why you smoke.
> - Think of other things to hold in your hand instead of a cigarette.
> - Think of habits or routines to change.
>
> **3 Days Before Your Quit Date**
> - What will you do with the extra money when you stop buying cigarettes?
> - Think of who to reach out to when you need help.
>
> **2 Days Before Your Quit Date**
> - Buy the nicotine patch or nicotine gum.
> - Or see your doctor to get the nicotine inhaler, nasal spray, or the non-nicotine pill.
>
> **1 Day Before Your Quit Date**
> - Put away lighters and ashtrays.
> - Throw away all cigarettes and matches.
> - Clean your clothes to get rid of the smell of cigarette smoke.
>
> **Quit Day**
> - Keep very busy.
> - Remind family and friends that this is your quit day.
> - Stay away from alcohol.
> - Give yourself a treat, or do something special.
>
> **Smoke Free—CONGRATULATIONS!!!**
>
> If you "slip" and smoke, don't give up. Set a new date to get back on track.
> - Call a friend or "quit smoking" support group.
> - Eat healthy food and get exercise.
>
> **For More Help**
>
> For help in quitting smoking, call the National Cancer Institute's Smoking Quitline.
>
> Toll-free: 1-877-44U-QUIT.
>
> U.S. Department of Health and Human Services Public Health Service—May 2003
>
> *Internet Citation: You Can Quit Smoking. Follow this 5-Day Countdown to Your Quit Day. Consumer booklet, May 2003. U.S. Public Health Service. Agency for Healthcare Research and Quality. www.ahrq.gov/consumer/tobacco/5daybook.htm*

Jabr: "We really didn't finalize the birth control approach. What have you decided to do, Lauren?"

Lauren: "Well…I am not seeing anyone and finally decided that my break from the pill or patch would be much better for my health at this time. So …I stopped using them. We will see how it goes."

Jabr: "Well, it is a tough choice. I am pleased that you were able to come to a decision. Please remember that you need to use barrier protection at all times when sexually active; and there are some protections for you as well. As you are probably aware, using barrier protection helps to prevent AIDS transmission, herpes, and other sexually transmitted diseases. If you decide to restart the pill, make sure that you include barrier protection for at least one complete month after you start the pill again. But talk to me about this if you find you want to return to the pill."

Jabr: "Here is my business card with my phone number and alternative emergency contact number. Let's check back again in another 4 weeks."

Lauren: "Thanks so much, Nasir. I will make an appointment for follow up with Joe at the check-out area again."

Jabr updates her profile and the summary to send to the physician (see Figure 10-7).

Figure 10-3 (continued). Case 1 Counseling Materials

Questionnaire: Stop Smoking

Patient: Lauren Smith **Date Completed:** first return visit

Instructions: Think about the following questions before you try to stop smoking. You may want to talk about your answers with your health care provider.

1. Why do you want to quit?

Lauren's response: *I don't like thinking I am making myself sick by smoking. I also don't like my appearance and having to cover up my breath.*

2. When you tried to quit in the past, what helped and what didn't?

Lauren's response: *I would chew gum and eat celery. These would help me. I would also try to relax - take a hot bath, do some sewing.*

3. What will be the most difficult situations for you after you quit? How will you plan to handle them?

Lauren's response: *Being around smoke. I will try to avoid it, but if I am going somewhere where there is smoke, I will take the chewing gum.*

4. Who can help you through the tough times? Your family? Friends? Health care provider?

Lauren's response: *I have a good girlfriend who doesn't smoke and has been on me to quit. I will contact Nasir if I am failing.*

5. What pleasures do you get from smoking? What ways can you still get pleasure if you quit?

Lauren's response: *I will try to expand my cooking and will also try to do my sewing hobby more.*

Here are some questions to ask your health care provider.

1. How can you help me to be successful at quitting?
2. What medication do you think would be best for me and how should I take it?
3. What should I do if I need more help?
4. What is smoking withdrawal like? How can I get information on withdrawal?

Quitting takes hard work and a lot of effort, but you can quit smoking.

Figure 10-4. Sample Smoking Questionnaire Completed by Lauren

Pharmacy Profile for:					
Patient: Smith, Lauren			New Patient	Print	Close Record
Demographic	OTC / Allergy		Insurance	Diagnosis	Contacts
General Health	Care Plans	Surveys	Account Status	Current Therapy	
General Information	Illnesses	Systems Review	Vital Signs	Lab Values	

Pharmacist's Progress Note - continued: Date: 02-10

S: Compliant with antibiotic and signs and symptoms resolved no burning or discomfort for several days. Headaches continue.

O: BP #1 150/102 seated, BP #2 148/99 seated. Scored 5 of 10 on Fagerstrom test—moderate dependence upon nicotine and classified at the "attempting to stop" in stages of change phases.

A: UTI resolved—patient complied with antibiotic and took until gone. Mild, intermittent headaches responsive to Advil. Advil may worsen fluid/sodium retention—contributing to hypertension. Headaches probably secondary to sinus discomfort or possibly allergies; worsened by smoking. Stage I hypertension. Both headaches and hypertension may improve if eliminate Advil use and smoking. Patient is ready to quit smoking. Patient is not comfortable with use of barrier method of birth control despite the risk–benefit discussion that has taken place.

P:

#1 – Urinary Tract Infection

P: Counseled patient to drink 8–10 glasses water/day and contact immediately if symptoms return. Patient confirms understanding.

#2 – Headaches

P: Use acetaminophen instead of Advil to decrease risk of fluid retention and worsening of hypertension. Patient agrees to use acetaminophen instead of Advil.

#3 – Hypertension

P: Initiate hydrochlorothiazide 25mg, 1 tablet every morning per hypertension protocol with Dr. Joyce Miller. Reassess in 3 weeks. Patient given a prescription and instructed BP will be rechecked in 3 weeks.

#4 – Smoking

P: Initiate smoking cessation program. Provide counseling materials and prescription for chewing gum. Follow up at next visit regarding medication compliance.

#5 – Method of birth control

P: Patient considering options. Will follow up at next visit to determine choices that patient has made.

Figure 10-5. Pharmacist's Progress Note Prepared about Patient Visit with Pharmacist in Community Pharmacy

Nasir Jabr, Pharm.D., R.Ph.

Werbert's Pharmacy
6907 Detroit Avenue
Detroit, MI 48169
Phone: 501-4279
Fax Number: 501-4280
Emergency contact: (313)498-2765

Patient Name: Lauren Smith

Appointment Date/Time: 3-3 at 2 pm

If you have any questions, please don't hesitate to contact me.

Figure 10-6. Business Card with Return Appointment

Pharmacy Profile for:

Patient: Smith, Lauren

Demographic	OTC / Allergy		Insurance	Diagnosis	Contacts
General Health	Care Plans	Surveys	Account Status	Current Therapy	
General Information	Illnesses	Systems Review	Vital Signs	Lab Values	

Pharmacist's Progress Note - continued: Date: 02-10

S: Headaches decreased in frequency and intensity, but continue. Response to acetaminophen. Patient reports no smoking for 12 days. Chose to quit birth control pill and use the barrier method. Presently sexually inactive
O: BP #3 126/82.
A: Responsive to acetaminophen, not using Advil. Questionnaire reveals smoke exposure and environment where smoking takes place as triggers. Responsive to hydrochlorothiazide, no smoking for 12 days and lack of Advil use.
Plan:
#1 – UTI—Problem resolved—no return of signs or symptoms.
#2 – Headaches—Continue use of acetaminophen as needed.
#3 – Hypertension—Continue hydrochlorothiazide.
#4 – Smoking—Monitor for 4 weeks.
#5 – Method of birth control   Will follow up at next visit to determine if patient has continued with the choice.

Figure 10-7. Pharmacy Profile Updated After Return Visit

CASE 1: SPECIFIC QUESTIONS

1. Given Lauren's age and social circumstances, what might you anticipate changing in her situation to challenge her ability to quit smoking?
2. If acetaminophen did not provide acceptable relief, what other medicines should Nasir Jabr recommend to Lauren for self-treatment?
3. What are the specific points that Lauren needs to be counseled about in order to maximize her use of the nicotine polacrilex gum (Nicorette gum)?
4. What aspects of implementing a care plan were demonstrated well by Jabr? What aspects need improvement? Support your opinion using the methods described in the chapter.

CASE 2

Christine Johnston implements the care plan with Mr. Montanez and Maria and conducts a care visit for monitoring and follow up.

Christine Johnston describes the plan that she, Mr. Montanez, and Maria have produced through the conversations in the visit.

Johnston: "Now that we have discussed these areas, do you have any additional questions?"

Mr. Montanez: "No, I understand."

Maria: "I do, too, Christine. However, I am concerned that our memories will not keep up with so much. There is a great deal of information that we have covered."

Johnston: "Yes, you are both right. I have some written materials to help us all remember and review. There is a great deal to learn. It is possible to do so if you have information to read. However, the most important things to do immediately are to

- Make the appointment with the eye doctor.
- Cut down on alcohol to no more than 1 drink a day.
- Take the two medicines for diabetes (glipizide and metformin).
- Read the materials I give you so that we can talk next time.
- Start to change your diet to improve diabetes control."

Mr. Montanez: "I will. Thank you." (He looks at Maria who nods her head affirmatively.)

Johnston: "There are many things we should do to help you take care of yourself. We have covered a great deal of information today. We will need to visit several times to understand how to best approach these needs. Please plan on another visit in 4 weeks, and we will see how you are progressing."

She prepares the progress note (see Figure 10-8).

Mr. Montanez: "Sí...Maria and I will visit again. Gracias." Christine provides both Mr. Montanez and Maria with her business card.

Christine Johnston conducts her care visit for monitoring and follow up with Mr. Montanez.

Johnston: "It is wonderful to see you, Mr. Montanez. We have several areas to assess regarding your progress and satisfaction. How do you feel about the visual correction?"

Mr. Montanez: "It is wonderful. I am pleased that I now have it." (The conversation continues through all of the issues in **Figure 10-9**.)

Johnston: "I am giving you a prescription for hydrochlorothiazide. This medicine is to help keep your blood pressure lower so that you do not have hypertension. The medicine is mild, and I am giving you a low dose."

Mr. Montanez: "Why do I need to take this?"

HEART OF TEXAS SYSTEM CLINICS	Patient Identification (Stamp)
PROGRESS NOTES	Name: **Eduardo Montanez**
	Reg.No. **16254**

Appt. _____ Call/Walk In_____ Primary Physician _____ /Staff _____ Date: 6-19

Progress Note

S: Does not like blurriness; leg pain continues; nocturia continues.
O: Possible retinopathy. Fasting Blood Sugar—220 mg%. Patient has total cholesterol—410 mg/dL; and High Density Lipoprotein=130 mg/dL.
A: EM is non-compliant with his diabetes care plan. He self treats and uses alcohol excessively. Evaluation is complicated by possible drug interaction with cactus flower plant consumption. Needs ophthalmologic evaluation now by someone who specializes in diabetes. Follow-up retinopathy status. Leg pain likely secondary to diabetes. Nocturia continues secondary to poor blood sugar control. Newly diagnosed hypertension needs management.

#1 vision
P: Please initiate referral to Dr. Jones, an ophthalmologist, for evaluation of retinopathy status and need for visual correction.
#2 diabetes neuropathy in legs
P: Control Diabetes
#3 Nocturia
P: Control diabetes
#4 Diabetes poorly controlled
P: Patient education provided about:
1. The relationship between controlling blood sugar and his symptoms,
2. Interaction with cactus flowers and his diabetes medication,
3. Educate to stop using the cactus flower treatment,
4. Educate to stop alcohol consumption,
5. Reinforce compliance of glipizide 5mg po daily and metformin 500mg po bid.
6. Schedule follow up for blood sugar and urine protein in two weeks.
#5 Hypertension
1. Patients blood pressure at 146/96—needs treatment.
2. Educate patient about relationship between diabetes and hypertension.
3. Discuss dietary control
4. Discuss need for treatment. Risks and benefits of treatment vs. no treatment—consult primary care provider.
#6 Immunization status
   Check immunization status—next visit.
#7 Dyslipidemia
1. Recommend dyslipidemia therapy to primary care MD
2. Initiate dietary counseling and establish goals.
3. Reduce cardiovascular risk. Start on once a day 325 mg aspirin.
#8 Allergy status education
   Reeducated the patient that he does not have an opioid allergy.

Pharmacist's Signature/Pager: Christine Johnston, Pharm.D.   Date: 06-19

Figure 10-8. Pharmacist's Progress Note for Patient Clinic Visit with Pharmacist

Problem	Status	Plan of Action	
Vision	Not corrected	P:	Outcome successful: Assessed response to Mr. Montanez's visual correction. He is complying with wearing his glasses and finds this an improvement.
Diabetes	Poorly controlled	S:	Maria states that he continues to use cactus flowers and yucca. However, he is taking his Glipizide every day and his metformin twice a day as he is supposed to.
			Fasting Blood Sugar—200 mg%.
		O:	He is partially adherent to this regimen—taking his oral medication but also allowing his relatives to treat him. Overall, his blood sugar has improved but is not ideal.
		A:	1. Encourage continuing the oral medication and reinforce with Maria how good it is that his blood glucose has decreased. Keep up the good work. Do not work at reducing home treatments at this time. Continue to monitor for the potential for hypoglycemia as he gets closer to goal blood glucose.
		P:	2. Address alcohol use. This must be reduced to a drink a day. Work at this goal to improve glycemic control.
			3. Monitor HgbA1c at next visit; expect lower value than 12.5 mg%
			4. Monitor Fasting Blood Sugar; expect lower value than 200 g%.
Neuropathy— Secondary to diabetes	Painful	A:	Neuropathy not noticeably improved.
		P:	Consider pharmacologic therapy if no improvement in comfort once diabetes is controlled.
Nocturia	Long standing	P:	1. Control diabetes
			2. If not corrected with improved diabetes control, consider alternative causes.
Suspected hypertension		O:	Patient blood pressure at 147/98
		P:	Initiate thiazide-type diuretic. Given his age and concurrent conditions—may be responsive to 12.5 mgs po qd for blood pressure control. Initiate prescription.
Immunization status		A:	Interviewed Mr. Montanez about history. Reviewed medical charts available. Provided the following immunizations: Tetanus diphtheria; MMR; pneumoccal vaccine.
		P:	Outcome successful: Immunizations up to date.
Dyslipidemia		P:	1. Take statin therapy at bedtime to maximize effect.
			2. Schedule visit with dietitian for dyslipidemia, diabetes and hypertension.
			3. Confirm patient is not adherent to aspirin. He is afraid it will cause a stomach bleed because this happened to a close friend. We decided not to continue the aspirin at this time; I want to gain more confidence in me and my intentions with the patient.

Figure 10-9. Problem Assessment

Johnston: "This is medicine that will keep your blood pressure lower. Keeping it lower will reduce your risk of strokes or heart attacks. You will get to enjoy your family and loved ones longer."

Mr. Montanez: "You know…I can read the label. This is a change!"

Johnston: "Good! I will give you more to read then!" (Mr. Montanez smiles. The visit concludes after the care plan modification discussion ends, and Johnston provides her business card.)

Johnston documents the patient progress and outcomes in the record.

CASE 2: SPECIFIC QUESTIONS

1. What approach did Christine Johnston adopt with Mr. Montanez to improve her chances of successful implementation?
2. Prioritize the problems that need to be addressed. How would you organize the tasks and responsibilities within each of the visits?
3. Prepare a progress note using all of the available information displayed here among Christine Johnston, Mr. Montanez, and Maria.
4. Discuss your plan with others. Are there other considerations you might incorporate into the plan?

CASE 3

Luisa Rodriguez implements the care plan for Huong Tran and has him return for counseling and follow up 1 month later.

Luisa Rodriguez contacts Dr. Morris to have him order the contracted service interpreter for Huong's family. She also discusses it with the social worker Ms. Sheri Turner.

Rodriguez: "Sheri, I think this family is going to have a hard time if we don't engage someone to translate the medical information and instructions."

Turner: "I agree. And I can see this really deteriorating as a problem in the community for Huong as soon as he arrives home. I work with a colleague who is in Huong's area. I wonder if he couldn't take the medication plan and orders intended and have one of the residents in the community translate this until we get a better solution?" (This started Luisa thinking.)

Rodriguez: "You know, Sheri, if your colleague were able to take Huong as the case, I could contact the local pharmacies in the area to see if there was someone who could provide support and feedback to the family. Ideally, a pharmacist who speaks Vietnamese may be a large part of the solution for them."

Turner: "You are right. Let's work on that."

Rodriguez goes back to the floor and reviews the Medication Administration Record (Figure 10-10), determines the discharge medication plan for the patient, and prepares the discharge prescriptions for Huong Tran to be countersigned by Dr. Morris (Figure 10-11). Luisa contacts several pharmacies and discovers one pharmacist who is willing to help Huong Tran. She prepares a discharge counseling note for Huong with the pharmacy information and has it ready when the interpreter and social worker Sheri Turner are present with her and the family.

Rodriguez: "It is a pleasure for me to introduce you to Xi Chang, our interpreter." (Xi repeats the introductory remarks.)

Memorial Hospital and Health System
MEDICATION ADMINISTRATION RECORD

INJECTION SITE CODE
A (R)Deltoid   H (L) Upper Quad
B (L)Deltoid   I (R) Lower Quad
C (L)Lat. Thigh   J (L) Lower Quad
D (R)Lat. Thigh   K (L) Glutial
E (R)Ant. Thigh   L (R) Glutial
F (L)Ant. Thigh   M (L) Ventro-Glutial
G (R)Upper Quad   O (R) Ventro-Glutial

DIAGNOSIS: ACUTE ASTHMA EXACERBATION

ALLERGIES:

Name: **Huong Tran**
Reg.No. **2364590**

GENERATED:
FOR PERIOD:
THROUGH:

START	STOP	MEDICATION	ORDER#	07:01-15:00	15:01-23:00	23:01-07:00
		ALBUTEROL 2 PUFFS Q 6 HRS	1246987	0600 1200	1800	2400
		FLUTICASONE 50 MCG Q 12 HRS	1246989	0900	2100	

Figure 10-10. Medication Administration Record for Huong Tran's Hospitalization

```
Dr. Morris                                    DEA No. AC 1269478

            Memorial Hospital and Health System
Patient: Huong Tran                           Date: April 4

Rx    Fluticasone 50 mcg twice daily - inhaled
Disp: 1 inhaler

Refills:  11
                                      Luisa Rodriguez/ Dr. Morris
_____       _____
Dispense as Written                   May Substitute Generic/Therapeutic Equiv
```

```
Dr. Morris                                    DEA No. AC 1269478

            Memorial Hospital and Health System

Patient: Huong Tran                           Date: April 4
Rx:  Albuterol two puffs every 6 hours
Disp: 1 inhaler


Refills:  11
                                      Luisa Rodriguez/ Dr. Morris
_____       _____
Dispense as Written                   May Substitute Generic/Therapeutic Equiv
```

```
Dr. Morris                                    DEA No. AC 1269478


            Memorial Hospital and Health System

Patient: Huong Tran                           Date: April 4
Rx:  Spacer Device for hand held inhaler
Disp: 1


Refills:  1
                                      Luisa Rodriguez/ Dr. Morris
_____       _____
Dispense as Written                   May Substitute Generic/Therapeutic Equiv
```

Figure 10-11. Discharge Prescriptions for Huong Tran

Rodriguez: "I have the medication prescriptions for you, Huong. These medications must be taken to a pharmacy in order for them to be dispensed. I have contacted a pharmacy that is able to provide these and also speak Vietnamese. I have written down the name and address of the pharmacist who will help you. I would also like to visit with you in a month or so. To accommodate this, Sheri Turner, our social worker, has made arrangements with another social worker in your area to visit and assess how you are doing. She will bring you back here for an educational visit with me in the pharmacy within 4 weeks or so. Here is my business card so that you have the information. I am so pleased to work this out with you."

Luisa Rodriguez conducts patient counseling and follow up 1 month later for Huong.

Huong Tran returns with the social worker for a follow-up visit to determine how he is doing with his asthma control.

Rodriguez: "Hello, Huong. I am so happy to see you! I hope that your family is well."

Huong: "Yes, Luisa, they are very good."

Rodriguez: "I am pleased to know that. How has your breathing been?"

Huong: "Much better. I haven't had to come to the Emergency Room."

Rodriguez: "That is good, too."

Luisa Rodriguez proceeds to ask a series of questions as a follow up that are provided by the National Asthma Education and Prevention Program (see page 295). Luisa then proceeds to provide education following the approach, as outlined in Figure 10-12. **She directly observes and reinforces correct inhaler use behavior as shown in** Figure 10-13. **But Huong is an 8 year old. He may not be able to respond to all of these questions, as asked here in this manner. After asking a series of questions, Rodriguez determines that Huong's overall asthma status is improved and does not believe there is a need to change his medication.**

Rodriguez: "Please show me how you use your inhaler."

Huong: "Okay, Luisa." (He makes a few mistakes, and she assists him to correct this.)

Rodriguez: "You have done an excellent job of using your inhaler regularly, Huong. I am so pleased it has gone well. Please keep getting your prescriptions refilled with the help of the social worker and your family."

Huong: "I will, Luisa. Thank you."

Recommendations for Initial Visit

Assessment Questions	Information	Skills
"What worries you most about your asthma?" "What do you want to accomplish at this visit?" "What do you want to be able to do that you can't do now because of your asthma?" "What do you expect from treatment?" "What medicines have you tried?" "What other questions do you have for me today?"	What is asthma? A chronic lung disease. The airways are very sensitive. They become inflamed and narrow; breathing becomes difficult. Asthma treatments; two types of medicine are needed: ■ Long-term control: medications that prevent symptoms, often by reducing inflammation ■ Quick relief: short-acting bronchodilator relaxes muscles around airways Bring all medications to every appointment. When to seek medical advice. Provide appropriate telephone number.	Teach or review and demonstrate the use of the inhaler (see Figure 10-13) and spacer/holding chamber use. Check performance. Self-monitoring skills that are tied to an action plan: ■ Recognize intensity and frequency of asthma symptoms ■ Review the signs of deterioration and the need to reevaluate therapy: ■ Waking at night with asthma ■ Increased medication use ■ Decreased activity tolerance Use of a simple, written self-management plan and action plan

Recommendations for First Followup Visit (2 to 4 weeks or sooner as needed)

Assessment Questions	Information	Skills
Ask relevant questions from previous visit and also ask: "What medications are you taking?" "How and when are you taking them?" "What problems have you had using your medications?" "Please show me how you use your inhaled medications."	Remind patient to bring all medications and the peak flow meter to every appointment for review. Self-evaluation of progress in asthma control using symptoms and peak flow as a guide.	Teach or review and demonstrate use of a daily self-management plan. Review and adjust as needed. Use of an action plan. Review and adjust as needed. Peak flow monitoring and daily diary recording. Correct inhaler and spacer/holding chamber technique.

Figure 10-12. Delivery of Asthma Education by Clinicians during Patient Care Visits

Steps for Using Your Inhaler

1. Remove the cap and hold inhaler upright.
2. Shake the inhaler.
3. Tilt your head back slightly and breathe out slowly.
4. Position the inhaler in one of the following ways (A or B is optimal, but C is acceptable for those who have difficulty with A or B. C is required for breath-activated inhalers):
    A. Open mouth with inhaler 1 to 2 inches away.
    B. Use spacer/holding chamber (that is recommended especially for young children and for people using corticosteroids).
    C. In the mouth. Do not use for corticosteroids.
    D. NOTE: Inhaled dry powder capsules require a different inhalation technique. To use a dry powder inhaler, it is important to close the mouth tightly around the mouthpiece of the inhaler and to inhale rapidly.
5. Press down on the inhaler to release medication as you start to breathe in slowly.
6. Breathe in slowly (3 to 5 seconds).
7. Hold your breath for 10 seconds to allow the medicine to reach deeply into your lungs.
8. Repeat puff as directed. Waiting 1 minute between puffs may permit second puff to penetrate your lungs better.
9. Spacers/holding chambers are useful for all patients. They are particularly recommended for young older children and adults and for use with inhaled steroids.

Avoid common inhaler mistakes. Follow these inhaler tips:

- Breathe out *before* pressing your inhaler.
- Inhale *slowly*.
- Breathe in through your mouth, not your nose.
- Press down on your inhaler at the *start* of inhalation (or within the first second of inhalation).
- Keep inhaling as you press down on inhaler.
- Press your inhaler only *once* while you are inhaling (one breath for each puff).
- Make sure you breathe in evenly and deeply.

NOTE: Different types of inhalers may require different techniques.

Figure 10-13. Steps for Using Your Inhaler

CASE 3: SPECIFIC QUESTIONS

1. Was Rodriguez successful in the implementation of the care plan for Huong? Why or why not?
2. Why should Rodriguez take responsibility to ensure the continuity of Huong's medication management care after he is discharged?
3. What did Rodriguez do well that supports her effectiveness in promoting Huong's compliance with his inhaler therapy?
4. Were any clues provided by Huong to suggest that a change was needed in his drug therapy?
5. Visit the questions provided for use by the National Asthma Education and Prevention Program shown in Figure 10-12. How would you rephrase these questions in a way that an 8-year-old child is more likely to be able to understand?

CASE 4

Michael Jones implements a care plan for Mr. Robinson in the hospital, and prepares him for medication management post-discharge.

Michael Jones follows up on interpreting the laboratory tests ordered so that he may confirm the appropriateness of the anticoagulation dose and begin the education process needed with this drug. His therapeutic monitoring of Mr. Robinson is described in the progress note (**Figure 10-14**). Michael Jones is reviewing another patient's chart when Dr. Rangert shows up on the patient floor.

Jones: "Good morning, Dr. Rangert."

Dr. Rangert: "Morning Michael. How is Mr. Robinson doing?"

Jones: "He appears to be doing well. His laboratory parameters indicate that the use of warfarin is appropriate. We are evaluating his response to using a 4-mg per day dose."

Dr. Rangert: "I am looking at discharge 2 days from now or so if all goes well. Will that be enough time to stabilize his warfarin?"

Jones: "If no dosage change is indicated tomorrow based upon his INR, this will be appropriate. I will contact you in the morning if there is an unexpected result. Otherwise, I will begin the anticoagulation education of Mr. Jones and, if possible, his acquaintances Althea Jones and Dorothy Roberts."

Dr. Rangert: "Sounds like a good plan. Thanks so much. I will countersign the orders."

Michael Jones prepares Mr. Robinson for medication management post-discharge from the hospital.

Michael Jones follows up the next morning and finds that Mr. Robinson's INR has risen to 1.7 (a good rise in response to the dose of warfarin being used). He looks over the remainder of the chart notes from others and decides that warfarin 4 mg orally every day is a good plan for discharge for Mr. Robinson.

Jones (enters Mr. Robinson's room): "Good morning, Mr. Robinson."

Mr. Robinson: "Good morning.' I am pleased to see you today. I am ready to go home!"

Jones: "Well, it sounds like everyone around here thinks it's time for you to go home too. So this is good news. I know that a social worker is going to be by soon to discuss your at-home needs. I am here to talk about your warfarin—we sometimes refer to it as your blood thinner. We will go through this patient education sheet together. I will also get your prescriptions ready for you so, when you leave, you will be all set."

Mr. Robinson: "I am so pleased we are able to do this. This medicine really scares me, and I want to do it right."

Jones: "I know you will do well with this, Mr. Robinson. I also believe it is good if you let me educate your friends

Madison Hospitals and Health Systems	Patient Identification (Stamp)
	Name: Samuel Robinson
	Reg. No. 02946372
	Location: INPT 347-1
PROGRESS NOTES	Date: 09-2

Anticoagulation Care Progress Note by Pharmacist

9/2 4:30 p.m.
S: No evidence of bleeding or skin discoloration.
O: Hgb = 14.1; Hct = 42; platelets = 350K; prothrombin time = 16; INR = 1.4; stool guaiac = (-)
A: The patient is an acceptable candidate for continuing warfarin therapy.
P: Dr. Rangert has determined the target INR goal range to be 2.0–3.0. Begin warfarin at 4 mg po daily.

9/3 9:10 a.m.
SR is a 76 yo African American male who was referred to this service to initiate warfarin therapy for prophylaxis for atrial fibrillation
A: Continue warfarin 4 mg po daily.

Michael Jones, RPh
Pharmacist's Signature/phone extension or pager

Figure 10-14. Progress Note Prepared by Pharmacist Michael Jones about Samuel Robinson's Inpatient Visit

who have been visiting you regularly too. It is always better to have everyone around you informed about what your needs are and what the right things are that need to be done. They care about you a great deal and will probably feel some relief if they have the knowledge to do the right things."

Mr. Robinson: "Yes, son. I think you are right about that. I know that they would really appreciate it. Thank you for taking the time to do it." [Michael Jones begins the counseling using an anticoagulation teaching checklist **(Figure 10-15)** and completes a progress note afterward **(Figure 10-16)**. Jones leaves his business card with Mr. Robinson for use at home and also leaves one for the social worker.]

PATIENT NAME: Date of Initial Instruction: Previous anticoagulation Hx: ___None ___Yes Preexisting knowledge of AC: ___None ___Yes	Initial Instruction Completed	Additional Education Needed	Repeat Education Provided	Patient Unable to Understand after Repeat Instruction	Comments/ Initials
INSTRUCTION					
General information, ACS; diagnosis, expectations of therapy and patient obligations					
Explanation of warfarin with other medications. Discussed the risks and benefits of AC					
Need for regular blood tests					
Use of warfarin with other medications					
Symptoms to report to provider					
Pregnancy					
Missed pills/adherence					
Time of day to take pills					
Alcohol use					
Emergency department					
ID card and guidelines/book					
Calendar					
Call back/contacting care provider					
Activities of daily living					
Travel					
Diet (Vitamin K consistency/ETOH use/GI illness)					
Risk of bleeding, major and minor, and precautions (shaving/dentist visits/minor cuts, etc.)					
Patient comprehends all of the above information and is ready for AC outpatient therapy					

Pharmacist's Signature _____   Date:_____

Figure 10-15. Anticoagulation Teaching Checklist—Inpatient Service, Madison Hospitals and Health Systems

Madison Hospitals and Health Systems	Patient Identification (Stamp)
	Name: Samuel Robinson
	Reg. No. 02946372
PROGRESS NOTES	Location: INPT 347-1
	Date: 09-2

Anticoagulation Care Progress Note by Pharmacist

9/4   10:30 a.m.
O: INR = 1.7 after 3 days of warfarin 4 mg po daily.
A: Maintain warfarin 4 mg po every day. Will verify PT/INR in a.m. Expect this dose to be the stable dose for discharge.
P: Provided discharge counseling program for warfarin and completed patient education sheet with Mr. Robinson. Provided educational brochures, manuals, medication tracking chart, and medication organizer for daily medication use. Have requested social work to assess in home assistance based on IADLs. Follow-up appointment to check INR within 14 days of discharge.

Michael Jones, RPh
Pharmacist's Signature/phone extension or pager

Figure 10-16. Progress Note for Mr. Robinson

CASE 4: SPECIFIC QUESTIONS

1. Was Michael Jones effective at communicating his care plan for Mr. Robinson to Dr. Rangert? If yes, what did he specifically do to accomplish this?
2. Under what circumstances would it be appropriate for Michael Jones to also educate Mr. Robinson's friends Althea Jones and Dorothy Roberts? What should he do to ensure that this is appropriate?

REFERENCES

1. Anon. The other drug problem. New York Public Television Station WLIW; 1997.
2. Anon. Available at: http://www.statehealthfacts.org/profileind.jsp?sub=66&rgn=1&cat=5. Accessed May 2011.
3. National Ambulatory Medical Care Survey: 1998 Summary, Advance Data from Vital and Health Statistics. No. 315; July 19, 2000.
4. Hash M. Health Care Financing Administration, Department of HHS, prepared statement, Subcommittee on Health and the Environment, House of Representatives, U.S. Congress; September 28, 1999.
5. Kuyper AR. Patient counseling detects prescription errors. *Hosp Pharm*. 1993; 28(Dec):1180–1, 1184–9.
6. Greenwald JL, Halasyamani L, Greene J, et al. Making inpatient medication reconciliation patient centered, clinically relevant and implementable: A consensus statement on key principles and necessary first steps. *J Hosp Med*. 2010; 5:477–85.
7. Galt KA, Backes JB, Sondag LD. Identifying noncompliance by combining refill audits with telephone follow-up. *Am J Health-Syst Pharm*. 2000; 57:219–20.
8. Pozsik CJ. Compliance with tuberculosis therapy. *Tuberculosis*. 1993; 77(6):1289–1301.

9. Shaw E, Anderson JG, Maloney M, et al. Factors associated with noncompliance of patients taking antihypertensive medications. *Hosp Pharm.* 1995; 30(3):201–7.

10. Happ MB, Naylor MD, Roe-Prior P. Factors contributing to rehospitalization of elderly patients with heart failure. *J Cardiovasc Nurs.* 1997; 11(4):75–84.

11. Daniels DE, Rene AA, Daniels VR. Race: An explanation of patient compliance—fact or fiction? *J Natl Med Assoc.* 1994; 86(1):20–5.

12. Frazier PA, Davis Ali SH, Dahl K. Correlates of noncompliance among renal transplant recipients. *Clin Transplantation.* 1994; 8:550–7.

13. Serfaty D. Medical aspects of oral contraceptive discontinuation. *Advances in Contraception.* 1992:8(suppl 1) 21–33.

14. Hamilton WR, Hopkins UK. Survey of unclaimed prescription in a community pharmacy. *J Am Pharm Assn.* 1997; 3:341–5.

15. Shea S, Misra D, Martin H. Correlates of non-adherence to hypertension treatment in an inner-city minority population. *Am J Public Health.* 1992; 82(12):1607.

16. Galloway R, McGuire J. Determinants of compliance with iron supplementation: supplies, side effects, or psychology? *Soc Sci Med.* 1994; 39(3)381–90.

17. Okuno J, Yanagi H, Tomura S, et al. Compliance and medication knowledge among elderly Japanese home-care recipients. *Eur J Clin Pharmacol.* 1999; 55:145–9.

18. Matesui ME. Drug compliance in pediatrics: clinical and research issues. *Pediatric Clinics of North America.* 1997; 44(1):1–14.

19. Kern RM, Penick JM, Hamby RD. Prediction of diabetic adherence using the BASIS-A Inventory. *The Diabetes Educator.* 1996; 22(4):367–73.

20. Marder SR. Facilitating compliance with antipsychotic medication. *J Clin Psychiatry.* 1998:59 (suppl 3) 21–5.

21. Safdar N, Baakza H, Kumar H, et al. Non-compliance to diet and fluid restrictions in haemodialysis patients. *JPMA.* 1995; 45(11):293–5.

22. Geest SD, Borgermans L, Germoets H, et al. Incidence, determinants, and consequences of subclinical noncompliance with immunosuppressive therapy in renal transplant recipients. *Transplantation.* 1995; 59(3):340–7.

23. Eisen SA, Miller DK, Woodward RS, et al. The effect of prescribed daily dose frequency on patient medication compliance. *Arch Intern Med.* 1990; 150:1881–4.

24. Lask B. Understanding and managing poor adherence in cystic fibrosis. *Pediatr Pulmonol Suppl.* 1997; 16:260–1.

25. Dew MA, Roth LH, Thompson ME, et al. Medical compliance and its predictors in the first year after heart transplantation. *J Heart Lung Transplant.* 1996; 15:631–45.

26. Baily JE, Lee MD, Somes GW, et al. Risk factors for antihypertensive medication refill failure by patients under Medicaid managed care. *Clin Ther.* 1996; 18(6):1252–62.

27. Monane M, Bohn RL, Gurwitz JH, et al. Noncompliance with congestive heart failure therapy in the elderly. *Arch Intern Med.* 1994; 154:433–7.

28. Mason JS, Walker R. Management of steroid reducing regimens by patients. *Intl J Pharm Pract.* 1993; 2:77–81.

29. Hargrave R, Remler MP. Noncompliance—letter to the editor. *J Natl Med Assn.* 1988(1):7,11.

30. Hamilton RA, Briceland AA. Use of prescription refill records to assess patient compliance. *Am J Hosp Pharm.* 1992; 49(7):1691–6.

31. Singh N, Squier C, Sivek C, et al. Determinants of compliance with antiretroviral therapy in patients with human immunodeficiency virus: prospective assessment with implications for enhancing compliance. *AIDS Care.* 1996; 8(3):261–9.

32. Myint T, Htoon MT, Win M, et al. Risk factors among defaulters in the urban leprosy control centre of Thaketa Township in the city of Yangon, Myanmar, 1986. *Lepr Rev.* 1992; 63:345–9.

33. Takaki S, Kurokawa T, Aoyama T. Monitoring drug noncompliance in epileptic patients: Assessing phenobarbital plasma levels. *Ther Drug Monit.* 1985; 7(1):87–91.

34. Atwood JR, Aickin M, Giordano L, et al. The effectiveness of adherence intervention in a colon cancer prevention field trial. *Prev Med.* 1992; Sep:21(5).

35. Leirer Vo, Morrow DG, Pariante GM, et al. Elders' non-adherence, its assessment, and computer assisted instruction for medication recall training. *J Am Geriatr Soc.* 1988; 36:877–84.

36. Parrilla JJ, Coll C, Bajo JM, et al. Analysis of compliance with oral contraception in Spain. *The European Journal of Contraception and Reproductive Health Care.* 1996: 337–47.

37. Kovacs M, Goldston D, Obrosky S, et al. Prevalence and predictors of pervasive noncompliance with medical treatment among youths with insulin-dependent diabetes mellitus. *J Am Acad Child Adolesc Psychiatry.* 1992; 31(6):1112–9.

38. Conrad P. The meaning of medications: Another look at compliance. *Soc Sci Med.* 1985; (20)1:29–37.

39. Anon. Patient barriers to compliance with cancer pain regimens. *Oncology News Intl.* 1998; 7(8):34–5.

40. Mcrea JB, Ranelli PL, Boyce EG, et al. Preliminary study of autonomy as a factor influencing medication-taking by elderly patients. *Am J Hosp Pharm.* 1993; 50:296–8.

41. Davidson AR, Kalmuss D, Cushman LF, et al. Indictable contraceptive discontinuation and subsequent unintended pregnancy among low-income women. *Am J Public Health.* 1997; 87(9):1532–4.

42. Meyerson MD. Many cultures/more compassion. *J Clin Pharm Ther*. 1994; 19:215–8.

43. Johnson JA. Self-efficacy theory as a framework for community pharmacy-based diabetes education programs. *Diabetes Educator*. 1996; 22(3):237–41.

44. Hoover H. Compliance in hemodialysis patients: A review of the literature. *J Am Diet Assoc*. 1989; 89:957–9.

45. Brus H, Van de Laar M, Taal E, et al. Compliance in rheumatoid arthritis and the role of formal patient education. *Semin Arthritis Rheum*. 1997; 26(4):702–10.

46. Geest SD, Abraham I, Moons P, et al. Late acute rejection and subclinical noncompliance with cyclosporine therapy in heart transplant recipients. *J Heart Lung Transplant*. 1998; 17:854–63.

47. Morisky ED, Mabotte CK, Choi P, et al. A patient education program to improve adherence rates with antituberculosis drug regimens. *Health Education Quarterly*. 1990; 17(3):253–67.

48. McCaffrey DJ, Smith MC, Benahan BF. Why prescriptions go unclaimed. *US Pharmacist*. 1993; Aug:58–65.

49. Brooks CM, Richards JM, Kohler CL, et al. Assessing adherence to asthma medication and inhaler regimens: A psychometric analysis of adult self-report scales. *Medical Care*. 1994; 32(3):298–307.

50. Berman RS, Epstein RS, Lydick E. Risk factors associated with women's compliance with estrogen replacement therapy. *J Women's Health*. 1997; 6(2):1997.

51. Miller J. Parkinson's disease patients show poor compliance, knowledge. *Am J Health-Syst Pharm*. 1994; 51:2554.

52. Bittar AE, Keitel E, Garcia CD, et al. Patient noncompliance as a cause of late kidney graft failure. *Transplantation Proceedings*. 1992; 24(6):2720–1.

APPENDIX 10-1
Medication Reconciliation Form for Hospital Admission

FAIRVIEW SOUTHDALE HOSPITAL
HOME MEDICATION ORDERS

Addressograph

The nurse has listed the medications known to be taken by the patient prior to admission, clarified as well as possible. The physician should indicate whether or not to continue the drug, any changes, and sign at the bottom. *If no indication is made, the drug will not be continued without further orders.*

Scheduled & PRN Medications						
Drug	Dose (mg)	Route	Frequency	Continue in Hospital?	Comment/ Changes	Time of Last Dose Before Admission
				☐ yes ☐ no		
				☐ yes ☐ no		
				☐ yes ☐ no		
				☐ yes ☐ no		
				☐ yes ☐ no		
				☐ yes ☐ no		
				☐ yes ☐ no		
				☐ yes ☐ no		
				☐ yes ☐ no		
				☐ yes ☐ no		
				☐ yes ☐ no		
				☐ yes ☐ no		
				☐ yes ☐ no		
				☐ yes ☐ no		
				☐ yes ☐ no		
				☐ yes ☐ no		
				☐ yes ☐ no		
				☐ yes ☐ no		
				☐ yes ☐ no		
				☐ yes ☐ no		

Herbal Medications						
Drug	Dose (mg)	Route	Frequency	Continue in Hospital?	Comment/ Changes	Time of Last Dose Before Admission
				☐ yes ☐ no		
				☐ yes ☐ no		
				☐ yes ☐ no		
				☐ yes ☐ no		
				☐ yes ☐ no		

Nurse taking history/date　　　　　　　　　　　　　　　　　　　　　　　　　　　　Physician signature/date

APPENDIX 10-2

Assessment of Factors That Influence Medication Adherence

Present	Factor
	Access Barriers to Obtaining Medications—Economic
	■ Not able to purchase medications—cost too much/financial[8-14]
	■ Not willing to purchase medications
	■ Using sample medications and not continuing medications after these are gone
	■ Lack of insurance to cover the costs of medications[15]
	Access Barriers to Obtaining Medications—Transportation
	■ Transportation is not available/dependable[7-10,16]
	■ Distance for travel to obtain medications is excessive/expensive/not convenient[9,16,48]
	■ Unable to pick up due to illness/hospitalization[7]
	Access Barriers to Obtaining Medications—Facilities and Services
	■ Inconvenient clinic hour
	■ General practitioner prescribe[17]
	Social Support
	■ Lack of general social support—self-care[9,18-22]
	■ Living alone associated with difficulty with adherence[9,21,23]
	■ Lack of assistance provided from people living with makes adherence more difficult[9]
	■ Family disorganization associated with lower adherence[24]
	■ Single (not married or partnered) persons have more difficulty with adherence[9,11,15,21,22]
	■ Lack of care provider[24,25]
	■ Church affiliated leads to active support
	■ Home health or assisted living improves adherence
	■ Low health care provider visits[11,15,26]
	■ Three or more meals per day[17]
	Complexity of Condition—Medication
	■ Poly pharmacy[27]
	■ As number of medications increases, adherence decreases[9,18,20,24,26-33]
	■ As number of doses/day increases, adherence decreases[18,24,26,30]
	■ Lack of drug free holiday when needed for treatment response[9,34]
	■ Medication class affect adherence[9,26]
	■ Self-limited need for med[7]

APPENDIX 10-2 (continued)
Assessment of Factors That Influence Medication Adherence

Present	Factor
	Complexity of Condition—Condition
	■ Severity of disease[20,24,32,35]
	■ Duration of illness/need for med[9,19,28,29]
	■ As number of chronic conditions increases, adherence decreases. Nonadherence is common with these types of chronic conditions: alcoholism,[15] anger and hostility symptoms,[25,29] anxiety,[20,24-26] arthritis, asthma, congestive heart failure, dementia,[16] depression,[12,20,21,24,25,29,31,36] diabetes, high blood pressure—proxy for adherence is the number of times BP taken[11] or evidence that the BP is primarily checked in emergency room,[15] high cholesterol, poor cycle control,[13] psychiatric disorder,[37] seizure type and duration of seizure control,[29,33] stomach disorders, substance abuse problems,[15,20] tobacco use,[11,15] and transplantation stress.[12,52]
	Perceived Effects of Medication
	■ Past-current adverse event associated with non-adherence[7-9,13,16,20,24,2,9,36,38-41]
	■ Past or current failure of therapy associated with non-adherence[7,8,24]
	■ Desired reversal of symptoms—if low then non-adherence
	■ Patient perceives no impact on disease—use of avoidance behavior[8,18,25]
	Health Effects
	■ Belief that medication works associated with improved adherence[9,12,16,20,42]
	■ Self efficacy with health—improved adherence—health locus of control[12,21,29,43,44]
	■ Self efficacy associated with improved adherence—Self esteem[22,37,43,45,46]
	■ Health beliefs support need associated with improved adherence[43]
	■ Satisfied with health providers associated with improved adherence[8,16,20,43]
	■ Lack of insight related to lower adherence—shouldn't have to take med[20,39]
	■ Denial of illness related to lower adherence—do not need medication[8,14,20,40,41,44]
	■ Low family value of medical care related to low adherence[20]
	■ Stigma attached to illness related to lower adherence[47]
	■ Belief that MD orders improve health associated with improved adherence[44]
	■ Use of home remedies related to lower adherence[9]
	■ Express concern about missed meds associated with improved adherence[9]
	Coping Skills
	■ Fewer coping skills developed associated with lower adherence[31]

APPENDIX 10-2 (continued)
Assessment of Factors That Influence Medication Adherence

Present	Factor
	Patient's Characteristics
	▪ Age[9,11,15,21,22,24-27,29,31-33,49,50]
	▪ Sex[11,15,22,25-27,31-33,49]
	▪ Socioeconomic status[11,18,44]
	▪ Occupation[32,44]
	▪ Employed[9,15,31]
	▪ Number of drug allergies[9]
	▪ Recent hospitalization[27]
	▪ Race/ethnicity (influence side effect profile)[20,31]
	▪ * Spirituality as a determinant of health or healing—would like to include, however, no prior useful research in area to assist us with this.
	Patient's Health Cognition
	▪ Forgetfulness[8,9,14,20,39,48]
	▪ Knowledge of disease[8,9,16,20,24,43,51]
	▪ Knowledge of drug regimen[8,9,13,16,20,22,24,36,43,47]
	▪ Reading level
	▪ Grade level completed[9,11,21-23,44]
	▪ Functional health skills (psychomotor)
	▪ Physical impairment/accommodation status
	▪ Vision impairment/accommodation status
	▪ Hearing impairment/accommodation status
	▪ Ability to open medication containers[16,35]
	▪ Ability to self-administer medications
	▪ Language is a health communication barrier[42]
	Other—Process Steps Associated with Improved Adherence
	▪ Physician–patient communication[18]
	▪ Formal education program about proper medication use[25]
	▪ Able to administer own medication[17,33]
	▪ Counseled by pharmacist[17]
	▪ Single dose pack of medication[17]
	▪ Receive medication in emergency room[15]

APPENDIX 10-3

Checklist for Patient Care Plan Implementation, Revision, and Follow Up

Check	Step in Care Plan Implementation
	Recommend the care plan to the appropriate individuals: patient, health care providers, caregivers
	Ensure that medication orders and/or prescriptions are written to facilitate patient monitoring
	Ensure patient receives medications and supportive technologies
	Conduct counseling relevant to the care plan
	■ Patient resources
	Use methods of counseling to optimize patient adherence
	Document care provided in the patients' record
	Follow up with health care providers as appropriate assuring your responsibility in medication reconciliation process completed
	Document patient/caregiver response to care plan
	Document appropriate type of note in the patient record
	Educate patients about how to contact you and other health professionals
	■ Business card
	Ensure patient follow up is scheduled

Check	Step in Care Plan Revision and Follow Up
	Evaluate the results and outcomes from implementation of the care plan
	■ Assess patient status and condition
	■ Assess achievement of desired endpoints
	■ Evaluate reasons for success or failure in achievement of desired endpoints
	■ Assess need for additional or missing information/data
	Determine changes to the care plan you would recommend
	Recommend the care plan to the appropriate individuals: patient, health care providers, caregivers
	Ensure that medication orders and/or prescriptions are written to facilitate care and monitoring of the patient
	Ensure patient receives medications and supportive technologies
	Conduct counseling relevant to the care plan
	■ Patient resources
	Use methods of counseling to optimize patient adherence
	Document recommended changes to the patient's care plan
	Communicate with the primary health care provider
	Document patient/caregiver response to care plan
	Document types of notes documented in the patient record
	Educate patients about how to contact you and other health professionals
	■ Business card
	Ensure patient follow up is scheduled

Glossary

Action Plan—a proactive document that describes your goals, what actions you will take, and when you will take them.

Acupuncture—an original Chinese practice of puncturing the body with needles at specific points to cure disease or relieve pain (as in surgery).

Adherence—the act, action, or quality of consistently behaving in a manner that is expected; used in the context of medication use or care plan steps.

Advocate—a person who pleads the cause of another.

Ambulatory Care Setting—care provided in outpatient and clinic environment(s).

Audit—an examination or review that establishes the extent to which a condition, process, or performance conforms to predetermined standards or criteria.

Auscultation—listening to the sounds made by various body structures and functions as a diagnostic method, usually with a stethoscope.

Biofeedback—the technique of manipulating unconscious or involuntary bodily processes (e.g., blood pressure) made perceptible to the senses (e.g., sphygmomanometer—blood pressure cuff) by conscious mental control.

Biomedical Model—the conceptual framework for the practice of Western medicine. The model describes disease in terms of symptoms and the pathology that, in part, is attributed to the cause of these symptoms. "Health" in this model is the absence of disease.

Care—assistive, supportive, or facilitative acts toward, or for, another individual or group with evident or anticipated needs to ameliorate or improve a human condition or life way.

Caring—direct and indirect nurturing and skillful activities, processes, and decisions related to assisting people in a manner that reflects behaviors that are empathetic, supportive, compassionate, protective, educational, and others; and dependent upon the needs, problems, values, and goals of the individual or group being assisted.

Centers for Disease Control and Prevention (CDC)—the lead federal agency for protecting the health and safety of people at home and abroad, providing credible information to enhance health decisions and promoting health through strong partnerships. CDC serves as the national focus for developing and applying disease prevention and control, environmental health, and health promotion and educational activities to improve the lives of people in the United States.

Chiropractic—a system of therapy using manipulation and specific adjustment of body structures such as the spinal column. It is based upon the premise that disease results from a lack of normal nerve function.

Clinical—relating to the direct observation of a patient to determine the course and symptoms of a disease or condition.

Clinical Guideline—an evidence-based, systematically developed statement to assist practitioners and patients in making appropriate decisions for specific clinical circumstances.

Clinical Performance—a method to monitor the extent to which the actions of a health care provider conform to clinical performance guidelines.

Clinical Reasoning/Clinical Problem Solving—terms used interchangeably to refer to the problem solving process that clinicians employ with patient problems.

Clinical Reasoning—a major component of expert clinical problem solving. It is a dynamic, cyclic, reiterative process in which observation, analysis, synthesis, deduction, induction, hypothesis generation and testing, inquiry-strategy design, and the skills of examination are all interrelated.

Clinical Research—patient-oriented research conducted with human subjects (or on material of human origin such as tissues, specimens, and cognitive phenomena) for which an investigator (or colleague) directly interacts with human subjects.

Clinician—the person encountering the patient in a professional relationship who evaluates the patient and recommends care.

Collaborative Practice Agreement—agreements by which practitioners of medicine, osteopathy, podiatry (or others), and pharmacists enter into voluntary, written agreements to improve outcomes for their mutual patients using drug therapies, laboratory tests, and medical devices. These agreements usually describe how one practitioner delegates authority to another to act within the scope of practice of another practitioner (e.g., pharmacist prescribing medication under a physician's delegated authority).

Compliance—see the term "adherence."

Computerized Physician (or Practitioner) Order Entry (CPOE)—a method of entering orders for patient care into a computerized system. It is intended to replace the use of paper.

Confidentiality—entrusted communication of information that is considered private and implies an ethical or legal principle.

Consumer Empowerment—the investment of power or authority in those who purchase goods and services.

Continuity of Care Record—a core dataset to be sent to the next health care provider whenever a patient is referred or transferred or otherwise uses different clinics, hospitals, or other providers. Both the content and specifics of the data elements are defined by a standard entitled, "ASTM E2369-05 Standard Specification for Continuity of Care Record (CCR)."

Critical Literature Evaluation—a process of determining the overall credibility of an information resource, emphasizing an evaluation of the internal and external validity of a study.

Culture—a set of guidelines, both explicit and implicit, which individuals inherit as members of a particular society, and which tells them how to view the world and how to behave in relationship to other people.

Cultural Competence—refers to the ability to interact effectively with people of different cultures. Cultural competence comprises four components: 1) awareness of one's own cultural worldview, b) attitude towards cultural differences, 3) knowledge of different cultural practices and worldviews, and 4) cross-cultural skills. Developing cultural competence results in the ability to understand, communicate with, and effectively interact with people across cultures.

Decentralized Practice—a professional practice in areas other than the central pharmacy within a hospital or health system (e.g., on the patient care floor).

Delegated Authority—authority to prescribe medications, order tests, or perform procedures given from a practitioner with that power to another practitioner who normally does not have this authority under the law.

Department of Veterans Affairs (VA)—department established on March 15, 1989, succeeding the Veterans Administration, that it is responsible for providing federal benefits to veterans and their dependents. Headed by the Secretary of Veterans Affairs, VA is the second largest of the 15 Cabinet departments and operates nationwide programs for health care, financial assistance, and burial benefits.

Disease—any abnormal condition affecting either the whole body or any of its parts, which impairs normal functioning.

Documentation—the process of recording relevant patient care information in a readily retrievable format.

Drug Information—the core knowledge that describes the characteristics of drug entities, their actual and potential uses, efficacy, effectiveness, and safety.

Drug of Choice—the pharmaceutical considered optimal, or the first one generally considered most appropriate, to be used for a particular diagnostic, treatment, or prevention.

Drug Utilization Review—review of a prescription, at the time of dispensing (concurrent) or after the fact (retrospective), for appropriateness based on a patient's medical condition, other medications the patient is already receiving, or patient-specific factors that might make the prescribed drug a poor choice. The term can also be applied to retrospective review of large numbers of prescriptions for appropriateness.

Durable Medical Equipment—any medical equipment used in the home to aid in a better quality of living. It is a benefit included in most insurance plans.

Electronic Health Record (EHR)—data from a subset of each institution's EMR that is agreed on by the institution. An EHR may also reside "entirely within one institution" and link various affiliated practice sites together. An EHR can only be present if the participating sites all have an EMR in place that is interoperable. With the EHR, a common repository structure is developed and managed by a parent organization, most commonly referred to as a regional health information organization (RHIO).

Electronic Medical Record (EMR)—the set of databases (or repositories) that contains the health information for patients within a given institution or organization. Thus, an EMR contains the aggregated data sets gathered from a variety of clinical service delivery processes such as laboratory data, pharmacy data, patient registration data, radiology data, surgical procedures, clinic and inpatient notes, and others.

Empathy—intellectual and emotional awareness of another person's thoughts, feelings, and behavior, even those that are distressing and disturbing. Empathy emphasizes understanding the ability to sense the patient's experience and feelings accurately as well as communicate that understanding back to the patient.

Ethnic—pertaining to or characteristic of a people, especially a group sharing a common and distinctive culture, religion, language, or the like.

Ethnocentricity—the interpretation of one culture using the norms of another culture, usually one's own.

Evidence-Based Practice—an approach to health care practice where the clinician is aware of the evidence in support of a particular practice, the strength of that evidence, and the appropriate application of that evidence to the practice. It is the conscientious, explicit, and judicious use of current best evidence in making decisions about the care of individual patients. Evidence-based clinical practice (or evidence-based health care) requires integration of individual clinical expertise and patient preferences with the best available external clinical evidence from systematic research, and consideration of available resources. Definition accessed at: http://www.jamaevidence.com/glossary?glossaryID=35 40126#g3540126 February 2011. The integration of the best available research with clinical expertise in the context of patient characteristics, culture, and preferences. American Psychological Association. (2006). Evidence based practice in psychology - APA presidential task force on evidence based practice. *American Psychologist*. Vol. 61, No. 4, 271–285 DOI: 10.1037/0003-066X.61.4.271

Expert—having, involving, or demonstrating great skill, dexterity, or knowledge as the result of experience or training.

Extended Care Setting—care provided in nursing homes, long-term care residences, assisted living, and other partially independent care arrangements.

Genuineness—the ability to be oneself in a relationship and not hide behind a role or façade.

Health—a state of well being that is mainly known and expressed in cultural meanings and ways, values, and beliefs. The concept of a state of well being varies greatly based upon the cultural and values-based context.

Health Literacy—the ability of a person to understand and process the health information available to him or her.

Heuristic—to find out; encouraging or promoting investigation; conducive to discovery.

HIPAA—abbreviation for the Health Insurance Portability and Accountability Act of 1996. The HIPAA regulates the use and disclosure of protected health information by covered entities.

Holistic—considers man as a functioning whole, or relating to the conception of man as a functioning whole. This term is related to holistic health.

Holistic Health—a system of preventive medicine that takes into account the whole individual, his or her own responsibility for well being, and the total influences— social, psychological, environmental— that affect health including nutrition, exercise, and mental relaxation.

Home Care Setting—care provided in one's home/residence.

Homeopathy—a system of medical practice that treats a disease, especially by the administration of minute doses of a remedy that would in healthy persons produce symptoms similar to those of the disease.

Hypothesis—descriptions of disease processes, pathologic processes, clinical entities or syndromes, etiologic or psychological processes, or social or economic factors that best explain the possible causes for a patient's problems. Initial hypotheses are working guides in clinical reasoning and change with accumulated knowledge.

ICD-9-CM or ICD-10-CM (International Classification of Diseases) Code or Diagnostic Code—a system for assigning a disease label for the diagnosis assigned to a patient's medical problem.

Ill-Structured Problem—a problem that is characterized by inadequate information about the cause and lack of readily definable guidelines to approach solving it.

Illness—a term used by a patient to express a comprehensive view of not being well, feeling sick, or feeling unhealthy; a patient's personal experience of ill health.

Inspection—see the term "observation."

Intuition—to have a direct understanding without reasoning.

Malpractice—illegal or immoral conduct; practice contrary to established rules; specifically, the treatment of a case by a surgeon or physician in a manner that is contrary to accepted rules and productive of unfavorable results.

Manipulation—see the term "palpation."

Medical Chart—the permanent record of patient information that is used by health care providers to communicate and document the patient's progress in response to care. The medical chart may serve as a legal document.

Medicare—a benefit in the form of a health care service or supply that is paid by the federal government to qualified U.S. citizens.

Medication Order—a written order of a qualified physician for a medication to be used in the institutional setting. This is the equivalent of a prescription in the outpatient setting.

Medication Reconciliation—the process of comparing a patient's medication orders to all of the medications that the patient has been taking. This reconciliation is done to avoid medication errors such as omissions, duplications, dosing errors, or drug interactions. It should be done at every transition of care in which new medications are ordered or existing orders are rewritten. Transitions in care include changes in setting, service, practitioner, or level of care (definition based on The Joint Commission).

Metacognition—the continuous process of deliberation and reflection during problem solving.

Monitoring Parameter—a measurement, sign, symptom, or impression that represents the status of a patient in relationship to a specific outcome. Monitoring parameters are both quantitative and qualitative in form.

Monitoring Plan—the temporal use of outcome indicators to measure or observe a patient's response to care.

National Practitioner Data Bank—the Data Bank, consisting of the National Practitioner Data Bank (NPDB) and the Healthcare Integrity and Protection Data Bank (HIPDB), is a confidential information clearinghouse created by Congress to improve health care quality, protect the public, and reduce health care fraud and abuse in the United States. You may learn more by accessing: http://www.npdb-hipdb.hrsa.gov/topNavigation/aboutUs.jsp.

Naturopathy—a system of disease treatment that emphasizes the use of natural agents (such as water or sun exposure, and physical means like manipulation) rather than medications or surgery.

Normal Range—usually determined by applying statistical methods to results from a representative sample of the general population. The normal range represents the range of values where a large percentage (95%) of normal people (i.e., without the illness in question) fall. The average value plus or minus two standard deviations is usually taken as the normal range.

Nutraceutical—a term coined by Dr. Stephen DeFelice from "Nutrition" and "Pharmaceutical" in 1989. The term nutraceutical is being commonly used in marketing but has no regulatory definition.

Observation—visual evaluation or assessment of the patient.

On-Line Resource—an information resource found through connecting to other computer resources (e.g., Internet access to a web site via high speed cable).

Outcome—the resultant effect that a health care intervention or system change has on patients, systems, organizations, or communities. Outcomes are usually measurable and represent the clinical, economic, or humanistic domain. They represent a change in a patient's current and future health status that can be attributed to antecedent care.

Palpation—touching or feeling the patient with the hand to augment the data gathered through inspection.

Patient—a person who receives care and services from health care professionals.

Patient-Centered Care—organizations and practitioners involve patients in their own care and redesign systems to be more patient-centered to respond to patients' needs. Patient-centeredness requires recognizing both the capabilities and limitations of the patient and reconfiguring the care plan and its delivery to maximize the former and minimize the latter. It requires learning about patients' needs and wants and system redesign to fulfill them.

Patient Encounter—the interchange between the pharmacist and patient during which the pharmacist gathers background information through conducting an interview and assessment to determine the patient's problems and develops a care approach. It is through the encounter that you develop and provide a therapeutic relationship with the patient.

Patient Interview—the communication component of the patient encounter during which you use questioning, listening, and observation skills to gather background information about the patient.

Patient Portal—the online applications that connect patients so they may interact and communicate with their health care providers, hospitals, and clinics where they receive care. The implication of a portal is that it is available to the patient around the clinic via Internet connectivity.

Patient Profile—a general term used to describe the documentation record maintained about the patient database that is updated throughout the pharmaceutical care process by the pharmacist. It is common to see this term used in community and hospital pharmacy practice.

Percussion—striking of the body surface lightly but sharply to determine the position, size, and density of underlying structures as well as to detect fluid or air in a cavity.

Personal Health Record—a computer-based patient health record intended primarily for use by consumers to maintain and manage their health information in a private, secure, and confidential environment. The PHR is a patient-controlled record that will accompany the patient throughout his or her entire life and may contain additional information that is entered by the patient that the patient perceives as important such as self-care behaviors, self-initiated treatments, and preventive care activities that are not recorded in the provider-controlled records.

Pharmaceutical Care—the direct, responsible provision of medication-related care for the purpose of achieving definite outcomes that improve a patient's quality of life.

Pharmacotherapeutic Regimen—the drug name, strength, dosage form, route of administration, duration of treatment, and schedule for use of a medication being taken by a patient.

Physical Assessment—the process of evaluating the health status of the patient through identification of the normal state and deviations from this state using the assessment techniques of inspection, palpation, percussion, and auscultation.

Pictogram—a symbol or icon that tells a story. The picture is used to replace written and verbal language that communicates a specific message.

Practitioner—one who exercises a profession.

Prescription—directions written for the preparation and administration of a drug.

Primary Resource—the publication that contains the original research or works, usually found in biomedical journals.

Problem List—a prioritized list of the patient's problems determined through clinical reasoning applied to the various sources of information that support the patient database. The problem list is the guide to care plan development and monitoring, and is updated as the pharmaceutical care process is applied.

Professional Care—cognitive and culturally learned behaviors, techniques and processes, or patterns that enable or assist an individual, family, or community to improve or maintain a favorable healthy condition or way of life.

Provider—one who practices, especially one who practices a profession.

Proxy Outcome—a measure that represents the likelihood of a particular outcome by virtue of its inherent relationship to that outcome.

Public Health—the science and art of preventing disease, prolonging life, and promoting health and efficiency through organized community effort.

Qualitative Monitoring Parameter—monitoring that provides information about the patient's perceived response to interventions and their effectiveness.

Quantitative Monitoring Parameter—monitoring that provides specific measures which are useful to choosing and monitoring therapeutic interventions and determining effectiveness.

Residency—a postgraduate program of organized training that meets the requirements of a residency accreditation body.

Respect—the ability to accept the patient as a unique person as he or she is and to suspend critical judgment.

Secondary Resource—resources that index or abstract the primary resource literature found in biomedical journals.

Self Care—activities that individuals, families, and communities undertake with the intention of enhancing health, preventing disease, limiting illness, and restoring health.

Self-Efficacy Theory—behavioral change facilitated by a personal sense of control. A person who believes in being able to cause an event can conduct a more active and self-determined life course.

Setting—the place where patient care occurs (e.g., community pharmacy, hospital, nursing home, outpatient clinic, emergency room).

Social Learning Theory—the likelihood of a behavior occurring in a given situation is a joint function of the individual's expectancy that the behavior will lead to a particular reinforcement and the extent to which the reinforcement is valued.

Systematic Review of the Literature—a structured literature review that summarizes a topic in a systematic fashion using preset criteria and guidelines for conduct.

Telehealth—services provided through remote access connections to the local communities where people live.

Telepharmacy—services provided through remote access connections to local communities where a pharmacy facility is available but no pharmacist is present.

Tertiary Resource—professional publications that contain a summary of information in full text such as textbooks, review articles, compendium, handbooks, and electronic full-text references.

Therapeutic Monitoring—the process of assessing outcomes associated with a treatment to determine the need for modification for the purpose of optimizing the desired outcome.

Therapeutic Relationship—a relationship established between the patient and pharmacist that is characterized by trust, empathy, respect, authenticity, and responsiveness.

U.S. Food and Drug Administration—a scientific, regulatory, and public health agency that oversees items accounting for 25 cents of every dollar spent by consumers. Its jurisdiction encompasses most food products (other than meat and poultry); human and animal drugs; therapeutic agents of biological origin; medical devices; radiation-emitting products for consumer, medical, and occupational use; cosmetics; and animal feed.

Web Site—an electronic file system accessible through the World Wide Web. The address for a web site is called a URL (Universal Resource Locator).

Western Measures of Health—Western conventional or mainstream health care that treats disease, using surgery and prescription medications or drugs, leading to outcomes representing the absence of disease.

World Health Organization—the United Nations specialized agency for health established on April 7, 1948 (www.who.int/en/).

Index

A
access, 3
acetaminophen, 247, 258, 283, 288, 289
activities of daily living (ADLs), 94
acupuncturist, 225
additional information, 163–164
additive response, 212
adherence cycle, 278
administration route, 244
Administration Simplification provisions, HIPAA, 117
administrative personnel, 125
admission note, 277
    review case, 147–148
admission tests, 133
adverse drug reaction, 38, 160, 188
Advil, 74, 100, 109, 141, 142, 143, 258, 265, 288, 289
advocacy behaviors, 250
age, 92, 245
Agency for Healthcare Research and Quality, 157, 281
albuterol, 76, 104, 147, 148, 225, 226, 294, 295
allopurinol, 70–71, 72
alteplase, 35
American Health Information Community, 115
American Health Information Management Association (AHIMA), 121, 123
American Medical Association (AMA), 47, 92
American Medical Informatics Association (AMIA), 123
American Pharmacists Association (APhA), 281
    Code of Ethics, 119
American Society of Health-System Pharmacists (ASHP), 281
    nondiscriminatory pharmaceutical care, 119
    Project HealthDesign program, 123
    Statement on Pharmaceutical Care, 30
amitriptyline, 188
angry patient, 98
antibiotics, 244, 245
anticoagulation
    assessment record, 110–111, 230–231
    services, 50–51
    teaching checklist, 301
antipsychotics, 245
Asheville Project, 51
aspirin, 149, 183, 263, 291
assisted living facilities, 45
attentive silence, 87–88
audit use, 126
"Authorization to Release Medical Information," 117

B
background information, 60, 63, 159–160, 163–167
bai guo ye, 180–182, 225
Bayer aspirin, 216
behavior/mental status, 130, 138
biographical data, 127
biomedical health model, 22–23
blood products, 246
Blue Cross/Blue Shield, 126
business card, 289

C
cactus flowers, 259–260
calcium channel blocker, 243
Campbell Collaboration, 157
Carative Factors of Watson, 30
care, 30
    behavior skills, 29–30
    delivery, 268–277
    documentation, 130, 139
    goals, 64, 242–243
    provisions, 68–72
care plan, 139
    development, 22
    documentation, 276–277
    patient/caregiver response, 277
care plan change
    case, 280
    documentation, 280
    recommendations, 279
care plan implementation, 34, 270
contacting health professionals, 275
counseling, 274–275
    ensuring patient takes medications, 274, 275
    ensuring patient receives medications, supportive technologies, 273–274
    follow-up scheduling, 275

medication orders, prescriptions, 270–271
medication reconciliation, 272–273
revision, follow up checklist, 280, 309
transfer of medication orders, 271–272
care plan recommendation, 268–269
approach, 269
directly to patient, 270
pharmacist-initiated to primary care provider, 269–270
responding to formal consult, 270
caregivers, 62–63
Cathflo, 35
celecoxib, 246
Centers for Disease Control and Prevention (CDC), 125
Certification Commission for Healthcare Information Technology (CCHIT), 115
change
readiness, 6
stages model, 6
chart note, 69
chief complaint, 132
Chinese herbs, 8
chlorpropamide, 179
choice, 2–3
clarification of orders, 129
clinical assessment skills
plan, 133
skills, 28–29
clinical guidelines, protocols, 214
clinical practice skills, 28–29
clinical reasoning, 31–32, 64, 209–210, 270
heuristics, 214–215
medication use assessment, 215–220
skills, 210–214
clinical signs, symptoms, 130
clonidine, 149, 246
close-ended questions, 86–87
Cochrane Collaboration, 157, 168
code situation, 91
cognitive impairments, 246
collaborative care, 62, 114–115
drug therapy management, 36
collaborative practice
agreement, 221, 238–240
application, 233–235
regulations, 236–237
common ground, 25
communication
exchange, 212–213
skills, 29, 164
community pharmacies, 45, 49

complex regimens, 38
compounding/formulation, 188
computerized practitioner order entry (CPOE), 129
concurrent disease characteristics, 242–243
confidentiality, 116–121
case, 120
Connection for Health's Common Framework, 123
consensus-building procedures morality, 33
consent forms, 128
CONSORT randomized trial report checklist, 201–202
consultation, 38, 70, 130, 131, 139
notes, 277
services, 51
consumer drug information sources, 170, 171
consumer empowerment, 114
consumerism, 114-115
continuity of care record (CCR), 121, 122–123
continuous quality improvement, 48
contraceptive patch, 141
coordination of care case, 35
corporate privacy, confidentiality policies, 119–121
Cortisporin Otic, 244
co-trimoxazole, 176
counseling materials, 284–285, 286
Covey, Stephen, 27
critical care, 38
Crossing the Quality Chasm, 123
cultural issues/factors, 243
awareness, 9
background, 90
bias, 8
competency, 9
desire, 9
encounter, 9
influences, 7–9
knowledge, 9
skill, 9
sub-groups, 7
current drug therapy problems, 243
Current Procedural Terminology (CPT) codes, 53

D

Declaration of Patient-Centered Healthcare, 2
diagnostic procedures, 131
difficult patient, 98
digoxin, 1, 149, 216, 245
direct patient care, 35
discharge care plan, 130, 277
case, 276
discharge prescriptions, 271, 295
disease/condition

-centered practice, 20, 21
experience, 24–25
prevention, 25
states, 38
dispensing
responsibility, 35
services fees, 53
documentation skills
care provision, 68–72
patient care plan, 250, 252, 254
patient encounter, 94
patient progress, outcomes, 279
skills, 31
dofetilide, 149
dosage, 244
schedule, 188–189
drug
availability, 188
of choice, 189
compatibility/stability, 188
cost, 247
frequency, 244
interactions, 189
-related characteristics, 244–245
routes, 244
simplicity, 247
drug information, 29, 63
gathering, 167–170
request origins, 157–159
sources, 167–170
worksheet, 161–162, 174–175, 178–179, 181–182, 184–185
drug therapy
adherence factors, 246
problems, 139
drug use review, 38

E

educational use, 126
e-Health, 45
e-health information exchange (e-HIE), 116
electronic data interchange, 117
electronic health information, 140
electronic health record (EHR), 115, 119, 121, 122
electronic medical record (EMR), 121–122
electronic protected health information (EPHI), 118–119
electronic records, 62
electronic transmission of orders, 129
empathy, 31, 60, 211–212
employer-based medication management service, 51
employment salary, 53

empowerment, 2–3
enalapril, 48
endpoints of indicators, 248
enoxaparin, 276
environment, patient interview, 84
environmental health model, 4, 23
esomeprazole, 66, 73
ethnic background, 246
ETHNIC mnemonics model, 9, 10
ethnocentricity, 8
evidence, published, 167–170
evidence-based clinical reasoning, 215
evidence-based practice, 155–157
skills, 29
Web sites, resources, 206–207
Excedrin PM, 216
experience, 214
expert opinions, 63–64, 171–172
expertise development, 33–34
eye contact, 89

F

facial expressions, 89
facilitation, 87
Fagerstrom test for nicotine dependence, 257
Fairview Pharmacy Services (Minnesota), 51
family background, 91–92
famotidine, 11
feelings, descriptive words, 213
financial factors, 243
financial/insurance data, 127
fluticasone, 294, 295
folk healing, 8
follow up, 274, 275
Food and Drug Administration (FDA), 125, 163
formal consultation, 69
"From the Source: 20 Tips to Help Prevent Medical Errors," 281
functional illiteracy, 92

G

gender, 92, 245
general pharmacy practice, 35, 36
general reference evaluation, 198
gentamicin, 164–167
genuiness, 60, 213
geriatric patient, 38, 96–97
ginkgo bilboa, 216
glipizide, 101, 261, 290, 291
glucophage, 101
glucotrol, 101

Google, 169
    Scholar, 169
graphic records, 129–130

H

Health and Human Services, 115, 120
health behavior, 5–7
health beliefs model, 4–5
health concept
    health care professionals, 3–4
    patient, 4
health information exchange (HIE), 115
Health Information Privacy and Accountability Act (HIPAA), 61–62, 63, 117–118
Health Information Security and Privacy Collaboration, 119
health information technologies (HIT), 44, 45
Health Information Technology for Economic and Clinical Health Act (HITECH Act), 119
Health Information Technology Standards Panel (HITSP), 115
health literacy, 92, 250
health model, 23
    definitions, 4
Health on the Net Foundation, 171
health promotion, 25
health record, 113–114
health care delivery
    physical settings, 44–45
    physical/virtual integration, 46
    structure, 43–46
    systems, 46–48
    virtual settings, 45
health care principles, 2–3
health care providers, 62
hearing impaired patient, 97–98
heparin, 35
herbal remedies research, 177–179
home care services, 49
home health care, 45
home test kits, monitoring devices results, 131
hospital health care professionals, 125
hospitals, 44–45
hydralazine, 48
hydrochlorothiazide, 48, 149, 216, 283, 288, 289, 290, 291
hydroxyzine, 48

I

ibuprofen, 183, 246
Identidex, 189
identification, 189
illiteracy, 92

illness experience, 24–25
individualized assessment, 215–218
    medication use, 217–218
    patient preferences and needs, 217
indomethacin, 71, 72
information, 3
    reliability, 171
inpatient
    admissions, 127–128
    collaborative drug therapy practice case, 56
    general patient-oriented pharmacy practice case, 56
    medication orders, 137, 271
    pharmaceutical product availability, 49
    rounding, 51
Institute of Medicine, 115, 123
instrumental activities of daily living (IADL), 94, 96, 229
instrumental egoism and simple exchange morality, 33
interchangeable response, 212
International Alliance of Patients' Organizations (IAPO), 2
Internet pharmacies, 50
Internet-based clinical support services, 46
Internet-based information services, 46
interpersonal concordance morality, 33
interpreter, working with, 97
interventions, 139
intuition, 21

J

Jabr, Nasir (pharmacist case study), 39
    care plan implementation, 282–290
    consultation with Lauren Smith, 255–259
    encounter with Lauren Smith, 74, 100
    evidence for Lauren Smith, 173–176
    outpatient pharmacy services, 55
    prescription, 141–143
    values, care preferences, 220–222
Johnston, Christine (pharmacist case study), 39
    care guidance, 223–224
    care plan development, 259–260, 261
    collaborative drug therapy practice, 55
    encounter with Eduardo Montanez, 75, 101–102, 104
    herbal remedies research, 177–179
    monitoring, follow up, 290–293
    patient health record information, 144–146
Joint Commission
    anticoagulation management, 50
    National Patient Safety Goal No. 8, 272
Jones, Michael (pharmacist case study), 40
    care plan development, 262–265
    care plan implementation, 299–302
    encounter with Sam Robinson, 77, 106–109

inpatient collaborative drug therapy practice, 56
medical record review, 149–151
problem list, 226–232
vitamin E and warfarin research, 183–185
Journal of the American Medical Association, Users' Guides Series, 157
journals online, 170

K

Kohlbert's Stages of Moral Development, 33

L

laboratory
    data, 130–131
    data, assessment, 138
    test order, 151
lactation, 190, 245–246
lanolin, 188
lansoprazole, 48
law and social order morality, 33
levofloxacin, 245
levothyroxine, 245
Lipitor, 216
listening skills, 87–88
literacy, 92
literature
    evaluation, 170–171
    search, 156
    search record, 163
    search strategy, 160, 163
Lo-Ovral, 142, 176
low molecular weight heparin, 245

M

mail order pharmacy, 49
malpractice suits, 125
measurable endpoint, 248
Medicaid, 53, 126
medical chart, 61–62
    entries, 68–69
medical health model, 4
medical history summary, 145
medical record, 121–124, 125
    content, 127, 128
Medicare, 36, 126
    Part D, 51, 53
Medicare Prescription Drug Improvement and Modernization Act of 2003, 36-37
medication adherence, 38, 275
    assessment, 306–308
    compliance history, 138–139

medication administration record (MAR), 62, 127, 134, 294
    IV, STAT, one-time orders, 136
    p.r.n. medications, 135
medication errors, 47
Medication List Summit, 124
medication management post discharge, 299–302
medication orders, 270–271
    inpatient, 137
medication organizer, 93
medication reconciliation
    case, 65, 66, 68, 73
    form, 305
medication therapy management services, 36–37, 50
    fees, 53
medication use, 6
    assessment, individualized, 217–218
    evaluation, 138
    process, 46–47
    systems of care issues, 219
MEDLINE, 169
mental status assessment, 93–94
mentally incompetent patient, 98–99
metacognition, 31, 211
metformin, 101, 261, 290, 291
method of administration, 190
Micromedex, 189
Mini-Mental Status Examination (MMSE), 94, 95
monitoring data assessment, 278–279
monitoring plan
    design, 65
    case, 249
    endpoints of indicators, 248
    follow-up, 249
    frequency, 248
    proxy outcome indicators, 247–248
Montanez, Eduardo (patient case), 15
    care guidance, 223–224
    care plan development, 259–260, 261
    encounter with Christine Johnston, 75, 101–102, 104
    herbal remedies research, 177–179
    monitoring, follow up, 290–293
    patient health record, 144–146
moral reasoning, 31, 211
multiple prescription medications, 38
mutual respect, 269

N

National Association of Boards of Pharmacy, VIPPS accreditation, 50
National Asthma Education and Prevention Program, 296

National Center for Biotechnology Information, 169
National Coordinator for Health Information Technology, 119
National Council on Patient Information and Education, 281
National Governors Association, 119
National Guideline Clearinghouse, 157
National Health Information Network (NHIN), 115, 116
National Library of Medicine, 169, 170
national model for technology development, 116
National Patient Safety Goals, 50
National Practitioner Data Bank, 26
Nationwide Health Information Network, 116
Net Generation, 114
Nicorette gum, 283
nicotine
    dependence test, 257
    gum, 258, 283
nitroglycerin, 244, 246
nonsteroidal anti-inflammatory agents (NSAIDs), 183, 245, 247, 263, 265
nonverbal communication, 88, 212
nursing
    admission data, 130, 150
    care plans, 130
    interventions, 130
    notes, 130

O

obedience morality, 33
observable endpoints, 248
occupation, 246
Office for Civil Rights, 120–121
Office of National Coordinator for Health Information Technology (ONCHIT), 115
omeprazole, 11, 65, 66
online information, 7
    sources, 168–169
open-ended questions, 84, 86–87
operating room procedures, 131
opiates, 244
oral response documentation, 70
Ortho-Evra, 173, 174, 175, 176
Oscal-D, 216
outcomes, 163
outpatient
    collaborative drug therapy practice case, 55
    pharmaceutical product availability, 49–50
    pharmacy services case, 55
    prescription records, 137
    prescriptions, 271

    visit, initial, 127–128
over-the-counter drugs, 191

P

pantoprazole, 245
paralinguistics, 212–213
patient, 1–3
    access to records, 125
    advocate, 28
    autonomous, independent, 11
    characteristics, 90–92, 245–247
    chart note, 254
    communication barriers assessment, 89
    consumer, 11
    counseling skills, 29
    culture, 7–10
    dependent, 11
    health-related goals, 242, 243
    involvement in health care, 3
    medical needs identification, 216
    medication use process, 46–47
    optimal health information, 12–13, 14
    -pharmacist encounter, 79–80
    -pharmacist relationship, enhancing, 25–26
    portals, 124
    preference/behavior, 246
    problems, 138, 244
    relationship, 6, 27–28
    resources, 281
    response to care assessment, 73
    safety, 47
    safety case, 48
    seeking care, 28
    support, 250
    values and beliefs, 3–10
    view of pharmacist, 11
    vulnerability, 115
patient assessment, 277
    endpoints achievement, 278
    expected outcomes, 279
    missing, additional information/data need, 279
    status and condition, 278
patient care
    continuous quality improvement, 48
    needs assessment, 60–64, 159–160, 163–167
    prioritization, 37–38
patient care plan
    care goals design, 64
    care provision documentation, 68–72
    core elements worksheet, 252

documentation, 250, 252, 254
evidence in, 172
implementing, 66–73
initiating, 67–68
monitoring, 65
pharmacist consultation note, 253
pharmacotherapeutic regimen, 64–65
recommending, 66–67
support needed, 65–66
patient education, 130, 139, 250, 275
asthma treatment/inhaler use, 297, 298
databases, 251
patient encounter, 60–61, 80
closing, 94
documenting, 94
space boundaries, 213
patient health care
goals, 242, 243
needs identification, 28, 215
patient health information, 114–116
clinic admission form, 256
conduct issues, 116–121
optimal, 12–13, 14
request case, 159
patient health record, 124–134
medical record, 121–124
organization, 126–127
patient history, 132–133
form, 81-82, 107-108, 227–228
patient interview, 60, 80, 84
assessment of communication barriers, 89
case, 93
environment, 84
interacting, 90
listening skills, 87–88
nonverbal communication, 88–89
opening, 90
organizing, 89–90
patient questions response, 88
preparation, 84, 85
protocol, 103
questioning skills, 84, 86–87
skills, 83
patient profile, 62, 137–138, 142
Patient Safety Task Force, 115
patient-centered care plan
design, 241–242
implementation, 267–268
practice, 20, 22-23
practice settings, 50
process, 59

providing, 23–26
workforce realities, 52
payment, 52–53
pediatric patient encounter, 94, 96
penicillin, 65, 66
personal beliefs, 27
personal health record (PHR), 121, 123
pharmaceutical care practice, 20, 22
pharmaceutical product availability, 49–50
pharmaceutical-centered practice, 20, 21
pharmacist
care plan, 107–108, 243
care provider, 12
consultation note, 253
continuous quality improvement, 48
expertise, trust, 12
healer, 12
information expert, advisor, 26
medication use process, 46–47
merchandiser, 12
-patient encounter cases, 100, 101–102, 104–105
patient safety role, 47
practitioner, 26–35
primary care provider, 26
role of, 19–20, 26
treatment plan, 26
pharmacists' notes, 138–140
pharmacoeconomics, 190
pharmacokinetics, 190
pharmacology, 189
pharmacotherapeutic regimen
characteristics, tertiary literature, 192–196
design, 64–65
options, 243–247
selecting optimal, 247
pharmacy practice
direct patient care, 35
evolution, 20–22
pharmacy profile, 176, 289
form, 222
pharmacy records, 134, 137–140
phenytoin, 69, 244
philosophy of practice, 26–27
physical assessment, 61, 93
functioning, 130, 138
limitations, 246
skills, 28
physician
consultation, S.O.A.P. note, 72
examination, assessment, 138
orders, 128–129

-pharmacist encounter, 67
Physicians' Desk Reference, 189
poisoning, 191
practice infrastructure needs, 51–52
practitioner
    personal beliefs, professional judgments, 27
    practice philosophy, 26–27
pregnancy, 190–191, 245–246
pre-printed routine, standard orders, 129
prescription, 270–271, 283
    records, 137
    vending machines, 49–50
prescriptive authority, 36, 37
present illness history, 132
PreserVision soft gels with lutein, 216
Prevacid, 216
PricewaterhouseCoopers, 114
prickly pear cactus, 178–179
primary general reference, critical evaluation checklist, 199–200
primary information sources, 168
privacy, 116–121
    violation recourse, 120–121
Privacy Act, 117
Privacy Rule, 118
probe, 87
problem assessment, 292
problem list, 64
    establishment case, 216
    religious, economic, personal values case, 219
problem-oriented medical record (POMR), 126
professional behavior skills, 30–31
professional judgments, 27
program evaluation, 126
progress notes, 70
    care plan documentation, 261
    clinical reasoning, 225
    patient-centered care plan, 263, 265, 277, 288, 291, 300, 302
    patient health record, 133–134
protected health information (PHI), 117–118
proxy outcome indicators, 247–248
public health, 125
Public Health Department, 125
PubMed, 169, 170

Q

Quality Improvement Initiative, 115
quality of care, 48
questions
    classifying, 160
    formulating, 160
    framing, 160
    by request classification, 188–190
questioning
    skills, 84, 86–87
    strategies, 164–167
quinidine, 248
QUOROM
    meta-analysis of trials checklist, 203–204
    statement flow diagram, 205

R

racial background, 246
ranitidine, 188, 216
referrals, 134
regional health information organization (RHIO), 122
registries, 124
reimbursement, 53
religion, 246
research use, 125
respect, 2, 60, 214
response
    formulation, 163
    time-frame, 160
review of systems (ROS), 132
    approach, 93
Robert Wood Johnson Foundation, 123
Robinson, Samuel (patient case)
    background, 16
    care plan development, 262–265
    care plan implementation, 299–302
    encounter with Michael Jones, 77
    medical record review, 149–151
    pharmacist–patient encounter case, 106–109
    problem lise, 226–232
    vitamin E and warfarin research, 183–185
Rodriguez, Luisa (pharmacist case), 49
    admission note review, 147–148
    bai guo ye research, 180–182
    care plan development, 260, 262, 263
    care plan implementation, 293–299
    counseling, follow up, 293–299
    encounter with Huong Tran, 76, 104–105
    inpatient general patient-oriented pharmacy practice, 56
    progress note, 224–225
Rogers, Carl, 60

S

S.O.A.P., 70–72, 276–277
Schon, Donald, 211

scientific information, 167
scope of practice, 31–33
search engines, 168–169
secondary info sources, 168
secure e-mail communications, 46
security, 21, 116–121
Security Rule, 118
self-care, 6–7
self-correction, 214
self-empowered consumer case, 11
self-monitoring forms, 134
sensory limitations, 246
sign-off note, 277
simvastatin, 101
skilled nursing facilities, 45
Smith, Lauren (patient case)
    background, 15
    care plan implementation, 282–290
    consultation and care visit, 173–176, 255–259
    encounter with Nasir Jabr, 74, 100
    evidence, 173–176
    prescription to Jabr, 141–143
    values, care preferences, 220–222
smoking cessation, 220, 282–290
    questionnaire, 287
    stages, 258
social cooperation morality, 33
social factors, 243
social networking, 115
socioeconomic background, 90–91
Solu-medrol, 147, 148
spacer for hand held inhaler, 295
specialized pharmacy practice, 35, 36
specialty clinics, 49
specialty therapy, 50–51
spirituality, 91
STAT laboratory test result, 146
support, 3
synthroid, 149, 183, 264
system factors, 243
systematic review, 156

T

"Taking Care of Myself," 281
telehealth services, 45
telepharmacy services, 45
temporary information, 134
teratogenicity, 190–191
tertiary information sources, 168
    literature content matrix, 192–196
    reference evaluation, 198

tetracycline, 244
therapeutic core qualities, 60
therapeutic drug monitoring test results, 131
therapeutic options, 64
therapeutic relationship, 27–28
therapeutics, 189
thiazide diuretic, 258
To Err is Human, 115
toxicology, 191
Tran, Huong (patient case)
    admission note review, 147–148
    background, 16
    bai guo ye research, 180–182
    care plan development, 260, 262, 263
    care plan implementation, 293–299
    counseling, follow up, 293–299
    patient–pharmacist encounter case, 76, 104–105
transcribed orders, 129
transfer note, 277
transfer of medication orders, 271–272
trimethoprim–sulfamethoxazole, 143
Tylenol, 258

U

uncommon drug products, 191
Unified Health Communication (UHC) approach, 92
United Nations NGO Health Committee, 2
urinalysis test results, 146

V

Vagisil Gel, 74
validity, 278–279
value-driven health care, 114
vancomycin, 35
Veterans Affairs, Department of, 127
Vicodin ES, 101, 261
visually impaired patient, 97
vitamin
    B complex, 216
    D, 216
    E, 109, 149, 183, 263, 265

W

warfarin, 77, 149, 159, 183, 216, 226, 264, 265, 276, 300
warfarin/heparin therapy, 245
Web sites, 169–170
    resources, 206–207
wellness health model, 4, 23
whole person understanding, 25
work environment, 50–52
workforce realities, 52

World Health Organization health model, 4, 23
written orders, 129
written responses, 68–69

Y
yucca root, 102, 104, 178–179

Z
Zellmer, William, 27
Zocor, 101
Zyrtec, 216